# Lambent Traces

## Franz Kafka

# Lambent Traces
# Franz Kafka

*Stanley Corngold*

PRINCETON UNIVERSITY PRESS

PRINCETON AND OXFORD

*Library of Congress Cataloging-in-Publication Data*
Corngold, Stanley.
Lambent traces: Franz Kafka / Stanley Corngold.
p.  cm.
Includes index.
Includes bibliographical references.
ISBN 0-691-11816-7 (alk. paper)
1. Kafka, Franz, 1883–1924 — Criticism and interpretation.  I. Title.
PT2621.A26Z6645 2004 833′.912 — dc22      2003057399

British Library Cataloging-in-Publication Data is available

This book has been composed in Sabon

Printed on acid-free paper. ∞

www.pup.princeton.edu

Printed in the United States of America

1   3   5   7   9   10   8   6   4   2

For Walter Sokel

*Das Früchtchen fällt nicht weit vom Stamm.*

Slanting through the words there come vestiges of light.

—Franz Kafka, *Dearest Father*

A mild and lambent light of Prophecy may be considered as encircling the Jews' whole constitution.

—Frederic Myers, *Catholic Thoughts on the Bible and Theology*

For the incomprehensible and unforgettable thing was that this law *glowed*: it radiated, it scorched and destroyed.

—Elias Canetti, *The Conscience of Words*

# CONTENTS

# PREFACE

FRANZ KAFKA WAS BORN on July 3, 1883, into a German-speaking Jewish family in Prague, the capital of the Czech Lands of the Austro-Hungarian Empire. This piling up of ethnic particulars right from the start should suggest something of the complexity of Kafka's predicament as it is reflected in his stories, novels, and confessional writings. Kafka's situation, like his city's, is mazy, intricate, and overly specified by history, lending his life an exceptional danger and promise: the danger of becoming lost in impenetrable contradiction that finally flattens out into anxiety, apathy, nothingness; and the promise, too, of a sudden breaking open under great tension into a blinding prospect of truth. At various times you see Kafka laying weight on one or the other of his identity elements in an effort to mark out his way—he understood Yiddish, learned Hebrew, toyed with Zionism; he espoused socialist ideals that aligned him with the aspirations of the Czech-speaking working class; and he sought literary fame by competing with masters of German literature living and writing in the German-speaking capitals (chiefly Berlin, hardly at all Vienna, which he disliked).[1] But the way he took—and to judge from his posthumous fame, found—was, with few interruptions, the way of writing.[2]

The "way" is a figure of speech that is meant to confer a special distinction on Kafka's decision to write. The work that he actually produced and published in his lifetime is not huge by ordinary standards of literary greatness, consisting of seven small volumes, four of them devoted to single stories. Yet on the strength of "The Judgment" ("Das Urteil"), "The Stoker" ("Der Heizer"), and *The Metamorphosis* (*Die Verwandlung*), all of which he published early, in single volumes, in the years 1913–15, Kafka enjoyed an indubitable literary esteem. His stories were admired by writers of the order of Robert Musil and Rainer Maria Rilke, and publishers like Ernst Rowohlt and Kurt Wolff pressed him for more of his work. There stood in his way, however, for most of his life, the mass and difficulty of his professional duties: he was a high official—Senior Legal Secretary—at the partly state-run Workers' Accident Insurance Institute.

Kafka's writing arose as an empirical practice, at a place—a desk—at a time—between eleven at night and three in the morning. To accomplish what he did, he had to construct a kind of salient around this time and place: he required an almost unimaginably deep degree of protection for his writing. Yet for as long as he was employed by "the office," he could not feel free of its demands. His best known story, *The Meta-morphosis*, which recounts the transformation of a traveling salesman into a verminous beetle, suggests the omnipresence of just this office as a threat. Soon after Gregor Samsa wakes at four (read: just as Kafka "wakes" from his creative "dream" spent writing), the household is invaded by the office head, who knocks on his door, demanding Gregor's loyalty and attention to his job. The imposition on the hero of a ver-minous body connects in Kafka's imagination with the "monstrous" reduction of himself at the instant his private redoubt is invaded. In this story the daily logic of cause and effect is reversed: here the monstrosity is the harbinger, and not the result, of the invasion. Kafka wrote that if he did not write, there would be nothing left of him; and if he were not let in peace, there would indeed be nothing left of him. At the end of *The Metamorphosis*, the charwoman says, "Look, you don't have to worry about getting rid of the stuff next door. It's already been taken care of" (M 42).

Kafka prepared for his profession from early on: he attended the Ger-man National Altstädter Gymnasium; took his law exams at the Ger-man Charles University; and, thereafter, on his own account a token Jew among Germans (and after 1918 a token German among Czechs), worked, and was advanced, for fourteen years in the office that released him only after his tuberculosis asserted the greater claim. With almost pathological modesty, he suppressed the knowledge of his achievement on behalf of workmen's compensation (his activity is not to be confused with that of "little" clerks like the young Italo Svevo or Fernando Pessoa). Time and again, he was obliged to bring home masses of docu-ments to prepare for court defenses of the Institute's cases. That the writing of *The Metamorphosis* was, to Kafka's mind, ruined by the "business trip" he had to take while in the throes of composition is well known. Less well known is the fact that this business trip was a com-plex legal defense that he won, obtaining a solid settlement for the Insti-tute (LF 69).

There is, however, another, and altogether productive, sense in which the world of the office enters his stories, shaping the spaces, for exam-ple, in which the hero of *The Trial* encounters the officials of the court that has arrested him for an unnamed crime. The attics and personnel of lower-middle-class tenements also contribute to the scene—the rough world that Kafka knew through his erotically charged city walks and the clamor of the beneficiaries of the insurance he helped to disburse. Kafka's literary greatness as an analyst of modernity, of the fusion of bureaucracy and technology as the governing principles of everyday life, would not have been achieved were it not for his immersion in the phantasmagoric hell of office life.[3] And still this burden drained him and threatened to leave nothing over for what finally mattered to him: "literature." It is only from literature and never, to Kafka's mind, the benevolent aspect of his professional work that he could imagine his justification.

Kafka lived his secretly excruciating bachelor's life within a radius of a few miles from the Old Town Center of Prague, held captive until 1923, the year before his death, by the city he called this "old crone" with "claws" (L 5). During this time he made trips, often with friends, fairly far afield — to Paris and London and Como and Berlin, and in the last year of his life did indeed live in Berlin. But what he felt with almost unbearable intensity — leading him, especially at the time of his writing his first important stories and just before beginning *The Castle*, to fear that he was going mad — were the elements of his personality in tension. At best this tension worked to produce a sort of claustral space between himself and the din of the world that did not exclude the entrance of subliminally selected productive atoms. He was responsive to politics and history and public culture, but he sought to translate this polemical complex, for his safety, into a private, recondite, even "dreamlike" text, whose purest expression is his writing.

It is in light of the crucial importance of writing for Kafka that this book intends to intervene in the present state of Kafka studies. Owing to the accumulation of information about his involvement in the culture of his time, he is perceived as a man drowning willy-nilly in its complications; and worse — as one who, all the time he drowns, does so with a bad conscience, swallowing its stereotypes while pretending, by his effort of writing, to be not a drowning man but an ecstatic. Yet it is not as if he were unaware of the difference: "The man in ecstasy and the man drowning," he wrote: "both throw up their arms. The first does it to signify harmony, the second to signify strife with the elements" (DF 77). In the view, however, of a number of sharp readers today, he was the drowning man only pretending to ecstasy; and now his stories, like so many stomachs, can be pumped to disgorge contents that were merely ordinary. As this method reaches its apogee in the works of two redoubtable critics — Sander Gilman, in a book entitled *Franz Kafka: The Jewish Patient*, and Elizabeth Boa, in *Franz Kafka: Gender, Class, and Race in the Letters and Fictions* — I will include in chapter 11 a detailed critique of their arguments.

My Kafka is an ecstatic. This bliss, this feeling himself "at the boundary of the human," is connected to his writing, although as a feeling it has no immediate linguistic content, since

for everything outside the phenomenal world, language can only be used allusively [as an allusion (*andeutungsweise*)], but never even approximately in a comparative way [as a comparison, in the manner of an analogy (*vergleichsweise*)], because, corresponding as it does to the phenomenal world, it is concerned only with property and its relations. (D1 58; DF 40, GW 6:237)

All of Kafka's writing turns on this ecstasy — its hiddenness, its warning, its power to justify a ruined life — but it cannot name directly what is nothing in respect of material things and the signs dependent on them. We know of Kafka's horror of metaphor, his frustration at "writing's lack of independence of the world" (D2 200–201). Still, there is the call of "real" writing, whose purpose is to bring about a "constructive destruction" of the world of experience (DF 103).[4] Real writing, however, is not something that Kafka can summon up at will. In times of failure, the good death of ecstatic writing is haunted by terror of the death of a misspent life — misspent, because "God does not want me to write — but I, I must" (L 10). Only a writing that flows from a full immersion could justify the risk. If it is less than wholehearted, it is only a great shame; and, then, for Kafka — like Joseph K., the hero of *The Trial* — it would seem as though nothing more than his shame could survive him (T 231).

There are these two sorts of death in Kafka — the good death of self-loss in writing and the "boisterous" ("*brausenden*") death of an unjustified life (D1 316, GW 10:211). They are at the heart of this book. One involves the denial of the empirical ego, and survival; the other, the refusal of "the sensate world," and extinction. They separate, come together, split apart, stream into one another, drawing the figure of Kafka's spirit in his work — elliptically. It is in such a manner — elliptically — that I mean to describe Kafka's spirit, recalling Walter Benjamin's view of Kafka's work as an ellipse whose twin foci are profane empirical urbanity, on the one hand, and mystical experience, on the other.[5]

I think of this tension as the tension between two longings, which arise in response to the two kinds of death that disturb him. One strains for the cultural immortality promised by literary works that deserve to survive; but it, too, is not without the ecstatic, the mystical dimension of creation. The other craves to find in death, before or beyond obliteration, a form of the "intensified redemption" ("gesteigerte Erlösung") vouchsafed to Kafka's *soeur semblable*, the mouse-singer Josephine (CS 376, GW 1:294). Both ecstasies are sought and feared, suspected and affirmed. Neither is simple, and neither is otherworldly. Cultural immortality is also a contingent affair of being published and read by persons who live in cities and feed (on) the media. And real death occurs in a context of tradition shaped by historical Judaism and types of Gnostic teaching rampant in Prague in Kafka's lifetime.[6]

Everything, however, depends on perceiving which of these foci — the worldly matrix or the imagination of redemption elsewhere — exerts the stronger pull. One could misunderstand their relation by simplifying it, since Kafka's mystic refusal of the world also involves its necessary inclusion: "what we call the world of the senses is the evil in the spiritual world" (DF 39, GW 6:236–37). His gnostic élan makes its way through a universe of medial, sensate inscriptions: K.'s visit to the Castle is organized by telephone; Kafka found bliss in trashy movies, just as he devoured pulp novels about colonial exploits in savage lands.[7] But these are cartoonlike reflexes of what truly mattered to him, the inescapable attraction of flexible genius to its own mockery.[8] Kafka's real longings are not local and contemporary and least of all an affair of cultural politics. They are apocalyptic. They seek "the strongest possible light" by means of which "one can dissolve the world"; they would "raise the world into the pure, the true, and the immutable" (DF 295, D2 187). With these chapters I hope to reestablish the dominant motive in this unequal play of forces.[9]

A note to the reader: In *Finnegans Wake* Joyce warned against "film[ing] in the elipsities of their gyribouts those fickers which are returnally reproductive of themselves."[10] I fear that I have violated this commandment in certain respects. In this book you will run across repetitions of key citations from Kafka supporting arguments that also recur from chapter to chapter. I promise you that these citations from Kafka warrant attention more than once: they are subtle, surprising, and cryptic. As for the fact that some of my arguments recur, I have found it somehow natural to repeat portions of them as reminders of stages of the way we have come.

This "way," I will note, includes chapters, "segues," and, at the close, an excursus on method. The segues are so called because they gather up themes from the preceding chapters and inflect them in a different direction, to a different starting point for further reflection. The excursus on method in the final two chapters is meant to naturalize the conclusions of this study somewhat, by shifting the focus from Kafka to Kafka studies as an entity, from the exalted singularity of Kafka's life and works to the discipline of its recovery, which bears generally on the way that modern writers are being read.

# ABBREVIATIONS FOR KAFKA CITATIONS

B     *Benjamin über Kafka, Texte, Briefzeugnisse, Aufzeichnungen,* ed. Hermann Schweppenhäuser. Frankfurt a.M.: Suhrkamp Taschenbuch Verlag, 1981.

BF     *Briefe an Felice,* ed. Erich Heller and Jürgen Born. Frankfurt a.M.: Fischer, 1967. See LF.

Br     *Briefe, 1902–1924,* ed. Max Brod. Frankfurt a.M.: Fischer, 1958. See L.

BrM     *Briefe, 1900–1912,* ed. by Hans-Gerd Koch. Frankfurt a.M.: Fischer, 1999.

C     *The Castle,* trans. Mark Harman. New York: Schocken, 1998.

CS     *Franz Kafka: The Complete Stories,* ed. Nahum N. Glatzer. New York: Schocken, 1971.

DF     *Dearest Father,* trans. Ernest Kaiser and Eithne Wilkins. New York: Schocken, 1954.

D1     *The Diaries of Franz Kafka, 1910–1913,* trans. Joseph Kresh. New York: Schocken, 1948.

D2     *The Diaries of Franz Kafka, 1914–1923,* trans. Martin Greenberg (with the assistance of Hannah Arendt). New York: Schocken, 1949.

GrW     *The Great Wall of China,* trans. Willa and Edwin Muir. New York: Schocken, 1960.

GW     *Gesammelte Werke* in zwölf Bänden, nach der Kritischen Ausgabe, ed. Hans-Gerd Koch. Frankfurt a.M.: Fischer Taschenbuch Verlag, 1992.

H     *Hochzeitsvorbereitungen auf dem Lande und andere Prosa aus dem Nachlaß,* ed. Max Brod. Frankfurt a.M.: Fischer, 1953.

L     *Letters to Friends, Family, and Editors,* trans. Richard and Clara Winston. New York: Schocken, 1977. See Br.

LF     *Letters to Felice,* trans. James Stern and Elizabeth Duckworth. New York: Schocken, 1973. See BF.

M       *The Metamorphosis*, trans. and ed. Stanley Corngold. New
        York: Norton, 1996.

NS2     *Nachgelassene Schriften und Fragmente II*, ed. Jost Schillemeit.
        Frankfurt a.M.: Fischer, 1992.

Pp      *Der Proceß*, in der Fassung der Handschrift, ed. Malcolm
        Pasley. Frankfurt a.M.: Fischer, 1990.

Pr      *Der Process*, "Historisch-Kritische Ausgabe sämtlicher Hand-
        schriften, Drucke und Typoskripte," ed. Roland Reuß in
        cooperation with Peter Staengle. Basel/Frankfurt a.M.:
        Stroemfeld/Roter Stern, 1998.

T       *The Trial*, trans. Breon Mitchell. New York: Schocken, 1998.

V       *Der Verschollene*, ed. Jost Schillemeit. Frankfurt a.M:
        Fischer, 1983.

# Lambent Traces

---

## Franz Kafka

# BEGINNINGS

"KAFKA IS NOT systematic, but he is coherent."[1] Yet for all the progress made in cataloguing the stereotypes of Kafka's social environment (sexual politics, family politics, ethnic politics, technics of script and the other media), the fundamental figures of his thought remain unsolved.

After more than a half-century of investigation, one would think, there ought to be an answer to the question, What, then, is Kafka's argument? And yet a critic as incisive as Erich Heller, addressing the question of the meaning of *The Trial*, throws up his hands in the end, asking: "What *is* [K.'s] guilt? What *is* the Law?"[2] And, what, indeed, is Kafka's Law? Here, as in everything in Kafka, it seems, in the words of Friedrich Hölderlin's hero Hyperion, "an instant of reflection hurls us down."[3]

I cannot say what *the* argument is, though I will discuss various constellations of images, tropes, narratives, aperçus, and aphorisms that resemble arguments. They are the exploding patterns of Kafka's thought. Walter Benjamin saw Kafka's work as a nebula of Kabbalah and Eddington; Theodor Adorno, as a cryptogram of the waste products extruded by late capitalism on its way to fascism; Walter Sokel, as the expanded myths of "authority and the self"; Gerhard Kurz, as the product of drastic awakenings. More recently, in *Schriftverkehr* (textual intercourse), Gerhard Neumann and Wolf Kittler have uncovered the modern medial dimensions of Kafka's stories of communication and failed communication.[4] Within this giant, endlessly ramified complex, argument-like figures of thought readily emerge. But these sequences do not fit the patterns of lived experience of persons generally or the customary dialectical or deconstructive moves that inform contemporary analysis. Kafka's "business," it appears, like "our business," according to Jean-François Lyotard, "is not to supply reality but to invent allusions to the conceivable."[5] The most important word is "allusions."

Consider a text of Kafka's, not chosen entirely at random, that illustrates the sort of conceptual difficulties I am envisioning. In spring 1922, in a notebook entry that is exceptionally clear and seemingly accessible to analysis, Kafka constructed one of the many parabolic houses that abound in his confessional writings. A building arises from his failure to write; or better, as he literally says,

> Writing denies itself to me. Hence plan for autobiographical inves-
> tigations. Not biography but investigation and detection of the
> smallest possible component parts. Out of these I will then con-
> struct myself, as one whose house is unsafe wants to build a safe
> one next to it, if possible out of the material of the old one. What is
> bad, admittedly, is if in the midst of building his strength gives out
> and now, instead of one house, unsafe but yet complete, he has one
> half-destroyed and one half-finished house, that is to say, nothing.
> (DF 350)

How intelligible this is. It is easy to understand what it might mean to
live in a house that is unsafe, to want to build another, in doing so to
want to justify even the elements of the first failed enterprise, to redeem
them even, in proving them good enough to be reused. We understand,
too, how one's strength might give out, and where would one be then?
Neither at home in the first building nor the second, the first imperfect
and yet complete, the second merely half-built: the builder is stranded
between them. This is where the aphorism could end, and this is where
we might reasonably conclude that here is a narrative intelligible on the
grounds of its analogy with lived experience. But this is not where it
ends. It continues:

> What follows is madness, that is to say, something like a Cossack
> dance between the two houses, whereby the Cossack goes on scrap-
> ing and throwing aside the earth with the heels [Absätze] of his
> boots until his grave is dug out under him. (DF 350, H 388)

The leap (it is swifter and less traceable than a leap) to another order
of the imagination, where thought-in-images races, takes us out of a
system of binary opposites—of "writing" versus "autobiographical investigations"—and out of a pattern of plausible reference to the building of a new house from the elements of the old. It takes us to another
kind of literary intensity. The Cossack dance dances into the text, as
text; the dance is without prototype in what has so far been given by
the text and without fitting conclusion at an order of insight and reflection. The Cossack dance dances into the text as the very act of producing text. Protruding from the dancer's scraping boots are heels and, by
association, pens—for *Absätze* means at once "heels" and "para-
graphs"—while, quite consistently, Kafka's verb "scraping" (*scharren*)
and the act of writing (*schreiben*) also share a root. This is to stress the
art-character of the dance, the literal product of that "freedom of true
description that releases one's foot from lived experience [Erlebnis]"
(D1 100, GW 9:71).
    Meanwhile, the qualifier "Cossack" adds another braided supplement

of meaning, invoking Kafka's history of relations to the "Russian" friend of "The Judgment"; to the Russian wastes in the diaries as a paradigm of indifference; and to the Russian killing agents of pogroms.[6] In pointing to a cold climate, it gathers together all the associations that Sokel has noted in this "existential sign"—connotations of isolation, asceticism, fanaticism, exile.[7] But that this Cossack dance as another sort of *writing* should finally dig one's own grave turns reason and worldly experience upside down. It is "madness," for writing in the normal case would raise one up out of the deathlike anonymity of unarticulated life. Writing may be an act of inscribing, as one implication of "scraping" has it, and may even represent, as Benjamin remarked, the death of an intention—the death, by degrees, of an empirical self—but it also surely amounts to a construction of sorts.

There are different types of writing here to look at. Recall how the passage began: the speaker has lost touch with "real" writing, which can only be real in the sense of transcending a merely empirical self, the creature of affects and stereotypes; and he has failed. So, barred from real writing, he seeks to write autobiography, a kind of writing that on the face of it is dedicated to building up and affirming the empirical person. But that too has failed and passed into another figurative action of writing that is unlike "real" writing because the death that this new dancing implies is more grievous than the figurative death of an empirical intention; and it is unlike autobiographical writing, because it does not construct a house for the ego (L 82). But if, in being unlike autobiographical writing, it is, as writing, more like real writing, then it does not only dig out a metaphorical grave; it constructs another sort of apparatus, contributing to the manufacture of Kafka's portable house of art. And if, in being unlike real writing, it is more like autobiographical writing, then certainly, it, too, has an ego-building dimension. So what, finally, is the relation of this *third* kind of writing—the enigmatic "construction of the grave"—to the house of art and the half-built house of the ego?

I do not think this narrative is, on the face of it, susceptible to a Hegelian—triadic, subsumptive—model of thought. And a deconstructionist model that stresses the eternally supplementary, delaying character of the third term—the Cossack dance that undoes the ostensible binary of the houses—understates the power of the third term to produce an entirely new sequence of truth claims even from the dreadful finality of the grave as well as on the heels of the cultural reference that digs it. Nonetheless, the passage began as a sequence of restricted arguments: "Writing denies itself to me. Hence plan for autobiographical investigations." Such sequences recur in even the most unpredictably image-saturated and argumentatively torqued of Kafka's stories. And, in this case, some of this argument points to one or another of Kafka's strife-torn identity elements, elements of his chief predicament. Kafka's work, as Benjamin noted, "argues nothing but is so constituted that it can at any time be inserted in an argumentative context" (B 41).

In the two houses above, even half-built, one discerns a pattern, a genealogical reminiscence of the two houses into which Kafka was born, for he is the son of two fathers.[8] He is the bourgeois flesh-and-blood of Herrmann Kafka, the entrepreneur and dealer in curses; and he is also someone else's son, the son of another father of whose family he is the "formal necessity" but who remains unknown.

> He does not live for the sake of his personal life; he does not think for the sake of his personal thoughts. It seems to him that he lives and thinks under the compulsion of a family, which, it is true, is itself superabundant in life and thought, but for which he constitutes, in obedience to some law unknown to him, a formal necessity. Because of this unknown family and this unknown law he cannot be exempted. (GW 269)

Kafka's task is to reconstruct himself along the imaginary lines of this paternity. Readers acquainted with Benjamin's readings of Kafka may see in this formulation a domestic version of Benjamin's famous aphorism:

> Kafka's work is an ellipse; its widely spaced focal points are defined, on the one hand, by mystical experience (which is, above all, the experience of tradition) and, on the other hand, by the experience of the modern city-dweller.[9]

This genealogical pattern has plain ramifications. If Kafka's father, the urban parvenu, is not his true father, then for one moment Kafka is fatherless, he is half-orphaned. He lives in another "country," a wilderness in which, separated from his parents, he is at once exile and orphan; he is a foreigner, an "American," in search of a new Zion.[10] Yet at other times — times that are startling — Herrmann Kafka is also the valuable, the authentic instigator of the son's search for the other father — the father of the "second" son who, at the beginning of Kafka's intellectual and artistic career, is represented by the bachelor, the writer. Consider this remarkable sentence from "Letter to His Father": "My writing was all about you," wrote Kafka.

> All I did there, after all, was to bemoan what I could not bemoan upon your breast. It was an intentionally long-drawn-out leave-taking from you, only although *it was brought about by force on your part*, it did take its course in the direction determined by me. (emphasis added, DF 177)

Now lines of relation have been laid down that Kafka's stories can accommodate, in which a father may be loved as the source, ignored as the imposter, and hated as the usurper. The sequence is not logical ("systematic"), since it violates the law of the excluded middle, but it is coherent, in the sense of constituting a pattern. This makes at least one empirical feature of Kafka's stories immediately cogent: his propensity for twinning—viz. "I"/the Praying Man (in *Description of a Struggle*); "I"/You, the Bachelor (in "'You,' I Said . . ."); Georg Bendemann/the Russian friend (in "The Judgment"); Lieutenant Gregor Samsa/the monstrous vermin (in *The Metamorphosis*); Old Commandant/New Commandant (in "In the Penal Colony"); businessman/schoolmaster (in "The Village Schoolmaster"); jackals/Arabs (in "Jackals and Arabs"); K. the land surveyor and the life he left behind (in *The Castle*); and, in the same novel, K.'s indistinguishable apprentices, the two Friedas, and Sordini/Sortini. Perhaps the root disturbance in this doubling—the last example is vivid—is their difference precisely in the midst of so much resemblance—a sameness that emerges only as "marred" by difference, a difference that emerges only as marred by sameness.[11]

If such distinctions sound abstruse, they are nonetheless productively played out in Kafka's novels, as par excellence, in the haunting repetitions of *The Trial* and *The Castle*. The endless resemblances of the Castle-world without qualities are full of a foreboding of danger. This world of doublings is prefigured by the sinister paintings in *The Trial* offered for sale to Joseph K. by the painter Titorelli:

> "A landscape of the heath," said the painter, and handed K. the painting. It showed two frail trees, standing at a great distance from one another in the dark grass. . . . "Here's a companion piece to that picture," said the painter. It may have been intended as a companion piece, but not the slightest difference could be seen between it and the first one: here were the trees, here was the grass, and there the sunset. . . . "You seem to like the subject," said the painter, and pulled out a third painting, "luckily enough, I have a similar one right here." But it was not merely similar, however, it was exactly the same landscape. (T 163)

In the Castle-world the barren "heath" is covered in a snow eternally blanketing differences. The lower inhabitants are even less distinguishable from one another than Sordini and Sortini. When K. says that his place lies somewhere between the peasants and the Castle, the teacher objects, saying, "There is no difference between the peasants and the Castle" (C 9). Klamm's men, too, cannot be told apart at first sight. Confronting Arthur and Jeremiah, the assistants furnished by the Castle, K. is puzzled: "'This is difficult,' said K., comparing their faces as he had often done before. 'How am I supposed to distinguish between you? Only your names are different, otherwise you're as alike . . . as snakes'" (C 18).

Such indistinction defines the architecture of the place. The village housing the Castle is a maze of ramshackle buildings. Even as a putative surveyor, K. cannot discern the village from the Castle, which is itself "only a rather miserable little town"; the snowed-in world allows for no distinctions of rank (C 8). Everywhere in the Castle-world lowers the presence of something not so much downtrodden as subhuman — pre-historical — visible in the faces of the peasants, their heads as if beaten flat under the weight of archaic authority. Here, the effect is of another sort of doubling: the sameness/difference pair operates to produce a sense of the contemporaneousness of the archaic and the modern — that fusion of aeons in Kafka originally noted by Benjamin.[12] The danger for the hero, the surveyor K., who appears to have wandered into the village at the same time that he claims his right to live there, is to founder in unknown dimensions of indistinction. There are

> hours in which K. continually had the feeling that he was so deep in a foreign place as no man before him, a foreign place in which even the air had no ingredient of the air of home, in which one must suffocate on foreignness and in whose absurd allurements one could do nothing more than go further, go further astray. (C 41, translation modified)

Repetition and difference operate their effects even as abstractions. Reflecting on "The Judgment," Kafka declared, not obviously with disapproval: "The story is full of abstractions. . . . The friend is hardly a real person, perhaps he is rather what father and son have in common" (LF 267). The factor that the father and the son finally have least in common, against all odds — I shall spring for this point — is the factor of paternity. The outcome of the entire complex of thought and action involved in Kafka's writing "The Judgment" is not his paternity, which remains an abstraction throughout: he cannot give himself the name of father. In the moment of writing the conclusion of "The Judgment," Kafka may have thought, as he declared to Max Brod, of "a strong ejaculation";[13] but when it came to reflecting on this story in one of the several diary entries that followed its composition, he said it came out of him "like a regular birth" (DI 278). A recent thesis on fatherhood helps to explain Kafka's fascinated aversion to abstractions:

> Fatherhood is a physical relation, but not enough of one — hence it needs to be constructed culturally, solidified institutionally, established by law, *becoming* the law. As the imposition of the abstract

on the material, it becomes the figure of abstraction itself, *the abstraction that has constituted and organized civilization as we know it.*[14]

Later in life the real father and the ideal father function as archrepresentatives—they are progenitors—of worlds that Kafka calls material and spiritual. But their distinction, especially in the matter of what is owed to them, is never finally separate. If it seems tautologically binding that life should be lived in devotion to the "spiritual" world, Kafka will also write, "In the struggle between yourself and the world, back the world" (literally, "be the world's second") (DF 39). This is another illustration of his insatiable penchant for undoing antithesis:

> My repugnance for [antitheses] is certain. . . . They make for thoroughness, fullness, completeness, but only like a figure on the "wheel of life" [a toy with a revolving wheel]; we have chased our little idea around the circle. They are as undifferentiated as they are different. (D1 157)[15]

Quite in accord with Kafka's horror of antitheses, Mark Anderson redeems the famous aporia in Kafka between the desire for writing, on the one hand, and family, on the other, in the reached treasure and solid joy of an imagined Zion.[16] There is the Zion of the achieved written work, and then there is the Zion of political Palestine, which includes marriage:

> It is as if the idea of Zionism were inseparable from the idea of marriage and founding a family. Both prospects represented to him the decisive step into a community, a living Jewish community. . . . To an anxious, literarily ambitious but unproductive Jewish writer plagued by bodily ills and what he thought was the malady of urban life, both Zionism and marriage within Judaism represented the threshold to a new, healthier, if frightening existence.

This "new and improved" existence does not exclude the practice of the writer's profession (though one would wonder what shape it would take, flattened within a new social differential).[17]

Kafka's horror of antithesis, like his penchant for doubling, is driven by a dominant myth of the two fathers. In *The Myth of Power and the Self*, Sokel refers the root of such doubling to Kafka's "Gnostic sensibility," his responsiveness to the proposition that being arises through an act of divine self-betrayal, a defection of God from himself.

> What predisposes Kafka to this particular Gnostic perspective is not only the split in the self between two contradictory demands, each of absolute validity, but also the radical division in the source

of the law, the split in the father figures, power figures, and God figures of his life and work.[18]

The figure of the two fathers informs Kafka's imagination of Zion as the bliss of a self purified of division. The model for this bliss is therefore a sort of death, a death of the ego that is constituted by such apparently intractable divisions. Writing well, writing ecstatically, Kafka is relieved of this burden. After completing "The Judgment," he recorded "the fearful strain and joy, how the story developed before me, as if I were advancing over water. Several times during this night I heaved my own weight on my back" (D1 276). It is in relation to such "self-consumption" (*Selbstaufzehrung*) that Kafka also conjures a redemptive death (DF 87, GW 6:198). "I would put myself in death's hands," he writes. "Remnant of a faith. Return to a father [zum Vater]. Great Day of Atonement [reconciliation, Versöhnüng]" (D2 187, GW 11:167). The figure of this Zion, according to the translation of Martin Greenberg and Hannah Arendt, no mean interpreters of Kafka, is "a" father. I would choose "the" father, even if the definite article still leaves the identity of this father unspecified. What is so haunting is that Kafka casts the goal of self-dissolution, which implicates writing, along with an explicit Gnostic theology of world-refusal, as the journey to the right father.

⌐⌐

With the citation of a Gnostic theology, an irregular doublet has emerged, involving the terms "Gnostic" and "gnostic." The "doctrine" of the two fathers is rooted in historical Gnosticism, but I have also said that Kafka's writerly élan is "gnostic" — i.e., neo-Gnostic. What is the meaning of this difference?

  In the pages that follow, Gnosticism appears in an upper- and a lower-case version. Upper-case Gnosticism refers to systems of theological belief active in the Middle East around the second century A.D. until put down mercilessly by an endangered Catholic Church and by other orthodoxies — Persian and Jewish. Gnosticism views this world as the corrupt product not of the true god but of a demented demiurge;[19] nevertheless, traces of the true world can be intuited by the live spirit in ecstasy. Sparks fly up. The task is purification — not personal augmentation and not reproduction.

  Kafka had more than a passing acquaintance with the systematic theology of Gnosticism, including the "Gnostic edges of Kabbalah."[20] He owned Walther Köhler's *Die Gnosis*;[21] in discussion circles at the salon

Haus Fanta, he heard lectures on a type of Gnosticism called Marcionism. William M. Johnston offers this vivid precis:

> The gnosis that flourished at Prague between 1890 and 1930 resembled a Christian heresy known as Marcionism. Preaching in Anatolia and Rome, Marcion (ca. 85–ca. 155) had taught that the Creator God of the Jews was an evil demiurge, whose Creation had trapped men until Christ came to deliver them. Representing the supreme, benevolent God, Christ preached a Gospel of love which if heeded would abolish the tyranny imposed by a capricious creator. Marcion reprobated Jewish law, promising redemption after death from the despotism of the Creator. Hostility to law and yearning for a remote salvation characterize the Gnostics of Prague.[22]

Sokel's *The Myth of Power and the Self*, which considers Kafka's Gnosticism in depth, objects to the premise of a Marcionist influence on Kafka precisely on account of its hostility to Jewish law.[23]

Indeed, for all the glamor of this association of Kafka with Marcionism and other unusual theologies—Kabbalistic and Chinese—it is important to keep Johnston's proviso in mind: "Marcionism" was "similar to" the gnosis that flourished in Prague in Kafka's life; Kafka was at best similar to the "Gnostics of Prague"; and it is not trivially paradoxical to recall Kafka's own voiced concern, whether he was in any important way "similar to" himself.[24] This puts Kafka's writing at three removes from Marcionism. In a word, Kafka's Gnosticism is not Marcionist; pace Franz Kuna, Kafka did not "embrace" Marcionism.[25]

On the other hand, this exclusion does not rule out the perspective that views a number of themes in Kafka's work as refractions of Marcionist law and lore.[26] The most interesting of these, as I have suggested, is the "doctrine of the two gods."[27] In *The Metamorphosis* we have Gregor Samsa's agonized surmise:

> Truly, this was not the father he had imagined to himself. . . . And yet, and yet, could that be his father? . . . From under his bushy eyebrows his black eyes darted fresh and penetrating glances . . . [as he] advanced with a grim visage. (CS 120)

Here, it is worth noting, the Marcionist dualism is "estranged." For if the father who appears to his verminous son Samsa is "higher" than the invalid that Gregor had imagined, in Ireneaus's account of Marcionism it is precisely the "lower" of the contrasted gods who is warlike, concupiscent, and inconstant.[28] Granting that Kafka's relation to his reading is allusive and metamorphic, we could still find traces here of the Marcionist and other Gnostic gods at work. This is the view of Gerhard

Kurz, author of an incisive monograph on Kafka's death drive. "Kafka's literature of existence," he writes,

> speaks of border skirmishes between life and death — of anxiety, the experience of death, guilt, and suffering. Its recurrent metaphorical paradigms are . . . homelessness, the loss of orientation, impotence, "thrownness," exposure, vulnerability, anxiety, madness, sickness, imprisonment, alienation. All are metaphors of Gnostic origin.[29]

This origin evidently includes more than the principle of the evil creator. Clark Emery, a Blake scholar, has assembled a list of "characteristics considered normative for all Gnostic teachers and groups in the era of classical Gnosticism":[30]

> The Gnostics posited an original spiritual unity that came to be split into a plurality. As a result of this precosmic division the universe was created. It was created by a leader possessing inferior spiritual powers, a leader often having the appearance of the Old Testament Jehovah. A female emanation of God was involved in the cosmic creation.
>
> In the cosmos, space and time have a malevolently spiritual character and may be personified as demonic beings separating man from God. For man, the universe is a vast prison. He is enslaved both by the physical laws of nature and by such psychic laws as the Mosaic code. Mankind may be personified as Adam, who lies in the deep sleep of ignorance, his powers of spiritual self-awareness stupefied by materiality. However, within each natural man is an "inner man," a fallen spark of the divine substance.
>
> Since, within each man a spark of holiness exists, the possibility of an awakening from the present stupefaction exists. What effects the awakening is not obedience, not faith, not good works, but knowledge.
>
> Before the awakening, men undergo troubled dreams. The knowledge that awakens man from these dreams is not arrived at by cognition but through revelationary experience, and it is not an accession of information but a modification of the sensate being. The awakening (that is, the salvation) of any individual is a cosmic event. Since the whole universal effort is to restore the wholeness and unity of the godhead, active rebellion against the moral law of the Old Testament is enjoined upon every man.[31]

Some of these themes survive in Kafka, but few of them serve him as principles. It is true that for Kafka "the knowledge that awakens man from these [troubled] dreams is not arrived at by cognition but through revelationary experience" — it happens in the act of reckless writing.

And certainly, this knowledge is "not an accession of information."[32] On the other hand, there is little else of normative Gnosticism literally present in Kafka's writings, and much of it is altogether alien to him — viz. God's "female emanation" and "active rebellion against the moral law." But since several Gnostic characteristics have a haunting relevance to Kafka's wider concerns, they can be termed a Gnosticism suited to a reading of his work.

Gnostic elements permeate Kafka's writing; but because they do not supersaturate it, his writing is *tout dit* a lower-case gnosticism, importantly including mythic elements of his own devising. "I must create a System, or be enslav'd by another Man's," wrote another heterodox Gnostic William Blake.[33] Small "g" gnosticism is a descriptor of Kafka's experience of writing; as a *writer* he is a "Gnostic sort" of writer; his "writerly being" (*Schriftstellersein*) has a Gnostic character (Br 383). This is a type that I shall serially elaborate in the lower-case: it includes the writer's ecstasy and a sense of bodily detachment; writing as a consuming of or leaping off "experience"; and a vast, autonomous world of inspirations conveying the promise of a higher perception (D2 212).[34]

The key point remains that for all of Kafka's arcane learning, normative Gnosticism could never serve him as a *philosophy of composition*. There is a world of conceptual difference between a Gnosticism that perceives the beginning of wisdom in the wish to die and a gnosticism that allows for ecstasy in the act of writing and constitutes a moral justification for a life lived here and now in writing.

At certain times in his life, Kafka did experiment more seriously than at other times with normative Gnostic thinking. This is true especially for the years after 1917, when the diagnosis of his tuberculosis extinguished the extravagant hopes he harbored about living a life as a professional writer independent of his family, outside Prague. Now he turns to Gnosticism as a stay against a senseless death. At the same time it is no accident — it is utterly crucial — that these years 1917–1918, in which he devoted himself to thinking the Gnosis, were years in which he wrote next to nothing. His illness, which conjured his real death, constitutes a muted syncope, a hiatus in principle, between his gnosticism and his Gnosticism. The stories toward the end of his life (see chapter 6) are thereafter penetrated by formal elements consistent with Gnosticism: Kafka is all too conscious of a death that exceeds, alas, the "little death" of the writing ecstasy.

The distinction between the Gnostic versus the gnostic component in any given work of Kafka, however, cannot be prescribed in advance: like the terms writing and death, they mingle, separate, and return. In one sense the gnosticism of writing is consistent with most Gnosticisms: it stands in the way of paternity, it is a stay against paternity, it is consistent with Gnosticism's repudiation of this-worldly carnal existence. In another sense, such gnosticism is not a self-denying spiritual exercise. From the beginning Kafka means to write books good enough to be published and in this way secure a certain cultural immortality. One hears of Kafka's belief in writing as belief itself. In this sense he is this-worldly, he is not a Gnostic, and the time of Gnostic thought experimentation is an articulation and heightening of concerns that have always been present in his life as a writer.[35]

If Kafka is, generally speaking, a religious thinker, he is, as Ritchie Robertson puts it,

> a highly individual and challenging religious thinker. His thought does not proceed within the framework of any one religion, but defines itself against a number of theologies and philosophies. . . . One simplifies Kafka and denies his originality and his eclecticism if one locates his thought within any religious system.[36]

What this comes down to, for Kafka, is a remarkably intense attachment to writing — to its promise of a bliss of justification that includes a measure of cultural immortality — and, on the other hand, an aversion to life, a poorly suppressed longing to die.

We began this chapter by weaving a web to contain Kafka, but the web was attached to only one piece of one small text, the text of the Cossack dance. As a result, it was incomplete from the start. Will it come round at the end of (hermeneutic) time to the remainder of the aphorism?

In the meantime, a time of great patience, it will be useful to study the sources of Kafka's first great story, "The Judgment." "The Judgment," a struggle between father and son, is not least of all a decisive anchoring term in the Gnostic pattern of two fathers and the gnostic pattern of the writer's ecstasy and the writer's death. Anderson suggests that

> the search of so many of Kafka's characters for the Law, for a home, for artistic fulfillment, can be read metaphorically as a figure for Kafka's own search to reproduce the conditions and results of this single night in September 1912 when he wrote "The Judgment."[37]

It was the ecstasy of writing this story — and such premonitions as Kafka had before, while writing — that very likely prompted him in turn to study Gnostic mysticisms.[38]

*Chapter 1*

## IN THE CIRCLE OF "THE JUDGMENT"

> Kafka's work is dipped in the color of powerlessness. The
> work develops out of a lifelong diary that keeps going
> by questioning itself.
> —Elias Canetti, *"Dialogue with the Cruel Partner"*

THE IMPORTANCE FOR Kafka of writing his first great story "The Judgment" cannot be overestimated. He composed the piece on the night of September 22–23, 1912, in a single sitting, in a single inspired thrust, and it thereafter became a permanent reference to the stations of his career—his breakthrough and his vindication. What remained crucial was the way the story was written: it came out of him like nothing he had written before, in "a complete opening out of the body and the soul" (D1 276). Only work written in this fashion deserved to survive. Toward the end of that year 1912, after reading "The Judgment" aloud at a circle of relatives and friends, he noted in his journal, "The indubitableness of the story was proved" (D1 278).[1]

The production and reproduction, in the telling, of such ecstasy confirmed for Kafka his earlier promise as an author. The story looks back to many attempts to find the themes and forms that he could acknowledge as his children, offspring of a literary reproduction (he wrote in his journal: "The Judgment" "came out of me like a regular birth" [D1 278]). And the story also looks forward to a time of despondency, marked by such works as *The Metamorphosis* (written in 1912; published in 1915); *The Trial* (1914–1915; 1925); and "In the Penal Colony" (1914; 1919)—works about debasement and the failed promise of justification.

Erich Heller has noted a remarkable coded attestation of the importance of "The Judgment" for Kafka. During that night in which Kafka wrote the story, writes Heller,

> he felt, his diary records, that several times "I heaved my own weight on my back" and knew that "only *in this way* can writing be done." With his novel-writing, interrupted again and again, and stretching over years, he was, as we have heard him lament, "in the shameful lowlands of writing." Anyone having read and pondered these remarks cannot but think of them when the Lawyer in *The*

*Trial* speaks to K. of two classes of lawyers (lawyers are, after all, the professional writers of "petitions" on behalf of the accused): the ordinary type who leads his client "by a slender thread until the verdict is reached" and the superior type who "lifts his client on his shoulders . . . and carries him without once letting him down until the verdict is reached, and even beyond it" (where there is "verdict" in the English translation, there is *"Urteil"* in the German, "judgment"). There is little doubt that Kafka was thinking of the story of that name.[2]

This is only one of a number of such moments in Kafka's writing in which "The Judgment" is commemorated. The story "In the Penal Colony," which Kafka was to write in the midst of composing *The Trial* in 1914, two years after the composition of "The Judgment, also encodes the continuing intensity with which the night of "The Judgment" lived on in him. The German word for the prisoner in "In the Penal Colony" is "der Verurteilte" ("the condemned man") (CS 145; GW 1:167). The explorer, who is visiting the penal colony, asks with amazement: "He doesn't know the sentence that has been passed on him?" (The word for "sentence" is, again, "Urteil.") To this the officer-in-charge replies, "No" (CS 145).[3] A good deal of the mythic autobiography of the writer is packed into these lines. The obvious connection runs between the act of not knowing or no longer knowing — disowning, forgetting — one's story "The Judgment," on the one hand, and the punishment that such forgetfulness will call down. If Kafka has forgotten the promise of future achievement implied in writing "The Judgment," then, in a certain sense, he deserves to be sentenced to death.

The officer then explains why the prisoner has been kept in the dark: "There would be no point in telling him. He'll learn it on his body" (CS 145).[4] Consider that "The Judgment" is about the destruction of the hero's engagement to a woman whose initials are FB (Frieda Brandenfeld). Consider that Kafka actually dedicated "The Judgment" to his future fiancée Felice Bauer with the words "A Story for Ms. Felice B." Kafka, who, only afterwards, in July 1914, was to suffer a broken engagement with his fiancée, would then experience the meaning of the story in actual truth, on his own body, as it were. Part of the mythic greatness of "The Judgment" for Kafka can have been its prophetic character.[5]

Before writing "The Judgment," Kafka conveyed in journal entries the tension of his being part of a family from which he hoped to escape by writing. He began keeping a diary in the summer of 1909 with a few dissociated remarks about the ravishing dancer Eduardowa and his own unravishing body, e.g., "The auricle of my ear felt fresh, rough, cool, succulent as a leaf, to the touch. I write this very decidedly out of despair over my body and over a future with this body" (D1 11). These jottings amount to a semisystematic foray into types of medial perception—film, dance, and the physical sensorium as such: vision, touch, smell.[6] The diary entry that immediately follows, however, written around May 17, 1910, records a striking change of perspective. In this piece, a sort of prose poem—the first entry to be marked by a high degree of self-reflectiveness—Kafka sets down his reasons for keeping a diary. It begins:

> Finally, after five months of my life during which I could write nothing that would have satisfied me, and for which no power will compensate me, . . . it occurs to me to talk to myself again. Whenever I really questioned myself, there was always a response forthcoming, there was something in me to catch fire, in this heap of straw that I have been for five months and whose fate, it seems, is to be set afire during the summer and consumed more swiftly than the onlooker can blink his eyes. If only that would happen to me!
> (D1 11–12)

This passage points ahead to several of Kafka's great preoccupations. First, there is the image of "combustion," "taking fire," for truly radical writing, which will recur: "How for everything," he will note immediately after composing "The Judgment," "how for everything, for the strangest fancies, there waits a great fire in which they perish and rise up again" (D1 276). In one or another group of images, the factor of perishing, of death, as the punishment for impiety and also a blissful release, informs, invades, all of Kafka's major work.[7]

Throughout this chapter I shall be dealing with the second great factor, Kafka's conversation with himself. But before we leave this passage, let us note one detail, however inconspicuous: it is the number five—the *five months* of sterility, when Kafka does not address himself and is nothing more than a heap of straw, the dead time following a moment when that straw had taken fire. "Five months" turns out to be a hermeneutic clue of considerable importance.

What is finally decisive in the diary entry is how, five months later, the form of Kafka's taking fire becomes "real" self-questioning. "The special nature of my inspiration" arises from a flash of self-scrutiny—and not, say, from a sudden glance into his meager surroundings or from the need to settle a grievance (D1 45). A long early diary entry centering on a "reproach" (*Vorwurf*) does everything to anthropomorphize it, vary it, ring changes on it, turn it into an entire population of figures — everything except discharge it.

This claim to the self-addressed, self-igniting character of Kafka's diaries, which Kafka himself makes, differs from the account given by his friend and editor Max Brod — an inadequate account that informs the commentary even of Kafka's perceptive editor Hans-Gerd Koch.[8] According to Brod, Kafka's diary originated as a reply to a bet made by Brod during the period of stagnation dated in the diary entry above as early summer 1909. Brod had proposed a "sporting competition" between the two friends while both were traveling together: each would keep a record of his observations, and then they would compare results.[9] The first object of this competition was to be "the airplanes in Brescia," which did indeed become one of Kafka's earliest published pieces as a newspaper article with that title. Thereafter, writes Brod, Kafka produced a variety of descriptive sketches already having the character of the later diary entries.

The point of Brod's thesis is that in every case one can identify an empirical origin for each of Kafka's notebook entries, even those that display various kinds of writing not only autobiographical — stories, epigrams, and detached observations that unfold in self-conscious awareness of their own rhetorical figures. "It is thanks to me," Brod declares, "that this diary ever came into being; even Franz's quartos [notebooks] grew directly out of our little notes on our journeyings, were in fact in a certain sense sequels [Fortsetzungen] to them."[10] But this spatial logic of continuous extension from the minutiae of observed particulars to thought pieces is oversimple; and Brod himself even undermines his idea in adding that at the root of this "reportage," there existed "a conscious and already cultivated tendency of Kafka to render such an account of his experiences."[11] This "tendency" is another name for the "writerly being" (*Schriftstellersein*) that Kafka recognized in himself and indeed *as* himself (Br 383). Brod's account of the relation of descriptive writing to Kafka's thought pieces finally drowns in a welter of opposing terms and images: reportage is supposed to have provided "fresh nourishment" to this "tendency" while at the same time enabling its "systematic" development. But reportage is the opposite of system. The point that Kafka makes repeatedly is that the diary is an affair of self-questioning leading to a certain kind of self-immolation — a *dissolution* of experience — with the intent of producing "real" writing (L 82). If the term "systematic" is to be used, it should be "systematic dissolution." We have glimpsed the image of such immolation, the separation from experience, that surfaces memorably in the diary entry of October 20, 1911, concerning the very project of writing a descriptive novel with Max Brod: "The 18th at Max's; wrote about Paris. Wrote badly, without really arriving at that freedom of *true* description that releases one's foot from lived experience [Erlebnis]" (D1 100, GW 9:71; emphasis added). The liberating character of self-reflexive questioning and its proximity to "real" writing is confirmed in 1914, when after another drought, Kafka succeeded in immersing himself in the beginnings of *The Trial*, noting, in a diary entry of August 15:

> I have been writing these past few days, may it continue. Today I am not so completely protected by and enclosed in my work as I was two years ago [that is, during the period of composition of "The Judgment," *The Metamorphosis*, and most of the America-novel], nevertheless have the feeling that my monotonous, empty, mad bachelor's life has some justification. *I can once more carry on a conversation with myself [Ich kann wieder ein Zwiegespräch mit mir führen]*, and don't stare so into complete emptiness. Only in this way is there any possibility of improvement for me. (D2 79, GW 10:169; emphasis added).

The phrase "only in this way" recalls Kafka's celebration of writing "The Judgment"; and, again, the propitiatory way of invoking genuine writing is "holding a dialogue with myself." The diary begins to resemble literature only when, like literature, it too arises from preternaturally quick conversation — when "no distance divides the interrogator from the one who answers him" (D2 131).[12]

A difficult diary entry, written a year after the one of ca. May 17, 1910, with which we began, develops these topics:

> I have the unhappy belief that I haven't the time for the least bit of good work, for I really don't have time for a story, time to expand myself in every direction in the world, as I should have to do. But then I once more believe that my trip will turn out better, that I shall comprehend better if I am relaxed [gelockert] by a little writing, and so I try again. (D1 61, GW 9:32)

Immediately thereafter Kafka begins to set down the complex of fragments that Max Brod was to collate and publish as the intense, essential story, beginning " 'You,' I said. . . ." Koch, Kafka's editor, comments on the diary passage as follows: "When Kafka is blocked for literature, he never ceases to turn to his diary in order to loosen up, relax [sich auflockern] through 'a little writing' " (GW 9:351). But this idea of "loosening up" is not perspicuous, nor does it take into account the peculiar temporality of the events of the passage. At first, we read, a sort of paralysis inhibits writing; thereafter, we realize, writing has come first, preceding and preparing for more writing. What is important is the relation of diary writing to the ecstatic writing of fiction.

Kafka's "trying again," in the passage cited above, might be a sign of his beginning the fiction that follows an only preparatory writing. This is Koch's reading. Kafka has been writing about a way of being on a "trip." And if the trip is of the order of a trip to Italy, then the self that needs to be "relaxed" is the empirical self that goes on vacation, and the diary provides this sort of self-help. But if, as I suggest, the "trip" is imaginary, the kind of thing propelled by Pegasus—a conceit suggested by the idea of an "expansion in every direction"—then Kafka is already inside or, indeed, astride his fiction; and "relaxing" is a moment in the beating rhythm of the wings. *These nice questions are the questions that the diary entry asks of the author.*[13] In this medium of "real" questioning, the empirical self, the blocked author of the diary entry, its narrative persona, and the personae of the story become interchangeable, though in fusing they generate different and irrefragable distinctions of their own. The empirical self is dissolved in the rhetoric of these entries, and the final outcome *is* the story " 'You,' I said. . . ." In performing an implicitly multivalent, polysemous dialogue with itself, this diary entry performs the very enablement ("loosening up") that it says is its aim. Things are consistent, then, that when, following the story element " 'You,' I said . . . ," the empirical self reappears, it is as a higher type—as a *reader* of Dickens ("I have been reading about Dickens")—and his language is intensely poetological, famous and inspired:

> Is it so difficult and can an outsider understand that you experience a story within yourself from its beginning, from the distant point up to the approaching locomotive of steel, coal, and steam, and you don't abandon it even now, but want to be pursued by it and have time for it, therefore are pursued by it and of your own volition run before it wherever it may thrust and wherever you may lure it. (D1 61)

Kafka's diary entries exist to produce a draught of transformation in which their own beginnings can be blown away. Nothing can resist the antigravity of this draught, no weight is heavy enough to anchor the body caught in it ("Several times during this night I heaved my own weight on my back," wrote Kafka on the morning after composing "The Judgment" [D1 275–76]). Only a strong enough self-questioning could produce the kinesis of ascent; only a hot enough friction of self on self could turn the perceptions of actual things into "optical accidents."[14] There is, meanwhile—in principle and in fact—a weak self-questioning; and the name that Kafka gives such introspection is "psychology."[15] The task of empirical psychology could well be to strengthen and enable the practical personality, but the task of Kafka's self-scrutiny is to abandon this personality, *so* see it, see it *so*, as to annihilate it. To this end, on

May 17, 1910, Kafka will "talk" to himself again (the German is stronger: the verb *ansprechen* has the connotation of "forcing an encounter with"); he will address himself in an ardent and also in a stringent way.

By studying the manuscripts of the notebooks, Kafka's editor Koch has produced a number of conclusions supporting this analysis. At about the time of the "heap of straw" diary entry, Kafka began to set aside another notebook for his more plainly fictional pieces. This decision follows from his will to draw a fundamental distinction between the two kinds of writing.[16] One can imagine Kafka carried along by the diary entry far enough to reach, while in flight, for the second notebook. But this was not a practice he actually maintained. The following year, fictional pieces crop up immediately next to entries in the same notebook. It as if Kafka found himself in the middle of a fiction before he had time to register the boundary setting it off from the diary entry and take the prescribed step. As a result, it is not possible in every case to draw a line inside or outside the diary entry marking the border where the empirical self decisively passes away in favor of the fiction.[17] "I won't give up the diary again," he wrote, a year later.

> I must hold on here, it is the only place I can. I would gladly explain the feeling of happiness which, like now, I have within me from time to time. It is really something effervescent [moussierendes] that fills me completely with a light, pleasant quiver [Zucken]. (D1 33, GW 9:103)

That the elation can occur within the text of the diary entry while remaining inside its syntactical barrier is finally confirmed by the fact that Kafka wrote *first drafts* of at least some of these entries as opportunities for development, for effervescence. The quiver is in the elaboration.[18]

The intimacy of the two kinds of writing is an empirical fact (the blank space between them expands on the page to become something visible or contracts to invisibility), but their distinction is, according to Kafka in 1910, a priori. The great merit of Koch's edition is that in publishing the notebooks intact, he allows this state of affairs to come to light: the reader sees diary entries alternating with fictions of increasing complexity. Max Brod addressed this very point in noting that "the diaries have a significance for Kafka which is not only autobiographical and an aid to the mastery of his soul; in between remarks of a personal content stand the pieces which he then later took for his first book, *Contemplation (Betrachtung)*."[19] Thereafter, Kafka did once again attempt to keep these two sorts of entries separate from one another by reserving the second notebook for "purely" fictional texts. The repeated attempt is telling.

The notebooks inscribe the movement from self-questioning to self-combustion, from journal keeping to "real writing" — defined by its resistance to the dead weight of the empirical subject. Typical sequences are revealing when looked at in detail. I shall offer one last example of the sort of analysis that each and every one of these entries actually invites. The diary entry in the so-called Fifth Notebook for September 20, 1912, begins innocuously enough: "Letters to Löwy and Miss Taussig yesterday, to Miss B.[auer] and Max today" (D1 275). Yet these letters also belong to the project of self-questioning. The letter to Yitzchak Löwy is lost; in the letter to Elsa Taussig (who was to marry Max Brod the following year), Kafka thanks her for sending him pages of Brod's *diary*, which sets down experiences from Brod's Italian journey.[20] Kafka's letter to Brod also literally takes up the question of diary-keeping, containing, under the circumstances, the remarkable admonition: "You must not stop the diary" (L 86). Reading Brod's travel diary must have had the effect of concentrating Kafka's attention on his own and stoking the rapture that would issue *that very day* into his first letter to Felice Bauer, inviting her to begin a correspondence with him, and, two days later, into the composition of "The Judgment." Brod notes: "In the context of the diary there are many fragments of short stories which have got thus or thus far; they pile up, until suddenly out of the throng the first finished story of considerable length, 'The Verdict (The Judgment, *Das Urteil*)' shoots out like a jet of flame."[21] This is not wrong, but, for one thing, there are also letters in the "pile"; the letters to Max Brod and Felice Bauer, only initialed in the diary, belong to the sequence of diary entries and fictions leading to "The Judgment." They too must be reckoned way stages of the spiritual tension of "real" writing, a notion that Goethe, as it happens, also advanced, in noting that "the letter is a sort of conversation with oneself."[22]

The text of the "The Judgment," which Kafka wrote directly into this Fifth Notebook, is followed by a rich entry celebrating its composition. Its position and texture invite readers to regard it as part of the story itself, for it contributes decisively to its clarification. (See pages 34–35.) Thereafter Kafka returns to the more nearly journal-like aphoristic aperçu: "I, only I, am the spectator in the orchestra" (D1 276), which nonetheless contains the (rigorous, self-reflexive) question, Why, and to what end, am I this spectator? and thus prepares for new stories, fragments, and aphorisms.[23]

There is a good deal more to learn from the "heap of straw" diary entry of ca. May 17, 1910, which amounts to a sort of phenomenology of diary keeping. Kafka proceeds by describing his state of mind: "My state is not unhappiness," he writes, "but it is also not happiness, not indifference, not weakness, not fatigue, not another interest — so what is it then?" (D1 12).[24] This feels like a moment of ardent enough self-questioning, for here, too, the entry enacts its own argument: "That I do not know this is probably connected with my inability to write" (D1 12). So, real questioning must produce good enough answers along the way, but this answer is not good enough. It is not enough to say "I do not know." What, after all, is the cause of this "inability to write"? There would be some profit in getting to the root of this inability. But

> all those things . . . which occur to me, occur to me not from the root up but rather only from somewhere about their middle. Let someone then attempt to seize them, let someone attempt to seize a blade of grass and hold fast to it when it begins to grow only from the middle. (D1 12)

"*When it begins to grow only from the middle.*" This image is re-markable. The blade of grass, Kafka's thought, does not grow from the root up; hence, its way of growing, its way of being, cannot be traced back to the root. Kafka cannot get to the bottom of his thought. Between his being and any thoroughgoing self-knowledge that might arise from thinking, there is disparity — a gap between the root and the middle.[25] Every fair narration of what occurs in thought would have to begin in medias res. This may very well register the distinctive lack of orientation, the lack of a settled beginning, in many of his major narratives. Consider the uncertainty with which, for example, *The Metamorphosis* and all three of Kafka's novels begin — *Amerika* (or *The One Who Sank Out of Sight*) (written 1912–1914; published in 1927); *The Trial* (1914; 1925); and *The Castle* (1922; 1926).

It is bemusing that in this very early diary entry — the sort of thing that is dismissed as youthful gropings, as a text that can be discarded once we approach the canonical stories and novels, as if it were, in a Hegelian sense, sublated there — we find a sentence that has since been anthologized for expressing with inspired precision the mood of writers at the turn of the century. The fit with Hugo von Hofmannsthal's *Lord Chandos Letter* of 1902 is perfect; the two are perfectly *vegetal* when taken together.[26] Hofmannsthal speaks of words that dissolved on his tongue "like decaying mushrooms": the word is an organic thing only as it is belated. Hence, for Lord Chandos

> Disjointed words swam around me, congealing into staring eyes whose gaze I was forced to return; whirlpools they were, and I could not look into them without dizziness, their incessant turning only drew me down into emptiness.[27]

Recall Kafka's "Let someone attempt to seize a blade of grass and hold fast to it when it begins to grow only from the middle." Below the blade of grass is emptiness.

"There are some people who can do this, probably, Japanese jugglers, for example," Kafka continues, in a phrase that marks his obsessive Orientalism and his obsessive interest in *varieté* performers.[28] These performers

> scramble up a ladder that does not rest on the ground but on the raised soles of someone half lying on the ground, and which does not lean against a wall but just goes up into the air. I cannot do this—aside from the fact that my ladder does not even have those soles at its disposal. This, naturally, isn't all, and it isn't such a question that prompts me to speak. (D1 12)

Such a question—a question about missing support, about yet another (missing) person inside this psychic drama—is not evidently the right one: it is not rigorously enough self-oriented. The right question will have to be found as these entries develop: "But every day at least one line should be trained on me, as they now train telescopes on comets" (D1 12). Kafka has found in this "Night of the Comet" of May 18–19, 1910—a night when all of Prague is awaiting its appearance—a use for this news coming from the world. "And if then I should appear before that sentence, once lured by that sentence. . . ." (D1 12). But note that his goal is not to produce the shining semblance of a self as an object of intellectual recognition but as a fiery sign, a warrant of writing. The comet trailing fire through the night sky, with all of Prague's eyes on it, matters only as it corresponds to a moment of fiery disappearance; the empirical world is interesting for the intensity of its dissolution.[29] Kafka's task is not self-knowledge but a form of empirical self-destruction as the occasion of writing: "not shaking off the self"—as he will note some years later—a sort of flight, "but consuming the self," a profane apotheosis (DF 87).[30] "Self-obliviousness is the primary condition of writing" (L 334).[31]

In diary entries of the following year, 1911, Kafka defines the kind of ecstasy he is after. On February 19, 1911, he writes: "The special nature of my inspiration . . . is such that I can do everything, and not only what is directed to a definite piece of work. When I arbitrarily write a single sentence, for instance, 'He looked out of the window,' it already has perfection" (D1 45). Note the stress on the mode of writing: it is not intentionally aimed at an object, it is "arbitrary." The following month, Kafka visited Rudolph Steiner, the anthroposophist, saying:

> My happiness, my abilities and every possibility of being useful in any way have always been in the literary field. And here I have, to

be sure, experienced states . . . in which I completely dwelt in every idea, but also filled every idea, and in which I not only felt myself at my boundary, but at the boundary of the human in general. (D1 58)

In October of that year, he writes:

> Again it was the power of my dreams, shining forth into wakeful-ness even before I fall asleep, which did not let me sleep. In the evening and the morning my consciousness of the creative abilities in me is more than I can encompass. I feel shaken to the core of my being and can get out of myself whatever I desire. . . . It is a matter of more mysterious powers which are of an ultimate significance to me. (D1 76)

Given claims of this sort, it is likely that *all* of Kafka's stories and novels will reflect this drama of writing, the inability to write, and the impossibility of not writing.

We shall now be advancing to Kafka's fiction, which arises from a strict, nonsensuous self-questioning and is not an affair of empirical psychology. One self is struck off the other with the hardness, the non-psychological thinglike character of flint off metal: here "real writing" begins.[32]

We still need to ask, however, about the marker of genuine self-questioning, since not every entry can end in a thematized combustion or self-immolation. How can this "ignition" be detected as it advances, and when can it be said assuredly to be in motion? Evidently, it can only be read off from the way things are stated in the diary entry, from the way the question proceeds, unfolds, and sometimes explodes. What is then remarkable is that the logic of this evidence is not "philosophical," not Socratic: a question is not valid insofar as it engenders other (verbalized) questions but insofar as it engenders *theater*, a distinctive staging of figures of the inner life with a startling energy of gesture and movement. (Certainly, Kafka's experience of the Jewish theater in 1911 is important here). This point about the theatricality of the dialogue has been made well in a monograph by Anne Rother, whose starting point is "estrangement" (*Entfremdung*), a term I have not used but acknowledged all along as the condition of a splitting of the subject into questioner and answerer, of the engendering of a "field" that, for Rother, turns out to be more like a stage than a dialogue, more like the setting of an action than a rebuttal.[33] There is plenty of evidence of theatrical improvisations arising from moments of self-questioning, of self-soliciting; but it is important now to stress the porousness of the line between the dialogue and the theatrical interaction. These types of gesture go over into one another; "language as gesture" passes into theatrical action, if the theatrical improvisation is not to remain entirely mute.[34] "Estrangement," concludes Rother,

> is the motor of writing, which means to surpass itself by bringing movable textual bodies onto the stage. . . . To be able to continue to write within this situation depends on sustaining the kinesis that makes the forces and agencies of the inner world bodily and tremulous. (175)

We recall the ready population of the stage—quite literally in the case of the Japanese jugglers—that arises from such a moment of powerful self-questioning.

Soon after writing the inaugural major diary entry of ca. May 17, 1910, in which Kafka declared that every day at least one sentence should be aimed at him the way a telescope is aimed at a comet, he began to compose the cryptic and yet henceforth forever determinative story beginning " 'You,' I said. . . ."[35] It is driven by the transformation of language into and out of a mimesis of bodily gesture.[36]

The beginning of the story will not be surprising: it is an affair of questions and answers directed from the writer to a shadow self. One might wonder about one's right to view the narrator, the "I," as a mask of Kafka the writer, since on the face of it, he seems to be a sort of professional, held together by the desire for "a great complex of possessions" (D1 24) or by the imagination of such a desire. To call him the writer—isn't this to allegorize him impermissibly, to impose meanings on him that aren't there?[37]

Kafka, however, is no enemy of allegorical readings, as he is no enemy of abstractions. We have heard him insist that

> for everything outside the phenomenal world, language can only be used allusively [as an allusion], but never even approximately in a comparative way [as a comparison, in the manner of an analogy], since, corresponding as it does to the phenomenal world, it is concerned only with property and its relations. (DF 40)

The word "allusive," especially in its opposition to the word "analogous," states the time-honored distinction, strong in Goethe and Friedrich Schlegel—and thereafter in Walter Benjamin and Paul de Man—between the more nearly conventional, pseudonaturalistic claims made on behalf of metaphor and symbol as the warrant of "real" writing and the more disruptive, modernist claims made on behalf of an allegory that implies temporal disjunction, the loss of aura, and the nonrepresentability of the thing signified. The writer's chief business, for Kafka, is with "things outside the phenomenal world." Gerhard Kurz has noted how this principle of attending to things "outside the phenomenal world" becomes practice in "[Kafka's] texts themselves," which, Kurz writes,

> contain turns of phrase that provoke an allegorical reading, for example, in "The Great Wall of China" the phrase "that could obviously be meant only *in a spiritual sense*" (CS 239); "A Hunger Artist" is a "suffering martyr, . . . although in quite another sense" (CS 271); in "The Problem of Our Laws" there are "possible discrepancies that may arise in the interpretation of the laws" (CS 437); as the metaphorical play of "cover up" (CS 84) and [by implication] "uncover" in "The Judgment" suggests, there are truths which are covered up (*zugedeckt*) and truths which are uncovered (*aufgedeckt*).[38]

This is a general argument. The particular case of the story " 'You,' I said . . ." calls for seeing it as charged with allegorical reminders of the problematics of writing. The tormented narrator is more than a bourgeois: he does not belong to an identifiable type of Prague citizen but is hybrid, noting that "there is at the moment scarcely any difference between me and the bachelor" (D1 25). And with his "imagined or actual sufferings," as well as his "literary inclinations," he connotes, in noble parody, Kafka the writer who thinks of his practical affairs as consuming so much of him that his destiny as a writer is absurdly, monstrously reduced (D1 25). This word "inclinations" is loaded: in a letter to Felice Bauer, apropos of a graphologist's analysis of Kafka's handwriting that she had sent him, Kafka took pains to warn her that his preoccupation with literature was not an affair of an "interest": "I do not have literary interests [scil. "inclinations"]; rather, I am made out of literature, I am nothing and cannot be anything else" (LF 428, BF 444). The point about the diary entry is not that it is chiefly concerned with an empirical person—a citizen with more or less burning literary inclinations—but with a discourse that alludes to literature as something "outside the phenomenal world."

As to this matter of Kafka's allegory, now in the more traditional sense of the term, I noted earlier a numerological detail of importance in " 'You,' I said . . ." that connects the "I" who speaks in this story with the blocked writer of the first diary entry. Just as the diarist has been impotent, as a writer, for five months, so too has the "I" of the story lived "here," in the city of his distress, for "five months" (D1 29). These are the five months for which he has "worked to receive this invitation" to an auratic community that will "organize" his powers and fulfill him (D1 24).[39]

At the point in the story where we last left off, the narrator is interrupted by a phantasmal "You." A key dimension of the struggle for justification has emerged. This figure whom the I-speaker addresses with so much bitterness—"the bachelor"—appears to be an insurmountable aspect of the writer's self. It is inconsistent with everything we know of Kafka to suppose that, à la Karl Kraus, his concern here is with excoriating in the figure of the bachelor some simply hated empirical person or type. The speaker abuses the bachelor as a dreaded possibility of himself—dreaded because this bachelor-shape may be the inseparable shadow of his becoming a writer, its necessary and yet not sufficient condition—whence arises the horrible surmise that the sexual deprivation and renunciation of family that bachelorhood entails might turn out to be an only devilish lure, and the profit of it nothing more than false fire. Such a possibility of oneself calls for anger, commination—indeed, whipping.

In this story Kafka splits himself into an "I" and "You," yet fluidly assigns to both of them dimensions of a common self—features that are partly plausible and partly grotesque. If there was a time when the bachelor "felt his depth lastingly," now the narrator feels *his* "depth much too often and much too strongly to be able to be even halfway satisfied" (D1 26, 25). "The bachelor has only the moment"; and yet this more nearly integral citizen laments, at the end, "When I look back . . . I don't know at all whether there have been any nights, everything looks to me . . . like one day without any mornings, afternoons and evenings, even without any differences in light" (D1 25, 29). Interestingly, at the conclusion of Max Brod's composite text, both voices fuse in a soliloquy of the I-narrator that dispenses with the quotation marks of direct address (D1 28).

Since "there is at the moment scarcely any difference" between the narrator and the bachelor, it is impossible to say throughout who is functioning as the superior questioner; who is en route to manifesting a "true" self ("If only I could be sure you are telling me the truth," complains the speaker to the bachelor); and who figures as the mask to be destroyed. Features of the bachelor repeatedly emerge alongside those of the I-narrator as the inescapable conditions of writing. The bachelor "went astray" at the moment of discovering his "depth"; it is the depth of an exceptional—we will say, literary—existence,

> the way one suddenly notices an ulcer on one's body that until this moment was the least thing on one's body—yes, not even the least, for it appeared not yet to exist and now is more than everything else that we had bodily owned since our birth. (D1 26)

This poverty of the physical life alludes, dialectically, to what Kafka will afterwards call "the tremendous world I have in my head" (D1 288). In the months coming, he addresses his dwindling body:

When it became clear in my organism that writing was the most productive direction for my being to take, everything rushed in that direction and left empty all those abilities which were directed toward the joys of sex, eating, drinking, philosophical reflection, and above all music. I atrophied in all these directions. (D1 211)

In "'You,' I said . . . ," this original assertion produces a fundamental displacement of attention: "If until now our whole person had been oriented upon the work of our hands, upon that seen by our eyes, heard by our ears, upon the steps made by our feet, now we suddenly turn ourselves entirely in the opposite direction, like a weather vane in the mountains" (D1 26). This is an opportunity that must be grasped, yet the bachelor does not, and so he bears the meaning of an original possibility that has been betrayed. Without an experience like his, there will be no literature; but an experience too much like his invokes a disaster, for "instead of . . . running away, [which] could have kept him on the tips of his toes, . . . he lay down, as children now and then lie down in the snow in winter in order to freeze to death" (D1 26).

Not so the narrator, who, toward the close, appears to have taken fire from their exchange: "Already, what protected me seemed to dissolve here in the city. I was beautiful in the early days, for this dissolution takes place as an apotheosis, in which everything that holds us to life flies way, but even in flying away illumines us for the last time with its human light" (D1 28). There resurges in this figure a reminiscence of the comet, with its qualities of brilliance and evanescence. It is an extraordinary moment, linking beauty with self-dissolution and hence with the artist's destiny. Recall the aphorism "not shaking off the self [Selbstabschüttelung] but consuming the self" (DF 87, GW 6:198). The condition of this dissolution is a withdrawal from the flux of life. And the code word for this withdrawal, as its necessary condition, is the "bachelor."

But, then, do bachelors take fire? Or do bachelors die of ice, of icy abandonment, in faraway St. Petersburg? At this point, Kafka appears to have in his possession all the themes and forms he needs to write "The Judgment," except for one, which could be termed "the metaphorical factor."

A crucial diary entry for January 19, 1911, details Kafka's discovery of the expulsive power of words when they assume unwonted literal and/or metaphorical meanings. This reminiscence turns on an uncle's judgment (literally, *Urteil*) condemning a literary effort of himself as a child. "The usual stuff," the uncle says—a verdict that grows material enough, in Kafka's recollection, to drive the author out into "the cold space of our world" (D1 44) into which, in his story, he has only fictively condemned both brothers.[40]

A month later Kafka wrote into his diaries a little (unfinished) story called "The Urban World," which advances his coded theorizing of rhetoric. This story centers on an angry, a dangerous conversation between son and elder—here, the father. The son, Oscar, is an "older student," whose father is furious with him (D1 47).[41] In his first harangue the father exhibits the rhetoric of what Kafka will call "family language"—a tissue of threatening banalities in which words stick out like things.

> "Silence," shouted the father and stood up, blocking a window. "Silence, I say. And keep your 'buts' to yourself, do you understand?" At the same time he took the table in both hands and carried it a step nearer to Oscar. "I simply won't put up with your good-for-nothing existence any longer. I'm an old man. I hoped you would be the comfort of my old age, instead you are worse than all my illnesses. Shame on such a son, who through laziness, extravagance, wickedness, and—why shouldn't I say so to your face— stupidity, drives his old father to his grave!" (D1 48)

Compare Kafka's diary entry some months later (March 24, 1912) on the topic of family language:

> In the next room . . . they are talking about vermin and corns. . . . It is easy to see that there is no real progress made in conversations of this sort. It is information that will be forgotten again by both and that even now proceeds along in self-forgetfulness without any sense of responsibility. But for the very reason that such conversations are unthinkable without absent-mindedness, they reveal empty spaces which, if one insists, can be filled only by thinking, or, better yet, by dreams. (D1 258)

Kafka will insert violent elements of his dreamlike inner life into the blank spaces of family conversation. Now we are brought to "The Judgment."

⌒

We began by setting out some prefigurations of the main elements of "The Judgment": the factor of self-division; the coding of this division as the struggle between the citizen and the bachelor-writer; and the submission of their struggle to a higher court, as represented by the father. Kafka's discovery and mastery of a new device is crucial: the "family language" of "The Urban World" — the cliché, the dead metaphor, that, as in the diary entry of January 19, 1911, has the uncanny power to come to life when taken literally and inserted into the struggle between the litigant-self and its judge.

To dramatize the struggle between these parties as the struggle to establish the literal and metaphorical dimensions of words: this technique is crucial to "The Judgment." The word "dramatize" is meant to be important. It points once more to the influence on the composition of "The Judgment" of the Jewish theater that captivated Kafka in the fall of 1911. But beyond this it refers to the histrionics that flow into and intensify the inner theater of self-questioning in Kafka's earliest diary entries.

In "The Judgment" the struggle between father and son turns on the son's effort to make literal his father's words, as if this were the way to turn him into a thing, and thence to seize and possess him. Their struggle is a contest for the power to make metaphors.

At the outset it is Mr. Bendemann, the father, who displays his mastery of this deadly game. The struggle turns on a word that the reader may recall from Gerhard Kurz's remarks on allegory: the word *zudecken*, meaning, literally, the act of "covering with a blanket." The father asks his son Georg twice: "Am I well covered up?" seeming, the narrator remarks, "to be strangely intent upon the answer. . . . 'Don't worry, [replies Georg,] you're well covered up.' 'No,' cried his father. . . . 'You wanted to cover me up, I know, my young sprig, but I'm far from being covered up yet'" (CS 84). And here he seems to mean, "I'm not dead and buried yet." The father is reading the word with elaborate metaphorical stress, which might also include such secondary meanings of *zudecken* as "to cover" a subject (so thoroughly as to bury its sense); "to heap meanings of one sort or another on someone," as "to cover with reproaches"; finally, "to fit words to a meaning" with the negative implication of covering it up.[42] Here, the term *zudecken* has what Gilbert Ryle calls "a higher-order function": it is a word connoting the intention of the speaker to "cover" a matter thoroughly, evoking the capacity of words to bury meaning.[43] And it is these various metaphorical senses that the father may be said to have uncovered in his son through the emphasis with which he pronounces the words "cover up."

Observe the sequence of moves in this rhetorical drama. The father's first tactic is to draw Georg into a scene where words seem to mean what they literally say. Georg accedes and reads the act of "covering up" his father in the required, literal way. This is the father's ruse to flush out his son's unconscious desires and then to ridicule them. And so it is with some shock value that the father trumpets out the son's repressed metaphorical meaning: "You wanted to bury me! You wanted to have the last word!" This is the first hostile act in the speech war that will amount to a fatal humiliation of Georg. Georg has been caught out seeming blind to the metaphorical meaning of (his) words.

The father takes fresh confidence from his victory. On attributing to Georg the metaphorical meaning of *zudecken*, he exults to think that Georg can have imagined that he (Georg) could ever have "covered him up." Here, where the word *zudecken* has a higher-order function, to take this figure literally, as the father initially pretends to do, means to deny his son a higher-order consciousness of the son's desire—to bury his father—and also to seem to acquiesce in a literal reading of himself, the father, as a stupid old Herrmanneut.

At this point, we are emphasizing the father's mischief. It is the cruelty of one who would trick or coerce another into taking his own figures literally. Certainly, one could also do "metaphorical violence" to an-other—crush him precisely by inserting his literal features into a violent metaphor. This, as Saul Bellow has claimed, would then lead to the sense that the hapless victim is owed "special consideration."[44] The fact, how-ever, that in "The Judgment" so little consideration is shown the victim may follow from the story's self-reflexive reversal of this relation. Instead of the speaker's inflicting "the violence of metaphor," we see the speaker of metaphors—Georg himself—turned into the product of violence—the opaque thing. By reading triumphantly Georg's word *zudecken* as an intended violent metaphor ("you mean to bury me"), the father convicts Georg of opacity, of blindness to his own intention: he makes him consent to his own absence of mind. The narrator confirms this point exactly:

> A long time ago . . . [Georg] had firmly made up his mind to watch closely every least movement so that he should not be surprised by any indirect attack, a pounce from behind or above. At this mo-ment he recalled this long-forgotten resolve and forgot it again, like a man drawing a short thread through the eye of a needle. (CS 85)

With this figure we move into a turbulence of metaphors and acts of reading metaphors. The image of a man drawing a short thread through the eye of a needle thrusts itself out, struts as a lure to the reader to enter into this mad game of reading persons to death. And the reading demanded of the reader will be beset, too, by moments of remembering how to understand it and as promptly forgetting it, for it is so elusive. What, otherwise, is the status of *this* figure, inserted into a charged field of metaphorical turmoil by a not so innocent narrator?

Meanwhile, the game between father and son becomes more and more deadly, as George turns his father's revelation of the metaphorical underlayer of ordinary language into a parricidal weapon. The father says tauntingly to Georg, "I've established a fine connection with your friend and I have your customers here in my pocket" (CS 86). Georg now seems besotted by the impulse to literalize his father's words—to deny, to refuse the lesson he has just learned: only metaphorize. And yet he must deny this rhetorical lesson because the meaning of his exposed metaphor is so damning—it is the desire to kill his father! For: look how the desire persists. Georg thinks, "He has pockets even in his shirt!" and that "with this remark he [Georg] could make him [the father] an impossible figure for all the world" (CS 86). Here, the aggressiveness of Georg's project is less transparent for the English than for the German reader, who will pick up the implicit metaphor. German knows the proverb "Das letzte Hemd hat keine Taschen" ("the last shirt has no pockets"); the last shirt is a funeral shroud. Georg's remark is cruel in a double register: he mocks his father by literalizing the pocket of "in my pocket," and toys with the idea of parricide by literalizing the shirt of "the shirt without pockets." To this ploy the father responds, as if deliberately to provoke more of the same aggression on Georg's part: " 'How you amused me today, coming to ask me if you should tell your friend about your engagement. . . . He knows everything a hundred times better than you do yourself. . . .' 'Ten thousand times!' said Georg, to make fun of his father," but, as Georg takes his own bait, "in his very mouth the words turned into deadly earnest" (CS 87). Kafka could not have made the point plainer: Whoever reads the metaphor literally—as an image—condemns it to the solitude of a thing; and as whoever reads the metaphor literally, kills it, whoever, as a metaphor, is read literally, turns monstrous or dies. Georg is making the fatal mistake of attempting to read his father as a feeble, toothless, old *thing* in soiled underwear, but his father is more than this!

He calls Georg "a devil." And, indeed, Georg's "devilishness" has been to deprive his father of a necessarily metaphorical existence, for the *father* cannot be defined as an assemblage (what Heidegger calls a *Gestell*) of literal characteristics—the features of his old body. And now Georg, the literalist, is appropriately disarmed when the father issues him a death sentence: "And therefore take note: I sentence you now to death by drowning!" (CS 87). Where it would serve Georg to let his father's language assume an only metaphorical resonance, he cannot: he has been turned into a creature who can only make his father's words thinglike. Now he is literally driven to his death by drowning, moist by his own petard.

So much, for the moment, to the mechanism through which the struggle between father and son is fought. What is the meaning of "The Judgment" as a whole?

⌐⌐

Readers feel obliged to produce a hypothesis about the meaning of the end, quite as Theodor Adorno warned: not to do so would mean to be destroyed as if by the force of an onrushing locomotive. "Each sentence of Kafka's says 'interpret me,'" and this is especially true of the conclusion of "The Judgment."[45] One needs to get beyond the sense that Kafka's execution of George is a mad, unjustifiable destruction of life. For what we have, after all, is horrendous: a son is condemned to death by his father, a life sentence is revoked and rewritten as a death sentence. Yet, at the end, Kafka, not alone among his readers, felt an ecstatic sense of relief, imagining (as Brod remembers from a conversation with him) "a strong ejaculation"![46] How can this bliss be squared with the horror of a family execution?

To be entitled to such joy, one must understand Georg as a figure for something not yet alive, something whose value is less than "real life"; he must be an only factitious mask of the author, who arranges Georg's fall and who says, *after* Georg has let himself fall: "At this moment an unending stream of traffic was just going over the bridge" ("In diesem Augenblick ging über die Brücke ein geradezu unendlicher Verkehr") (CS 88, GW 1:52).[47] With its multivalent image of "traffics" and its fusion of contradictory temporal ecstasies, the conclusion radiates elements of bliss and horror. One recalls Kafka's aphorism of the drowning man: "The man in ecstasy and the man drowning—both throw up their arms. The first does it to signify harmony, the second to signify strife with the elements" (DF 77).

We need to grasp the threat to Kafka that the personality of Georg represents. Aside from his ugly struggle with his father, Georg has also chosen to stay engaged to his fiancée rather than keep faith with his bachelor friend. As a result, Kafka, the narrator, whose perspective at this point is very nearly identical to Georg's, faces a crisis. The bachelor friend is an inescapable reminder of the writing destiny. And now, as someone who breaks faith with literature, how can the narrator continue? He proceeds, in a perspective distorted by anxiety, to envision the father. This is a coherent move—for the son, too, means to embark on family life. But what follows in this perspective must not be what can actually happen to Kafka in life; the world depicted in "The Judgment" is the world as it must *not* be. The father reveals himself to be the true father of the Russian friend, the semblance of the writer. If Kafka is to grasp the life of literature as sponsored by the father, as his "ideal" offspring, then writing becomes an only compulsive behavior, the neurotic offshoot of the father's vitality. We recall that Kafka did indeed write, in his "Letter to His Father," imagining the worst, "My writing was all about you; all I did there, after all, was to bemoan what I could not bemoan upon your breast."[48] In this perspective, writing cannot be preferred to marriage. The decision to marry becomes a compelling alternative at the same time that it becomes worthless, for this is the institution that perpetuates neurosis. Being Georg, the narrator cannot turn anywhere and escape guilt: guilt toward the fiancée, guilt toward the friend, and worse, the knowledge that this guilt is itself nothing — a "psychological" event, an instance of family language, and not an essential concern of the self. If this is the case, then Kafka has been sentenced to death.[49]

How, then, could such a crisis turn to ecstasy? It would, by the logic of catharsis. Georg's destruction provides an intense, explosively concentrated relief to a mind "above" him that has arranged the perfect annihilation of a dreaded fate. With this sentence, Kafka identifies and expunges a disastrous inclination of his personality.

But the cathartic route is not the strongest way to read this ending. It is a seductive hypothesis, of course; and it is in fact doubly seductive. The story has presented the father in a stereoscopic perspective. In one respect, he is the empirical father, a reminiscence of Herrmann Kafka; as such, he too crashes to his death. In this case another piece of (illicit) bliss is produced through the logic of purgation: both the negativity of the mask (the bachelor) and the negativity of its sponsor (the real father) are extinguished. But the father can be seen — and felt — otherwise. In another, stronger perspective, his influence works in an entirely positive way. He deals not in curses but in blessings. If the bachelor is the "true son" of the father, then this father is the "true father" of the writer. In this case, the energy of the final scene flows out of a wish-dream come true: the father is splendidly vital. "His insight made him radiant" (CS 85). And it is this being who loves and approves his son precisely on the condition that he be the bachelor, a condition of the possibility of being a writer. Franz Kafka, the bachelor-writer, is the true son of the loved father. His tormentingly doubled persona having been refined down to its writerly essence, there is no longer any need for such a thing to exist as the genealogical line of Herrmann-father and Georg-son — the practical, marrying businessman. If only Kafka's true father would bless his bachelorhood — his, in the family sense, sterility, yet, in the extraordinary, literary sense, fertility. In the conclusion to this story, vision becomes event.

This is the core of Kafka's ecstasy, conveyed by the movement following the judgment that drives Georg into the river to drown: Banish the nightmare of an eternal, monotonous, familylike procession of the will that must not be the case; allow it to transport the wish-dream of the ascetic.

I have said that with this sentence, we have to do with a voice surviving Georg's. In this fictional world, it is a moment occupied entirely by the narrator, the narrator who, from the start, has only pretended to identify his optic with Georg's but has in fact designed his execution.[50] What else does this moment convey?

To answer this question, we must look again at the diary entry that

Kafka wrote with a fine elation, the night after he spent composing his story:

> This story, *The Judgment*, I wrote at one sitting during the night of the 22nd–23rd, from ten o'clock at night to six o'clock in the morning. I was hardly able to pull my legs out from under the desk, they had got so stiff from sitting. The fearful strain and joy, how the story developed before me, as if I were advancing over water. Several times during this night I heaved my own weight on my back. How everything can be said, how for everything, for the strangest fancies, there waits a great fire in which they perish and rise up again. . . . The conviction verified that with my novel-writing [the "America-novel"]. I am in the shameful lowlands of writing. Only *in this way* can writing be done, only with such coherence, with such a complete opening out of the body and the soul. . . . Many emotions carried along in the writing, joy, for example, that I shall have something beautiful for Max's *Arkadia*. (D1 275–76).[51]

*Joy that I shall have something beautiful for Max's "Arkadia."* This "judgment," conveyed by joy, tends to confirm the jubilant reading of "The Judgment" as the wish-dream that invokes paternal protection of the bachelor-friend at the cost of the destruction of the fiancé-Georg; and here both Kafka's father and Max Brod function as ideal representatives of the public world.

Consider, further, that the word "judgment," while designating as a synecdoche a certain action within the story world (the sentencing of Georg), also designates the totality of the story's action. And furthermore, it designates the judgment that Kafka twice made on the factual life of the story itself. This tripleness is preserved in his remark, "The indubitability of the story was proved." Some of its compact wittiness may have gone unnoticed: the indubitability that was confirmed is not only that of the story, is not only that of Kafka's first diary judgment on the story, it is also that of its afterlife, its survival in the empirical world where stories are read aloud and published.

The critic David Schur stresses the point that, with this story, Kafka would have "something beautiful" for *Arkadia*; here, the empirical reality of publishing has thrust itself in advance into the conclusion of the story.[52] The story intuitively mimes a coming reality; this moment completes the exhilaration of the moment at the outset when the real comet in the telescope thrust itself into the journal—and completes the circle of "The Judgment." With the annihilation of Georg, whose goal is marriage, we have the decisive fictional achievement: the empirical person of the diary entry is extinguished for the sake of the fiction he shall become.

Is this a merely conventional allegorical interpretation? In one sense it is: the story *codes* it. In another sense it is not an imposed or arbitrary allegory. It is a riddle. The story does no more than direct the reading along this allegorical path to an achieved piece of writing, in vivid contradistinction to Georg Bendemann's mendacious letter to a friend. If the story is coded, the code has to be struggled for. The result is driven along by the son's and father's struggle for the friend as a putative figure of authenticity, the "true son" of a "true father."

We have a marker of this consciousness of achievement in the story itself, one clear enough to have provoked the happy verdict that Kafka pronounced after composing the story and then, a few days later, after reading it "at Baum's." The story seemed strong enough to have survived its violent birth. Weight falls again on the bliss of the dream come true that the father be the friend and support of the bachelor's bizarre fertility; for the friend, as "the link between father and son . . . [and] their strongest common bond" (D1 278), can mean only: their procreativity. The father, in this wish-dream, wants his son to be the bachelor-writer and wants his first real "offspring" — the story itself — to be born into the world. In the sexual imagery of the closing sentence, "The Judgment" pronounces the judgment on the story itself as a warrant of Kafka the writer's afterlife. Kafka foresees that with this story he will survive Georg, his dreaded antiself, exposed as a false and lying mask; and by his death, Kafka the bachelor, his father's true son, will enter the stream of literary renown. That is the sense of the "infinite stream of traffic that flows over the bridge." For all its demotic imagery, it is a being superior to the individual life; it is the confirmation of Kafka's promise as a writer as the promise of cultural immortality. A gnostic truth shelters in a Gnostic text.

A current of affirmation continues to flow from "The Judgment" into the diary entries written immediately afterwards. We have seen this elation marked in more than one place in the story itself. "The Judgment" creates a father after the son's own heart — the son who is a writer. The father rises up "radiant" with "insight" (CS 85) — a phantasmatic projection of the father who bears the insight that is the son's own and that the son imputes to him: Recognize that you are the father of the writer I am.

The true son of the father is the writer perishing of solitude. The father wants him to write: he is the herald of the new commandant of "In the Penal Colony," no longer the comminatory Jewish God who does not want him to write. "The Judgment" imagines the father as an active principle, the neverceasing author of the son's transformation into the writer. He answers to the god who says: "This man is . . . to come to me" (DF 35). He is the true father, and "The Judgment" is a moment of return to him.

And yet Kafka could not himself assume the patriarchal virility wishfully depicted there. When he reviews his story, some months later, at the beginning of the new year, in a diary entry for February 11, 1913, it as one who stands outside patriarchy, figuring as the *mother* of the story "that came out of me like a real birth" (D1 278). To be neither the good father nor the good father's son will mean to be subject to further coercion, willy nilly, at his actual master's hand, who retains the power to be cruel and false. And now, indeed, in the winter of 1912, Kafka's father is the empirical father Herrmann Kafka with a vengeance, the investor in an asbestos factory, who needs his son for asbestos work: how must Kafka have suffered together the images of the conflagration he was and the dealer in asbestos his father wanted him to be. These are figures in the counterlife to the fiery act of writing: (1) Felice Bauer, (2) the paterfamilias Herrmann Kafka, and (3) asbestos. Kafka was driven to thoughts of suicide.

From November 17 to December 7, 1912, in a period of despondency following the composition of "The Judgment," Kafka wrote *The Metamorphosis*. The monstrosity of the vermin is the measure of its disparity from the son who bathed in his father's radiance, the son who was born some months before as a being who could walk on water. *The Metamorphosis* marks a transformation, indeed; the core transformation is Kafka's being marked negatively as a writer, as a desolate fate. Here, his plan to marry Felice Bauer acquires a higher potency and a higher danger: it can exclude his fulfillment as a writer. Equally, his father's plans for him as a factory manager: what of the plans his other father had for him? The conflict between the two fathers is extreme, is critical. The monster that appears at the outset of *The Metamorphosis* is the transmogrified, the distorted, the damaged form of the new creature he has become: the writer in extremis. And if he is never to fulfill the promise of the new being affirmed in "The Judgment" — his genuine being? — he will remain until his death the monster, the family invalid.

The outcome of *The Metamorphosis* is appalling: Kafka paints the small bliss of the dissolution of Gregor Samsa next to the wide bliss of the dissolution of Georg Bendemann and the apotheosis of the empirical self of Kafka the author. It is as if even the empirical gloom impacted in the vermin were itself so diminished, so abject, that there is little left to burn, and even the elation of death must be dimmed down in a being sunk so low.

*Chapter 2*

---

## *THE TRIAL*: THE GUILT OF AN

## UNREDEEMED LITERARY PROMISE

ACCOUNTS OF KAFKA'S "guilt" are by now legion — his guilt is over-determined — yet this is not a category that can easily be ignored. In adding more words to the account, one might simplify it or lend it an energizing direction. "Kafka never missed an opportunity to accuse himself," writes Detlef Kremer, "always quick to assume the position of the guilty party." According to Kafka's script, "the harmony of the family Kafka was disturbed only because of him, the one son Franz, for he is a failure, *since he writes* and hence never leaves the family."[1] Christ was a figure of great interest to Kafka, notes Leo Lensing, because "he was not only the Christian Messiah but also a Jew shaken by crises, a teller of stories, *and the bachelor par excellence*" (emphasis added).[2] Kafka must remain a guilty bachelor until he too has grasped the kind of being he has in relation to his father. He acknowledged this conundrum, writing simply and trenchantly: "In German the word *sein* stands both for the verb *to be* and for the possessive pronoun *his*" (to belong to him, to be another's property) (DF 39). But for Kafka the matter is even more questionable: *from* whom, then, was he independent, and *to* whom did he belong? The precariousness of this situation is conveyed by the emotional and conceptual reality of his having two fathers, with both of whom he needs to be on good terms. He is the son of his father Herrmann Kafka, and he is another father's son, whose nature is hidden — and thus he can be guilty in both relations. One requires progeny, as the condition of his blessing; the other blesses, on the condition that there be separation: it is the Gnostic divinity, the source; its way of working, per negation, and it authorizes Kafka's way per negation. Herrmann Kafka does not want him to write, and he does. Worse is that the "God [of his fathers] does not want . . . [him] to write" (L 10), and he does. To complicate matters, this tribal god usurped the Hebrews' Gnostic roots.

It never becomes any easier to separate these paternal figures. In a well-taken tirade against the "psychological" criticism of Kafka, Erich Heller remarks:

> If, for instance, the writer believes he has discovered the meaning
> of his senselessly tormenting feud with his father . . . — that he

should find his place within a true spiritual order of divine authority—the psychological reader will insist that the author "really" means his father.[3]

One is inclined without much further ado to disdain this "psychological reader," but in his naivety he has nonetheless hit part of the mark, because the two fathers are not separable—or, to adapt a phrase from Walter Benjamin, apropos of semblance and essence under the force of the "expressionless": they are not separate, *and* they do not mingle.[4]

How in this situation of twinned paternity, should Kafka not be guilty? His writing can only aggravate, it cannot repair, his fault. If he writes, he is guilty of failing to live; if he does not write, he has sinned against the spirit. If the world were one, he could not be guilty: in being part of it, he would stand opposed to nothing. But as the world is two, he is always part of the one or the other, stands opposed to one or the other, and so is guilty of offending it.

And writing—as such? Reflecting, toward the end of his life on the "father-complex" of psychoanalysis, Kafka preferred to grasp this complex as one bound up with the father's Jewishness (but that factor must be twinned into the four-times-a-year assimilationist Judaism of Herrmann Kafka and a type of Jewish Gnosticism we shall discuss in chapter 5). Kafka's argument, which turns on the "impossibility of writing," concludes with the assurance that

> the despair [of the complex] could not be assuaged by writing, was hostile to both life and writing; writing is only an expedient, as for someone who is writing his will shortly before he hangs himself— an expedient that may well last a whole life. (L 288)

Writing puts marks into a land outside family, an "Ausland," and, hence, there is Kafka's affinity in his fiction for images of desperate persons in exile—Georg Bendemann's "friend" in Russia, Karl Rossmann in "America," K. in the wastelands of the Castle. To live in exile is to stand in a guilty relation toward one's home, bearer of the irremediable curse—it must feel like this—of having forever hated one's home. One thinks of the "natural" proclivity of the miserable man (*der Elende*), in Nietzsche's aperçu, to consider himself "without a land of his own."[5]

From 1911 on, Kafka's preoccupation with guilt—and guiltless ecstasy—is more and more densely entangled in his concern with writing. Early in his life, when writing well, he knew ecstatic moods of an intensity that, outside of Nietzsche, has few precedents in the history of German literature. The famous words with which Kafka wrote about the composition of "The Judgment" were words he was never able to use again: "Only *in this way* can writing be done, only with such coherence, with such a complete opening out of the body and the soul" (D1 276). "The Judgment," which, like *The Trial*, ends with a death sentence carried out at the behest of an inexplicably potent authority, allowed Kafka to realize a portion of the "creative abilities" of which we have heard: "mysterious powers which are of an ultimate significance to me" (D1 76), "powers that concentrate themselves as literature at a depth that is uncanny."[6] Recall, however, that in late 1914, with work on *The Trial* at low ebb, Kafka began writing "In the Penal Colony"—another approach to the themes of guilt and ecstasy—and there, in the figure of the explorer, noted of the abject prisoner awaiting execution, "He doesn't know the sentence that has been passed on him." (These words, cited from the standard translation, badly miss the fact that, for "sentence," Kafka wrote the phrase "sein eigenes Urteil," "his own judgment" [scil. Kafka's story "The Judgment"].) Since Kafka's "happiness, abilities, and every possibility of being useful in any way," had always been in "the literary field," to "forget" such things would be to provoke at least his moral death (D1 58).

The fate of Joseph K., a high-ranking bank official—the hero of *The Trial*—would seem to have little in common with the fate of the modern writer.[7] And yet other diary entries decisively prefigure the analogy between Kafka the writer and his feckless hero on the grounds of their common relation to a third term, the higher court. In 1910, Kafka wrote: "How do I excuse my not yet having written anything today? In no way [mit nichts]. . . . I have continually an invocation in my ear: 'Were you to come, invisible judgment [Gericht]!' " (D1 36, GW 9:106). Between 1910 and 1914 the claim of the court sounded more and more insistently. In 1913 Kafka described himself to his fiancée Felice Bauer as a man "chained to invisible literature by invisible chains [who] . . . screams when approached because, so he claims, someone is touching those chains" (LF 308). This image can have generated a scene in *The Trial* in which an accused gentleman in the law offices screams when Joseph K. touches his arm "quite gently." The usher explains: "Most defendants are so sensitive" (T 71). "Chained" to their guilt, which gives them a sensitive surface, they are like Kafka, "chained" to literature, an inexhaustible source of guilt as a higher promise only intermittently redeemed.

*The Trial* also alludes to Kafka's own concerns as a writer by suggesting that the verdict on Joseph K. is a judgment, not on the unexplained accusation with which he is confronted at the outset, but on the way in which he conducts his case. As the chaplain explains in the great cathedral scene, "The proceedings gradually merge into the judgment," and here he seems to have K.'s reliance on others foremost in mind (T 213).[8]

"You seek too much outside help . . . ," he says, "particularly from women," a remark that could refer to K.'s sexual dalliances with the student's lover following the first interrogation scene and with Leni in the chambers of Lawyer Huld ("Grace") but especially to his hopes aimed at the slightly higher type of woman, the petty-bourgeois typist Fräulein Bürstner (whom he has nonetheless sexually molested) (T 213). In the closing chapter of *The Trial*, as K. is half-dragged, half-escorted to his death, he glimpses her figure ahead of him, and for one moment she seems to provoke, if only inadvertently, a moment of insight (concerning "the futility of resistance") (T 227). It had always been K.'s habit to overvalue women for their effectiveness in his case, as the chaplain has maintained: "A woman's hand indeed works quiet wonders," K. had said to himself right from the beginning (T 22). Perhaps he is supposed to have learned a little at the end in discarding his impulse to keep Fräulein Bürstner steadily in view ("he could do without her now"), or perhaps he drops her out of apathy (T 228).

What, though, has K.'s sex-besotted manner of conducting his trial to do with Kafka's behavior as a writer, since it is precisely as a writer, immured in the subterranean space of writing, that Kafka would seem to be proof against sex? One cannot, however, overlook the autoerotism of the writing "intensity" for Kafka. Yes, "writing is a form of prayer" (DF 312). But it is also a deeply private, subversive affair. It stands opposed in his consciousness, of course, to married sex, and yet it is not sex — or, better, it is that sex that does not want to be seen as sex — the pseudoascetic delight for which Kafka also has the dubious names "dilettantism" and "sensuality" and that for him has nothing redemptive about it (GrW 264, L 334). In saying this, we should not forget, however, that it is also impossible for Kafka to construct the opposite pole of married sex as a kind of innocence to which it would be a proof of worth to attain. He knew that he had bound himself to Felice Bauer at least in part to secure a token of the nourishment he needed in order to stay sane enough to write. But one of his finer impulses is to sublate this relation so that there comes to light a law that he codes in his fiction: the writer, the anguished ascetic, like the accused in *The Trial*, is attractive to women, who in making love to these martyrs, make love to the suffering quester in them. So that everywhere Kafka turns, he sees himself "creative in self-torment" but no less creative in finding and accusing himself of perverse forms of pleasure; the finding and the accusing are the same things. In all of this, there is a jot of defiant pride. In 1920, he wrote the summary aphorism concerning a person called "He":

All that he does seems to him, it is true, extraordinarily new, but also, because of the incredible spate of new things, extraordinarily dilettantish, indeed scarcely tolerable, incapable of becoming history, breaking short the chain of the generations, cutting off for the first time at its most profound source the music of the world, which before him could at least be divined. Sometimes in his arrogance he has more anxiety for the world than for himself. (GrW 263–64)

Here, still, the pleasure of writing appears as something less than the ascetically prepared, ecstatic self-loss of writing and, certainly, less than the sexual act of maintaining "the chain of generations." The association of writing with an only perverse delight recurs throughout Kafka, who, finally, in the famous letter to Max Brod of July 5, 1922, links the writing destiny to a mania for pleasure (*Genußsucht*) and for this reason damns it as "devil's work" (L 332–35, Br 384–86). Kafka writes, not as a hunger artist, but for the complex pleasure writing gives: the pleasure of writing is the sex of the ascetic and hence part of an economy of guilt. So it is predictable that when, in late July 1914, just at the time that the world war had broken out, Kafka began writing *The Trial*, he would write defiantly, and in the language of what is called denegation, "I am hardly moved by all the misery and more determined than ever. . . . I will write in spite of everything, absolutely; it is my fight for self-preservation" (D2 75). And as the idea of self-preservation includes the pleasure of "the individual subject" — which, as Hegel puts it in *The Philosophy of Right*, "*as such* has the guilt of its evil" — self-preservation here will produce a heightened sense of guilt.[9] Without positing some such efflux of the guilt attaching to the very project of writing *The Trial*, it will be otherwise difficult to understand the readiness of Joseph K., who is Kafka's "alias," "twin," and, in a demonstrable sense, "hypocrite reader," to acknowledge a "trial" for which every ordinary, civil-legal justification is missing.[10]

The conflict between the pleasure of writing and of married sex had furthermore become especially acute for Kafka in late July 1914. The onset of composition was dictated by twin catastrophes: On July 23, Kafka's engagement to Felice Bauer was broken off at the Hotel Askanischer Hof in Berlin, which Kafka called "the court of justice in the hotel" (D2 65). And, on July 28, Austria declared war against Serbia. In a mood of jubilation, based (one may imagine) on the anticipation of his own explosive destruction, Kafka attempted to enlist but was rejected. As a result of the general mobilization, though, he was obliged to move out of his parents' apartment and "receive the reward for living alone. But it is hardly a reward; living alone ends only with punishment" (D2 75).

Since we are acquainted with the promise of ecstasy impacted in Kafka's writing project (the condition of which, for Kafka, until 1923, was living without a woman), this description of his newfound solitude will seem only half-true and contestable. In fact, in late 1914, he was able to write on *The Trial*, and to write well on it, for several months. Something of his extreme determination to succeed is visible in an extraordinary compositional maneuver. As a result of feeling that he would never be able to bring his previous novel *Amerika* (*The One Who Sank Out of Sight*) to a close, and that, therefore, in such a work he was stranded in "the lowlands of writing," he was determined to make certain that *The Trial* should have an ending (D1 276). And so in his initial assault on the novel, he wrote the first chapter "The Arrest" together with the final chapter "The End" and, moreover, left a coded marker in the novel of what he had done. We have here a sign of what has been called by Malcolm Pasley "the parallel process run through by fictional events [in *The Trial*] and the acts of writing that produced them."[11] It is worth noting that the German word for *The Trial*, which Kafka, moreover, spells "*Process*," means precisely this in English — "process." As a result, there is a specific connection between Joseph K.'s trial and Kafka's own "trial," so to speak, in writing this novel: these two processes or trials act and react together and in some instances, as Pasley notes, seem actually to fuse. In this matter of the parallel of beginning and end, on the way to his execution, K. urges himself to stay "calm and analytical," adding: "Do I want to show now that even a yearlong trial could teach me nothing? . . . Shall they say of me that at the beginning of my trial I wanted to end it, and now, at its end, I want to begin it again?" (T 228). This reflection is remarkable when one realizes that Kafka did indeed want to end his writing of *The Trial* at the very beginning (of his writing it); and now, at its end, he did want to begin it again. Writing these lines, Kafka was in the very process of ending his own *Trial* or *Process* at its beginning, in order to begin again, where he had left off, with Joseph K.'s arrest. A specific difference in valence within the symmetry of Joseph K. and Kafka thus begins to open up: what Joseph K. in no way wants to be said on his account, Kafka wants, above all, to be said on his account. This difference is a measure of the differing consciousness of their predicament. Kafka wrote *The Trial* precisely as he did because, unlike Joseph K., he was unable to declare himself innocent.

Kafka began his project, then, with defiant expectancy, but, as his mood darkens, something like a guilty, punishable quality to the entire process sets in. It is tellingly cast as the specific invidious comparison Kafka made between this process and that of the time of breakthrough in 1912. On August 15, 1914, he noted: "Today I am not so completely protected by and absorbed by my work as I was two years ago [that is, during the period of the main composition of *Amerika* (*The One Who*

*Sank Out of Sight*), "The Judgment," and *The Metamorphosis*]; nevertheless I have a direction, my regular, empty, insane bachelor's life has a justification" (D2 79). The act of writing *The Trial* more and more takes on the distinctive stake of establishing the author's superiority to his hypocrite brother Joseph K., which appears to become harder and harder to come by. Yet it is clear that if Kafka could not succeed in coherently finishing off Joseph K., it is precisely he himself who would be finished. One implication of the major story "In the Penal Colony" (which I read as a sort of reflective sequel to *The Trial*, though it was written in the course of it, in late 1914) is that it preemptively releases the author from the constraints of the monstrous system of justice that risked executing him as well, as the overweening and deluded hanging judge.

Thereafter, there are few happy diary entries during the process of writing *The Trial*. By the beginning of the next year, the project would have run into the sands. But what is plainly at stake for Kafka throughout all the writing of *The Trial* goes beyond alleviation of his empirical miseries — his personal failures as a dodger both of his engagement to Felice Bauer and of the draft. He seeks "justification" — redemption "into the [greater] freedom that perhaps awaits me" — a result that depends on his writing purely while continuing to condemn Joseph K. (D2 92). There is, however, a visible tension between these goals: the novel is unusual in Kafka's oeuvre for its steadily maintained lack of sympathy for its hero. Another way of looking at the fact that Kafka composed the scene of his hero's brutal execution right at the outset is that he needed to make sure that Joseph K. would be destroyed; hence, he would finish him off at the start before the temptation could set in of finding grounds to pardon him, which would exonerate Kafka impermissibly, or grounds to flee the project through one or another form of suicide. Yet by the time of writing the lawyer episode or — the same thing — shortly after accomplishing the meditation of "In the Penal Colony," Kafka appears not to know how to justify his administering K.'s punishment. The demonstrated fact of his harshness can be understood as a reflex of the intensity of his desire to annihilate his own empirical ego as the bearer of a life situation that he could barely endure — that of the writer who does not write or does not write well enough — at the same time that, as a writer — as the warrant of ecstatic self-annihilation — he means to survive. Hence, nothing can be linear in Kafka, and nothing he does or writes is not without its aspect as a cunning subterfuge plotted against the "invisible court," as he was the first to acknowledge. Even Joseph K.'s condemnation in advance is arranged along ingenious rhetorical lines that cast doubt as to its probity.

In its first manuscript appearance, the opening sentence of *The Trial* reads: "Someone must have slandered Joseph K., for one morning, without having done anything truly wrong, he was *held* [or *caught* (*gefangen*)]" (emphasis added). Thereafter Kafka crossed out the word "held" and replaced it with the word "*arrested*" ("*verhaftet*"), introducing the more obviously legal term. The shift into legal language supplies Kafka with his inner design for the novel, which he kept elaborating as he wrote it. The design may be grasped as the requirement that Joseph K. come to terms with his sense of guilt by insufficient — indeed, by childish means.

Joseph K. supposes that he will be brought to trial by a court constituted like a civil court, which, even in the absence of specific charges, will exonerate him. But in this way, he merely repeats Kafka's authorial leap into a seeming legality and, hence, takes the lure that will lead to his death, for it becomes more and more evident that there are no ordinary legal means available to rescue him. It is Kafka as author who has made the leap ahead of him in replacing the word "caught" with "arrested": the author is guilty of this treacherous leap of thought before his puppet is. The manuscript inscribes the impulse to flee an existential drama for a legal one as the very move that Joseph K. will be punished for making. Joseph K. acts at odds with the truth of his situation, but in forcing him to do so Kafka does not obviously establish K.'s difference from himself, who has obliged K. to misunderstand his situation while only hinting all along at the kind of truth it has. That truth exists essentially as something K., the nonwriter, will never grasp.

In proposing to see this truth as an efflux of the guilt that originates with Kafka's *Schriftstellersein* (his writer's-being), have we succeeded in affirming Kafka's superiority to his victim? The narrator cannot bring this question to a conclusion. And so we are returned to Joseph K., to a guilt the remoteness of whose origin compels it to remain an enigma. It is monstrous to be required to witness Joseph K.'s being stabbed to death, especially since it is impossible to say whether it is or is not deserved. This very impossibility, however, sustains *The Trial* as an indispensable work of literary consciousness.

# Segue I

---

## ON CULTURAL IMMORTALITY

*Where the main motifs of the preceding chapters are taken
up and inflected toward the media.*

THE CRAVING FOR the immolation of the empirical self; the guilt of writing or not writing; ecstasy; the risk of crossing over the limits of the human — all this involves choice and free activity. Kafka represents these longings and troubles as intelligible, as things about which he can make up his mind to pursue or to resist as dangerous. At the same time, however, he is a philosopher of constraint — of the force exercised on him by the patriarchy above all. And in his imagination, a crucial subdivision of this authority is its system for the transmission and preservation of its signs of power — in short, the media.

Kafka and Kafka's works are attentive to modern medial technology, as witness his intense curiosity about his fiancée's work as *Prokurist* for a company (Lindstrom Parlograph) manufacturing recording and telecommunicative devices. His medial imagination flourishes in *Amerika* (*The One Who Sank Out of Sight*), with its full-fledged prophecies of technical prowess in cycling information (the "information givers" at the Hotel Occidental are human machines). In the later novels, scenes of telephonic communication are staged between higher instances of authority and the supplicant figure Joseph K. in *The Trial* and K. in *The Castle*. Here, the distribution of power and authority runs across lines demarcated by the flows of information.

In "In the Penal Colony" the body itself becomes a medium to be inscribed; "deciphering" it, the prisoner is illuminated. This event is registered by an entire society, which assures a relative cultural immortality for the moment of insight. The moment of recognition is also a sort of medial inscription in the social body.

At the same time, the cost of the exemplary body's saturation by signs is its death. The fate of an illuminated death is linked to the fate of a medium, which is here consumed by the very signs it is meant to accommodate. The illumination communicated to the cult of the penal colony arises from the prisoner's fleeting grasp of his own body as a medium of communication; but what he actually grasps is that here there is a medium and nothing more — and certainly not a message (see chapter 4). A

moment of meconnaissance inscribes itself into the mind of the social
body as the illusion of an act of successful reading; the true kernel of
the experience, however, to judge from current editions, is the prisoner's
failure to read his inscription. Kafka's imagination of medial misrecog-
nition persists until the end in the hapless performances of the hunger
artist and the pantomime of Josephine, the mouse-singer. Kafka is a
philosopher-poet of medial power.

The phenomenon of unwilled self-loss in medial appropriation engaged him, as it engages his readers. What was at stake for him was the
loss of the self that could dribble away in the senseless messages he
wrote.[1] What is at stake for his readers is the loss of his manuscripts,
which he claimed to want to have destroyed but were nonetheless sal-
vaged by Max Brod and recently, in the most dramatic way, by the new
technical media.

To Kafka's first concern, Gerhard Neumann has emphasized Kafka's
meditation on and display of the *sign*, his

> semiotic concerns — his interest in the ordering of signs, whose play
> unfolds in the zone between power and flight: chiefly, the orders of
> the sign in the strict sense, which are articulated differently in his
> world: in the scriptive play of exchanged letters, which situate fig-
> ures who write and read; in the scriptive play of literature . . . as a
> flow of relations between persons, into which a third element se-
> cretes itself — the parasite, at once disrupting and enabling this
> communication; in the rustle of language, which denudes itself
> of meaning; in the "white signs" of the writer in exile that flow
> through the modern communications media; and, finally, in the dia-
> lectic of the local and individual peculiarities and the foreignness of
> signs, as documented in an exemplary way by Kafka's confronta-
> tion with "Jargon," the Yiddish language.[2]

Meanwhile, the appropriation of Kafka's manuscripts (and the expro-
priation of their intended destiny of being cast into oblivion) is something every reader of Kafka confronts whenever he holds in his hands
one or another edition of Kafka.

These are issues of self-mutilation and medial denaturing: what stands
behind them is the threat they mount to the idea of cultural immortality,
since that is, at times, the chief predilection in the ascetic economy of
Kafka's self-making. "It," this impersonal self, is produced for the sake of
writing and is in turn its product. Furthermore, cultural immortality
would also appear to be the goal (both as a promise and a catastrophe) of
the media that circulate and preserve the writer's words. Besotted by the
thought of one's contingency, one's ever approaching annihilation, one
must, without such an institution or concept of cultural immortality, go

mad. Yet, however torn and jumbled our time, it is one in which we suppose we have not yet gone mad — a state of affairs that suggests that an idea of cultural immortality is still afoot. The postmodern "world" is not finally the drift of contingencies it is held to be: it is held together, differently, by the principle of its sanity. We take for granted a notion of cultural survival: I know only a few readers — of Kafka or of anyone — who have made peace with a shadowless extinction.

Early modernity had its privileged sites of metaphysical longing: first, theology, that guaranteed the immortality of the soul; then, negative theology, that conjured a virtual redemptive agency through a sufficiently intense consciousness of its absence.[3] But I doubt that many readers now look to either of these places, and hence not to Kafka, if he should be held to be a surveyor of these places (he did look to both — though intermittently, and with pained irony).[4] It is in this sense of our not looking for metaphysical comfort that Foucault, like the late Nietzsche, could write of the "death of man":

> Man is an invention of recent date. And one perhaps nearing its end. If those arrangements were once to disappear as they appeared, if some event of which we can at the moment do no more than sense the possibility — without knowing either what its forms will be or what it promises — were to cause them to crumble, then one can certainly wager that man would be erased, like a face drawn in sand at the edge of the sea.[5]

But it is no longer so difficult to "sense the possibility" of that event. We are in the midst of it, and, as I glare back at my computer screen, I know that this possibility is medial. We are like a face drawn with a cursor on the brink of deletion, beginning to fear that there is a hand bold enough to strike this key.[6]

Look more closely where I am looking now — at the screen archive, the Web, a covert form of cultural survival. What does it tell us about Kafka — and our reading of Kafka — aside from what we find on Alta Vista?

Our medial immersion is, first of all, a source of resistance to Kafka the metaphysician. If Kafka studies are enjoying a renaissance of sorts — through and against cultural studies — then this has something to do with Kafka's own attentiveness to the media.[7] The resistance to Kafka the metaphysician has led not to an overthrow of Kafka but to a heightened interest in Kafka as a thinker of the media. His preoccupation with bureaucracy represents a forestage of his philosophy of the archive. These interests situate Kafka precisely in the history of the awareness of cultural immortality at a point of late modernity, on the cusp between negative theology and the philosophy of the medial archive.[8]

I stress, in this segue, the oddness (and the resistance to this oddness) of Kafka as the metaphysical poet bent chiefly on introducing into probable-seeming narratives, without consistent empirical reference, a transcendent aura, an aura of the perpetual and the abysmal having something to do with the truth. If his stories and concerns seem strange to us today, it is not because we have no use for what they suggest but because one sort of transcendent reference is already so secure, so much taken for granted through our mediawork, that we can hardly imagine experience without it: I am thinking, with respect to the media, of

- their infinite expansibility of the ordinary, as one item of information is connected to countless other items;
- their infinite reproducibility of the ordinary, as it is made universally accessible;
- their "memories" (of the ordinary), more capacious than any man's or woman's;
- and their immeasurably great resources of recorders, archivists — and archives;

so that, for us mediaworkers and surfingkeyboarders, the media might suggest that we are part of an eternity now — an infinitely expansible, world-immanent, supersaturated and supersaturating endlessness of reference.[9]

To this side of things, the cybertheorist Andrew Piper comments:

Few writers [Kafka notwithstanding] have been able to capture the logic of the database [our electronic Library] [. . .] its lexicon of infinity, its redundancy, its elusiveness. . . . As the invisible architecture of the database slowly spreads among us — an architecture "whose center is everywhere," as Borges wrote of his metaphorical Library, "and whose circumference is nowhere" — we are suspicious that it is there, recording, but uncertain as to exactly where.[10]

With "whose center is everywhere and whose circumference is nowhere," Borges is quoting Empedocles' definition of the One God.[11] Meanwhile, the cybertheorist Jonathan Rosen is similarly inspired to compare the Internet to the Talmud on grounds of the likeness between verbal "boxes" and windows, the totality of a tradition, and the user's sense of exile on a centerless periphery.[12]

The triumph of the Internet assures us a spatialized transcendent reference even while we are alive. Furthermore, these media will very likely assure us safe passage, too, after we are dead. Search with Alta Vista, and you will find *your* essentials there, a benefit that Kafka's heroes must do without: the Hunter Gracchus dies but cannot find an archive to lay his head down in.

This book on Kafka is concerned with how a feeling for an archaic (Gnostic) transcendence informs — and is informed by — Kafka's ethics and philosophy of writing. But consider, now, the effort of Kafka's demythologizing, empiricizing mediacritics to banish this concern. The mediacritic has been well-served by his discovery in Kafka of a brother mediacritic and by the medial reproduction of Kafka's manuscripts. These enterprises go hand in hand. Just when books of considerable power began to be written on Kafka's technophilia by wired readers of Gerhard Neumann's and Wolf Kittler's pathbreaking *Schriftverkehr* (Textual intercourse), whose path was itself opened by Friedrich Kittler's *Aufschreibesysteme 1800/1900* (Discourse networks), the great effort was begun by K. D. Wolff, Roland Reuß, and Peter Staengle to produce a media-facilitated edition of Kafka's manuscripts.[13] The remanufacture of Kafka's scripts, with its justified claims to "save" them from yellowing and decay, can enjoy the good conscience of treating Kafka in a manner that reflects both his empirical interests and the referential texture of his work bearing on the media of modern technology (typewriting, photography, telephones, wireless communication as such). The medial attention paid to Kafka is a reflex of the fascination, horror, and analytic intensity that Kafka's manuscripts brought to the media.

One material factor needs to be added: the driving force behind the enterprise of producing an "authentic" edition of Kafka's writings with the help of advanced computer printing technology is capitalist and appropriative. Whatever love of truth undoubtedly accompanies the enterprise of Stroemfeld/Roter Stern, it is also attentive to the market niche, no small one: the market of the German-speaking library and archive and household, each of which might be supposed to want to own — and consume? — one modality of the complete works of Franz Kafka. The Roter Stern enterprise arose as the felt need to bring into the maw of the new technology Kafka's dormant manuscripts, true; but this challenge has been sustained by the existence of a rival enterprise, the Fischer *Kritische Ausgabe in der Fassung der Handschrift*, which, from 1982 on, has already cornered most of the German market. No accident, here too, that the complete paperback edition of this work was rushed into the market by Fischer to capture in late 1994 the Christmas spirit of gift-giving.

In this struggle for publisher's fortunes — another sort of cultural immortality — the coupling of the concept of cultural immortality with the medial archive has been mobilized in the most explicit way. Along with its economic interest, Roter Stern has based its desire to proceed with its facsimiling on its claim, on the example of Kleist's manuscripts, that only in this way could the permanence of the manuscripts be assured: they might crumble in the fullness of time but, once computer-imaged, would endure forever (as long as computers do not crumble and apocalyptic-minded hackers are restrained). What we finally have is the surreptitious substitution of one ideology of cultural immortality for another. If mediacritics thought they had demythologized Kafka the metaphysician, they have succeeded in mythologizing their own media as the token of a new cultural immortality.

One remarkable innovation, if not a plain advantage, of the Reuß facsimile vis-à-vis the standard "complete" Fischer edition (see chapter 10) is the way it redistributes the authority of Kafka's writings. Since every reader can now own a reproduction of Kafka's manuscripts, the work becomes that entity that he or she is free to "edit" according to his or her own lights. That new entity is not a "work" in a traditional sense, since it no longer has the imprimatur of a single editor making decisions about the correct ordering of chapters or their exact word sequence. Instead, readers are free to decide how they wish to sequence the fascicles of Kafka's notebook pages and treat Kafka's visible crossings-out and half-crossings-out. We have here an unwonted democratization of the authority to confer cultural immortality.

Kafka had mixed feelings about wanting his work — let alone his unfinished work — to survive him, ranging from his saying that very little of it ought to survive to implying that it all ought to survive, since he entrusted his last testament to a friend, Max Brod, who he knew would never destroy a word of his work. What would Kafka have made, however, of the medial appropriation of his manuscripts? He would have been fascinated, and he would have been appalled. Aside from the horror of their universal exposure, how much of them would be on display, and in what form? Would the ghosts of the digital machine suck up the last erotic filaments threading about the words that Kafka wrote to himself?

Kafka was interested in his cultural survival, so he would have been enthralled by the time warping involved, by a technical, medial device of sufficient complexity to assist him in his pursuit of justification — justification being a matter of what one leaves behind. This is exactly where the Web comes in; in transcribing and preserving Kafka's manuscripts from decay, it lifts them from the medium of the material page into cyberspace and promises them a sort of paraphysical immortality.

Not the least advantage of the facsimile edition, however, is that it puts a good version of the manuscript of *The Trial* in our hands and allows us to consider — and to solve — a famous crux: this is the subject of the next chapter.

---

# Chapter 3

# MEDIAL INTERVENTIONS IN

# *THE TRIAL*; OR, *RES* IN MEDIA

FROM THE START, the narrative of *The Trial* displays various kinds of media. The basic medial device is theater.[1] This theatrical performance in turn includes ("intermediates") two other medial types—first, popular literature, especially travel literature; and second, the archive, the very manuscript or manuscription from which the diegesis, the world of the novel, emerges.[2] Kafka's talent for dramatizing different modes of presentation (*Vorstellung*) and of reading includes even the ways that readers read—ways of reading and interpretation, "symbolic" and "allegorical," that themselves amount to different kinds of media. "Types of Kafka interpretation can be identified and their validity measured by a scrutiny of the work, which unfolds as the adventurous combat of principles authorizing interpretations."[3] This sentence was written in 1973. Now, thirty years later—after guerilla theater; after the emergent claim that literary modernism is defined by its absorption of popular culture; above all, after the expansion of the electronic archive—this point about Kafka's wide consciousness of the medial constraints on interpretation still seems correct.

In *The Trial*, the scenic element of theater—the "show" ("die Schaustellung") (T 9, Pp 15), the "farce" ("die Komödie") (T 7, Pp 12)—foregrounds a scriptive element (*das in Schrift Gestellte*), "the book" ("das Buch") (T 5, Pp 9), "the document" ("das Schriftstück"), "papers" ("die Papiere") (Pp 12). This scriptive element mirrors the grand medium of the narration as such, the incomplete book of *The Trial*. With this, something of the problematic relation of the visible Court (*Gericht*) and the in principle readable Law (*Gesetz*) is reflected; they cross as the media cross—the visible and the readable—*res* in media. The outcome of this medial intersection will not be the "clarification" ("Klarstellung") (T 14, Pp 22) that K. requires but his death sentence in the quarry.

Consider how these medial intersections play out. From the very first page, *The Trial* sets the stage for a play within a narrative. On awakening, Joseph K. is put out not to have been brought his breakfast: it is past eight o'clock and Anna the cook, a holdover from *The Metamorphosis*, usually brings him his breakfast before eight o'clock.[4] Upon noting the absence of cook and breakfast, K. does immediately notice the presence of something. This is a scene made instructive by Jean-Jacques Rousseau's *Second Walk*, in which Rousseau, having fallen unconscious as a result of a collision with a Great Dane ("un gros chien danois"), awakens — and bit by bit perceives — and hence constitutes, as if for the first time, the human world as a pastoral: "the sky, some stars, and a little greenery" ("le ciel, quelques étoiles, et un peu de verdure").[5]

> This first sensation was a delicious moment. I still had no feeling of myself except as being "over there" [par là]. I was born into life at that instant, and it seemed to me that I filled all the objects I perceived with my frail existence. . . . A rapturous calm pervaded my whole being. (translation modified)[6]

Otherwise with Joseph K., who on awakening, sees — what? Another's stare; for, from his pillow, he saw "the old woman who lived across the way, who was peering at him with a curiosity quite unusual for her" (T 3). K. constitutes his world as the event of being stared at by another, so that anything he thereafter sees and does falls under the sway of another's stare. His moment of awakening out of his bewilderment is to see himself figure as the element of another's seen world. His attempt to constitute a world enacts another's world, meaning that he is no longer a subject — which is to say: the protected spectator of his own actions — but the exposed object of another's spectatorship — he is an "actor." And now it is as if every judgment he makes on his own experience must be referred to a complex of forces stemming from others, must be seen as capable of aggravating or, then again, as mitigating the judgment implicit in the stare of others: henceforth his judgments can be made only in spite of them or in accord with them. It all must figure as something of a clamp, as if to be "arrested" (*verhaftet*) were principally to be trapped in the niche of the prisoner of the panopticon.

On next ringing for his breakfast (and with this ringing of the bell: Let the play begin!), Joseph K. is amazed by the appearance in his bedroom of a man he has never seen before. The man is wearing a jacket suggestive of a tourist's, "with a variety of pleats, pockets, buckles, buttons and a belt" — one that looks "eminently practical" although "its purpose remained obscure" (T 3–4).

The fit of this event with the event of being seen is perfect: the effect of being seen (and hence judged in the act of seeing) by a remote pair of eyes — hence, quite possibly always thus being seen — must provoke the next question: With the inevitable appearance of another (real) human counterpart, how shall one figure the stare of this stranger? Does it belong together with the stare of the abstract stranger projected by the old woman in her loge? The question on the face of it is undecidable —

and as worrisome as it is undecidable. The only relief might be in the superidentification of this other person, his minute specification. Scrutinized with great precision, do the colors he wears rather suggest his allegiance to the party of the others or his independence of it: is he friend or foe?

One could recall, for corroboration of this gesture, the moment in the initial inquiry when K., at his most paranoid, studies

> The faces that surrounded him! *Tiny black eyes darted about*, cheeks drooped like those of drunken men, the long beards were stiff and scraggly, and when they pulled on them, it seemed as if they were merely forming claws, not pulling beards. Beneath the beards, however — and this was the true discovery K. made — badges of various sizes and colors shimmered on the collars of their jackets. They all had badges, so far as he could see. They were all one group, the parties on the left and right, and as he suddenly turned, he saw the same badges on the collar of the examining magistrate. (emphasis added, T 51–52)

His paranoia is accomplished.

Now, at the opening scene of his process, K. studies the rich specificity of the tourist figure before him, the abundance of pleats, pockets, buckles, buttons, and belts sewed into this fetish-bearer whose name will be: Franz — K.'s, Kafka's, monstrous and seductive bisexual alienness within — but here outed and exposed in the service of an adversarial world. The entire structure of relations is unsurprising in an author who wrote, "In the struggle between yourself and the world, second the world" (DF 39).[7] This "Franz" is now a killing agent of the Court.

But beyond perceiving the purposiveness of his costume or mask, K. cannot tell what its purpose is and hence cannot tell the purpose of the figure. This mysterious abundance, this surplus of signs without meaning, points to a certain remoteness in relation to the scene: and indeed this Franz is a traveler, though we cannot say whether it is because he is now prepared to travel away from Joseph K.'s bedroom, with Joseph K. in tow (his black jacket might anticipate the deadly black "frock coats" [Gehröcke] (T 225, Pp 305) worn by K.'s executioners in the final chapter); or, perhaps, more tellingly, whether he is a traveler whose long journey has now come to an end with his arrival at K.'s; and the pleats, belts, buckles are to serve a purpose that K. will experience at first hand, at home. Says the warden: "You'll feel it eventually" (T 9), or, more potently, more menacingly: "You'll find out first-hand" ("Sie werden es zu fühlen bekommen") (Pp 15).

This, now — after the theater or indeed inside the theater — is the second medial allusion, an allusion to Kafka's ongoing preoccupation with travel literature and especially, as one learns from John Zilcosky, an allusion to Kafka's beloved imperial adventure novels, *Schaffsteins Grüne Bändchen* (Schaffstein's little green books) (1910ff.).[8] Zilcosky's work suggests that Kafka dreamt of traveling to a newfound land — on the model of his Uncle Alfred, who did indeed become director general of the Spanish Railways in Madrid.[9] Kafka then abandoned the dream; and the punishment for the abandonment of the dream is to stay at home and become the destination of another's travels, the second self who went away.

The presence of a second self is marked, as I have said, by the name "Franz"; and I am proposing "paranoia" as the perverse of Kafka's green-book-colored travel lust, which invariably has a fin de siècle sexual and exploitative character. The charm of foreign lands is that they offer a pool of available "subjects" of erotic and sadistic exploitation. What would it mean to abandon guiltily — not renounce — but abandon through anxiety and lassitude one's erotic and sadistic desires if not to court the punishment that is its mirror obverse: to become oneself the impending subject of erotic and sadistic exploitation by the traveler who does travel, who does set off on the long journey that will bring him into the bedroom of Joseph K.?

Mark Anderson suggests that K. has been raped; Zilcosky develops the argument:

> This [black tourist's] suit is one of Kafka's trademark symbols of *Verkehr*, a conceptual node that, through the word's double meaning, connects "traffic" with "(sexual) intercourse" [scil. Anderson].[10] The guard's suit, as a marker for *Verkehr*, points to what Anderson refers to as the "rape" of K.[11] K., we remember, claims to have been "pester[ed]" or "molested" (*belästig[t]*) in his bed — dressed, like a Kleistian rape victim, only in a blouse-like nightshirt [T 5, Pp 10]. As we discover later, the man in the traveling suit leaves K.'s room with his usual sexual trophies (K.'s underwear). . . .[12]

The rape is K.'s undercurrent projection: the wider name for his predicament is paranoia; the more anodyne term: "performance" — a play: K. will perform a play to escape his paranoid arrest or seizure, by clarifying it.[13] With this gesture (the play), the more drastic workings of his paranoia will be delayed, just as the violence of his sexual imagination will be pushed into the background until it too springs out.

The analogy of K.'s opening moves with the opening of a play is evident. K. says to Franz: "I have no wish to stay here, nor to be addressed by you, until you've introduced yourself" ("Ich will weder hierbleiben noch von Ihnen angesprochen werden, solange Sie sich mir nicht vorstellen") (T 4, Pp 8). The act of "introducing himself" (*Sich-*

*vorstellen*) is not forthcoming in the bedroom and hence dictates that if there is to be such a "(theatrical) presentation" or *Vorstellung* of sorts, it will have to be provoked by K. and take place in another room. With perfect consistency, "the stranger" ("der Fremde") — "Franz" — "opened the door of his own accord" ("öffnete nun freiwillig die Tür") (T 4, Pp 8). This way K. can escape the oppression of his bedroom, the world of "Fr-," exchanging it for the adjacent room, Frau G.'s sitting room (thus, by connotation, also exchanging Frieda — Felice Bauer's cover name — for **Grete Bloch/Grubach**), a room that appears unchanged except for seeming less cluttered, more open: the impression is of the deck having been cleared, of a room that has been turned into a stage, now in the service of a play, in which K. will attempt to affirm his public authority.[14]

More than once, it is K. who imposes the metaphor of the play onto his effort to escape his situation of being seen. He thinks: "If this was a farce, he was going to play along" ("War es eine Komödie, so wollte er mitspielen") (T 7, Pp 12). This prepares the language of his protest to the inspector: "You ask what sense it makes [to telephone the public prosecutor], while you stage the most senseless performance imaginable?" ("Sie wollen einen Sinn [dafür, daß ich dem Staatsanwalt telephonieren will] und führen das Sinnloseste auf was es gibt?" (T 15, Pp 23). Even of his killers, at the close, he says, to diminish their power, "They've sent old supporting actors for me . . . ," and to them: "Which theater are you playing at?" (T 226).[15]

Now, in Frau Grubach's sitting room, the second warder, not Franz, is the first to speak, in effect ordering K. to return to his bedroom, whereupon K. replies, "What is it you want, then?" ("Ja, was wollen Sie denn?") (T 5, Pp 9) and with this "wollen" appears to constitute this other person as "Einer, der was will [someone who wants something]," "einer, dessen Willen eine Absicht zugesprochen wird [someone, to whose will an object is attributed]," "einem Willen" — or, put simply: "Willem." That is the name the guard is given, in this scene of name-giving; and later we have a corroborative formulation, for, on replying to K. he is identified as "the guard who had been named Willem" ("der Wächter, der Willem genannt worden war") (Pp 15) and not as Breon Mitchell has it, in his otherwise admirable translation, "the guard called Willem" (T 9). To this extent, not only a situation, with charges and countercharges, but even named persons are constituted performatively.

Consistently, in this scene of naming, the main import of what Willem says is to refer K. to the second warder, who is now formally introduced as "Franz," a gesture that produces K.'s — Kafka's? — wondering stare — Franz? — as one might expect. (It is not surprising, with touches like these, that Kafka and his listeners, when Kafka read this chapter aloud to them, could not go on for sheer mad hilarity). So what we have chiefly had, then, in this scene, is an exchange of glances between K. and a man reading a book by an open window and then a glance back to Franz before K. must experience with a renewed impact his situation as a player of a play. The window, even as an open window, is not an opening out and away to a freer zone but a space filled entirely by the perception of being perceived, for "through the open window the old woman was visible again, having moved with truly senile curiosity to the window directly opposite, so she could keep an eye on everything" (T 5). Moments later, too, "He [K.] saw the old woman, who had pulled an ancient man far older than herself to the window and had her arms wrapped about him" (T 9); and that's not all:

> Across the way, the old couple were again at the opposite window, but their party had increased in number, for towering behind them stood a man with his shirt open at the chest, pinching and twisting his reddish goatee. (T 12–13)

They are members of the audience to join the gaping cast already on stage. Even K. identifies the figures in the window as such: "There's more of the audience over there" ("Dort sind auch solche Zuschauer") (T 15, Pp 24). A persecutory audience on all sides seals the theatrical space: *fenêtres closes*.

Whereupon K., depriving Willem in advance of an answer to the question of what he wants, answers the question for him: "I'd still like Frau Grubach — " ("Ich will doch Frau Grubach — ") (T 5, Pp 9). Just as in the first instance of his perceiving himself being perceived, Joseph K.'s remedial move was to ring for a woman — Anna, Frau Grubach's maid; now, again perceiving himself being perceived, he demands Frau Grubach: the woman will rescue him from this space of windows opening onto yet other windows to reveal the stare of others reflecting himself. Woman as beneficent reality, woman as the antiparanoid: "I just wanted to hear your judgment on the matter [Frau Grubach]," K. will say later on, "the judgment of a sensible woman, and I'm glad we agree about it" (T 23–24).[16] Is this not a figure in small for the construction of interpersonality throughout the entire book? The chaplain, moreover, will reprove K. for this expedient; we recall: "You seek too much outside help, . . . particularly from women" (T 213).[17]

## THE ARCHIVE

What has been happening at the order of scenic event and gesture is now mirrored in remarkable fashion at the order of verbal exchange: the third — and most surprising — medial intrusion.

In response to Joseph K.'s *Willensäußerung*, to the expression of his will, Willem throws down his book. In response to Joseph K.'s "I'd still like Frau Grubach," Willem produces his key reply: "No, . . . you may not go, you're being held" ("Nein . . . Sie dürfen nicht weggehen, Sie sind ja gefangen") (T 5, Pp 9), with the word "ja" connoting, "as things are" or "as anyone can see" or "right?" It is evident from Reuß's manuscript edition that Kafka indeed wrote the word "gefangen" (held, caught) (Pr, fascicle entitled: "Jemand musste Josef K. verläumdet haben," 9). Yet in the older, until recently standard German edition — that of Max Brod — the sentence reads: "Sie sind ja *verhaftet*";[18] and, hence, in the older, until recently standard English translation of Willa and Edwin Muir, as revised by E. M. Butler, the sentence reads: "You are arrested."[19] It is as if Willem has found his (correct) lines in the script/manuscript that he was reading and can now toss "the book" aside and speak his line — a line that, with its little word "ja," is very productive and very apt at the outset of this drama. Why?

Consider that the opening lines of a drama, which need to be spoken, are more limited in their power to stage a scene than the principally long and reflective lines of epic. The opening lines of a drama require the greater suspension of the demand for intelligibility by an audience or by a performer who does not have the script in advance, because neither we nor he knows the world to which the words refer. Every successive line is in principle clearer, since it has more evidence within the stage world to refer back to; the first lines have nothing. What is now eye-catching and fitting is the little word "ja" with which Willem announces K.'s being "held" or "caught": its thrust is to move the drama back to a virtual moment when an understanding had already been reached, as if the communicative situation among the players were already well established. The "ja" endows the referentially deprived opening lines of the drama with the suggestion of thick intelligible reference.

Now, this little play within *The Trial* is, to be sure, a play within a *frame* narrative. Hence, a certain kind of precedence does go to the frame in which it is embedded, though that precedent narrative is brief, consisting only of the sentence: "Someone must have slandered Joseph K., for one morning, without having done anything truly wrong, he was arrested" ("Jemand mußte Joseph K. verleumdet [Reuß: "verläumdet"] haben, denn ohne daß er etwas Böses getan hätte, wurde [Reuß: "war" crossed out] er eines Morgens verhaftet [Reuß: "gefangen" crossed out]") (T 3; Pp 7; Pr, ibid., 2). This is a rhetorical moment of great importance. In the manuscript, the German word "gefangen" (held, caught) is crossed out and replaced by "verhaftet" (arrested). In chapter 2, I mentioned this substitution of the word "verhaftet" (arrested) for "gefangen" (held, caught) in order to stress the absoluteness of Kafka's decision to punish Joseph K.: he will plunge him into what Joseph K.

takes to be a standard legal case — one that he has no possibility of winning, since his plea of innocence is vacuous in the absence of a charge. But now we shall be looking at this revision as one moment in a series of revisions opening up to a wider discovery about Kafka's writing strategy. We must keep this frame sentence in mind, since it will establish the crux that I now intend to resolve.

We now return to Willem's remark, "Sie sind ja gefangen" ("You're being held") (T 5, Pp 9). Clayton Koelb was the first to elaborate the speech-act implications of the little word "ja," to point out the performative character of this sentence owing to this little word, since the intelligibility of the sentence is not based on anything that precedes it in the diegesis: its intelligibility must be constituted for the first time by the person to whom it is addressed — here, Joseph K. — who is free to (1) consent to a prior understanding, which the sentence assumes; (2) deny it explicitly; (3) evade it; or (4) simulate any of the foregoing.[20] Any reply must amount to an acknowledgement of (or a refusal to acknowledge) the communicative situation as such, since this "ja," meaning, "Well, isn't it so?" refers to a communicative state of affairs presumably established earlier between the speakers. Finally — the bottom line — with either a yes or no answer, K. is agreeing to perform the speech-act scripted by another and to accede to his own captivity. So with typical, but in this instance quite understandable indecision, K. replies: "So it appears" ("Es sieht so aus") (T 5, Pp 9), which is just enough to keep the communicative situation unsettled but intact and *The Trial* in motion.

What follows is indeed a crazy speech, a discussion about K.'s bribing his warders with silk underwear. It is talk of the rhetorical ilk that Kafka calls "family language," of the kind reported in the 1912 passage from the *Diaries*, beginning, "In the next room . . . , they are talking about vermin and corns. . . ." Here, again, is Kafka's brilliant analysis:

> It is easy to see that there is no real progress made in conversations of this sort. It is information that will be forgotten again by both and that even now proceeds along in self-forgetfulness without any sense of responsibility. But for the very reason that such conversations are unthinkable without absent-mindedness, they reveal empty spaces which, if one insists, can be filled only by thinking, or, better yet, by dreams. (D1 258)

This act of critical augmentation, in the absence of dreams, is exactly what we are attempting.

Finally, we need to look at one more short exchange; for I plan to resolve the crux concerning the terms "gefangen" and "verhaftet" in their various appearances by means of a segue to the manuscripts.

A few pages later, then, after K. has asked why Frau Grubach wasn't permitted to enter, Willem says: "She's not allowed to. . . . After all, you're under arrest" ("Sie darf nicht. . . . Sie sind *doch* verhaftet" [emphasis added]) (T 8, Pp 13). Thus the manuscript sequence has read, beginning with the frame narrative: Joseph K. was "gefangen," which was crossed out and replaced by "verhaftet" (Pp 7); next: "You're being held" ("Sie sind ja gefangen") (T 5, Pp 9); thereafter, "After all, you're under arrest" ("Sie sind doch verhaftet") (T 8, Pp 13).

In a previous paper on this question, I argued for emending the word "gefangen" in the second case, à la Max Brod, to "verhaftet," on the putative grounds that "Kafka nodded," in order to bring this moment into the hermeneutically rich force field established by the two other instances of "verhaftet," the one preceding it and the one following it.[21] I concluded: "What effect on Koelb's discussion of the interesting manner in which the authority of the Court is constituted recursively has Malcolm Pasley's and Roland Reuß's 'purification' of Brod's version of the second of the three instances from 'verhaftet (arrested)' to 'gefangen (held)'? For, in the present situation, the third exchange no longer returns to the second (since the third is about being 'verhaftet [arrested]' but the second is about being 'gefangen [held]'); and, hence, the entire argument about how the authority of the Court is constituted by an endless recursiveness of the performative utterance (from 'doch' [after all] back to 'ja' [implying 'Well, isn't it so?'] and the pseudo-agreement of 'so it appears') is unsettled. Or does the purification, in the second instance, of 'verhaftet' to the original 'gefangen' somehow make matters more interesting?"[22]

That is what I hope to show. Let us attribute to Kafka himself, the author of *The Trial*, a complete knowledge of the process of composition. Then he is fully aware of a history of events occurring not only at the level of the diegesis but at the level, too, of scription—the making of the manuscript. It would not be surprising if events of the first order ("figures of scription") would impress themselves on the diegesis. What would help us now is a general rationale for thinking about the migration of such figures in *The Trial*.

Here we are again well served by the work of Malcolm Pasley. In chapter 2, we saw Pasley pinpoint several intersections of the worlds of scription and plot as part of "the parallel process run through by fictional events and the acts of writing that produced them."[23] These intersections produce effects of wit, as the forcible yoking together of dissimilars. "The two processes—the two 'trials,'" Pasley continues, "reciprocally determine one another and at certain places even appear to fuse—in an amazing way."[24]

Pasley's prize example of this fusion, we recall, occurs in "Ende" ("Conclusion"), the chapter Kafka wrote as he was writing the first chapter "Verhaftung" ("Arrest"). K. is on the way to his execution and urges himself to "keep my mind calm and analytical to the last," adding: "Do I want to show now that even a yearlong trial could teach me nothing? . . . Shall they say of me that at the beginning of my trial I wanted to end it, and now, at its end, I want to begin it again?" (T 228).[25] This play of beginnings and ends is amazing when one recalls that of course Kafka did want to end his writing of *The Trial* at the very beginning (of his writing it, with K.'s execution); and now, at its end, he did want to begin it again, with chapter 2. What K. in no way wants to be said on his account, Kafka wants, above all, to be said on his account. These semiprivate games are, Pasley continues, citing a phrase of Goethe's, "quite serious jests."[26] They are effects of authorial superiority too striking to suppose that Kafka did not arrange them.

Pasley offers another example of "the parallel process" that is even more amazing, if this is thinkable. Around the beginning of October 1914, Kafka asked for leave from the office in order to get on with *The Trial*. Meanwhile, in a passage that Kafka appears to have written at this time, Joseph K. plays with the idea of asking for leave from the bank so that he can devote himself uninterruptedly to composing the "petition" (*Eingabe*) that he means to submit to the Court. The text of *The Trial* reads:

> If he couldn't find time for it at the office, which was quite likely, he would have to do it nights at home. And if the nights weren't sufficient, he would have to take a leave of absence. Anything but stop halfway, that was the most senseless course of all. (T 126–27)[27]

And thereafter:

> The days that lay ahead! Would he find the path that led through it all to a favorable end? Didn't a painstaking defense . . . simultaneously imply the necessity of cutting himself off as far as possible from everything else? Would he successfully survive that? And how was he supposed to do that here at the bank? It wasn't just a matter of the petition, for which a leave might perhaps suffice . . . ; it was a matter of an entire trial, the length of which was unforeseeable." (T 132)[28]

This "petition" is a manuscript that will cover up, so to speak — "zudecken" — the script, the papers, the book of the Law.[29]

What is remarkable about this sentence is that it was actually composed by Kafka in the present tense: "it *is* a matter of an entire trial" ("es *handelt* sich um einen ganzen Process") (emphasis added). The present tense gives the allegory away. And furthermore, before writing the word "Dauer" (length, duration), Kafka initially wrote "Länge," which also means "length" or "duration" but with connotations both of "longlastingness" and even of "body length," for which reasons Pasley presumably considers the first word to fit Kafka's own lifelong "process" better than the trial of Joseph K.[30]

Having been alerted to the active presence of Kafka the author *in* his text, we can return to the specific matter at hand: his choice of "gefangen" over "verhaftet" and then back again. Given our knowledge of the manuscript, we are now better able to understand Willem's declaration to Joseph K.: "Sie sind ja gefangen!" ("You're being held!") As naive readers, our puzzled response had been: "How so? Joseph K. isn't just 'being held'; he's been 'arrested.' You have only to recall the opening of the text, you have only to read the book of his 'Trial' — the book in which Willem was reading and has now emphatically tossed aside." But, in the light of the manuscript, this response is no longer valid, because, here, Willem is reciting to Joseph K. from the manuscript *before* Kafka emended the first line of it. *At this moment Kafka has not yet made the change from "gefangen" to "verhaftet" in the first sentence of the novel.* This is my thesis, and I know no other, short of the punitively deficient one that Kafka blundered and required the editorial ministrations of Max Brod to set him right. The word "gefangen," offered in this instant by both the manuscript and the printed edition, is the same word that concludes the first sentence, Joseph K.'s special sentence, in its *original* conception: Joseph K. was "gefangen." What else can Joseph K. — who can be held to be conscious of the first sentence — say now to what actually confronts him in the world of his plot except, "So it appears" ("Es sieht so aus"). Furthermore, through the uncertainty of Joseph K.'s utterance, the author appears to be registering his own nascent uncertainty about this word and category choice. On the one hand, there is the word "gefangen," with its at once exaltedly metaphysical and primitively naturalistic connotations — since in addition to meaning "being held," it can mean both "captured," as in the gravitational field of mortality, and "caught," as in the child's game Gefangen — quite in the way that the word "Böses" (truly wrong, evil) (T 3, Pp 7), which figures centrally in the opening sentence of the novel, can mean, as Breon Mitchell points out, both preternaturally "evil" and also merely "naughty."[31] (The two terms — Böses" and "gefangen" — support one another in this way.) On the other hand, there is the category "verhaftet," for which Kafka finally opts, with the definitive connotation of a civil-juridical technical term of law. And so Kafka returns to the opening sentence and makes the change.

It is only some pages later, during another discussion between Willem and K., that the news of the emendation appears to have arrived from the archive (news of which Willem, unlike K., might be said to have been subcutaneously informed), announcing that the conclusion to the opening sentence of the manuscript has now been changed from "gefangen" to "verhaftet." Ergo, says Willem, "Sie sind *doch* verhaftet" ("After all, you're under arrest"), meaning: the word choice *is* "arrested." As an agent of the Court, he is entitled to have or to allege a better insight into the Law (Gesetz) and its now no longer alterable "letter" (Schrift).

Willem, as authorial agent, has registered the change in the first sentence from "gefangen" to "verhaftet." Kafka's serious jest is to have Willem be au courant with the script or manuscript of K.'s trial and to have him inform K. of the truth of his arrest. But unlike the wardens of the Court, K. is to be denied direct access to the text of his trial: he has been alienated from the author; he knows only the first "sentence" of his "Process"—where we read of his likely reaction in advance to the fact of being held—but he is not allowed to see any of the further protocols. "The records of the Court, and above all the writ of indictment," as he is afterwards told by his lawyer, "are not available to the accused" (T 113); and all the connings of it by K. and his lawyer are only expressions of the commentators' despair. Having heard earlier from Willem that he had been "gefangen," how can he react now, on learning that he is "after all, . . . under arrest," except to cry out, "How can I be under arrest" ("Wie kann ich denn *verhaftet* sein?") (T 8, Pp 13). It is then entirely consistent that the conversation immediately following should turn on the legitimacy of various sorts of "papers" ("Schriftstücke"). "Here are my papers," says K., "now show me yours" ("Hier sind meine Legitimationspapiere, zeigen Sie mir jetzt die Ihrigen") (T 8, Pp 13). K. offers up a puny text, but we may now imagine what papers the Court has access to.

Here is my summing up: Kafka can have introduced into the world of the novel a manuscript "figure"—the (irregularly) crossed-out word choice. He can have incorporated the event of emendation into the sequence of plot events. Certainly this conceit gains support not only from Pasley's reflections, as above, but from Roland Reuß's way of requiring that moments of uncertainty in Kafka's manuscript—Kafka, as it were, between emendations—be left uncertain and active.[32] All these voices together make uncertainty, especially the uncertainty as regards the choice of the words "verhaftet" and "gefangen," a forcible poetic event.

Interesting, noteworthy, and corroborative, too, is the way in which the inspector subsequently mentions the fact of K.s being under arrest. "You've been arrested, *that's true*" ("Sie sind verhaftet, *das ist richtig*") (T 14, Pp 22; emphasis added). Why this emphasis, uncalled for in context, if Kafka weren't here working out the conclusion of his uncertainty?

The contributions of these various critics appear to hold together: I am in the same cathedral as Pasley and Reuß, but then again I am in a different pew, because I need to underscore a hermeneutically important difference. In the examples that Pasley gives, there is a rather striking omission, and that is the lack of any mention of a key difference between them. In the first instance of an imbrication of manuscript and diegesis at the close of the novel, "Conclusion," K. is ignorant of the irony that is being played out around him or through him or over his head. The ironist is Kafka; the fall guy, Joseph K. But that is not at all the case in the second example: here Kafka the author and K., the potential author of a petition, fuse.

In my own example, where the news of the emendation of "gefangen" to "verhaftet" at the opening of The Trial is only belatedly introduced into the narrative, K. is again the fall guy; the jest is on the side of the author, who here sides with Willem and the inspector. The court knows the score—or script—as K. does not. But it is quite revealing that the first example of such medial intervention that Pasley gives—K.'s reluctance at the end of the novel to begin his trial all over again—and my example—the delayed introduction into the novel of the news of the emendation—were both written at about the same time (August 11, 1914) and are quite consistent in marking Kafka's distance from K.—his more than formal authorial distance. The mode is distantiation and the goal is murder, with Kafka functioning as loyal officer, friend of the court, and executioner. With some indignation, Brod retitled Günther Anders's incisive polemic against the fatalistic, demoralized character of Kafka's heroes "Die Ermordung einer Puppe" (The assassination of a puppet).[33] This is an accurate description of things at the outset of the scription of The Trial (after the chapters "Arrest" and "Conclusion") but not as the diegesis begins to unravel and Kafka becomes less and less capable of imagining his superiority to K. and of functioning as officer of the Old Law. (We recall that Kafka wrote "In the Penal Colony" midway through the writing of The Trial, in which it is the machine, and not the initial culprit, that shatters: "It's the organization that's guilty" ["Schuldig ist die Organisation"] [T 83, Pp 112], just as K. had maintained; and no identification on Kafka's part with this murderous law is any longer defensible.)

What is at stake in my reading of the "gefangen"/"verhaftet" crux is Kafka's reflection on how K.'s entire process is to be figured. I restate the question: Is K.'s plight to be "caught" (Gefangensein), with its at once natural and metaphysical openings (corresponding to the at once brutally natural—infantile—and also metaphysically open sense of *Böses*), or is it to be a "being under arrest" (*Verhaftetsein*), corresponding to a category in civil law? What self has been fixated: the animal/ metaphysical—the "natural" self—or the civil/legal public identity?

The author Kafka's final shift from "gefangen" to "verhaftet" requires K. to figure the trial as a civil/legal affair, but the minute he does so he is doomed: he cannot be "saved" by playing the role of the person accused in a civil/legal sense, since, in the absence of a charge, his protestations of innocence have no role to play in a court of law; his is a fundamentally different sort of case. K. is doomed by this message broadcast into his world through Willem, from the archive, the world of the manuscript. More than "gefangen," he has been "verhaftet"— "that's true" ("das ist richtig") (T 14, Pp 22): he is condemned to think his case through the prism of a civil arrest, and for this blunder he shall surely die.

With this decisive change of descriptor from "gefangen" to "verhaftet," Kafka not only sentences K. to death but implicitly sentences his authorial personality to death as K.'s guilty executioner. "Death," here—the death of the author—means precisely: Kafka's failure as author to survive K., the impossibility of his bringing *The Trial* to a close on a note of mastery. "Er kennt sein eigenes Urteil nicht?" ("He doesn't know the sentence that has been passed on him?"), it is said of the culprit in "In the Penal Colony," which is surely an allusion to the author who does not know the mastery he once possessed as author of "The Judgment" (GW 1:167, CS 144–45).[34] That means that in 1914 Kafka was unable to reproduce the authorial-manuscriptive-diegetic structure of 1912, in which he could literally survive the death of his puppet as "an unending stream of traffic" that "was just going over the bridge" (CS 88).[35] To be sure, he was otherwise preoccupied.

POSTSCRIPT

Two further examples of interventions "from the archive" are interesting to note—one occurring early in the manuscript and one at the very end, though written at approximately the same time as the beginning, around August 11, 1914. On returning home the evening of his arrest, K. encounters at the house landing the porter's son, who says to K., after K. has shown some signs of impatience

"Is there anything I can do for you, sir? Shall I get my father?" "No, no," said K. with a note of forgiveness, as if the fellow had done something *truly wrong* [*Böses*, Pp 31], but he was willing to forgive him. "That's all right," he said, and passed on; *but before he went up the stairs, he turned around once more.* (emphasis added, T 21)[36]

Now what on earth can have prompted K. to whirl around except the recurrence of the key word "Böses" not in the immediate context of his world but in the immediate context of the script, the narration of his world? It is as if K. had just remembered the first sentence of his life-text and grasped the coincidence of the word that has just occurred to him with the sinister marker "Böses," which had been introduced at the outset but then dismissed as a likely explanation of K.'s capture or arrest.

That first "Böses" to which this "Böses" returns, I stress, is not part of the consciousness that has been given to the Court. It is part of the text, "spoken" in thought by K. or by a narrator who at this stage of the game maintains his sly advantage of attitude over him — a piece of language or thought that precedes the first event in K.'s world at which the Court is present, the event of his awakening to his capture or arrest.

A second remarkable moment of scriptive intervention has been noted by May Mergenthaler in the last line in the manuscript of the concluding chapter.[37] Here, after Joseph K. has been brutally stabbed, Kafka's narrator observes, "it seemed as though the shame was to outlive him" ("es war, als sollte die Scham ihn überleben") (T 231, Pp 312). A look at the manuscript shows that Kafka formulated three versions of this concluding piece of a sentence (Pr, fascicle entitled "Ende," 25). After writing the phrase " 'Wie ein Hund!' sagte er" (" 'Like a dog!,' he said"), he wrote a first, then a second, rejected sentence that reads "bis ins letzte Sterben blieb ihm die Scham nicht erspart" ("up until his last dying moment, shame was not to be spared him"). At this point, a line in the manuscript is drawn through each one of the words *except* the last word on this line, which in the German is "Scham" ("shame"). The word "shame" survives the crossing out.

The *word* "shame" outlives Joseph K. If one needed additional confirmation of the haughty distance that Kafka was able to maintain toward his hero/victim at the outset (though not as the writing of *The Trial* advanced), one could scarcely find stronger evidence. Kafka the author is in control of the scription as K. is not; Kafka generates K.'s world through scription when the illusion produced by the diegesis is that K.'s world is at least co-constituted by his perception of it. Not true, not true even of his gravest moment, of his dying instant. Dorrit Cohn has written that "No instant of life (if one can call it that) highlights more dramatically [the distinction of fiction]." For fiction is able "to represent an experience that cannot be conveyed by 'natural' discourse in *any* manner or form. This may well be why novelists — great realists no less

than great antirealists—perennially give us the mimesis of a dying consciousness."[38] But here it appears to be less a mimesis of a consciousness
than, finally, a "logomimesis" that Kafka has given us.[39] A shame so
great that it survives K., a consciousness of shame that might be attributed to the dying hero and so might be reckoned his achievement, is in
fact an accident of the scription: not K.'s shame but Kafka's *word*
"shame" survives him for not having been crossed out. This haughty
distance will close.

Before leaving this issue, I will consider one further implication of the
closing sentence. Recall that Pasley offered two examples of earlier "intersections," "half-serious jests": (1) Kafka writes sentences for Joseph
K. at the time of his death that also pertain to his own concerns as the
author, the producer of a manuscript; (2) Kafka writes sentences for
Joseph K. that also pertain to his own concerns as the empirical person
needing to become an author. But it is more than a half-serious jest for
Kafka to ironize to such a degree Joseph K.'s struggle to make sense of
his life on his dying day. It is sadistic and has nothing whatsoever in
common with the rhetorical gestures through which he identifies his
own "case" with Joseph K.'s. This sadistic moment, however—Kafka's
using the word "*Scham*" in the scription to mock his victim's effort to
justify his death with a healing insight—appears to be poetically productive: Kafka fuses in his consciousness the contingent dimension of
the signifier at the order of the scription with the hero's insight at the
order of the diegesis—the insight into his own death as an affair of a
shame that would survive him. This latter connection of ideas would
then inspire the representation of signs inscribed into the unresisting
flesh of the victim of "In the Penal Colony," with the final result, once
more, of ironizing, undercutting, and ultimately depriving the victim of
a redeeming insight.[40]

Given the evident heuristic fruitfulness of this principle of "scriptive
intervention," with the onset of electronic and electronically generated
reproductions of Kafka's manuscripts, a vast and "profitable entertainment" now awaits his reader in this age of mechanical solitude (DF 69).[41]

# Chapter 4

# ALLOTRIA AND EXCRETA IN

# "IN THE PENAL COLONY"

IN THE MIDST of writing *The Trial*, a process that continually sputtered, Kafka composed "In the Penal Colony," which reads like a dreamt commentary on the themes of *The Trial*. In "In the Penal Colony," the bureaucracy of *The Trial* has been turned into a medial apparatus, a murderous writing machine. This transformation is an event in Kafka's ongoing allegory of writing, a torture machine depicted as an intermedial translation device, converting the signs of one medium — written texts and embellishments — into the signs of another — the stabbed tattoo — a machine not in principle unlike its more beneficent brothers and sisters the player piano and the mixed-media film projector or recording device. But it is meant to be murderous — ethical, not aesthetic.

One can begin to understand the machine in the light of certain oddities of the scene in which it is embedded. Some of these features have hitherto been neglected; the category word I give to half of them is itself peculiar — "allotria." Allotria and excreta are two dimensions of upheaval in Kafka's representation of medial function: medial machines run on power, and power generators spew the remains of their fuel — excreta; and machines can also spin their wheels, engage in footling "play" — allotria.

We have already represented Kafka's relation to the electrically driven media as "interested"; in this story the consummate medial device becomes at once a demonic agency of mythical power and a crude material failure, sublime in its promise and trashy in practice.

My reading of "In the Penal Colony" is guided by two mottoes, both of which are riddles. The point of the first, from Hölderlin's drama *Empedocles*, is quickly felt: "Nothing is more painful . . . than unriddling suffering" ("Nichts ist schmerzlicher . . . denn Leiden zu enträtseln").[1] The second motto, by Lionel Trilling, reads: "To comprehend unconditioned spirit is not so very hard." I am thinking of how easy readers have made it for themselves by grasping uncritically the moment of alleged enlightenment in the old commandant's penal process. "But," continues Trilling, "there is no knowledge rarer than the understanding of spirit as it exists in the inescapable conditions which the actual and the trivial make for it."[2] In writing about allotria and excreta in "In the Penal Colony," I have in mind a nonsimple form of the trivial (allotria) and the actual (excreta), two products of human activity whose meaning is hardly self-evident.[3]

Put the most radically serious quest for justification side by side with foolishness and nonsense: put the strongest, most intensely felt life side by side with inattentiveness and giddy play: allotria must trouble the consciousness of every reader of "In the Penal Colony." There is a good deal of difference between how this story has come down to us, as a systematically pure and grave conceptual meditation on the one hand; and, on the other, how it actually reads. Then we will be struck by the emphasis on such matters as blood and vomit and sputum and muck and oil and the disposal system laid out to contain them; and we will be struck by the high jinks, horseplay, capers, antics (it turns out that there are a great many words for this neglected category) involved in this construction.

"Allotria" means what's irrelevant (*das Nicht-Sachgemäße*), what's nonsensical (*Unfug*) — clowning about, cutting up — exactly what the officer in "In the Penal Colony" calls "childish nonsense" ("den Unsinn eines Kindes") when he is unable to convince the explorer of the value of the penal system he represents.

> It did not look as if the officer had been listening. "So you did not find the procedure convincing," he said to himself and smiled, as an old man smiles at childish nonsense and yet pursues his own meditations behind the smile. (CS 160)

Not to find the procedure convincing — a serious matter, seriously argued — is, the officer concludes, senseless resistance. But to note this is to smile and "pursue [one's] own meditations behind the smile." Perhaps this is explicit instruction on how to read allotria in "In the Penal Colony," read the several pages in the story dramatizing such childish nonsense, for one is beset by them, and they are a hermeneutic puzzle.

> The explorer, down below, watched the [officer's] labor uninterruptedly, his neck grew stiff and his eyes smarted from the glare of sunshine over the sky. The soldier and the condemned man were now busy together. The man's shirt and trousers, which were already lying in the pit, were fished out by the point of the soldier's bayonet. The shirt was abominably dirty, and its owner washed it in the bucket of water. When he put on the shirt and trousers both he and the soldier could not help guffawing, for the garments were

of course split up behind. Perhaps the condemned man felt it incumbent on him to amuse the soldier, he turned around and around in his slashed garments before the soldier, who squatted on the ground beating his knees with mirth. All the same, they presently controlled their mirth out of respect for the gentlemen. (CS 162)

Or, again:

The soldier and the condemned man did not understand at first what was happening, at first they were not even looking on. The condemned man was gleeful at having got the handkerchiefs back, but he was not allowed to enjoy them for long, since the soldier snatched them with a sudden, unexpected grab. Now the condemned man in turn was trying to twitch them from under the belt where the soldier had tucked them, but the soldier was on his guard. So they were wrestling, half in jest. (CS 163)

"Childish nonsense," "beating his knees with mirth," "gleeful," "half in jest": what is the meaning of such things? They occur at a moment of crisis: the officer is about to lay himself on the machine. Or perhaps there is nothing further to say about them, and that is the point. If they are nonsensical, they are not recoverable. But if we insist on developing the point — one that is not self-evidently understandable — we will have to take another route.

"Allotria" is an other otherness, other to allegory (*allos*: Greek for "other"), especially to its most schematic form, to pedantry.[4] For all its oddness, this allotria has a distinguished past — and a future to Kafka, too, as in Thomas Mann's *Doctor Faustus*, where the word appears in a striking context: as a schoolboy, Adrian Leverkühn, the serious composer, could not be suspected of it.[5] "Allotria" does not occur in Kafka, but his story quickly enough identifies it as "childish nonsense," and the meaning of the word is found all throughout his work — in *The Metamorphosis*, for example. It is what Gregor Samsa practices en route to consolidating his identity as a vermin, playfully taking bits of food in his mouth and then spitting them out, aimlessly navigating the junk in his room. Allotria is the compulsory life content of the *vermin* — as long as he is not yet being tortured to death. It is also something that Kafka flashes out of the narrator's relation to his composition, as when Gregor is shown casting a bewildered glance upwards to the wall where the photograph hangs of Gregor Samsa, Army lieutenant, his hand on his short sword, ready to impale his dreadful Other; or when Joseph K. stares wonderingly at the tourist who has come to arrest him in a safari suit replete with pockets, pleats, buttons, straps — the name of this captor is Franz![6] And, most famously, now again at the mimetic level: the antics of the twin assistants in *The Castle* (whose element is described by the landlady as so much "filth and lechery") (C 253). This sort of thing made Kafka's audiences laugh aloud at his readings, but they did not laugh when he read "In the Penal Colony" in Munich in 1916 (three women are said to have fainted).[7] "In the Penal Colony" is no laughing matter.

One historical use of the term "allotria" can help us to conceptualize it. None other than John Wesley writes:

> We have no right to dispose of anything we have, but according to His will, seeing we are not proprietors of any of these things; they are all, as our Lord speaks, *allotria, belonging to another person*; nor is anything properly *our own*, in the land of our pilgrimage. We shall not receive *ta idia, our own things*, till we come to our own country.[8]

This allotria is the nontrivial inauthentic as such, and a good deal more significant than "time-wasting." It is lent us by God. The Wesley passage points up the dual nature of the thing: it is above and also below the civilized norm, it is divine and it is improper. Furthermore, if it is an essential quality of Gregor Samsa and all vermin (*Ungeziefer*), then it cannot be returned to God, as being (Middle High German: *ungezibere*) "unsuited for sacrifice," unacceptable to God.[9]

Why does Kafka allow, even encourage, such displays of allotria? The matter is certainly overdetermined. For one thing, since "all trials are a kind of theater," this scene of trial and punishment is a kind of theater.[10] The operation of the torture machine is *ein Spiel*—a play. "And then the performance begins" ("Und nun beginnt das Spiel"), says the officer (106, CS 147); and later we hear of the parliamentary assembly, too, as a mise-en-scène or "public spectacle" ("Schaustellung") (115, CS 158).[11] The events of "In the Penal Colony" comprise a theatrical play, with the chief spectator—the explorer—seated in a cane chair in the orchestra, the whole a kind of amphitheater, with palisades. And—to say this directly—allotria belongs on the principle that if this is a theater, then any amount of stage business is permissible. Indeed, you scarcely find a longer work of Kafka's without its complement of stage business. This is the legacy of his highly developed instinct for play and performance of the demotic kind: his heroes are never artists but they are *artistes*—trapezists, cabaret singers (the mouse Josephine), hunger artists—circus performers, players in the theater of alternative communication: staged, excessively public, fictional conveyances of feeling, altogether opposite to the immediate conversation that, as Kafka said, drained the life out of him.

Even the death-dealing machine itself clowns in a parody of the Taylor speedup system and the circus performance: it collapses as an extravagant excretion of its gears, as in the circus today an endless quantity of persons is expelled from a red Volkswagen. Here we verge on a crossing of allotria and excreta, allotria itself being a sort of excrescence on the normal social essence.[12] But I delay discussion of this element — waste matter, dejecta — until spelling out a few further motives for Kafka's vaudeville. His vaudevillian practice, in principle admissible into matters of high concern, marks his modernism as such — an impertinent mixing of genres and levels of communicated feeling, of medial feeling (we may think of artistes' bodies themselves as odder types of media). The point is that for all its impropriety and distastefulness, allotria works distractingly, and its plain function is the way it gives relief from horror. A sentence from *The Picture of Dorian Grey* once again proves Wilde's usefulness to readings of Kafka.[13] Dorian Grey, having heard a disturbing idea,

> listened, open-eyed and wondering. . . . He watched it [the bee] with that strange interest in trivial things that we try to develop when things of high import make us afraid, or when we are stirred by some new emotion for which we cannot find expression, or when some thought that terrifies us lays sudden siege to the brain and calls on us to yield.[14]

There is another, more home-based motive to Kafka's allotria here. In his diary entry of February 9, 1915, Kafka complained of "In the Penal Colony." He had written the story in the late fall of 1914 in the course of writing or failing to write *The Trial* but had not sought to publish the story, partly because he thought he had botched the ending. There is further evidence for this assumption in the presence in the diary entries for August 1917 of a number of sketches of alternative endings, none of which Kafka used.

But if he at first singled out the ending of "In the Penal Colony" as botched, he afterwards thought he had botched the entire story. On September 4, 1917, he wrote to Kurt Wolff:

> Perhaps there is some misunderstanding concerning the "Penal Colony." I have never been entirely wholehearted in asking for it to be published. Two or three of the final pages are botched [sind Machwerk], and their presence points to some deeper flaw; there is a worm somewhere which hollows out the story [der selbst das Volle der Geschichte hohl macht]. (L 137, Br 159)

If we rely on Kafka's evaluation, this worm alludes to a certain "element" that he apparently saw in another story he began writing in February 1915 which he calls the "dog story"; it has not survived. (This is not the splendid "Investigations of a Dog," written in 1922.) This dog story—if this is indeed the story that Kafka is thinking of when he continues his diary entry with the words, "Just now read the beginning"—is "in spite of all its truth wicked, pedantic, mechanical, a fish barely breathing on a sand bank" ("trotz aller Wahrheit böse, pedantisch, mechanisch, auf einer Sandbank ein noch knapp atmender Fisch") (D2 114–15, GW 11:77). "Mechanical," "sand bank," "fish" are clues that he is also or, indeed, immediately thinking of "In the Penal Colony," with the figure of the dog in "the dog story," as we shall see, supplying the subliminal connection.

For the words "mechanical" and "pedantic," we might substitute "allegorical" and "abstract": this is what the scholar Ingeborg Henel has done, representing to excess one tendency of Kafka's art as opposed to the liveliness (*Lebendigkeit*) that Kafka saw in abundance in "The Stoker," the first chapter of his "American novel," *The One Who Sank Out of Sight*.[15] It is not hard to guess what Kafka might have meant by pedantry, allegory, or abstraction in "In the Penal Colony": it is the machine and the law and the scenes of parliamentary wrangling conjured by the officer, none of which has ever had its "foot in lived experience" (D1 100). It is the outcome of what Henel terms "the translation of an idea into an image, pure construction."[16] But we are not obliged to accept Kafka's own judgment on the matter; it is too peremptory, and it leaves out too much of what in the story is not of the order of allegory but rather of allotria. Pieces of this work dance on the border of conceptual knowledge and rational narrative: mimetic allotria, bodily excreta, odd, unreadable signs; randomly functioning allusions; plays on words that have been expelled from the circle of communication and made thing-like; and the bag of fragmentary, unincorporated endings.

Allotria is a key term, as that being beside the point, that going off topic, that is unrecoverable as allegory. Itself an insubstantial irrelevance, allotria both is—and is attracted to—elements that are extruded and expunged from healthy, directed life—life's excreta. Children and madmen, who are drawn to excreta, whose antics are, or can be judged as, so much excreta, cannot but seem foolish, or worse, in the eyes of adults. They are at best distractions from, at worst obstacles to, the rational conduct of life. So it will not come as a surprise that Kafka is guilty of allotria because "on his own admission he is depraved and takes pleasure in filth (*Schmutz*)."[17]

The excremental speaks for itself—or does it? In this story—and in the history of its versions—the excremental functions as a species of speech . . . uncannily: it is the body's mute howl of pain, its *resistance* to the mortal threat to its substance. It is a marker of the body, of human embodiedness, of the all too tender and recalcitrant flesh that will not submit to discipline. It expresses itself as a protest; it is, like pain, "part of the body's obdurate resistance to intelligibility, its blind, obtuse persistence in its own being."[18] What is then disgusting about such expressions, such excreta, may be their half-living character: they are remains of the body even as they leave the body, neither at first altogether alive nor dead, an unwonted revelation (outside) of the body (an inside). Hence, they are forbidden objects of curiosity and an inducement, to the nonsqueamish, to play — allotria.[19]

In alluding to some excremental oddities in "In The Penal Colony" ("excremental" means, variously, "superfluous," "nonnutritive," and "of matter to be evacuated"), one is in this way looking askance at and away from the story's great themes of just sentencing, truthful writing, canonical law, torture, and illumination. But this is only a way of making a return.

At this point, a quadrilateral of categories has begun to suggest itself. There are the facts of allotria and excreta at the order of the mimesis; and there are types of allotria and excreta at the order of the semiosis — the relation of the author-cum-narrator to the act of composition or scription. This is the matter that now needs to be explored.

There is allotria in "In the Penal Colony" at the order of the composition, at the order of the tropes, in Kafka's aberrant literalization of the metaphor "dog." This is a rhetorical display, but it connects to serious matters, belonging to an economy involving political power. Consider the metaphor of the prisoner as dog. The story is set, after all, in the *Tropen*, the tropics — décor for a scene of political terror — and it is also decorated with tropes, turns of phrase. The apparent allotria of tropic play belongs to an economy — the political administration of torture.

Consider politics as the decent (or indecent) application of power to persons, especially as this power is produced, stored, and conveyed by institutions — viz. the "apparatus" or "machinery" of the law in "In the Penal Colony" and the semiotic apparatus or machinery of the story "In the Penal Colony." This interinvolvement of the two sorts of power is plain in the first paragraph, which situates the apparatus of the torture machine and its spectators in its sandy amphitheater. The actor (and later spectator) most graphically represented is the prisoner, "a stupid-looking, wide-mouthed [wide-muzzled (breitmäuliger)] man with bewildered [abandoned by authority (verwahrlostem)] hair and face" — an animal-like creature, guarded — "led about" would be better — by a soldier, "who held the heavy chain controlling the small chains locked on the prisoner's ankles, wrists, and neck, chains that were themselves attached to each other by communicating links" (CS 140). Having been treated like a dog—he has even been struck on the nose by a whip—it comes as no surprise that he has become doglike. Kafka depicts this in the playful manner that is at once typical and fraught, as we have seen from the play of literal and figurative speech in "The Judgment" (see chapter 1). The text proceeds: "In any case [additionally (übrigens)— there is a world of significance in this harmless conjunctive phrase], the condemned man looked so like a submissive dog [so hündisch ergeben] that one might have thought he could be left to run free on the surrounding hills and would only need to be whistled for when the execution was due to begin" (CS 140). Doggishly submissive (*hündisch ergeben*) is a metaphor. But the intensifier *so* added on to *hündisch ergeben* literalizes that metaphor: the prisoner is now no different from a dog. These two kinds of coercion, political and rhetorical, are interinvolved. The man is brutalized by a violent application of political power; and the metaphor, too, is submitted to a kind of violence in being robbed of its floating status as trope and made more or less literal.

I now say "more or less" literal, for as becomes evident after a moment's reflection, every metaphor is in principle an *unsettled* semantic force field: this is Kafka's insight par excellence. To tamper with the relation between tenor and vehicle—thing compared and comparison— is to generate monsters even independently of the literal meaning of the metaphor "dog"; so even more is at stake here than that a man has been turned into a dog. The aberrant literalizing of the metaphor suggests that the prisoner has been turned into a monstrous collage of dog features and man features outside of any ordinary scale of things—neither man nor dog—more brutal than a man, more monstrous than a dog.

This literalizing moment is a crucial one for Kafka in the story. He hated, as I have said, the ending of "In the Penal Colony"; and unlike the case of *The Metamorphosis*, whose ending he also hated, he left behind several fragmentary versions of possible alternatives in his diaries. These are extraordinarily lurid. One reads:

"What?" said the explorer. The explorer felt too tired to give [any further] commands or [indeed] to do anything. He merely took a handkerchief from his pocket, gestured as if he were dipping it in the distant bucket, pressed it to his brow and lay down beside the pit. He was found in this position by the two men the commandant had sent out to fetch him. He jumped up when they spoke to him as if revived. With his hand on his heart he said, "I am a cur [Hundsfott] if I allow that to happen." But then he took his own words literally [wörtlich] and began to run around on all fours. From time to time, however, he leaped erect, shook the fit off, so to speak [riß sich förmlich los], threw his arms around the neck of one of the men [and] tearfully exclaimed, "Why does all this happen to me!" and then hurried back to his post. (D2 178; GW 11:152)

This diary entry dates from August 7, 1917; Kafka had written "In the Penal Colony" three years earlier, ca. October 15, 1914. Note the administration of political authority and also the mad, foolish play with figurative language (allotria of the signifier). This play is familiar to us from the first paragraph of the story, but here, as an unincorporated fragment, it is so much excreta.

We need to consider how the play with rhetoric connects with the seriousness of the political administration of terror. In these examples from the beginning and end of the story, the will and the ability to tamper with the metaphor go to the artist, who thereby obtains an extraordinary rhetorical power not without marginal political power, since metaphorical labelling lends itself to political use. This monstrous literalization is the rhetorical equivalent of the political, where the political, in this our painful modernity, has come to mean the construction of types of men and women by the application of force and the constructive destruction of men and women as persons as good as dead: rogues, outlaws, vermin.

It is not that Kafka *says* that the political and the rhetorical are involved in one another, duplicate one another, or cause one another. Rather, he shows this complication happening. The wordplay that has a great deal to do with torture-play is not merely marginal to the text and its time. But the answer to the question of what this connection is in truth — whether, as cultural studies has it, the political play contains and comprehends the rhetorical play; or whether the rhetorical play, marginally outside politics, in turn provokes political acts and a subtle knowing representation of political acts (J. M. Coetzee writes of "the freedom of textuality, however meager and marginal that freedom may be"[20]) — is something that Kafka's story cannot represent.

Addressing the rhetorical dimension of "In the Penal Colony" means addressing one sort of play, one form of the marginal, that has the power to usurp center stage. We will now look at three textual cruxes triggered by rhetorical details, all of which bear on the process of reading a work interrupted by allotria and excreta.

"Read it," said the officer.
"I can't," said the explorer. (CS 148)

The story gives no information on how the victim's act of reading his sentence is supposed to occur; it requires a strenuous and ultimately frustrating effort of interpretation on the part of the reader to have even a glimmer. The writing on the victim's body is of two types. The first is called "the actual [real] script(ure)" ("die wirkliche Schrift") and also "the [authentic] script(ure) itself" ("die eigentliche Schrift"). The second type of writing is ornamental, consisting of "embellishments" ("Verzierungen") (107; CS 149). One might be inclined to call the second type inauthentic, secondary, or derivative, employing the semiotic model of the metaphor: the real, authentic meaning, is borne along, as the tenor, by the trope, the metaphor as such, which can then pass away, its semantic work as vehicle having been done. But this cannot be right, this is not the function of the embellishment, since reading the ornament is *essential* to the work of justice, to "the kind of sentence we pass" (better: the form of our judgment [die Form unseres Urteils]) (103, CS 144). The form is not complete, the essence of the punishment is not revealed, until the ornament, too, has been deciphered.[21] At the same time there is no suggestion that it is the embellishments themselves, rightly deciphered, that deliver the message. The sentence stating the violated commandment is different from its embellishments, though it is not essentially different. In the *Tropen*, in the tropics, all are tropes (*Tropen*): the designation of the real, the authentic sentence, is already gnawed on by this secondary and derivative function; and so we are inclined to ask, *of* what are these embellishments the figures, *of* what are they the fictive (after all not real or authentic) script? But we are unable to say more than that they too are essential; like allotria, according to Wesley, they are the essential inauthentic. This artistic (*kunstvoll*), beautiful, but nonsimply beautiful handwriting, which is "no calligraphy [keine Schönschrift] for schoolchildren" (107, CS 149), evidently signifies something within what the officer calls "das Gesamturteil" (the general or broad-gauged judgment) (109, CS 151), but what?

Perhaps it has a formal sense, perhaps it signifies in an only *reflexive* manner, in the sense of mirroring or completing a structural parallel with the ostensibly trivial (allotria) and excremental in the story as such — the curlicues and embellishments being equivalent to the plethora of seemingly "useless" details. They are marginal — and yet they suspend any possible assertion of the precedence of issues of justice over issues of art and aesthetics. Here we can take note of the historical dispute about modes of literary classification in respect to "In the Penal Colony." Is it, as a story of a punishment that raises substantial questions of law and justice and just sentencing, to be grouped with *The Meta-*

*morphosis* and "The Judgment" (as Kafka explicitly intended it to be), stories that also treat of punishment; or should it be grouped with, par excellence, "A Hunger Artist," as a story of art and performance for which no audience any longer exists?[22] "Nor did the colony itself betray much interest in this execution": this citation immediately resonates with the opening of "A Hunger Artist" (100). But these are taxonomic formalities. The matter of the embellishments poses the crucial question: if the epistemological status, as we say, of the ornamental script(ure) is undecidable, if the relation of trope to diegesis is incomprehensible, what then is the status of the understanding that is given to the prisoner's faculty of reason (*der Verstand*) in the sixth hour?

This question has hardly ever been stated as a problem before. In the sixth hour the culprit understands his sentence—so runs the conventional interpretation—but does he? The officer claims to have seen the prisoner's enlightened face as he grasps the verdict. This is what the officer *says*. But even his account of the medial process does not allow for this conclusion—first, because the process requires a *twelve-hour* deciphering; second, because what Kafka (unlike his English translator) has written is that the process requires a twelve-hour *"deciphering"* ("Entziffern") (108). This phrase immediately calls attention to the signifier (*Ziffer*), but you would not think so, reading the Muirs' translation of "es geschieht ja nichts weiter, der Mann fängt bloß an, die Schrift zu entziffern" as "Nothing more happens than that the man begins to understand the inscription [the script(ure)]" (CS 150). What is wrong with this translation is the tendency that it advances; this "begins to understand" is meant to recall the rational illumination allegedly produced in the sixth hour, when "enlightenment [better: understanding] comes to the most dull-witted" ("Verstand geht dem Blödesten auf"), encouraging the reader to conclude that the victim's "understanding the inscription" in the sixth hour is the same thing as his apprehending through reason the truth of an ethical commandment. And that truth is? Whatever it is, it is *not* the truth of the verdict. One must read the German! The moment of ecstasy is not that of *understanding* the script(ure); it is a moment of *understanding* that here there is script to be *deciphered*. "Script(ure) [die Schrift]," as the prison chaplain in *The Trial* informs Joseph K., "is immutable" ("unveränderlich"); in its own impregnability, it is irreducible to interpretation (T 220, Pp 298). In "In the Penal Colony" we deal not with combustion of the script (à la Walter Benjamin) but with the ineradicability of a fact: that here there is writing, that here is the task of the translator. And if the prisoner were somehow to decipher the script with his wounds, then—since at the end of things he is nothing more than his wounds—perfection of justice would consist in wounds deciphering wounds or, equivalently, script deciphering script, leaving no margin for interpretation. "How the inscrip-

tion takes form on the body" ("wie sich die Inschrift im Körper voll-
zieht") is by no means equivalent to the "happening of justice" ("daß
Gerechtigkeit [geschieht]"), if by the latter is meant the prisoner's understanding his sentence (106, 111). He could not understand his sentence until he is emptied out of his substance, until he has been *excreted*
by the script.[23]

In making these claims, I am referring to conceptions of understanding and interpretation as they figure in a German hermeneutical tradition shaped especially by Friedrich Schlegel and Friedrich Schleier-
macher. The concept of "deciphering" or "decoding," however, with its
connotations of automaticity and of transformation only along the axis
of the material signifier, constitutes a departure. Here, one could well
think of Kafka's early fantasy of himself in the act of writing as inscribing "all [his] anxiety" in the paper in a writing process that excludes the
consciousness of an interpreter (D1 173). An aphorism from 1922 ban-
ishes interpretation altogether: "It is enough that the arrows fit exactly
in the wounds that they have made" (D2 206, GW 11:203).

As readers of Kafka, we have been concerned with an understanding
of what truly occurs within the story as a whole. Is it possible to achieve
a proper understanding of the prisoner's tormented reading process as
such? The effort is made even more difficult by two minor, marginal,
rather excremental-seeming cruxes at the order of scription — one *parenthesis* and, according to Max Brod, one *crossing-out*. Matter to be
excreted has an exact semiotic correlative in the parenthesis: it is excluded from the sentence while still belonging to the economy of the
sentence in the way that excreta — half-organic, half-alive — is retained
within the economy of the body until it is expulsed. The parenthesis is
unique as a syntactical element in requiring no corresponding adjust-
ment in the sentence as a whole in order to accommodate it, just as
there is a provision in every body for matter to be excreted that does
not disturb the economy of the whole, allowing it to function as it nor-
mally functions.

The parenthesis occurs at the close, following the mutilation of the
officer. In the edition of Paul Raabe, an edition admired by both Brod
and Sokel, the passage reads:

> And here, almost against his will, he [the explorer] had to look at
> the face of the corpse. It was as it had been in life; (no sign was
> visible of the promised redemption); what the others had found in
> the machine the officer had not found; the lips were firmly pressed
> together, the eyes were open, with the same expression as in life,
> the look was calm and convinced, through the forehead went the
> point of the great iron spike. (121, CS 166)

Thereafter come three asterisks and the unsatisfactory ending.[24]

Who says—on what authority—that the officer found no trace of the promised redemption? Even in death the officer remains "convinced"; he has not registered the shortfall in the promised revelation. But his is the only authority we have for the existence of any such redemption.

I suggest that the uncertainty of the claim that "no sign was visible of the promised redemption" in the death of the officer is emphasized by the parenthesis: it contains within it the excremental detail at the order of rhetoric. This is an odd piece of orthography of a sort I have never seen anywhere else in Kafka's stories as printed—and yet it is a "detail" of utter importance. It is a paradoxical construction, implying, to begin with, a sort of tentativeness of statement. For what is the meaning of the marker "parenthesis" except to indicate an addition, an *übrigens* (moreover), a remainder, an only secondary reflection, whose retention in the body of an argument may not disturb the argument, which has more serious, forward-looking concerns? The argument, as it is designed outside the parenthesis, takes precedence: the writer will not undertake to integrate the parenthetical matter; and yet, in this case, regarding the question of whether the officer found meaning in his ordeal—the answer, No, not a trace of it was to be found!—is of crucial importance. It is the story's leading idea. How can the story's leading idea be put between parentheses?

It is as if what is contained in the parenthesis, a bracketing off—meaning: nonpertinence, what is off the point, scarcely belonging—were provisory only, subject to revision, even to reversal. And yet precisely what is at stake is nothing less than the meaning of the whole of the story. Was there ever in truth such a procedure as the glorious operation of the machine? Was there ever so worthy an alternative to the inefficient justice of liberal states? Could a death ever be justified in the consciousness of the victim in this way? Could the truth of one's derelict life ever be inscribed on the heart?[25] And could, moreover, Nietzsche's account of the genealogy of morals be affirmed—was there ever a moment of dawning moral enlightenment powerful enough to irradiate and transfigure an entire people? Sane societies require a token of hope, the promise of a future. The punishment in the penal colony is such a token, because it promises the transfiguration of an entire community before death.

These are some of the questions taken up in a parenthesis in "In the Penal Colony" as published—overwhelming questions to which Kafka's answers are belied by his parenthesis. They are implicitly taken up again, and answered differently, in the three or four fragmentary endings found in the diaries. One pertinent item stands out: it involves a moot crossing-out. The latest Fischer (so-called) manuscript edition—a printed transcription by and large faithful to the manuscripts—prints a portion of an alternative ending, as follows: "Und wenn auch alles unverändert war, der Stachel war doch da, krumm hervorragend aus der geborstenen Stirn" (GW 11:353). In my translation, this reads: "And even if everything was unchanged, the spike was still there, protruding crookedly from his shattered forehead." But if you read the standard English translation of the diaries, you get something different: "And even if everything remained unchanged, the spike was still there, crookedly protruding from his shattered forehead *as if it bore witness to some truth*" (D2 178, emphasis added). The addition of this last phrase is explained in a footnote by Max Brod: "The clause, 'as if it bore witness to some truth,' was struck out by Kafka in the manuscript" (D2 322). So this footnotation "as if it bore witness to some truth," having, then, precisely, parenthetical status, returns to a *crossing-out*, leaving undecided whether, in the matter of the empirical transmission of the manuscripts, the phrase "as if [his shattered forehead] bore witness to some truth," though crossed out, should be retained. If truly crossed out, the sum of things is left intact and pure, and *no* trace of the promised redemption was indeed to be seen. But if this velleity is preserved—it is *not* preserved in the manuscript edition of the story—then one would find in the officer's report the positive substance of justice, conveying a most important nostalgia and imaginative yearning on Kafka's part, he who had written (while still young) of his desire not only to write his being into the depths of the paper but to draw up that writing into him.

The words "as if it bore witness to some truth" are remarkable words to cross out. Kafka's own editing confirms the reader's suspicions. This is not a story about true sentencing but about its disappearance in the intricacies and hollows of fiction. What we have had throughout is the narration of the reception, on the part of the explorer, of a narrative produced by a fanatic of a ceremony. This intricate narratological state of affairs does no more than imply that a prisoner's attempt at deciphering his sentence is achieved with his death. The truth of this process is then nullified when it is empirically enacted by the same fanatic on himself. But what we have lost as an "acquist of true experience," we have gained as a tolerable experience of allotria and the excremental.[26] What is tasteless in the actual and trivial is etiolated, bled of its loathsomeness, by this multiplication of narrative foci and foyers—a gesture which, by driving truth out of art, enlarges its scope. In this work, allotria and the excremental (a kind of expressiveness) are symbols together of the distasteful that now has a place in art and can be borne. Their "meaning" is reflexive only, in pointing to the vast, unlimited, because truth-bled, order of the signifier uncoupled from its referent. This is a conclusion perfectly consistent with Hegel's view of the end of art as the end of any art that would need to be validated by the truth it can no longer represent.[27]

# DEATH AND THE MEDIUM

Where the main motifs of the preceding chapters are taken
up and inflected toward death.

KAFKA, AS WE know, was acquainted with a kind of death that brought
him a maximum of enjoyment, an ecstasy that carried him to the limits
of human experience. It happened in connection with his nocturnal
writing. The most important of the early texts that tells of this bliss is
the story assembled by Kafka's editor Max Brod from Kafka's notebook
fragments, beginning, " 'You,' I said. . . ." (1910). The narrator is a hybrid figure, part bourgeois with "literary inclinations" and part emaci-
ated bachelor-figure in a state of existential extremity. Together they
prefigure the complex that Kafka would call, in a nonce word, "writerly
being" (*Schriftstellersein*). The narrator declares:

> Already, what protected me seemed to dissolve here in the city. I
> was beautiful in the early days, for this dissolution takes place as
> an apotheosis, in which everything that holds us to life flies away,
> but even in flying away illumines us for the last time with its hu-
> man light. (D1 28)

The "everything that holds us to life" is the bodily ego with its material
cravings — its love of food, sex, and philosophy. But there is light impacted in it that may become visible upon its destruction. This is the
Wordsworthian moment of which J. M. Coetzee has written beautifully:
"As the sense-organs reach the limit of their powers, their light begins
to go out. Yet at the moment of expiry, that light leaps up one last time
like a candle-flame, giving us a glimpse of the invisible."[1] It is striking
that even in the early days of Kafka's writing his text, he envisions the
ecstasy of "early days" as already past, their beauty vanished.

On the face of it, Kafka's account of his apotheosis says little about
its connection with writing. But in context the association cannot be
missed. It anticipates, for one thing, the feelings that Kafka recorded
after writing "The Judgment" in 1912, which came out of him "in a
complete opening out of the body and the soul" (D1 276). He noted

> the fearful strain and joy, how the story developed before me, as if I
> were advancing over water. Several times during this night I heaved

> my own weight on my back. How everything can be said, how for
> everything, for the strangest fancies, there waits a great fire in
> which they perish and rise up again. (D1 275–76)

Observe once more the brilliance, the fire, that accompanies a moment
of disintegration.

In diary entries written the year before, in 1911, Kafka spoke of having "experienced states [in "the field of literature"] . . . in which I completely dwelt in every idea, but also filled every idea, and in which I not
only felt myself at my boundary, but at the boundary of the human in
general" (D1 58). These are "time[s] of exaltation, time[s] more feared
than longed for, much as I long for . . . [them]; but then the fullness is
so great that I have to give up" (D1 152). Earlier he evoked "the power
of my dreams, shining forth into wakefulness. . . . It is a matter of more
mysterious powers which are of an ultimate significance to me" (D1
76). Such experiences of "ultimate" transformation are connected to
writing as their source and their goal. Yet these experiences were
scarcely ones that Kafka could reproduce at will. He never forgot them;
he called this bliss — this "constructive destruction" — "self-consumption"; but henceforth, with the way to such literary ecstasy closed — viz.
the 1922 notation, "Writing denies itself to me" (DF 350) — the term of
self-consumption acquires the somber, anxious character of death, no
longer "self-consumption" but a "shaking off the self" (DF 87).

These two forms of separation haunt Kafka's imagination. The first is
a "kind" of death — literary, poetological. One could think of Stephan
Dedalus's aperçu: "The personality of the artist, at first a cry or a cadence or a mood and then a fluid and lambent narrative, finally refines
itself out of existence, impersonalizes itself, so to speak."[2] The second
kind of death is not literary: it is a matter of personal extinction *tout
pur*. Of the first, Kafka will note

> the strange, mysterious, perhaps dangerous, perhaps saving com-
> fort that there is in writing: it is a leap out of murderer's row [deed-
> observation deed observation (Beobachtung)]; (it is a seeing of
> what is really taking place). This occurs by a higher type of obser-
> vation, a higher, not a keener [schärfer] type, and the higher it is
> and the less within reach of the "row," the more independent it
> becomes, the more obedient to its own laws of motion, the more
> incalculable, the more joyful, the more ascendant its course. (D2
> 212, GW 11:210)[3]

But this joy is contested by another, more murderous way of registering
separation. "What we call the world of the senses is the evil in the
spiritual world . . ."; and so "one of the first signs of a beginnings of

understanding is the wish to die. This life appears unbearable, another unattainable" (DF 39, GW 6:236–37; DF 35, GW 6:230).

The issue that concerns us throughout this book is the relation of these two modalities of self-abnegation — of author mysticism, on the one hand, and of naked life denial, on the other. The first can be called gnostic; the second, Gnostic. One path seeks through literature the negation of the empirical ego, and survival; the other seeks the negation of "the sensate world," and death. These two streams separate, come together, split apart, and return to one another, and in the end define the circulation of Kafka's work. We could note how the imagery of the apotheosis in the city (D1 28) participates in both flows of ideas.

In some of Kafka's stories, the tension between these flows is explicit: "The Judgment," *The Trial*, and "In the Penal Colony" figure both writing and real death. But consider this proviso from the start — Kafka's references in his art to the act of writing are infrequent and mostly inexplicit. His later works feature a trapezist, a hunger artist, and a singing mouse; but they are *artistes*, not artists or writers.[4] And yet the figure of the writer might be contained in dramatic representations of what we have called Kafka's medial imagination. This imagination, as Gerhard Neumann and Friedrich and Wolf Kittler have shown, is an imagination of the sign, of its embodiment, and of the tension between its contingent material substrate and the temporal awareness — the elation — of the meaning it constitutes. The medium is the code of the material substrate that embeds the sign, is its support.

Consider now the writer Kafka, the being whose essence is "writerly being." He himself is the higher reference of a sign, a sign conscious of its own semiotic character; he is a memory come alive. Such a being is continually alert to the tension between the opaque, unconstrainable, and inarticulate materiality of his body, of the muck below *and* the hand that writes, and the virtual, ideal meaning constituted by things written; and he might strive to discharge this tension by detaching himself entirely from his material substrate, whether conceived of as a levitation through, or a plunge into, things written. Recall, in this light:

> The strange, mysterious, perhaps dangerous, perhaps saving comfort that there is in writing . . . : This occurs by a *higher* type of observation [Beobachtung], a *higher*, not a keener [schärfer] type, and the higher it is . . . , the more joyful, *the more ascendant* its course. (emphasis added, D2 212, GW 11:210)

If Kafka's interest in the sign is broad, ranging from its sensuous particularity, its medial specificity, to its "higher" being, as an allegory of "the writer," this one vector of his interest recurs: to release from the material sign the elation it contains.

One of the concrete ways this desire works is to strip his prose of ornament. Think back to "In the Penal Colony," where a preponderance of unreadable ornament stands in the way of illumination. What Proust said of Flaubert could be said with equal cogency of Kafka, who was devoted to Flaubert: You will look in his works in vain to find a single lustrous metaphor.[5] The elation of the sign is not a function of the ostensible surprise or sparkle of its substrate but a movement away from the substrate. "Wrote badly," wrote Kafka in his diary once, "without really arriving at that freedom of true description that releases one's foot from lived experience [Erlebnis]" (D1 100; GW 9:71). In this remark Kafka mainly has in mind what is termed "the referent" and not the material mark (sound-look) of the sign and other automaticities of language. And yet "lived experience" necessarily includes a sense of the materiality of familiar language and its stereotypes — and hence of the substrate of the sign. The categories — referent and substrate — converge in Kafka's imagination, as witness his famous lament at writing's "lack of independence" of metaphor (D2 200–201).[6] The release from lived experience verges on apotheosis. It is called "freedom" and is not a matter of unriddling things or storing up meanings. The meaning of things encountered is "the writer in me"; but this meaning is a riddle, "since such a figure has no basis, has no substance" (L 334).

Kafka's passion to identify himself with the higher valence of written things gives rise in his work to a constellation of images of hybrid beings — part man/part text — textual man, man-into-text — the text constituting the higher, the "meaningful" part. *The Metamorphosis* is the transformation of a man into his metaphor ("This man is a louse"), whereupon the creature gains, along with the horror, an acrobatic lightness of being. The prisoner's wounds in "In the Penal Colony" are said to decipher the text of his sentence on the verge of an illumination. The "eleven sons" of the story of the same name — "Eleven Sons" (1917) — are, according to Max Brod's recollection of Kafka's own words, "quite simply eleven stories I am working on this very moment"; and only as stories, one might say, are they children after the very own heart of this father, the writerly being.[7] Oneself become sign: the person addressed in "On Parables" ("Von den Gleichnissen") is adjured to become a parable, *Gleichnis*, which, in a strong reading by Walter Sokel, means "rhetorical figure" — figure of speech, trope, allusion.[8] Letterlike, stick-figure self-portraits populate Kafka's notebooks, in which the empirical man becomes textual signs.

The "text" is refined inscription, a webwork of signs — like the webbing that the acrobat climbs to ascend to his perch and then lets fall — part of a trajectory that leads from "the depths" of the body to the "joyful ascendancy" of the word. We could advance the following ratios: body is to text as the material substrate of the sign is to its combustion, its illumination. The model for the material envelope consumed by the meaning is the body consumed by the text. The force of these ratios is evident in the craving that Kafka announced early, in 1911,

> to write all my anxiety entirely out of me, write it into the depths of the paper just as it comes out of the depths of me, or write it down in such a way that I could draw what I had written into me completely. (D1 173)

I am focusing, for the moment, on the second half of the notation: "write it [my anxiety] in such a way that I can draw what I had written into me completely." The written affect has the distinction of what is movable, airier than the anxiety that might sink into the depths of the paper. The "*words* of anxiety," in being reabsorbed by the body, alleviate a once bodily anxiety, turning it into a thing that is lightened, chastened, made acrobatic.

What is striking about this passage, however, is that it opens up a different vector of transubstantiation, *unlike* the verticality of the "higher" observation, *unlike* Kafka's wish "to raise the world into the pure, the true, the unchanging" (D2 187).[9] This movement is parabolic, plunging from one depth into another. Here, written words are not lighter or higher than bodily affect, than anxiety: they are weighty, too. They could break the skin of the paper and sink down deep into it. Consider an earlier formulation of this wish: "If I were ever able to write something large and whole, well shaped from beginning to end, then in the end the story would never be able to detach itself from me" (D1 134). A too, too solid story could not be born; it could not break out through the paper of the skin; it would be stillborn; it would lodge where it had been conceived. The full trajectory of writing is an ellipse projected by the expulsion of affect and then by words drawn back in. But if these words are heavy enough to sink into the depths of the paper, then could so *imposing* a text be integrated into the body without harm? The meaning of the German word *einbeziehen* is bigger than to "draw in": it suggests a physical entity that has been taken possession of and incorporated. Could so weighty a text — not airy after all — be the prelude to illumination, to the vanishing of bodily signs in a glimmer of light? When the small, hard apples thrown by Mr. Samsa like so many pieces of family language penetrate Gregor's back, the pain they cause is "startling, unbelievable," and Gregor very likely dies of them (M 28–29). Is it otherwise when the words are "one's own"?

Kafka's reflections on anxiety keep in reserve the question of the body's capacity to absorb written words without itself being broken (it is medially different!). The yearning "to write . . . [anxiety] down in such a way that I could draw what I had written into me completely" implies the knowledge that it is has not been possible to write in such a way and elides the knowledge of what the result might be of drawing into oneself a writing of anxiety that has not been written "in such a way." Such a prospect would not put an end to anxiety but become another anxiety, for the body could die, the medium could shatter from the intrusion of signs it could not consume, could not be enlightened by. A proverb of Primo Levi's anticipates this danger: "Perfection belongs to narrated events, not to those we live."[10]

The point is interesting for the way that it is enacted in "In the Penal Colony." Here this distinction is radical: the perfection of a narrated event emerges only at the moment of its perfect reading or reception, supposing that the narrative has been so composed that "I" could draw the written words completely into me. But to draw words completely into me is, in this story, to be wounded and destroyed by them. This truth is dispersed throughout Kafka's fictions. Where human being and the being of texts join, you get a hybrid that cannot live: as his textlike wounds, the prisoner in "In the Penal Colony" cannot live; as his metaphor, Gregor Samsa, in *The Metamorphosis*, cannot live; the moving "crossbreed" of lamb and cat—which, in the story of the same name, suggests the crossing of human being and writerly being—cannot live. The promise of elation through the sign at the limit does not give life— it marks the candidate for death. "Of course the writer in me will die right away," wrote Kafka to Max Brod; "such a *figure* has no basis, has no substance, is less than dust; is only a construct of the craving for enjoyment [Genußsucht]. This is the writer" (emphasis added, L 334, Br 385). I read "figure" as a strong figure of rhetoric, as a webwork of written signs.

The horror of one sort of being written to death is downplayed at first by the officer of "In the Penal Colony." He tells a story about writing that is meant to be effective. The body of the prisoner, having absorbed the writing of the "law," triggers an ecstatic insight for him and, moreover, becomes for its witnesses a site of future memory: the body of the victim is culturally reinscribed. The basis of this social festival is the interpretation of what Kafka called sardonically, in his own case, "the illumination of my dead body (die Illuminierung meines Leichnams")—at once a lighting up, with final insight, but also a furnishing of figural decorations for his corpse (L 334; Br 385). By narrating a process of medial inscription that involves scriptive ornament, the promise of illumination, cultural appropriation, and death, "In the Penal Colony" seems not just one particular story but Kafka's master narrative.

Under what conditions, then, and with what effect might the body, in becoming text, be dissolved? Kafka's procedure in "In the Penal Colony" is typical of the way in which he elaborates "problems" in fictive constellations. In the figure of the explorer he "explores" the matter—the fatality of extreme inscription—in a literal scene of writing. The story enacts his anxious hesitation before the view that body and writing might fuse in one elation, that the body might absorb and be exalted by a script that bears the meaning of its "law."

According to our earlier ratios, what is at stake is the possibility of an apotheosis of the material substrate of the sign in a pulse of light. Where there is text, there must be illumination—light at a higher place. Kafka had always been willing to submit to writing on the strength of the promise that the medial substrate might be dissolved in it, almost literally as a sort of rocket fuel that would take him to the moon: "we [writers] have lost ourselves for the sake of a homeland on the moon" (L 204).[11] "In the Penal Colony" opens auspiciously: the officer claims to have seen in the old days a look of enlightenment on the face of the victim—"the look of transfiguration, . . . the radiance of that justice achieved at last" even if it "fades so quickly!" (CS 154).

But this is not the story's last word. In the skeptical presence of the explorer, the question grows acute: can a body accommodate the sign-script inscribed in it as the condition of its ecstasy? Might not the first ecstasy, the saturation by signs, when taken to its end, *preclude* the second and, seen through the darkest lens, itself amount to physical annihilation—and nothing more? Writing's dependency on unenlightened matter stands in the way of a literary redemption—its

> lack of independence of the world, its dependence on the maid who tends the fire, on the cat warming itself by the stove; it is even dependent on the poor human being warming himself by the stove. (D2 200–201)

Writing has less in common with a language of transparent signs than with a kind of pact-signing that leads downward to darkness,

> the reward for service to the devil—this descent to the dark powers, this unshackling of spirits bound by nature, these dubious embraces and whatever else may go on below, of which one no longer knows anything above ground when one writes one's stories in the sunshine. (L 333, Br 384)

Kafka has an exact word for a philosophy of writerly mysticism that represses the defiance and danger of writing: dilettantism. What is always horribly beckoning is not this or that scriptive bliss but the truth of death. Words so good that their return could also tear a body apart.

Only in the best case does the inscribed body proceed from sobriety to ecstasy, which, at its far end, requires extinction, only in the best case is death the tain of the mirror of insight. "In the Penal Colony" performs a feat of synthetic imagination, bringing together, at the limit, the twin ecstasies of writing and death, imagining, with terrible intensity, that death is the condition of one's innermost truth coming to light.

But here the model of textual illumination veers toward death as a model of opaque dying. "In the Penal Colony" stages writing and death as the truth that literary ecstasy must end in death, although the reverse is *not* true: the writer's death might not be accompanied by ecstasy. Kafka cannot decide whether the death "In the Penal Colony" is anything more than manslaughter.

I am using the concept "undecidable" in a demonstrable sense. In the previous chapter I mentioned that Paul Raabe's edition of this story concludes by printing the sentence "(no sign was visible of the promised redemption)" ["(kein Zeichen der versprochenen Erlösung war zu entdecken)"] *in parentheses*. No sign guaranteeing the illumination is at once visible and not visible. Hence, no reading by the explorer correctly based on the victim's reading (or not reading) his sentence may have taken place. And even if it had taken place, for the victim, the moment of intellectual apprehension would have been transitory in an absolute sense — purely and only transitory; it would have occurred only as the subject-medium deliquesces into its wounds and dies. There is no energy released by dying.[12] In the best case, the illumination is purchased with death; in the worst case, nothing is purchased with death.

The grim outcome — either entirely grim, in being without a grace note; or grim with the grace note of understanding — forces the reader to look backwards and askance at the story. Then he becomes more than ever aware of the tension between the officer's original, eudaemonic account of the process of "reading" and one that never amounts to anything more than an incomplete "deciphering." A shadow passes over the officer's reminiscence of a look of enlightenment on the face of the victim — "the look of transfiguration, . . . the radiance of that justice, achieved at last and fading so quickly!" ("den Ausdruck der Verklärung . . . , den Schein dieser endlich erreichten und schon vergehenden Gerechtigkeit!") (CS 154, GW 1:178). The German word "Schein" is not the word for "radiance": this would be *das Leuchten, das Strahlen.* "Der Schein" means "the shining" and also "the *semblance.*" The entire process, as in the story "The Silence of the Sirens," is only "the semblance of an event," a *Scheinvorgang.*

In another respect, too, the English translation is misleading. The words "achieved at last and fading so quickly" suggest a sequential narrative, a Before and After, with the Before, the so-called radiance, having been achieved and consolidated for some finite length of time. The German actually provides another nuance: "endlich" can modify "erreichten" so as to highlight not time ("finally") but mode; the "achievement" is of the "finite, earthly" sort and hence is instantly shadowed by temporality and failure. In this sense the words "schon vergehend" ("already vanishing") appear to indwell and not to follow the moment of accomplishment. The moment is destroyed in the instant of its production: it never "is" except virtually, as "semblance."

The story presents a perfect paradox: the experience of the full text of one's sentence ("justice" ["Gerechtigkeit"]) is possible only as its impossibility, for the consciousness of it, occurring on the margin of death, has no duration. A paradox wrapped in a textual conundrum, for the sign of even the semblance of the radiance of the transfiguring insight is parenthetical.

And yet, and yet . . . the suspension of meaning within the brackets of undecidability also means that Kafka will not concede the negative conclusion without a struggle. A doubt persists — a parenthetical hesitation — as to the possibility of an illuminated death. Kafka struggles to introduce the lambent death of writing into brute death. The stake is immense, for failure means to be condemned to see the writing destiny as only so much allotria; or as an ascetic spiritual torment without reward; or as a nothing, the rehearsal of a senseless death. He writes, in some perplexity: "What is literature? Where does it come from? What use is it? What questionable things! Add to this questionableness the further questionableness of what you say, and what you get is a monstrosity [*ein Ungeheuer*]" (DF 246, H 276). For if literature is finally only this "monstrosity," then

> to die would mean nothing else than to surrender a nothing to the nothing, but that would be impossible to conceive, for how could a person, even only as a nothing, consciously surrender himself to the nothing, and not merely to an empty nothing but rather to a roaring nothing whose nothingness consists only in its incomprehensibility. (D1 316)

The "monstrosity of literature" is more than the merely structural impossibility of reading "the full text of one's sentence," since this very act of reading is as such excluded from the text. The monstrosity of literature exceeds even the paradox of the task that *is* the being one is — "You are the task" — at the same time that this task is impossible to accomplish, viz. "the impossibility of not writing, the impossibility of writing German, the impossibility of writing differently. One might also add a fourth impossibility, the impossibility of writing" (DF 36, L 289, Br 337–38). The monstrosity of literature is its never having been any-

thing other than a subterfuge of death, and even its ecstasy, the jubilation of a demon bent on one's early destruction.

"The task of literature," writes the critic Silvio Vietta, "is to realize a
capacity of the imagination to conceive of alternative kinds of action
and communication. In this light imagination is a dictate of rationality."[13]
Kafka's task becomes the continuation of his culture's task at large: to
imagine, under the head of "action and communication," an ecstasy
promising redemption — one better even than any possible ecstasy
promised by death alone.[14] This is the condition of his *life* as a writer.

But the task is threatened by the temptation it means to resist — of
supposing that, after the failure of any other redemptive illumination,
death itself, *as such*, might be redemptive. There seem to be but two
places for taking fire — the scene of writing and the scene of dying. Now,
with the diagnosis of Kafka's tuberculosis in 1917, the scene of redemption shifts from the desk to the bed. In 1914 Kafka had written that the
death-scenes in his novels, which were calculated to grieve his readers,
were for him "secretly a game," for he would lie "contentedly on my
death bed" (D2 102).[15] He is not inclined to claim that now. That con-
tentment, which appeared to be a consequence of having written well,
has passed away: "the devilish part of my writing is its vanity" (L 334).[16]
Writing, this profane thing, is subsumed within a general ethics, no better than all the other tasks Kafka was to allege in 1922 he had failed
at — "piano, violin, languages, Germanics, anti-Zionism, Zionism,
Hebrew, gardening, carpentering" (D2 209). Writing belongs to a general theology as only one opaque particular. After such profanation,
how could one surrender one's body to death? Without progeny, a secular death is insupportable; and Kafka's autocratic, nocturnal writing excluded any such issue. Josephine — the singing mouse, the spinster artiste — in dying "will rise to the heights of redemption" ("in gesteigerter
Erlösung") (CS 378; GW 1:294); and Kafka, the writer? the man? After
the loss of the writer's capacity for ecstasy, with the knowledge of death
palpable in his lungs, Kafka attends to a form of redemptive Gnosticism.[17] Gnostic theology gives another meaning to death, precisely on
account of the absence of progeny. During the entire period from
mid-1917 until early 1922, Kafka wrote very little and nothing at all
intended for publication.[18] In 1917–1918, however, he composed the
remarkable aphorisms entitled by Max Brod "Reflections on Sin, Suffering, Hope and the True Way," which pursue a higher "consolation" in
the Gnostic theology equating death with redemption from a fallen
world. In his last stories, Kafka moves well within the ambit of Gnosticism in the formal play of deconstructive logic (see chapter 5). The
staged deconstruction of his late work is driven by a salvific concern.

Such questions are probing and not only for him: How, beyond the possibility of a writerly illumination, could death be justified? Kafka's poetics, his poetology, is in the last resort a thanatology. He has to get his death under a God that sanctions it. The body is a specific, not a universal medium; for, following "In the Penal Colony," death *as such* might be conceived as a profusion of inflicted signs inassimilable to the code of the matter—the bodily medium. The model of the death of the prisoner in "In the Penal Colony" advances a general model of the dying subject—not only of the dying writerly subject but of the dying subject purely and simply. All deaths might be figured as a being (over) written to death—a writing impossible for the subject to read.

For to *become* one's (inflicted) words in the fullest event of reading would imply an impossible medial translation: the DNA, the code of bodily matter, cannot accommodate all and any signs. The virus of the word, like the computer virus, overwrites the code of life; and death is the result of this displacement—"a displaced name," as Paul de Man puts it, "for a linguistic predicament." In "In the Penal Colony," de Man's words assume flesh. This image responds to the picture of the victim who attempts to "decipher" his sentence "*with his wounds*" (emphasis added, CS 150).[19]

In "The Crossbreed" Kafka imagines a body accommodating strange DNA: the product is a hybrid with no claim to life, who invites the butcher's knife. The story concludes:

> Perhaps the knife of the butcher would be a release for this animal; but as it is a legacy I must deny it that. So it must wait until the breath voluntarily leaves its body, even though it sometimes gazes at me with a look of human understanding, challenging me to do the thing of which both of us are thinking. (CS 427)

But if this animal is also Kafka the writer—it clings to the narrator, it wishes to be inseparable from him, it has no other home than his lap—then the knife of the butcher is also a metonymy of suicide. There were times when Kafka thought of suicide but did not venture it. It was from an impulse to suicide that he began writing "The Judgment," but that story does not finish with the wish to die—rather: "Joy that I shall have something beautiful for Max's *Arkadia*" (D1 276). Kafka continued to write—especially at the end of his life, with a perspective that connects the secular gnostic and the theological Gnostic poles. (This is our way of rephrasing Benjamin's ellipse.)[20] But now we might ask, following in Kafka's traces: could there ever be a writing truly congruent with Gnosticism? The vision of death as an overwriting from *outside* is a stumbling block.

If it were possible to write stories truly congruent with a Gnostic perspective, death of both sorts could be figured as the good consumption of the self. It would proceed via the "impersonalization" of ego through the inscription of "higher" signs into the receptive body. But this idea is fragile. In conversations reported by Brod, Kafka spoke of "the *false* hands that reach out to one in the midst of writing."[21] At other times he said that what he had written and especially what he had published—and hence now belonged to others' light of day, or darkness—"led him astray" in his attempt to write new things.[22] At this point, a way of writing consistent with keeping to one's own path might be congruent with a good death, while taking false hands would amount to a death pure and simple, the "boisterous" death of an unjustified life (D1 316). The images of false hands and the detritus of past projects continue to allow for the distinction between higher medially motivated and random signs; but this distinction is hard or impossible to sustain.

> More and more fearful as I write. It is understandable. *Every word*, twisted in the hands of the spirits—this twist of the hand is their characteristic gesture—becomes a spear turned against the speaker. (emphasis added, D2 233)

It appears impossible to keep to one's own path while "reading" these assaults. And if death is figured as the outcome of opportunistic inscriptions, it cannot supply an insight true to *this* dying body; it has no meaning other than unreadable inscriptions—a text that calls for but does not allow deciphering. Kafka's death would then amount to an other-medial assault on the bodily ego, the result of which would be only a "shaking off the self." And—dreadful thought—it would follow that, as mere death might be figured as the assault of a foreign, heteronomous, unreadable writing, so might the "real writing" that had assaulted him. Any difference between the two deaths, other than a quantitative affair of intensity, would appear to be negligible. As the body is exhausted by the "inscriptions" of experience—by the "writing" of a life lived to its end—so too the writing self, whether exalted by genuine-seeming inscriptions or led astray by false inscriptions, is exhausted. The story of a redemptive writing that was entirely "one's own" would indeed be little more than a "craving for enjoyment"—an illusion, not unlike the vaunted entry into the Castle (L 334, Br 385).

In the closing pages of his diary, Kafka imagines the monstrosity of literature at once mythically and concretely, in conceiving of literature as the action of an antithetical "spirit." What writes, when "one" writes well, is not oneself but another. And this "spirit"? It might answer to the imaginative possibility of writing the "true" self, where the "truthfulness" of this self, as Sokel notes, "depends on the abolition of the writer's ego as the medium of the writing."[23] On the other hand, this annihilating "writer" might be none other than a spirit of destruction:

> It is astounding how I have systematically destroyed myself in the course of the years, it was like a slowly widening breach in a dam, a purposeful action. The spirit that brought it about must now be celebrating triumphs; why doesn't it let me take part in them? But perhaps it hasn't yet achieved its purpose and can therefore think of nothing else. (D2 195)

To strive to become what one writes as that which has been written on one is to be enthralled by a monstrosity, so that to write fully—and hence to be fully written upon—is to be overwritten, it is to die.

At various times, Kafka imagines death as the occasion of a great redemption. He also imagines death as a destructive abundance of heteronomous signs. The devilish surmise that this is also the case of his writing is something he must struggle against. This struggle is conveyed by a picture of Kafka on his death bed, when his body was fading from him, correcting proof texts, not yet relinquishing a mute solicitation of the writer's ecstasy. Did he know in this instant the "intensified redemption" of a body become text? The body being exchanged for the proof, the proof would be a thoroughly illuminated body. Many paths lead out of this struggle, and constitute a great provocation to cultural theory. The following chapters explore several of these paths in slower motion.

# Chapter 5

## NIETZSCHE, KAFKA, AND

## LITERARY PATERNITY

What things do we copy, writing and painting, we
mandarins with Chinese brushes [*mit chinesischem Pinsel*],
we immortalizers of things that can be written . . . ?
— Nietzsche, *Beyond Good and Evil*

Pardon that for a barren passion's sake,
Although I have come close on forty-nine,
I have no child, I have nothing but a book,
Nothing but that to prove your blood and mine.
— W. B. Yeats, *Responsibilities*

*Aut liberi aut libri.*
— old monk's saying

A GOOD DEATH consists in an illumination before dying. One such illumination is the prospect of cultural immortality, and yet it can seem odd
to describe the death that consists in an illumination before dying as an
affair of *cultural* immortality. But if we leave out of this account the
good Gnostic death — which Kafka did not die, as witness his deathbed
concern with the textual body of Josephine the Singer — both kinds of
death we have described involve a cultural reference. In the instance of
the ecstasy of writing, the product of Kafka's states is literary works
meant to be published, to see others' light of day. In the instance of the
final insight into one's own law as obtained by the victim of a writing
machine, the prisoner's epiphany is witnessed and interpreted by a crowd
of citizens.

Kafka is inclined to represent deaths as events that are witnessed, as
"always already" public. The disgraceful death of Joseph K. is witnessed by his killers, as is that of the murdered Wese of "A Fratricide":

Pallas, choking on the poison in his body, stood at the double-
leafed door of his house as it flew open. "Schmar! Schmar! I saw it
all, I missed nothing." (CS 404)

When Kafka reflects on the deaths of his heroes as secretly a game — for *he* intends to die contentedly — he imagines a plurality of readers who share his heroes' anguish:

> someone is dying, . . . it is hard for him to do so, . . . it seems unjust to him, or at least harsh, and the reader is moved by this, or at least he should be. (D2 102)

In "An Old Manuscript" the nomads "tear morsels out of the [ox's] living flesh with their teeth" in the public square in front of the emperor's palace (CS 417). The death of Gregor Samsa is an exception; but then again the story might have turned more than just "a bit horrible" ("fürchterlich") if the family or the boarders or the charwoman had been on hand to watch the monster expire (LF 58, F 116). Death is an opportunity for public recognition; the prospect of cultural immortality depends on the medial means to attain it.

In "In the Penal Colony," Kafka's reflections on a public, medial death were left unresolved. In this chapter, I mean to put these terms — the good death and the media (which involve the inscription of signs) — in conjunction once again, widening their context to include the example of a predecessor. My focus is Nietzsche's and Kafka's preoccupation with survival through their writings, which they sometimes figure as the offspring of a literary paternity.

In the matter of Nietzsche and Kafka we have alluded (and will continue to allude) to the diffuse and inexplicit presence of Nietzsche in Kafka's work. The task now is to address their relation directly. But the outcome will not be a small monograph on "Kafka as a Reader of Nietzsche," because there is nothing in Kafka's oeuvre resembling a direct, plainly articulated preoccupation with Nietzsche's writings of the kind one finds in the work of Kafka's contemporary Thomas Mann. Unlike other young Jewish intellectuals in Vienna and Prague in the 1890s — such as Herzl and Werfel and Buber and to some extent Kraus — Kafka was not ostentatiously engaged by Nietzsche. And yet he was well aware of him. According to Max Brod, while he and Kafka were both law students at Charles University, they attended a lecture on Nietzsche that irritated Brod. Kafka replied by defending Nietzsche; and knowing Kafka's character, we may assume he did so on the strength of having read him. To judge further from the evidence of a woman named Selma Kohn, we know that Kafka had read *Thus Spoke Zarathustra* — or at least parts of it: toward the end of her life she reported in a letter to Max Brod that in the summer of 1900, when she was a girl in Roztok, Kafka, a house guest, read her passages from *Zarathustra*.[1] Kafka's certifiable Nietzsche reception begins (and ends) with this probably unsuccessful attempt to seduce a young woman. We may conclude, then, that Kafka's earliest, strongest experience of reading Nietzsche was marked by sexual desire, irresolution, misogyny — and writing. (Kafka would not have failed to note that Selma was the daughter of the chief postman.) Thereafter, we have additional recollections by Kafka's friends that Kafka was interested in Nietzsche; yet in all his journals and correspondence, he never once writes the name "Nietzsche," so that except for Selma Kohn's letter to Max Brod, there are no irrefragably hard data connecting him to Nietzsche's works.[2] This state of affairs has led to the consensus that, like Thomas Mann in *Doctor Faustus*, Kafka did not have to mention Nietzsche by name since he is everywhere in his work, like salt in seawater.[3]

With the customary route of influence blocked, the relations of the two must be an affair of the critic's induction, of hermeneutic speculation. In selecting texts and topics of Nietzsche that lead to Kafka's themes and aperçus, one will be following one's own bias.[4] The path I shall take addresses Kafka as a reader of Nietzsche on the question of *literary paternity* — the relation of the producer of literature to his products as male parent to offspring. The issue is not one of a hypothetical paternal relation between Nietzsche and Kafka. That Kafka read Nietzsche as a young man and was captivated by what he read should not suggest that his literary personality came out of Nietzsche as, let us say, Kafka's story "The Judgment" came out of him, "like a regular birth" (D1 278). We have more than once mentioned Kafka's concern for a sort of cultural immortality through his writings; this concern has also come to be reflexively cast back upon him in the matter of the survival of his manuscripts. I am asking about this same issue in a different way. The question is Nietzsche's and Kafka's own views on literary paternity, a subject on which they did indeed have strong views; this allows us to formulate a relation between them on the basis of their shared illusions and critique.

Now, even to consider "literary paternity" of a "proper" or legitimate kind is to strike a defiantly modernist stance, for this stance is radically anti-Platonic, and, in Nietzsche's words, modernity is "the fight against Plato."[5] Literary paternity, the conjunction of male acts of writing with live proper offspring, joins what Plato's Socrates put asunder, even if this figure remains well within the orbit of his influence.

The metaphor of literary paternity is of Socratic origin, but the notion of a proper literary paternity is for Socrates untrue or incomplete. Plato's translator and commentator Benjamin Jowett sums up Socrates's position in the *Phaedrus*:

> Writing is inferior to speech. For writing is like a picture which can give no answer to a question, and has only a deceitful likeness of a living creature. It has no power of adaptation, but uses the same

words for all. It is a sort of bastard and not a legitimate son of knowledge, and when an attack is made upon this illegitimate progeny, neither the parent nor anyone else is there to defend it. . . . The living is better than the written word . . . : the principles of justice and truth when delivered by word of mouth are the legitimate offspring of a man's own bosom, and their lawful descendants take up their abode in others.[6]

The text of the *Phaedrus* actually succeeds less well in distinguishing the proper offspring of speech from the bastards of script. It describes the "right man," certainly, as one "who thinks that in the written word there is necessarily much which is not serious" but as one, too, who holds that "only in principles of justice and goodness and nobility taught and communicated orally and *written in the soul, which is the true way of writing*, is there clearness and perfection and seriousness; and that such principles are like legitimate offspring" (emphasis added).[7]

To suppose the contrary, that both Nietzsche and Kafka care for writing because writing might entail legitimate reproduction, is to second their fight against Plato—a fight for which they could find support in Aristotle, who, in *The Nicomachean Ethics*, wrote, "Poets, because they are exceedingly fond of their own poems, love them as if they were their children."[8] But the issue is too strong, too important, to be settled by an "as if." It is a question of the near *identity* of "poems" and children. I repeat this point: the question is whether writing might entail legitimate reproduction. This is by no means a settled matter.[9]

Let us look at these actual, complicated cases, beginning with the view of a recent reader of Nietzsche, Alexander Nehamas. In *Nietzsche: Life as Literature* Nehamas argues that Nietzsche succeeded, through effects of writing, in fathering a human personality. For Nietzsche's books amount neither to a philosophical system nor to a collection of aperçus but rather to the production of a "character." "In engaging with [Nietzsche's] works," Nehamas writes,

> we are not engaging with the miserable little man who wrote them but with the philosopher who emerges through them, the magnificent character these texts constitute and manifest, the agent who, as the will to power holds, is nothing but his effects—that is, his writings.[10]

Even acknowledging, as Nehamas does, that "the parallel between life and literature is" (to say the least) "not perfect," nonetheless his formulation more or less meets the conditions of paternity: the empirical Nietzsche produces ("constitutes and manifests") a personal being ("a magnificent character"), it being, for the moment, of secondary importance that the person fathered by "this miserable little man" Nietzsche is actually *himself*. The dwindling empirical personality produces, through acts of writing, another self, its deep self — it reproduces itself, becoming the self it was. Odd as this formulation may sound, we have no choice, on Nehamas's view, but to call Nietzsche's literary persona a human self, so clearly marked is it by the customary attributes: it is a speaking (or echoing) subject, stylized into a character of depth, variousness, and complexity, recognizable through its many appearances, endowed with moods, modulating its identity through the effects it imaginatively produces on its audience. This state of affairs can be confidently characterized as "literary paternity" — indeed at the very least as "literary" paternity, since it appears to verge closely on real paternity.

If, though, we are willing to entertain this view of Nietzsche as a father — and, indeed, as the father of himself — what are we to make of Nietzsche's polemical insistence on the difference between life and literature, in, for instance, *Ecce Homo*: "I am one thing, my writings are another matter"?[11] For this difference stipulates decisively the very distinction between real and artificial reproduction, from which there follows nothing less than the impossibility of literary paternity and hence the profoundly abusive character of this figure. For even if Nietzsche's life (or so-called experience) is literally and deeply entangled in his literature (or so-called rhetoric), nonetheless, "paternity" remains one of those knifeblade words mercilessly distinguishing literal and figurative meanings without further recourse: nation-states, for example, have traditionally required fathers to feed, clothe, and shelter their offspring but not their "offspring," i.e., their literary effects.[12] Nietzsche himself excerpted with interest this cautionary sentence: "Paternity [is] not something self-evident but rather a legal institution achieved only late."[13]

As it springs from Nietzsche's pen, the tense distinction between reproduction in life and literature produces some highly charged results. Toward the end of *Beyond Good and Evil*, Nietzsche writes: "The 'work,' whether of the artist or of the philosopher, invents the man who has created it, who is supposed to have created it: 'great men,' as they are venerated, are subsequent pieces of wretched minor fiction."[14] Consider, then: artistic "paternity" in this instance is but a bad fiction, a type of the minor fiction of so-called personal creation. In fact, it is the offspring who retroactively "invents" the personality of its supposed begetter. Nietzsche's key words here are "invents" ("erfindet"), not "creates" ("schafft"), "pieces of wretched minor fiction" ("kleine schlechte Dichtungen"), not truly "great men" ("große Männer"). The destructive force of this passage cannot be confined to a chiastic reversal of direction of the paternity metaphor. On the contrary, the passage annihilates the paternity metaphor purely and simply by degrading it to a wretched minor invention.[15]

*On the Genealogy of Morals* offers a more revealing example of Nietzsche's attack on the paternity metaphor. Nietzsche famously writes:

> One should guard against confusion through psychological *contig-uity*, to use a British term, a confusion to which an artist himself is only too prone; as if he himself were what he is able to represent, conceive, and express. The fact is that *if* he were it, he would not represent, conceive, and express it: a Homer would not have cre-ated an Achilles or Goethe a Faust. Whoever is completely and wholly an artist is to all eternity separated from the "real," the actual; on the other hand, one can understand how he may some-times weary to the point of desperation of the eternal "unreality" and falsity of his innermost existence — and that then he may well attempt what is most forbidden him, to lay hold of actuality [ins Wirkliche überzugreifen], for once actually to *be*. With what suc-cess? That is easy to guess.[16]

It is not so easy to guess. It might be easy to guess that the outcome would be disastrous, but our power to envision this disaster fails on account of our necessarily weak understanding of what it might mean "to lay hold of actuality, for once actually to be." It does seem imme-diately plausible to grasp this *"typical velleity* of the artist" as moving toward an act modeled on the sexual incursion that could father a child (the German suggests, along with "a laying hold," "a forced entry") and in so doing forge a fetter binding the artist to "the real." The fact is interesting, if we may look ahead for a moment to Nietzsche's critical counterpart Kafka, that Kafka, in the words of Walter Sokel, also "saw writing in its ideal form as a passionate penetration, a taking possession of language and, through language, of the social world."[17] But this is not to conclude, at this stage of the discussion, that Kafka's aesthetic position is a mere reversal of Nietzsche's. On this view, then, Nietzsche resists the fall from artistic ascesis into the sexual reality of the woman — into what is termed, in the critique of Wagner immediately following, the world of the "woman in need."[18]

This reading holds up. Immediately afterwards in this essay, the im-age of sexual transgression arises. We need to feel, as the argument unfolds, the heady ambivalence of Nietzsche's contempt for *and* attrac-tion to the act of "laying hold of actuality." It is crucial, for one thing, that the artist who is exemplary for caving in to the temptation "actu-ally to be" is his beloved adversary, the aging Wagner — and the fruit of his lapse, *Parsifal*. What kind of offspring — legitimate or bastard — is this?

A more nearly illegitimate one. The artist, Nietzsche writes, does vio-

lence to his own nature in becoming a kind of priest and metaphysician—a mystified propagator of ethical ideals. (One could say, he becomes "the wretched fiction" of a propagator of ideals.) According to
Nietzsche, Wagner's late, dubious achievement is to "utter *ascetic ideals*," an act, which, however, is not even original with Wagner but one
for which he had to gain "*courage* [from] . . . the prop provided by
Schopenhauer's philosophy." But this appropriation of influence is altogether improper, for, according to Nietzsche, Schopenhauer's philosophy itself has no designs on "'the real,' the actual," being the work of
"a genuinely independent spirit . . . , a man . . . who had the courage to
be himself, who knew how to stand alone."[19] (We should reflect on this
"standing alone" as a way of being that is not *actually* a way of being.)
But Wagner's use of Schopenhauer is a perversion; he turned Schopenhauer's private system into a public spectacle.

The force of Wagner's desire to "lay hold of actuality" drives him to
this violence. It made him vulnerable to poisonous influences, and it
overrode even his loyalty to himself—the loyalty his earlier aesthetic
position required from him, for (here quoting Nietzsche)

> There exists a complete theoretical contradiction between his ear-
> lier and his later aesthetic creed—the former set down, for exam-
> ple, in *Opera and Drama*, the latter in the writings he published
> from 1870 onward. Specifically, he ruthlessly altered . . . his judg-
> ment as to the value and status of *music*; what did he care that he
> had formerly made of music a means, a medium, a "woman" who
> required a goal, a man, in order to prosper—namely, drama![20] He
> grasped all at once that with the Schopenhauerian theory and inno-
> vation *more* could be done *in majorem musicae gloriam*—namely,
> with the theory of the *sovereignty* of music as Schopenhauer con-
> ceived it. . . . With this extraordinary rise in the value of music that
> appeared to follow from Schopenhauerian philosophy, the value of
> *the musician* himself all at once went up in an unheard-of manner,
> too: from now on he became an oracle, a priest, indeed more than
> a priest, a kind of mouthpiece of the "in itself" of things, a tele-
> phone from the beyond—henceforth he uttered not only music,
> this ventriloquist of God—he uttered metaphysics: no wonder he
> one day finally uttered *ascetic ideals*.[21]

In the new system, representing a "complete theoretical contradiction"
of the old, the ascetic priest plays the dominant, displacing the artist-
mediator; read: procurer, whose music drama arose from a sexual coupling. Wagner, the ascetic priest, does not grasp, however, that in this
way he himself becomes an invader of boundaries, an implicitly sexual
transgressor of what is forbidden in reality.[22]

In both cases, Nietzsche sexualizes Wagner's theoretical mise-en-scène of opera: explicitly, in the first case, as a scene of sexual intercourse — the masculine Word of drama impregnates music figured as Need; implicitly, in the second, as a scene of violation, in order that music, and with it the musician, "prosper" (*gedeihen*) — which means, reproduce.[23] I draw this reproductive conclusion with the support of other passages from Nietzsche, e.g., from *Thus Spoke Zarathustra*: "Everything about woman is a riddle, and everything about woman has one solution: that is pregnancy."[24] (It is no secret that Nietzsche has more interesting things to say about woman — who, in at least one instance, we are told is Truth and as such no longer the riddle but its solution.)[25]

At this point it is clear that Nietzsche, with Schopenhauer's help, has devalued the association of art with sexual reproduction. Yet we do not want to leave Nietzsche's argument without noting an important swerve — namely, that it will soon be Schopenhauer's turn to be excoriated. For, like Wagner, he too abuses art in his aesthetics by instrumentalizing it as a palliative against sexual desire. The contrary figure to Schopenhauer, for Nietzsche, is Stendhal (as the contrary figure to Wagner was Schopenhauer) — Stendhal, who does indeed acknowledge the power of art to "arouse" the will, for art is most truly a scene of sexual excitation.[26] But this sort of sexual charging can be safely preferred to Wagner's early aesthetic of impregnation, because it appears to identify art with male arousal or, better, masculinizes aesthetic excitation in opposing it to woman's need for reproductive fulfillment.

In the matter of this opposition, though, other texts of Nietzsche are regularly cited as tending to eliminate it. Sarah Kofman, for example, concludes from her reading of *The Genealogy of Morals* that "because the birth of a work of art is also the birth of a gifted child, Nietzsche uses the same economic hypothesis to understand it [and thus "the work of art draws on all the reserves and supplements of the force and vigor of animal life"]."[27] A work of art is like "a gifted child?" One is reluctant to criticize so progressive an idea. But this sort of intervention appears to arise from what Benjamin, in his *Elective Affinities* essay, terms "lightly-assumed liberalism" ("gespielter Freisinn").[28] I know of no sentence in which Nietzsche identifies the work of art with the birth of a gifted child. Indeed, in the preceding aphorism Nietzsche has the opposite to say about children — gifted or otherwise: "Every philosopher would speak as Buddha did when he was told of the birth of a son: 'Rahula has been born to me, a fetter has been forged for me' (Rahula here means 'a little demon')."[29] It would seem to be important that books precisely not be such little devils in any way whatsoever.

A couple of famous aphorisms from *The Gay Science* also suggest a link between authorship and male parturition. "Constantly," writes

Nietzsche, "we [philosophers] have to give birth to our thoughts out of our pain and, like mothers, endow them with all that we have in us of blood, heart, fire, pleasure, passion, agony, conscience, fate, catastrophe."[30] The same book, however, also offers an opposed account: "Spiritual pregnancy produce[s] the character of the contemplative type, which is closely related to the feminine character: it consists of male mothers." Note that the value for Nietzsche of "the contemplative type," let alone "the male mother," hardly goes uncontested. The point about spiritual pregnancy is a qualified one: "Pregnancy has made women kinder, more patient, more timid, more pleased to submit."[31] We recall that in just the same way "spiritual pregnancy produce[s] the character of the contemplative type," etc. The sexual charge on art is not improved by its dissipating into a submissive body.

Should one, then, be as sad as Laurence Rickels, who, noting Heidegger's misappropriation of Nietzsche, remarks: "Here we traverse an uncanny and barren landscape, one in which everything recalls to us that Nietzsche died without having had children"?[32]

Did Nietzsche want to have children?

The stage is set for the conclusive proclamations of *Ecce Homo*: "The good fortune of my existence, its uniqueness perhaps, lies in its fatality: I am, to express it in the form of a riddle, already dead as my father, while as my mother I am still living and becoming old."[33] Nietzsche thereafter develops the conceit, shrinking from his feminization: "At another point as well," he writes, "I am merely my father once more and, as it were, his continued life after an all-too-early death."[34] To the extent that Nietzsche's riddle is thinkable, his literary reproduction was confined to his incessantly reproducing himself *as his father*. Everything points to Kierkegaard, in *Fear and Trembling*: "The one who will not work fits what is written about the virgins of Israel: he gives birth to wind—but the one who will work gives birth to his own father."[35] Nietzsche kept on fathering his father whose task it was to father him. The notion goes back to the earliest years of Nietzsche's writing, to *Human, All Too Human*: "If one does not have a good father one should furnish oneself with one"; and things are always so, for "in the maturity of his life and understanding a man is overcome by the feeling his father was wrong to father him" (translation modified).[36] And so Nietzsche had, so to speak, to give birth continually to himself. Recall the prohibition against the artist's attempt "for once actually to *be*." As his already dead father, Nietzsche had his father's work to do—and did, a work without conclusion. Perhaps, though, he also rejoiced in it—an idea suggested by his conjuring a Demeter, "who, sunk in eternal sorrow, rejoices again for the first time when told that she may once more give birth to Dionysus."[37]

At this point, it might be observed, we have put forth claims border-
ing on Nehamas's — namely, that Nietzsche reproduced his genuine self
in his writing and that in this sense Nietzsche's work crosses the divide
between literature and life: but note the important difference in our
conclusion. Nietzsche does not *reproduce* himself so much as he perpetually produces himself *for the first time* as the one being he means to be.
This is not quite an affair of becoming the "philosopher" or "character" who transcends the "miserable little man" who writes. His task is
more fundamental still. He writes in order to be . . . something more
than a ghost.[38] This is not reproduction but a movement incessantly
repeating an inconclusive birth. Nietzsche had to locate the task of generation further back; he had first to set his genealogy to rights, then
strive to be the being he never yet was.

Something of this argument is present even in the triumphalist rhetoric of *Thus Spoke Zarathustra*. In "On Child and Marriage," Nietzsche
writes:

> You are young and wish for a child and marriage. But I ask you:
> Are you a man *entitled* to wish for a child? Are you the victorious
> one, the self-conqueror, the commander of your senses, the master
> of your virtues? This I ask you. Or is it the animal and need that
> speak out of your wish? Or loneliness? Or lack of peace with your-
> self?
>
> Let your victory and your freedom long for a child. You shall
> build living monuments to your victory and your liberation. You
> shall build over and beyond yourself, but first you must be built
> yourself, perpendicular in body and soul. You shall not only repro-
> duce yourself, but produce something higher! [Nicht nur fort sollst
> du dich pflanzen, sondern hinauf!] May the garden of marriage
> help you in that![39]

"On Child and Marriage" distinguishes the reproduction of a child in
marriage (*sich fortpflanzen*) from another sort of action which may be
sexual but is not reproductive (*sich hinaufpflanzen*). This action suggests an arousal of the will and hence artistic excitement. But for all its
instinctualization of the act of writing, the view is not the Freudian one
that considers such work as substitutive sexual gratification (especially
if the scene of gratification is conjugal and its tendency reproductive). In
urging the instinctual character of writing, Nietzsche means, on the one
hand, to elude the pitfalls of sublimation and the eternal series of reverse valorizations the concept engenders (the sublimated product, the
artwork, is "finer," but it is also "weaker" — and, hence, decadent). On
the other hand, Nietzsche wants the act of writing to be the immediate — read Dionysian — discharge of an affect, hence, more nearly a

squandering: this means, he wants to give away whatever there is of himself now. Perhaps he is preserved in a particulate way in this scattering of word charges (though "a living thing seeks above all to discharge its strength . . . ; self-preservation is only one of the indirect and most frequent results").[40] But there is no suggestion here of reproduction, let alone a welcome acknowledgment of his verbal offspring for containing the contribution of any other mother's charge (I am thinking here of Paul Rée, who dedicated a work to Nietzsche thus: "To the father of this text, most gratefully, its mother.")[41] Nietzsche's main concern is to resist any intervention or injury to his narcissism but his own—a narcissism that, by the way, is always only just about to glimpse itself. It feels itself as the will to the shattering that could bring it into being for the first time. And so it strives to accumulate its erotic charge around a point of possibly productive self-scattering. Hence, our conclusion must be paradoxical. Nietzsche reproduces himself as the being who must shatter, leaving behind only an ineradicable specter of the will that this action recur.

What task, now, was laid on Kafka, whose father would have very likely found it superfluous that Kafka give birth to him, being already "superabundant in life"?[42] Kafka's sense of the demand for reproduction was shaped by Nietzsche's conclusion. This is the main argument of this chapter, which is therefore attuned to the idea of a fuller consonance of Kafka's gnosticism with his Gnosticism at the end of his life.

I said earlier that there are no hard data bearing on Nietzsche's importance for Kafka, and that this state of affairs has led to the consensus that Kafka does not have to mention Nietzsche by name since he is everywhere in the work, like salt in seawater. I can agree with this figure to the extent that I am pursuing one line of salt tears involving Zarathustra, and that is Kafka's indubitable sorrow over paternity.

Maurice Blanchot surmises that Kafka's ordeal of writing takes place inside a (Jewish) religious conflict.[43] The drama runs as follows: Kafka cares inordinately for writing, and the mark of the extremity of his concern is his readiness to test God with it: "God doesn't want me to write," Kafka wrote, "but I, I must" (L 10). This struggle is also the measure of writing's oppositional character, which, at the order of religion, means its diabolism. This association was never far from Kafka's mind. The act of writing may be devilish; the wager, in writing, is for nothing less than salvation—the failure, nothing less than damnation.

Here in Blanchot's own words is Kafka's predicament:

Kafka needed more time, but he also needed less of the world. The world was first his family, whose constraint he bore with difficulty, never being able to free himself from it. It was next his fiancée and his fundamental desire to observe the law which requires man to fulfill his destiny in the world, have a family, children, and take his place in the community. Here the conflict assumes a new aspect, enters a contradiction which Kafka's religious position makes especially strong.

Blanchot proceeds to describe the difference in intensity between the predicaments of Kafka and Kierkegaard (to Kafka's disadvantage), and concludes:

> Kafka seemed to identify with the exigency of the work of art that which could bear the name of his salvation. If writing condemned him to solitude, made his existence that of a celibate, without love, without bonds, if however writing seemed to him . . . the sole activity which could justify him, it was because, at all events, solitude was a threat to him within and without, it was because the community was nothing more than a phantom and because the law which still speaks through it (the community) is not even the forgotten law but the feigned forgetting of the law. Writing becomes once more, then, . . . a possibility of fulfillment, a path without a goal perhaps comparable to that goal without a path which is the only one that must be reached.[44]

But the matter cannot be put (nor does Blanchot finally put it) so victoriously. A good deal of Kafka's work and imagery in the years following his first broken engagement suggests an intention to straddle both positions by producing a literary progeny pleasing to God. Kafka did imagine a *literary* paternity.

If an undistorted disgust of reproduction colors *Amerika* (or *The One Who Sank Out of Sight*), there is the ecstatic breakthrough of "The Judgment," which Kafka likened to a real birth. We have noted how the breakdown of the writing machine in "In the Penal Colony" suggests Kafka's despair of ever again producing a story as quick and vital as "The Judgment." In March 1917 Kafka wrote the extraordinary story "Eleven Sons," which, according to Max Brod, codes in the narrator's eleven children eleven stories that Kafka was writing. Readers acknowledging this allusion have mostly focused on aligning the right story with the right son, without raising the basic question underlying this connection.

According to Max Brod, "Eleven Sons" amounts to a powerful proof of the idea that Kafka craved—and, more, achieved—paternity. "In a story like 'Eleven Sons,'" he writes,

> this high esteem for . . . the patriarchal way of life . . . stands out clearly. . . . The prose piece "Eleven Sons" is, in my opinion, to be understood as a wishful picture of fatherhood, of founding a family, which can be held up against the father's example as something of equal value, that is to say, something just as magnificent and patriarchal. . . . This explanation is not contradicted by the fact that Franz once said to me, "'The Eleven Sons' are quite simply eleven stories I am working on this very moment." After all, stories were his children. In his writing he was accomplishing, on a remote territory, but independently, something which was analogous to his father's creative power—I am following Franz's conception of this point, not my own—and which could be set alongside it.[45]

Yet it is not obvious that Max Brod has accurately reproduced Kafka's mood. "I am following Franz's conception of this point, not my own," Brod writes immediately after having written the phrase "in my opinion." The comfortable affirmation of literary paternity, in which a "wishful picture" soon appears as an "accomplishment," resembles the lightly assumed liberalism of Sarah Kofman's "gifted child" thesis. The question missing from Brod's account of Kafka's position is whether this act of one-sided reproduction can count as paternity, since it is a paternity obtained without the advantages or (to speak plainly in the case of Nietzsche and Kafka) the imagined deficits of natural paternity, namely, sexual and social cohabitation with a woman.[46]

Wouldn't such literary paternity amount, in Kafka's case, to a trick to outwit the Jewish God? Wouldn't his offspring seem a monstrous, a devilish brood, and his demonstrable skill at fraud, taken to an extreme, proof of his desire to proclaim himself a (false) messiah?

But Kafka never allowed the fantasy of paternity to get so far. In the months before his death, when he expressed his sorrow of being "without forebears, without marriage, without heirs, with a fierce longing for forebears, marriage and heirs," he concluded, pointedly:

> There is an artificial, miserable substitute for everything, for forebears, marriages and heirs. Feverishly you contrive these substitutes, and if the fever has not already destroyed you, the hopelessness of the substitutes will. (D2 207)

Nonetheless, for several years, Kafka gave himself fully to the design of one distinguished substitute—to writing. The distinction of this substitute is heightened by a set of aphorisms, which places the ordeal of paternity in a metaphysical light. This light can be called Gnostic and shines especially strongly from 1918 on.

In January 1918, as we have heard, Kafka wrote in the series "Reflections on Sin, Suffering, Hope and the True Way," "There is nothing besides a spiritual world; what we call the world of the senses is the evil in the spiritual world" (DF 39). Ergo, there is a spiritual world, which might be heightened and augmented, while the sensory world, including the material creation and its demiurge, remain evil. In 1920, Kafka wrote: "In one of our ancient scriptures it is said: 'Those who curse life and therefore think not being born, or subjugating life, is the greatest or the sole non-deceptive happiness must be right, for the judgment concerning life . . .'" (DF 291). The text breaks off, as if to mark the Sisyphean labor of believing in, let alone acting upon, this ancient scripture.[47]

In 1920 Kafka composed a second series of aphorisms called "He." In January he wrote:

All that he does seems to him, it is true, extraordinarily new, but also, because of the incredible spate of new things, extraordinarily amateurish, indeed scarcely tolerable, incapable of becoming history, breaking short the chain of generations, cutting off for the first time at its most profound source the music of the world, which before him could at least be divined. Sometimes in his arrogance he has more anxiety for the world than for himself. (GrW 263–64)[48]

This passage is rich beyond telling, but note, for our purposes, that it conjures a "world" as first and foremost "destructible" and that Kafka's persona, who will accomplish this destruction, thereby acquires the god-like dimensions of a Zarathustra. The aphorism is, furthermore, Kierkegaardian in its inspiration, in a way entirely compatible with Nietzsche's theses on asceticism. According to Kierkegaard, no angel knows history: the end of history implies the end of sexual generation. Kafka's writing, which could bring about an end to history, entails a mighty ascesis, an envisioning of redemption on the far side of the body.[49]

Thereafter, in the same sequence of aphorisms, Kafka wrote:

He does not live for the sake of his personal life; he does not think for the sake of his personal thoughts. It seems to him that he lives and thinks under the compulsion of a family, which, it is true, is itself superabundant in life and thought, but for which he constitutes, in obedience to some law unknown to him, a formal necessity. (GW 269)

*His* family obligation has become an affair of occupying a certain "formal" position, which could again point to the formal operation of writing. This formal position has in it all the closeness to family he can and must endure.

A thesis on the transmission of a certain attitude toward paternity from Nietzsche to Kafka has now begun to emerge: Kafka's Gnostic inclination is informed by a reminiscence of the Zoroastrianism in back of (and sublated by) *Thus Spoke Zarathustra*. Kafka's recollection would then repeat the religious-historical relation of Zoroastrianism to Gnosticism. This connection is reinforced by the fact that in the first decades of the twentieth century, in Prague and elsewhere in Central Europe, Zoroastrianism, as a proto-Gnosticism, was very much in the air.[50]

Zoroastrianism, as it backgrounds Nietzsche's Zarathustra, became a privileged marker for Kafka of a moral dualism—and the possibility of its "overcoming." The way to that overcoming depends on the observance of a (barely readable) law or formal necessity and not, certainly, on any direct augmentation of "the world of the senses," which is idolatry. In this perspective, writing slides out from under the paternal, the reproductive metaphor: it has another purpose.

This different context of purposes can be put as follows. Kafka lives and writes from within a Jewish framework—the Judaism of Jehovah after the covenant with Abraham, with its ethic of tribal reproduction. The question of paternity of a literary or indeed of any other kind is connected for Kafka with this religious ordering of things. But as long as he stays within this framework, the problem for him *as a writer* is insuperable, for he is torn between two unacceptable positions. One is to be the father of Jewish children—but he cannot be this; because, two, he must write; but yet again writing might be only a miserable substitute for such paternity or only a gesture of diabolical defiance.

Kafka needs a thought model that holds bodily reproduction to be inessential. A Gnosticism consonant with the Judaism of the Old Testament *before the covenant* gives him this other frame. The Zoroastrian (or Persian-Manichean) strain is quite literally opposed to reproduction: in holding the soul to be a particle of light, it deplores reproduction, an act by which these particles of light are further shattered and "world harmony" destroyed.[51]

As a Gnostic, Kafka is relieved of the burden of thinking that his writing is only a miserable substitute, since that for which writing is only a miserable substitute is itself only a miserable simulacrum of the divine. In turning to Gnosticism, he accomplishes a turn within his own paternal dilemma. Accordingly, the defects of the second position, which advocates writing—the defects being that writing is a diabolical presumption or a miserable substitute—are chiastically attached to the first position: it is actually fathering a sensuous child that is a diabolical presumption and a miserable substitute. Writing is now freed to perform its task of the negative, of shifting the boundary between the spiritual and the sensate worlds.

Consider, now, Nietzsche's idea of a Zoroastrian Gnosticism, as it is spelled out in *Ecce Homo*. It contains the two familiar moments: Zoroaster was the greatest dualist; Zoroaster's dualism is a moral one, consisting of the two opposed moments: Good and Evil, Ormazd and Ahriman. Because Zoroaster was, for Nietzsche, "the first to consider the fight of good and evil the very wheel in the machinery of things, the transposition of morality into the metaphysical realm, as a force, cause, and end in itself," Zoroaster became "the first moralist."[52] In *Thus Spoke Zarathustra*, however—according to Nietzsche's commentary in *Ecce Homo*—Nietzsche's own creation Zarathustra negates and overcomes the principles of his historical predecessor: "Zarathustra created this most calamitous error, morality: consequently," writes Nietzsche, "he must also be the first to recognize it."[53]

In writing his *Zarathustra*, Nietzsche separates morality from activity, announcing a writing that shall be an *active* writing. We could call this writing, which rejects moral dualism, the language of the earth, a regained earth.

Kafka repeats Nietzsche in associating writing with a Zoroastrian struggle. But if Nietzsche's writing is driven by a repudiation of an original Zoroastrian moralism, Kafka's writing is driven by a Gnostic moralism consistent with the earlier Zoroastrianism. Kafka's position arises from a double negation: (1) he negates Nietzsche's overturning of a religious frame in order to (2) conceive of his writing as a new Kabbalah.[54]

Structurally speaking, Kafka repeats Nietzsche's negation of a dualism at a higher order by resituating the negative (writing) within the dualism. For if one thinks of the cosmos as the articulated space of a moral conflict, then Nietzsche extraterritorializes writing: writing begins where, with the overcoming of the dichotomy, man is brought into another space, a newfound land. Kafka, on the other hand, does not ever leave the moral dimension: he situates writing within the space of a moral struggle that contends for "the spiritual world" (DF 39).

This formulation take place against the background of *Thus Spoke Zarathustra*, which remained for Kafka an indelible reading experience: it stamps and shapes his position as Gnostic—and revisionist. For Kafka's Gnosticism is a metaphysical dualism that, in the absence of an indubitable gnosis, is capable, perhaps, of being "overcome"—that is to say, of being brought to a conclusion—by a type of practice: artistic practice. "The heavens assault Kafka's bodily ego," writes Harold Bloom, "*but only through his own writing*"[55]: writing is therefore also that place where the heavens can be resisted — or joined. The task of the negative might be accomplished through the sole bond on earth that Kafka could affirm: the covenant of writing. He turns, in a phrase of Walter Sokel's, to a "'Hebrew' variant of *Kunstreligion*"[56] — a mode of transcendence, an artistic practice, that is moral not because it "speaks ascetic ideals" but because it *is* this ideal, the sole appropriate form of a striving for purity and truthfulness. Kafka defines writing as the formal necessity of a Gnosticism consistent with an intensified, moralized, original Zoroastrianism. Nietzsche wrote: "Am I understood? — The self-overcoming of morality, out of truthfulness; the self-overcoming of the moralist, into his opposite — *into me* — that is what the name of Zarathustra means in my mouth."[57] Kafka wrote on September 25, 1917: "I can still have passing satisfaction from works like *A Country Doctor*, provided I can still write such things at all. . . . But happiness only if I can raise the world into the pure, the true, and the immutable" (D2 187). The lever is writing, a new Kabbalah. It is evident here that the identification of writing with a sort of paternity, a direct augmentation of the sensory world, has quite fallen away. Writing is something other than a miserable substitute for paternity.

Both Nietzsche and Kafka strove to put down the torments of failed paternity, either by thinking of their books as offspring — a wretched minor fiction they were too scrupulous to avow for long — or by finding an intellectual, moral, and feeling frame in which not having children would be pardonable.[58] They imagined they had found such a frame, and Nietzsche helped Kafka to this discovery. The frame that pardons them implies at the same time the unheard-of freedom of producing a self by an artistic will to destruction of the created world.[59] Nietzsche jubilantly proclaims this freedom on the brink of insanity. Kafka, lucid to the end, could not welcome this freedom except with a tremor of anxiety, indeed "sometimes . . . fearing more for the world than for himself" (GrW 263–64).

*Chapter 6*

# SOMETHING TO DO WITH THE TRUTH

## KAFKA'S LATER STORIES

KAFKA'S LATER WORKS continue his struggle to articulate the writer's task against its only justification — the *full* justification of his existence. These are the pieces produced in the years after 1915, following Kafka's abandonment of work on *The Trial*: they include diary entries, the aphorisms of 1917–18 that Max Brod entitled "Reflections on Sin, Suffering, Hope and the True Way"; and lengthier stories like "The Great Wall of China," "The Investigations of a Dog," "The Village Schoolmaster," "The Little Woman," and "Josephine the Singer, or The Mouse People." To employ Martin Greenberg's useful distinction, many of these are "thought stories" rather than "dream stories" — stories that lack the seductive appeal, the ostensible fullness and closure of the image. Here, the reader must make do with the reflections of a narrator absorbed in exquisitely refined "research" and, as befits the term, a perpetual air of experimentation, speculation, and inconclusiveness.[1] A piece like the unfinished 1922 story "The Investigations of a Dog" exemplifies this late style.

The inquiries of such narrators address a matter that often falls short of visual realization. "The Village Schoolmaster" ("Der Dorfschullehrer" [1915], also known as "The Giant Mole" ("Der Riesenmaulwurf"), for example, begins with the report of a giant mole:

> Those, and I am one of them, who find even a small ordinary-sized mole disgusting, would probably have died of disgust if they had seen the giant mole that a few years back was observed in the neighborhood of one of our villages, which achieved a certain transitory celebrity on account of the incident. (CS 168)

In fact, however, no reader of this story will be in even the slightest danger of suffering a fatal revulsion, since the image of the giant mole, like the village it was sighted in, "has long since sunk back into oblivion." The story develops, instead, as an account of the tortuous dealings of the narrator with the village schoolmaster, who was once important for having written a pamphlet on the incident. The passage in the narrative from the "sensate world" of the mole to a space of speculation on traces left by it in the learned world rehearses a major thrust in the late pieces that might be called Kafka's "Gnostic verve." I capitalize the adjective here because I mean this thrust to resonate with historical Gnosticism. These late stories exhibit the tension of a Gnostic world view, in which the created world consists of debased images of a transcendent source that has nonetheless left lambent traces in the mind.

Kafka's withdrawal from the visible world is vivid in an aphorism written a year before his death:

> The strange, mysterious, perhaps dangerous, perhaps saving comfort that there is in writing: it is a leap out of murderer's row [deed-observation deed observation]; (it is a seeing of what is really taking place). This occurs by a higher type of observation [Beobachtung], a higher, not a keener [schärfer] type, and the higher it is and the less within reach of the "row," the more independent it becomes, the more obedient to its own laws of motion, the more incalculable, the more joyful, the more ascendant its course. (D2 212, GW 11:210)[2]

The point is not a sharper perception of empirical actions and events but another, a "higher" kind of vision. It is learning to see with a view to the "incalculable" fate that catches up the image in another world. Here Kafka is writing not unlike Rilke's Malte Laurids Brigge, who is also "learning to see" — otherwise.[3] This "higher type of observation" appears to be a fascination with the verbal image precisely at the moment that it flies free of the empirical trace image: it is antimetaphorical in its intent. We shall see more clearly by the end of this chapter the kind of observation involved.

The interested reader may remember hearing earlier in segue 2 of this other kind of vision, where it served to illustrate the joy of Kafka's writerly (small-g) gnosticism. But there, in fact, it was explicitly contrasted with the Gnostic fragment that celebrates the wish to die. Here, however, I am saying that it is consonant with historical Gnosticism. How can this difficulty be explained?

The passage in question concerns the consolations of *writing*: it describes the kind of perception that writing provides through a leap into higher and more incalculable zones — and hence, with a "motion" that is freer than doctrine allows. But now I mean it to display a gnostic element in Kafka's writing compatible *from another aspect* with death-minded theological Gnosticism, for this Gnosticism construes death, as Kafka construes writing, as a determined flight from sensuous experience.

Kafka's late poetic gnosticism draws on selective features of the historical Gnosticism he assembled for his use. It is consistent with them but stays this (secular) side of a theology that in its radicalism would, after all, call for the renunciation of any writing whatsoever. Gnosticism does not want "creative" writers; for writing, as Kafka knows, is dependent on "the maid who tends the fire and on the cat warming itself by the stove," dependent on the ordinary fire of the world (D2 200–201). And yet it is through writing, which at times Kafka rates higher than belief — and which, at these moments, *is* belief — that he imagines he can redraw the line between the heavens and the earth.

We have had occasion to cite the aphorism from Kafka's 1917–18 "Reflections on Sin, Suffering, Hope, and the True Way" that can articulate his Gnostic concerns in a way compatible with his late writing. Here Kafka descries another — and altogether more tragic — tendency in his "higher" program of deflecting the empirical image:

> There is nothing besides a spiritual world [geistige Welt]; what we call the world of the senses is the evil in the spiritual world. (DF 39, GW 6:236–37)

The perspective is now that of the bare, thrown human existent and not the writer who writes or does not write. But once assumed, this perspective, which requires one or another sort of death, might fuse with, intensify the higher observation post of writing. In imagining the fate of Josephine the mouse — the whistling artiste — all of whose people are whistlers, Kafka speaks of the "heights of redemption" ("gesteigerte Erlösung") to which, on dying, this artiste-people rises (CS 376, GW 1:294). We have in both instances a fusion of horizons inspired by a single drive: to explode the pseudosolidity of the empirical world, deny its ontic givenness, especially that of its chief representative, the ego. In the late work, this facticity is juxtaposed with the "spiritual world," from which the writer hopes to snatch and focus a few gleams, since "by means of very strong light one can disintegrate the world" (DF 295).

As hard as they are to "understand," Kafka's late stories glint with another light. "Slanting through the words there come vestiges of light" (DF 261), Kafka communicates from a posthumously published fragment. These late pieces are full of delicately staged invocations of "the heavens" — but also mockeries of this passion, viz. "The Bucket Rider" ("Der Kübelreiter") (1917), in which the heavens figure as "a silver shield against anyone who looks for help from it" (CS 412), a delusive glitter with the power to harm.

Kafka's later work requires a metaphysical orientation — one that posits a division between this life and a higher life. "The joys of this life are not this life's joys," he writes, "but our fear of rising up into a higher life; the torments of this life are not this life's torments, but our tormenting of ourselves on account of this fear" (DF

45–46). The positing of the two domains entails a task: to survey the line between them—to think, complicate, and even risk transgressing it. In writing, Kafka will "assault" "the last earthly frontier," press against the divide between the flighty self and what he calls "the heavens," even when the difference between the two is a gulf so deep that it might in the ordinary sense be senseless to imagine this otherworldliness, in whatever form, let alone crossing over to it (D2 203, 233).[4] Kafka, however, insists on this adventure, with a view, above all, to the right customs of approach, the right *practical* logic.

This adventure is the task of writing, which in this sense is a practical enterprise: to force pathways from the empirical self toward the being which Kafka is pleased to call "the pure, the true, and the immutable," viz.

> I can still have passing satisfaction from works like *A Country Doctor*. . . . But happiness only if I can raise the world into the pure, the true, and the immutable [die Welt ins Reine, Wahre, Unveränderliche heben kann]. (D2 187, GW 11:167)

To do so would be to sustain all connections to the other world at the highest tension, by an act of "raising up" that necessarily observes the difference between these orders—a difference that comes to be represented as the difference between the world of the *living* and that of the *unborn* or the *dead*, between the *new* and the *ancient*, between the *filial* and the *patriarchal* (the dead, the ancient, and the patriarchal being possible metaphors of the eternal). It is a matter of inventing rites of intercourse between the daily and the eternal (in its metaphors: the said-to-be-*dead*, said-to-be-*ancient*, said-to-be-*patriarchal*), a series that can be extended to include all those pertinent forms of the not-self that, for Kafka, have a better claim on the infinite and eternal, abysmal and immutable, than the empirical person he is. So add on, from Kafka's standpoint, those figures of other persons to support as representatives of the higher world: the woman, who he is not; the judge of himself, who he is not; the mythic figures from antiquity, like Ulysses and Alexander the Great's war horse Dr. Bucephalus, who he is not.

With a view, then, to clarifying the practical logic of Kafka's life under the spell of writing, a logic informing both the life and the work—both, after all, having something to *do* with the truth—we can take our cue from an early diary entry, in which gnostic and proto-Gnostic elements conspire. Here Kafka declares that his writing has preempted in him all the ordinary joys of life, viz.

> When it became clear in my organism that writing was the most productive direction for my being [meines Wesens] to take, every-

thing rushed in that direction and left empty all those abilities which were directed toward the joys of sex, eating, drinking, philosophical reflection, and above all music. I atrophied in all these directions. . . . My development is now complete and, so far as I can see, there is nothing left to sacrifice. (D1 211, GW 9:264)

Thereafter, Kafka does not think of "real writing" as a type of philosophical reflection; instead, it constitutes "a way," a practical orientation, if indeed a hesitant one, for "there is a goal, but no way; what we call a way is hesitation" (DF 36). Still, it is possible that real writing might point towards the one goal that matters: "to become a good man and answer to the Highest Court." Yet it might also subserve a baser practice — as, "quite to the contrary," it contents itself with a philosophical survey of mankind, striving "to *know* the entire human and animal community, to recognize their fundamental preferences, desires, and moral ideals, to reduce them to simple rules [or laws (Vorschriften)]" (emphasis added). As he wrote to Felice Bauer on September 30/October 1, 1917, this entire effort of culture is undertaken with another view in mind,

> so that this way I should become thoroughly pleasing to all, and, to be sure, (here comes the jump) so pleasing, that, without sacrificing this general love, I might finally, as the sole sinner who will not be roasted, parade the meanness that dwells in me, openly, before all eyes. (translation modified, LF 545, BF 755)

Note that even in the worse case, this human "law," a matter of various requirements (*Vorschriften*), consists of "preferences, desires, and moral ideals" — of what we *want* and *do* and not of what we *know*. There is no mention here of perceptions, discriminations, and judgments, of cultural refinement or *Bildung*, as contributing to one's case at law, whether before the highest court or only that of men, "the court of Man."

This radical position is developed in Kafka's late theological aphorisms, in his "Reflections on Sin, Pain, Hope, and the True Way." It was here that we encountered Kafka's Gnostic view of "the evil of the sensate world." A second aphorism concerns the knowledge of good and evil given with the Fall.

Kafka's reflections on the Fall belong to a Hebrew tradition of biblical commentary and also to a German-language reinterpretation of Scripture that comes to the fore in the periods termed Classicism and Romanticism. This master narrative tells how the acquisition of the knowledge of good and evil spurs human perfection through the continual exercise of reflection and judgment on things good and evil. It is sometimes called the "triadic" view of ethical man and has been associated with Schiller, Hölderlin, Kleist, and Novalis. The narrative describes the passage from an original state of innocence into one of self-reflecting reflection — and hence of division, a sort of evil — en route to a wholeness of being and reflection at a higher synthetic order, to be achieved through a heightening of this very reflectiveness. Kafka's position is, however, the clearest possible *antithetical* position, and it is a good deal more radical than even the demurrer that simply doubts the concept of an "end," of "closure," to such a development. In Kafka's words, "It is only on the far side of this ability and knowledge that the real differences begin" (GrW 298–99).

What distinction is Kafka pointing to? The differences that matter — the "real differences" — lie not between the conceptual work one does and the conceptual work someone else does in producing judgments of an ethical kind (stress on judgments, on sentences, on propositions). The real differences lie between this pervasive and deficiently *conceptual* way of putting to work the knowledge of good and evil and the demand imposed by the acquisition of that knowledge. The first way, the way of experience, accumulates knowledge — perverting the commandment and evading its charge, assembling the images, simulacra, and logical phantasms or connectors Kafka calls "justifications" (*Motivationen*).[5]

So, what is the right response to the demand that comes with the Fall? It is, says Kafka, to *do* what one knows is required, act in the name of the good; for "no one," he continues, "can be satisfied with the mere knowledge of good and evil but must strive to act in accordance with it." An injunction not easy to obey. Once we hear its siren call, Kafka concludes, we will be obliged to destroy ourselves out of the awareness that we do not otherwise have the strength to act in conformity with the knowledge of good and evil.

Let us step back, for a moment, to review the stations of Kafka's itinerary of moral consciousness as they are set down in this aphorism. The first is the difference between conceiving distinctions of principle between good and evil and acting in accordance with the knowledge of these principles. There follows the impossibility of so acting — an awareness that must provoke in us, Kafka says, the decision to destroy ourselves. Finally, however, the strength to destroy ourselves is not given to us any more than the strength to act in accordance with the knowledge of good and evil. One thinks of Joseph K., at the end of *The Trial*:

> K. knew clearly now that it was his duty to seize the knife as it floated from hand to hand above him and plunge it into himself. But he didn't do so; instead he twisted his still-free neck and looked about him. He could not rise entirely to the occasion, he could not

relieve the authorities of all their work; the responsibility for this final failure lay with whoever had denied him the remnant of the strength necessary to do so. (T 230)

Moreover, unlike K., we shrink back from even the effort of conceiving its necessity. And it is this shrinking back that is the actual thrust of what is called aesthetic and intellectual culture, whence Kafka's (Gnostic) account of the work of art: "Our art is a way of being dazzled by truth; the light on the flinching, grimacing face is true, and nothing else" (DF 41). Taking aesthetic pleasure "with the various flourishes I might have talent for, . . . ringing simple, or contrapuntal, or a whole orchestration of changes on my theme," is part of his effort to undo the demand laid on the writer by the knowledge of good and evil (D2 184). "But," Kafka continues,

> what has once happened cannot be undone, it can only be muddied [getrübt werden]. To this end motivations [justifications (Motivationen)] arise. The whole world is full of them, indeed the entire visible world is perhaps nothing more than a motivation of the man or woman who wants to find peace for a moment. This attempt to falsify the fact of knowledge, to turn knowledge into something as outlandish as the goal [erst zum Ziel — the goal yet]. (GrW 299, GW 6:242–43)

The reader may recognize this moment from Nietzsche's *Birth of Tragedy*, where it contests the Socratic-Euripidean goal of wanting to turn everything into "concepts, judgments and inferences," a moment paraphrased by Norman O. Brown as "the great, and really rather insane tradition that the goal of mankind is to become as contemplative as possible."[6] Kafka's Gnostic verve is not, or does not stop at, contemplation. The stake is redemption, which is not an affair, as in the "triadic" scheme, of heightened reflectiveness. It is less Kafka than the German Idealist philosophers, who, in Walter Benjamin's phrase, compose "fairy tales for dialecticians."[7]

We have been examining Kafka's version of an Enlightenment critique. The knowledge of the Fall is ethical, yet not as an effort of interpreting and supplying justifications — the constructions that people invent to account for the way they act or fail to act in alleged ignorance of the law. Knowledge is rightly an affair of feeling the imposition of a command: do the right thing. Yet we are sooner inclined to forget this command or — what is the same thing — to do the work of culture, dream the various and easy dream of keeping the commandment in oblivion. Maurice Blanchot observed that, for Kafka, writing could amount to the promise of salvation as long as "the community was nothing more than a phantom and because the law which still speaks through the community is not even the forgotten law but the feigned forgetting of the law."[8] Culture is a prolonged denial, a slow, eccentric path to self-extinction never properly grasped. Its images, signs, and representations are simulacra in the sense of the excuses Kafka calls "justifications."[9]

So much, for the moment, for the question of the right, the practical logic of exploration of "the higher world," a practice in accordance with "the law" regulating such intercourse.

By what literary means does Kafka experiment with the rule of meta-physical division, the line dividing the physical from the metaphysical world? It will be interesting to observe the patterns of argument through which his late stories conjure — and erase — the impression of transcendent reference.

This process is a paradoxical approach to Being through rhetoric, a procedure implicitly recognized by Theodor Adorno when he noted that the meaning of Kafka lay in the abyss between the literal and the signifying moments of his work, out of which "blinds the glaring ray of fascination."[10]

This process can be identified in two major moments. The first presents this other space-time (the metaphysical or spiritual world) as devoid of morally interesting pathos, feature, or agency; it is unpromising and readily susceptible to negative interpretation, in the register of what is mute, futile, duplicitous, vacuous, and so forth. It can appear as that "everything" of the aphorism that begins "Everything is deception . . ." and concludes that "in every case one betrays the good" (GrW 291). It can appear in a parable, as in the aphorism of the crows: "The crows maintain that a single crow could destroy the heavens. Doubtless that is so, but it proves nothing against the heavens, for the heavens signify simply: The impossibility of crows" (GrW 285). In its more tangible form, this moment appears as the corruption emanating from presumed intercourse with the metaphysical or spiritual world. In "Investigations of a Dog," for example, the seven dancing dogs, who "conjure music from the empty air," seem ridiculous in their nakedness — "indecent," "abominable" (GrW 9, 14–15).

The second moment, often connected to the first, invokes the other world with a positive-seeming aura. That such a moment might be worth looking for up and down the length of Kafka's work is suggested by at least one other passage from "Investigations of a Dog." Here, the narrator, recollecting his researches into dogdom, describes an earlier trancelike moment. As a consequence of prolonged fasting, he has seen and talked to a splendid hunting dog—is it an "angeldog"?—who suddenly begins to sing. The investigator recalls:

Today, of course, I deny all such acquisitions of true experience [Erkenntniße] and attribute them to my excessive sensitivity at the time; but even if it was an error, nonetheless it had a certain magnificence—it is the only, even if merely seeming reality that, during the time I fasted, I rescued and *brought over into this world*; and it shows at least how far we can get when we are completely out of our senses [bei völligem Außer-sich-sein]. (emphasis added, translation modified, CS 314)

Both moments—negative and positive, frustrating and full, the latter even as a magnificent error—are presented through techniques essentially thematic or essentially formal. *Thematic* moments occur when someone in a story, including the narrator, explicitly acknowledges them as belonging to a quest for transcendent experience, as in the case of "Investigations of a Dog" or the aphorism of the crows or, most famously, "A Hunger Artist" (1922).[11] On the other hand, *formal* feints toward transcendence produce an aura of the abysmal by means of the rhetorical or logical negation of a series of conceptually articulated states of affairs. This movement of deconstruction, demythification, or disarticulation may go unreflected by persons in the story but will be perceptible to the reader. We shall examine this moment in such a story as "The [Spinning] Top" (1917–23) and in a late self-reflecting parable "On Parables" (1922–23).

Thematic moments have the logic of evidence that is manifested and then as swiftly disappears. One such movement occurs through the quick, accelerated passage from the private case to the communal, as in "The Village Schoolmaster." The story conjures a vastly idealized picture of community, having an aura of the fabulous and the archaic that functions as an allusion to the transcendent. The old schoolmaster, who has written an account of the sudden appearance of a giant mole in "one of our villages," imagines his pamphlet achieving a giant success through the support of his patron, "a noble protector [who has] risen for us in the city, a fine businessman" (CS 177). The schoolmaster soon sees himself at the center of a procession, accompanied by waving, welcoming, "chirping" crowds, but his vision evaporates: it had the air of a compensatory daydream, though not one that he acknowledges as such. Like "every new discovery, [it] dissolves into the whole [of knowledge] and disappears" (CS 180). The schoolteacher's imagination of community vanishes, but not before inducing in him an obdurate, inexplicable silence, as if it would take an eternity of reflection for him to absorb the shock of its disappearance. The outcome is an abandoned utopia, a virtual fullness never to be encountered here and now. This is a dream-like moment buried in a "thought story," having an archaic analogue in the scene of festival that, according to the officer in "In the Penal Colony," accompanies the illumination of the prisoner being tortured to death, another exemplary bearer of truth. "How we all bathed our cheeks in the radiance of that justice," declares the officer, but that moment, too, is no more (CS 154).

The little story called "A Little Woman" (1923) offers a related moment of totalization that then vanishes, though this total being suggests transcendence not as a festival but as a heightening of the whole of existence into a single negative. The narrator tells how very much a certain little woman is furious with him, so furious that even thoughts of improvement that occur to him seem useless, since the merest suggestion of his readiness to reform will only drive the little woman to new heights of fury. According to the speaker—and we have only his account to go on—there has never been a relationship of any sort between the little woman and himself. Her fury is gratuitous; it is real only as a private construction. Nor is she bent on changing things between them: "She does not care about my development," writes the narrator; "she cares only for her personal interest in the matter, which is to revenge herself for the torments I cause her" (CS 318). And he repeats this point in order to persuade himself that their quarrel does not deserve to be brought before the public.

What is especially striking is the extreme heightening of the stakes of a rather ordinary-seeming quarrel by a process that can be called "ontologization." The psychological aspects of a personal dispute turn into fundamental issues of human being (with its longing for transcendent peace). The change proceeds as the transformation of a quantum—the magnitude of the woman's rage—into a quale—the quality of an eternal imprecation that her rage becomes. All reality is contracted to the space of this tribunal and the time without end in which her charge recurs. The entire detail of life is absorbed into the all-governing principle of the woman's fury and the interminable delay of the crisis, which will never come.

The quarrel is set in a frame of metaphysical, of apocalyptic expectation. In the space of his trial the accused grows old, yet pieces of the situation "were always there from the beginning," in place from the beginning of time (CS 323).

Thoughts about the quarrel advance into an ontological register. The speaker (who is the sufferer) endures the brute, factlike existence of his being hated, which suggests that the whole of his case is only this: a "Being-hated-to-death." The quarrel with the little woman becomes the punishing truth of existence. And then, as swiftly, the quarrel becomes almost nothing at all, for "if I keep my hand over it, even quite lightly, I shall quietly continue my own life, for a long time to come, untroubled by the world, despite all the outbursts of the woman" (CS 324). We are acquainted from "The Village Schoolmaster" with this moment of the vanishing of a heightened world. In "The Little Woman," the story evokes, by means of a double negation, a sweet reclusive peace, in which the sufferer waits patiently for heaven: the abysmal pitch of suffering to which an ordinary life is brought is suddenly negated by a simple gesture of the hand. An absolute is evoked in the mind of a suffering character and then made to fall into oblivion.

Recall, too, "The Village Schoolmaster," where the discussion addressed not the giant mole but the manner in which the alleged sighting of the giant mole had been recorded and circulated and then the airy motives of the discussants themselves. The visible outlines of the giant mole get lost in the story, as Gnostic verve informs it. We noted earlier the same movement at the outset of "Investigations of a Dog," when the object of the investigations (dogdom) turned swiftly into "investigation" as an object of scrutiny in itself. Interpreters, in the poet Hölderlin's words, can also "*fall* upward."[12] Such "skyey," recursive flights that take leave from an initially posited subject matter are one of Kafka's Gnostic signatures.

In other thought stories, aphorisms, and fragments, moments of self-dissolution arise under the pressure of relentless speculation. To the extent that the logic of this train of thought goes unacknowledged by the narrator, they may be termed formal. In "Josephine the Singer," thought projects occur and dissolve: the narrator offers exquisite reflections on the great question of whether or not Josephine actually sings, which, left unanswered, flow into still more exquisite questions on time and death until they too, like Josephine herself, pass into oblivion. As with the "Investigations of a Dog," in the case of the investigations of the mouse people without a history, "Is it not as if nothing at all had happened?" (CS 285). Yet such refined hypothesizing leaves behind the virtual reality of implicit answers, tribute to Kafka's facility in turning apparent fact or proposition into a vacant surmise and then back again into a world absent but felt. As in Wallace Stevens's "The Snow Man," Kafka's narrator, "Nothing himself, beholds / Nothing that is not there and the nothing that is."[13]

The formal device in Kafka's late work most apt to generate the aura of the transcendent (in both positive and negative senses) is a type of deconstructive logic that works through what might be called "chiastic recursion." In such a pattern, each new term, consisting of elements syntactically and conceptually parallel to those of a previous term, arises by means of an inversion of these elements. This strategy of figural transposition gives Kafka the swiftest approach to an other world abysmally open and beckoning. We can observe its workings in the story "The [Spinning] Top."

A philosopher is convinced that mastery of a single event would lead assuredly to mastery of the whole, so he attempts to seize hold of the secret of the top that the children whip into movement. It is his seizing hold that kills the movement. At the close, "the screaming of the children . . . chased him away," whereupon, "he [the philosopher]," writes Kafka, "tottered like a top under a clumsy whip" (CS 444).

The properties of the first-named object (the top) revert to the first-named subject (the philosopher), whereupon a second-order subject comes alive, prompted by "the screaming of the children." This new subject operates a new, figurative whipping, whose object is the former subject, the philosopher. But now that the hare of recursion is running, it cannot be stopped: the movement conjures, in turn, another virtual, higher-order flagellation, in which the new subject, who wields a whip, himself turns into the object of another's frenzy. Of course, this transposition has already occurred—it cannot be missed; for the reader (following Kafka himself) knows the sadistic thrill of identifying the master's hand, Kafka's, in this torture ceremony.[14] It is the author's hand that wields this not so clumsy whip under which the virtual second-order whipper becomes, in turn, the object of his assault. But to what extent can this subjectivity—the author's, the master's—claim to be, unlike the philosopher's, something more than only another stage in the dizzy movement under the whip belonging to an unknown master? Borges wrote:

> God moves the player, he in turn the piece,
> But what god beyond God begins the round,

adding, with a pathos foreign to his precursor:

> Of dust and time and sleep and agonies?[15]

Yes, indeed—and what god beyond the god that starts the round?

Kafka is fertile in such transpositions and recursions. In the story "The Great Wall of China" (1917), a wall is being built to keep out the nomads of the North. The question arises, however: how can a wall afford protection when it is not built continuously? "Indeed, such a wall can not only not protect; it is itself in perpetual danger." For who will protect the protector? And now the clincher:

> These blocks of wall left standing in deserted regions could be easily pulled down again and again by the nomads, especially as these tribes, rendered apprehensive by the building operations, kept changing their encampments with incredible rapidity, like locusts,

and so perhaps had a better general view of the progress of the wall than we, the builders. (CS 236)

The key to the wall is its design. Its design is incomprehensible, except, perhaps, to the nomads whom it exists to ostracize. This fact, taken strongly, means that the builders are dependent on the beings from whom it is their entire purpose to obtain independence. At this point an abysmal paradox opens up.

The deconstructive movement can also advance to the metaphysical moment which, while positive — even alluring — still falls well short of being "redemptive": it is nonetheless marked by features assimilable to doctrine. "On Parables" ("Von den Gleichnißen") (1922–23) begins with the famous complaint about the uselessness of parables. After all, all parables do is allude to "some fabulous Yonder" ("irgend ein sagenhaftes Drüben") but succeed only in saying: the Incomprehensible is incomprehensible.

> Concerning this a man once said: Why such reluctance? If you only followed the parables, you yourself would become parables and with that rid of all your daily cares.
> Another said: I bet that is also a parable.
> The first said: You have won.
> The second said: But unfortunately only in a parabolic sense.
> The first said: No, in reality; in the parabolic sense you have lost.
> (GW 8:131, CS 457)

The argument brings to the fore the recursive moment — the perpetual postponement, in principle, of what seems in every case to be the final claim. Indeed, there is little here to prevent the second speaker — or the reader who speaks in his name — from answering, "I bet that is also a parable." The parable, however, also contains an allusion to a victory of sorts, especially in the redemptive figure posed along the way: the man-become-parable, the body become the paradox of a "truthful" writing.[16]

The conjunction of the recursive parable and a truth achieved by the embodied self is plainest in the aphorism that has guided the entire argument of this chapter — the supreme paradox found in Kafka's last diary entry. It may be grasped as the answer to the question that reads: How does the recursive field of rhetorical deconstruction relate to the writer who, in obedience to the moral law, seeks a truth higher than this field? Answer: He must first wander this field, immerse himself knowingly, unlike his characters, in the formally destructive element, in the experience of recursiveness, in the verbal but not only verbal phenomenon of feints toward an end that, like "justifications," appear to track only the failure to arrive at this end.

Kafka's last diary entry, written on June 12, 1923, reads:

More and more fearful as I write. It is understandable. Every word, twisted in the hands of the spirits—this twist of the hand is their characteristic gesture—becomes a spear turned against the speaker. Most especially a remark like this. And so ad infinitum. The only consolation would be: it happens whether you like or no. And what you like is of infinitesimally little help. More than consolation is: You too have weapons. (D2 233)

The fearful twist of the hand turns a spear against the speaker with the same gesture that informs Kafka's chiastic sentences: they turn back on their thrower, like the seeker of the spinning of the top who, in his failure and his hope, is spun like a top. These sentences tend to produce little parables of nonarrival.

And yet, says Kafka, something happens—"it" happens. What is "it"? It might be "every word," and it might be "infinity"; but neither referent taken alone gives the right force to the pronoun. What happens is *this movement*, which appears at first to be a play of language and logic finishing in the absence of an end. And yet this movement—chiastic and apparently self-cancelling—is, on the strength of another intuition, which Kafka means to place outside this series, an event. The event is the sign that a mark has been hit, that something has taken hold, "whether you like or no." And "what has once happened cannot be undone" (GrW 299).

In another posthumously published aphorism, Kafka wrote of the possibility of an approach to the truth: "Contemplation and activity have their apparent truth; but only the activity radiated by contemplation, or rather, that which returns to it again, is truth" (DF 97). One could adapt this aphorism to speak of the truth of a certain act of writing—the necessity of its recursiveness—as an event "radiated" by the contemplation of it. This event is then necessarily "returned" to (further) contemplation.[17] The existence of at least this one necessity—that recursive writing happens and its recognition happens—rewrites the ground rules of existence. Kafka thinks of the acknowledgment of this necessity as a "weapon." To have this weapon means to write with the strength of the flow between "contemplation" and "activity," contemplation and event.

The consequences of this realization are formidable. An experience of the phenomenon of recursiveness results in an event having practical effect. Consider again the conditions of this happening of truth: first, the setting into play of chiastic reversals; second, a contemplative, will-less attending on the event; finally, the emergence of this recognition with the force of an event. This pattern informs Kafka's late fictions. We can show him miming in language the recursive feints of a move on "the heavens." His words provoke the coming to light of the necessity of their own deflection. But the consciousness of such necessity in and through his fictions, he declares, heightens his power to act, to struggle, giving him something to *do* with the truth. Kafka does the right thing in taunting recursiveness — he writes it into being — and acknowledging its necessity, achieves a power that has something to do with the *truth*.

What is finally so important about this experience of recursion is that it instantiates a going over from the writing self, an intellectual-artistic being, to the practical self bent on justification. This movement responds to the dilemma that haunts all of Kafka's late stories and parables: the problem of justifying a life spent in writing in light of the command to act in accordance with the knowledge of good and evil, a command that Kafka understands as requiring his orientation toward what he calls "the spiritual world." The difficulty might be pictured as follows: Kafka is acquainted with two columns of his personality, the pillar of the constructed artistic self, which, in his view, is as often as not quite splendid; and the pillar of his ethical personality, which lies about him in ruins. The artistic pillar was constructed by the intellect, and the intellect, once stimulated, returns to it and contributes to its building. What delight to be building: how much better than to be supinely, mutely, fearfully lost in the contemplation of one's ruin!

The disturbing surmise, the defeat, however, would be to conclude that the two buildings are forever separate, that no amount of artistic-intellectual construction could ever succeed in erecting a moral personality that is any better proof against judgment than before — a moral being that would "refresh, satisfy, liberate and exalt me" (DF 91–92). In Kafka we see the severest bifurcation of an intellectual-artistic writing self and a moral self tormented by the command that it must destroy itself (for its strength is lacking). Kafka is free of this anguish only when absorbed in the practice of writing — for which he must find a justification.

And so the key question continues to resonate. Could more, or more whole-hearted, artistic experience (experience oriented away from the visible world) constitute a support for his broken, anxious moral self? The answer comes off Kafka's last diary entry: the strength he needs arrives as an event of artistic knowledge going over to the moral personality as a being disposed to write. If this movement could be maintained, it would amount to "more than a consolation," it would supply him weapons suited for "an assault on the last earthly frontier" (D2 202). Interesting for more than our contemporary theoretical concerns (read "deconstruction") is the fact that the measure of this power is its ability to endure the necessity of chiastic recursion.

# Chapter 7

# "A FAITH LIKE A GUILLOTINE"

## KAFKA ON SKEPTICISM

A faith like a guillotine, as heavy, as light . . .
— GW 6:243

KAFKA'S CLAIM TO justification is embattled: he is insomniac in his awareness of the disparity between the truth of a righteous life and his own ineptitude for living it. The question now is whether Kafka was inclined to palliate his consciousness of failure by assuming a skeptical attitude. According to the historian William M. Johnston, "Kafka outdid Marcion by contending that any gospel of hope was merely another delusion invented by an inscrutable demiurge."[1] This claim is more vivid than true.

Ancient skepticism issues into repose; modern skepticism, into a disquiet of mind that prevents it from remembering its origins in tranquility. Modern skepticism, the equivalent of doubt — of mordant doubt, in all things — will have despair as its outcome or, as in the case of Nietzsche, obligatory good cheer, or nothing at all. In the ancient kind, as in Sextus Empiricus's celebrated citation of Pyrrhonism, the outcome of an attitude of skepticism is *ataraxy*, calmness of mind. Sextus Empiricus wrote, "Skepticism is the ability which sets up antitheses among appearances and judgments in any way whatever: by skepticism, on account of the 'equal weight' which characterizes opposing states of affairs and arguments, we arrive first at 'suspension of judgment' and second at 'freedom from disturbance.'"[2] In what follows, as regards Kafka's modern skepticism, I shall frequently be orienting his own reflections toward this ancient model.

Skepticism of the verbal kind strikes an attitude of doubt toward statements that claim positions on difficult matters (let us call such statements "positions"). Skepticism doubts that any single position has the right to occupy such crucial states of affairs, since it knows of other positions with an equal right to do so. It turns states of affairs into open questions, and doubts that a position could be legitimately "staked" or "mapped" onto a question: this is the agnostic geography of skepticism.

With various positions "whirring and buzzing" around such issues as: Is the world intelligible? Can an individual human life be justified? Does art contribute to its justification? — positions eager to colonize these issues in their name — the skeptical mind sees only terra incognita, a reality that offers no purchase to positions.[3] The issue remains unmapped, uncultivated, like those bleak terraces on the island in J. M. Coetzee's novel *Foe*, awaiting the castaway who will bring corn to plant; but meanwhile there is none.[4] More, the skeptic disposition doubts that such an island could ever be mapped or made fertile. How unlike Valéry's Monsieur Teste, the master of certainty who, "knowing himself by heart," his "heart included," declares, "Bah! The whole earth is staked off, all the flags are flying over all territories."[5]

What gives skepticism its bite is its affective side. Not every skepticism matters — not the feeble position without teeth or hands or feet to settle (on) an issue. I said that the special affect of the modern type is despair, though on the example of Nietzsche and Nietzscheans one could also register elation:

> They know that Hamlet and Lear are gay;
> Gaiety transfiguring all that dread.[6]

Paul de Man, writing on literary-critical skepticism, declares that the affective content of a state of "suspended ignorance" is an entirely contingent affair: "The resulting pathos is an anxiety (or bliss, depending on one's momentary mood or individual temperament) of ignorance."[7] But in making room for a contingency of feeling in regard to ignorance, one must make room, too, for an *apathy* that is not "freedom from disturbance" or "calmness of mind" — an unnerving, a debilitating coldness that I count as an affect. De Man's conjuration of strong pathos — "anxiety," "bliss" — may be altogether too vital for modern skepticism, which is after all marked by its detachment from, or resistance to, pathos. It is a skepticism reluctant to admit a pervasive tone, as if, in its radicalness, it would itself refuse to be the matter that can be occupied by a position or saturated by an affect.

Especially in his *Diary* entries at the time of writing *The Trial*, Kafka excoriated his own "coldness of heart," his "monotonous, empty, mad, bachelor's life," bounded by a deeper constraint — "the last boundary": "apathy, . . . that forever comes back and forever has to be put down again" (D2 79, 98, 92). Supposing that the intellectual correlative of this affect is skepticism (I continue to call such "apathy" an affect), we could proceed to isolate and analyze this attitude in Kafka.

Despite Kafka's coldness of heart, pieces of Sextus's classic take on skepticism enter into Kafka's "aesthetics of skepticism," formulated exquisitely in the wish on Laurentian Hill (Laurenziberg), the "green hills" of "The Judgment," which is found in his diary entry of February 15, 1920. It begins:

> This is the problem: many years ago I sat one day, in a sad enough mood, on the slopes of the Laurenziberg. I went over the wishes that I wanted to realize in life. I found that the most important or the most delightful was the wish to attain a view of life (and—this was necessarily bound up with it—to convince others of it in writing), in which life, while still retaining its natural full-bodied rise and fall, would simultaneously be recognized no less clearly as a nothing, a dream, a dim hovering. (GrW 267–68)

The reclusive mood of the opening, attuned to delight, suggests the nascent aesthetic. As a "view" attuned by delight, it resembles the aesthetic proper. Finally, with the "writing" of a view attuned by delight, it *is* the aesthetic triumphant.

The life "retaining its natural full-bodied rise and fall" that figures in this view alludes to Sextus Empiricus's rising and falling components of "equal weight"; this equilibrium is counterbalanced in turn in being recognized "as a nothing, a dream, a dim hovering." The opposition is explicit: the "rise and fall" of life contrasts with its "hovering"; its "full-bodied" character contrasts with "Nothing." Here one could think of Sextus Empiricus's "opposing states of affairs and arguments" duly characterized by "equal weight." From Kafka's wishful staging of elements from the teaching of Sextus Empiricus, an aesthetics of skepticism arises. But Kafka's persona has failed to wish this beautiful wish rightly, and so we may now expect the collapse of a perfect "suspension of judgment" into—not "freedom from disturbance" but "disturbance."

The passage reads:

> A beautiful wish, perhaps, if I had wished it rightly. Considered as a wish, somewhat as if one were to hammer together a table with painful and methodical technical efficiency, and simultaneously do nothing at all, and not in such a way that people could say, "Hammering a table together is nothing to him," but rather: "Hammering a table together is really hammering a table together to him, but at the same time it is nothing," whereby certainly the hammering would have become still bolder, still surer, still more real and, if you will, still more senseless. (GrW 267–68, GW 11:179–80)

"Considered as a wish . . .": this is the Muirs' translation, but Kafka's construction is more complex. What Kafka writes is "Etwa als Wunsch einen Tisch mit peinlich ordentlicher Handwerksmäßigkeit zusammenzuhämmern," leaving undecided whether he is addressing the manner in which the wish ought to be wished and hence the manner in which the aesthetic *view* is to come about; or the manner in which the *object* of the wish, the aesthetic object (which happens to be the manufacture of a table) ought to come about.[8] In other words, it is uncertain whether Kafka is thinking of a manner of writing in general or the manner in which some particular construction might be produced, like the story, for example, "The City Coat of Arms" — or like the Tower of Babel, which figures as a construction within "The City Coat of Arms" (DF 103, GW 6:220). This leaves undecided whether or not, in this entire Laurenziberg fable, the table that is to be hammered together looks back to the properly wished-for view of life or forward to the properly depicted object of the wished-for view — namely, life "with its natural full-bodied rise and fall" (that is at the same time "a nothing, a dream, a dim hovering"). But this undecidedness is not itself nothing; it is precisely such creative destruction that supports the skeptic stance.

Kafka's figure for the act of wishing, viewing, or building truthfully is striking. A certain nothing, a senselessness, acts as a goad to the hammering together of a wish or a table and in no way undermines — indeed it even heightens — a boldness of activity. Even with the threat posed by the conditional "if"-sentence, the passage produces an impression of equilibrium. The difference between the act ("really hammering a table together") and the state ("it is nothing to him") survives as a balance of equal and opposing weights.

Kafka's word for this hammering is *kühn* (bold); and one could think of Nietzsche, who philosophizes with a hammer, and of the figure of Nietzsche behind Thomas Mann's Lever*kühn*, the artist whose frenzied musical hammering together is also stimulated by deep draughts of nothing. One thinks of Nietzsche especially when the qualifier *kühn* is taken together with other qualifiers describing the artist's activity — "sure" (*entschlossen*, better: "determined") and "senseless" (*irrsinning*, better: "insane"). I include Mann's Nietzsche to highlight the recognizable high modernism of Kafka's construction: a boldness and decisiveness of artistic purpose, aiming at a totality, verging on madness, and spurred by (a glimpse of) nothingness.[9] The outcome of a properly wished wish or a properly wished-for table-manufacture is, for Kafka, a bold, decisive, real, mad, *freedom* of activity (recall Sextus Empiricus's "freedom from disturbance," with which Kafka's terms share something).

I continue to emphasize the point that the text constructs a balanced ambiguity in the figure of the hammered-together table (that is also a nothing for the artist). Does the hammering relate to the proper manner of wishing to write or the proper manner of constituting the object of that writing, life with its full-bodied rise and fall that is at the same time a nothing, a dream, a dim hovering? The ambiguity is sustained by a pervasive structural parallel. In both the wish-work and the life that it has in view, we find the antithesis of a certain nothing and a bold something. In the case of the life, it is something "full-bodied," and in the case of the wish-work something "boldly, really, surely, madly" realized, with both objects — life and the table, whose manufacture is the goal of the wish — being shaped by a rhythmic internal opposition: the rise and fall of life, the rise and fall of the artisan's hammer. It would be wrong to deny a categorical difference between the two. Life proceeds "naturally" whereas the hammering proceeds with "painful and methodical technical efficiency": everything about the first suggests (to speak good Hölderlinean) the boldness of Nature, and everything about the second suggests the boldness of Art; but then again that is how both live and move according to their being.[10] So to wish rightly is to wish with the "authenticity" of one's being; the rightly wished view of life assures that the life thus perceived will be authentic. Or at least be spared the onus that Kafka elsewhere attaches to "constructions" ("Konstruktionen"), glimpsed "whitely [hence: anemic, unbold] merging in a corner."[11]

## A Prospect at Midpoint

Read in a totalizing way, the form of the wish displays qualities of the worldview that the wish means to attain as its content (as something bold and simultaneously nothing at all). This reading fuses together both subjective and objective senses of the "wish." But one can also stress the distinction between them, reading the "full-bodied rise and fall" of life as the manifest content masking the latent content of the wish — which remains, irreducibly, a certain manner of wishing (read: a certain manner of writing). Finally, according to a third way of reading, it is this writing itself that acquires an absolute distinction apart from any kind of writing that might correspond to the being or making of the object it has in view. Here, "writing" means the gerund of the intransitive verb "to write" — writing as a state of being, for which Kafka has the word *Schriftstellersein*.

This moving quadrilateral of nature/nothing; construction/nothing in the field of writing is Kafka's signature of what I am calling an aesthetics of skepticism. It would come about in Kafka's writing through the semblance of representing — with maximum technical efficiency — a subject matter that displays — with a maximum of naturalness — a rise and dying fall (that is at the same time a nothing, a dream, a dim hovering). It is a high modern aesthetic, and in its elementary structure, a brother of Nietzsche's tragic aesthetic of the resuscitated Dionysian, with the sharpest agonistic dimension subtracted. No doubt it remains discussable whether, without the agonistic side, the co-presence of the components of life and nothing and hammering and the dream and a natural rise and fall can qualify this aesthetics as Dionysian after Nietzsche. But this consideration finally, and significantly, falls away because, in Kafka's fable, a Euripidean affect of irony, an impotence of social origin, comes at the end to disrupt this aesthetic from its basis in the strong wish, in the strong thrust of fiction. The passage concludes:

> But he could not wish in this fashion; for his wish was not a wish, but only a vindication of nothingness, a justification of non-entity [better: a granting to Nothing of protection and dwelling rights (eine Verteidigung, eine Verbürgerlichung des Nichts)], a touch of animation [better: an air of gaiety (ein Hauch von Munterkeit)], which he wanted to lend to non-entity [Nothing (das Nichts)], in which at that time he had scarcely taken his first few conscious steps, but which he already felt as his element.[12] It was a sort of farewell that he took from the illusive world of youth; although youth had never directly deceived him, but only caused him to be deceived by the utterances of all the authorities he had around him. So is explained the necessity of his "wish." (GrW 267–68, GW 11:179–80)

I will say one more word about the constructive and destructive sides of the aesthetics of skepticism and the social origin of the poorly wished wish.

Bernd Hüppauf has written suggestively of an aesthetics of skepticism as an "aesthetics of destruction."[13] His work leads directly to the aphorism that Kafka composed apropos of Abraham's call to sacrifice his son Isaac:

> There is an enchantment accompanying his argument of the case. One can escape from an argument into the world of magic, from an enchantment into logic, but both simultaneously are crushing [erdrückend], all the more since they constitute a third entity, a living magic or a destruction of the world that is not destructive but constructive. (DF 103, GW 6:220)

For an "escape from an argument," recall the enchanting view of life that, dreamlike, "still retains its natural full-bodied rise and fall." For an escape from enchantment into logic, recall the "painful and methodical technical efficiency" of a proper wishing or writing. These moments, taken together in an aesthetics of skepticism, summon "a living magic" and are "crushing" — i.e., radiate conviction, brook no resistance, "work." The destructive moment is sublated. I am stressing the constructive side

of Kafka's "aesthetics of skepticism" that connects it to Sextus Empiricus.

But such an aestheticism, as we have seen, remains in the end a wish-
dream for Kafka. The collapse of the Laurenziberg-fable in the wish
improperly wished comes as Kafka's fall into the order of lament that
he addressed to that authority, his father:

> My writing was all about you: all I did there, after all, was to
> bemoan what I could not bemoan upon your breast. It was an
> intentionally long-drawn-out leave-taking from you, only although
> it was brought about by force on your part, it did take its course in
> the direction determined by me. (DF 177)

The course taken by "me" can have been distorted in advance by the
force of the originary impulse supplied by another, one of the authorities Kafka "had around him" in his youth. That force is crushing. At
the times when he attempted to recruit his father's approval for his
writing, he must have conceived the energy at the origin as indispensable for his purposes.

Kafka's complaint of having wished his wish improperly marks a shift
from the aesthetic into the moral register. The fable registers the origin
of the moral enterprise in the consciousness of the original sin of believing that an original sin had been committed against oneself—by "authorities," necessarily, since that is how "authorities" become what they
are.[14] Here, the fable has descended into the inferior domain of what
Kafka has elsewhere called "justifications"—a manufacture of alibis, a
reasoning that one hopes can obliterate the consciousness of having
failed to do the right thing. Recall the discussion in chapter 6 of the
aphorism beginning: "Since the Fall we have been essentially equal in
our capacity to recognize good and evil" (GrW 298). In its drastic
plainness, the complaint against the authorities reads like a parody of
this second fall into alibis.

In the Laurenziberg fable the aesthetic register gives way to that of
the Euripidean social-ethical; the authority cited at the close is that of
the family, and the aesthetics of the family is a contradiction in terms.
Recall, too, Kafka's sense of family language in the diary entry of March
24, 1912: "In the next room they are talking about vermin" (D1 258).
That is quite a different story from inventing Gregor Samsa. Consider,
further, this aphorism: "Puny life-force, misleading education, and
bachelorhood produce the skeptic, though not necessarily; in order to
salvage skepticism, many a skeptic marries, at least the idea thereof
[ideel], and becomes a believer" (DF 251, H 282). Here skepticism
slides into "self-consciousness" but because of the affective dimension is
more—and worse—than that. J. M. Coetzee points up this complaint

as a tradition: "The metaphor of self-consciousness as a disease is a commonplace in Europe by the 1860s. 'Self-contemplation . . . is infallibly the symptom of disease,' wrote Thomas Carlyle in 1831; only when 'the fever of Skepticism' is burned out will there be 'clearness, health.' "[15]

I cannot say the *one* single thing that this last socializing of skepticism means because of its exquisite glide from real marriage to a being wedded to the idea of its failure. What is still clear is that the point of marrying is not to "salvage" the groom from skepticism but to "salvage" skepticism itself — "at least the idea thereof."[16] The groom manages to preserve his skepticism, dogmatically; it may not have been necessary for him to remain a skeptic, but he is nonetheless trumped by the family-self even as he thinks he has trumped it in "salvaging" skepticism.

This concept of "salvaging" has the same function as does "believing" in an aphorism commented on by Michael Wood: "Think of Kafka's [sentence] 'To believe in progress is not to believe that progress has already occurred. That wouldn't be a belief.' This looks like a simple reminder about the meaning of words, but it is has the unnerving effect of making belief seem like an advanced form of doubt, so advanced that we can only deny it."[17]

Both aphorisms, especially the one ending in marriage, resituate Kafka's skepticism in the field of moral action, where its outcome is not repose but *Angst* — a fever forever underfoot.[18] In the beginning it seemed as if *Angst* could be employed by an aesthetics of skepticism and would in this sense be "practical": in 1910, at the age of 27, Kafka explained to Max Brod apropos of his writing that "Keeping hard on my own heels still is a joy that warms me . . . for it stirs in me that general excitement [better: disquiet (Unruhe)] that produces the only possible equilibrium" (L 70, Br 86). The same thought is evoked some twelve years later in the great diary entry of January 16, 1922, in which Kafka speaks of "an assault on the frontier" between man and the inhuman:

> There are doubtless several reasons for the wild tempo of the inner process; the most obvious one is introspection, which will suffer no idea to sink tranquilly to rest but must pursue [emporjagt] each one into consciousness, only itself to become an idea, in turn to be pursued [weiter gejagt] by renewed introspection. . . .
>
> This pursuit [Jagen], originating in the midst of men, carries one in a direction away from them. The solitude that for the most part has been forced on me, in part voluntarily sought by me — but what was this if not compulsion too? — is now losing all its ambiguity and approaches its denouement. Where is it leading? The strongest likelihood is, that it may lead to madness; there is nothing more to

say, the pursuit [Jagd] goes right through me and rends me asunder. Or I can—can I?—manage to keep my feet somewhat and be carried along in the wild pursuit. Where, then, shall I be brought? "Pursuit," indeed, is only a metaphor. I can also say, "assault on the last earthly frontier," an assault, moreover, launched from below, from mankind, and since this too is a metaphor, I can replace it by the metaphor of an assault from above, aimed at me from above. . . . All such writing is an assault on the frontiers. (D2 202, GW 11:198–99)

The restless pursuit of one idea by another is driven by the motor of an active skepticism. This pursuit, "originating in the midst of men," carries one in a direction away from them." Here we see Kafka backing out of the ethical sphere and turning toward something else, toward what we recognize at the close as art and rhetoric, with the same wild commotion. For all their turbulence, these flights might nonetheless "carry him along." The idea is to be borne along in the chase, as Kafka here envisions an imaginative triumph.

Later that year, however, Kafka would write to Max Brod that the price of this equilibrium (does it exist?) is devil's work and murders sleep. Writing, we recall, is "the reward for serving the devil," service that "take[s] place in the nether parts which the higher parts no longer know, when one writes one's stories in the sunshine. Perhaps there are other forms of writing, but I know only this kind; at night, when fear [Angst] keeps me from sleeping" (L 333–34, Br 384). Here, angst and art are incompatible or compatible only at the cost of life; hence, they cannot support a rational ethics. The putative "living magic" of the aesthetic only smuggles away the anxiety of skepticism in social practice, "in the midst of men"; the aesthetic is literally a mask, "a way of being dazzled by truth" (DF 41).

We have arrived once again at the central focus in Kafka's life and work: the disturbing sense of the tenuousness of aesthetic activity wielded by whatever sort of instrument. Kafka's great aphorism on Pascal goes directly to the point. This diary entry for August 2, 1917, reads:

Pascal arranges everything very tidily before God makes his appearance, but there must be a deeper, uneasier skepticism than that of a man cutting himself to bits with—indeed—wonderful knives, but still, with the calm of a butcher? Whence this calm? the confidence with which the knife is wielded? Is God a theatrical triumphal chariot that (granted the toil and despair of the stagehands) is hauled onto the stage from afar by ropes? (D2 173)[19]

This is a grand allusion to the scene of "redeemed" Greek tragedy, helping to highlight contrastively the finality of tragedy and the eternal indeterminacy of skepticism. And the grounds for this? The structural point, at least according to Nietzsche, is that tragedy couples Dionysian boldness with Apollinian illusion in order to make the dominant Dionysian visible. The bold, real, senseless Dionysian *appears*, as in a dream. Yet final redemption—reconciliation, the cessation of strife, the renewal of human life—can be produced only by a deus ex machina. This is utterly unlike that "deeper, uneasier" skepticism, in which the Dionysian and Apollinian are equipollently joined but neither is dominant, so that all life under its sway remains suspended. It is on the one hand the condition of an aesthetics of skepticism, on the model of the Laurenziberg daydream; on the other hand, it is rigor mortis. Neither condition suggests a renewal of ethical life.

It is striking that Kafka's "discourse" on skepticism, in the Pascalian scenario above, again involves metallic killing engines: we have had, in passing, the guillotine, the hammer, and now, knives; and I shall allude to spears or skewers in Kafka's final diary entry at the close.[20] This is to suggest the murderous stakes of this discourse.

Kafka's little essay on Pascal is plainly conscious of classic skepticism, connecting the terms argument, aesthetic performance, and calm—and finding them false. Pascal aestheticizes skepticism with "wonderful" arguments that have a calm about them, while Kafka's skepticism is driven by a deeper anxiety, which no amount of metallic incising can quiet. "A man cutting himself to bits with—indeed—wonderful knives" repeats perfectly the imagery of self-(over)writing in "In the Penal Colony." A truer anxiety, a deeper skepticism, cannot be lived: there is no living "delight" in being unable to hold fast to something—to believe. " 'It is not a bleak wall,' " Kafka writes, in a fictive dialogue,

> it is the very sweetest life that has been compressed into a wall, raisins upon raisins." — "I don't believe it." — "Taste it." — "I cannot raise my hand for unbelief." — "I shall put the grape into your mouth." — "I cannot taste it for unbelief." — "Then sink into the ground!" — "Did I not say that faced with the bleakness of this wall one must sink into the ground?" (DF 297)

"Man cannot live without a permanent trust in something indestructible in himself," Kafka writes, "though"—and here is the anti-Pascalian qualification—"both the indestructible element and the trust may remain permanently hidden from him," nothing like "a theatrical triumphal chariot . . . hauled onto the stage from afar by ropes" (DF 39, D2 173). The grounds for trust are given; but that is too little for that lawyer for incredulity, the psychological self. There is no good counsel there; it is apt to elaborate alibis against spiritual work as stupid as a poverty of life-force and faulty education and the doxa of authorities at home.

Which leaves Kafka at the famous juncture that can be put this way: "it is *not* only as an aesthetic phenomenon that existence and the world are eternally justified."[21]

For the late Kafka of Gnostic leanings, it is not "the world" that in its root is in need of justification. The world is already justified, for, as the familiar aphorism has it, "There is nothing besides a spiritual world" (DF 39). Kafka's moral skepticism goes rather to our absorption in "our present sinful state": "How much more oppressive [bedrückend] than the most inexorable conviction of our present sinful state is even the weakest conviction of the coming eternal justification of our temporality. Only strength in the endurance of this second conviction, which in its purity entirely comprehends the first, is the measure of faith" (DF 46, GW 6:208).

Contrary to expectation, it is now this irrefutable "measure of faith" and not our present misery that "in its purity" is "oppressive," even "crushing" ("bedrückend"). One could think of Rilke's angel: "and even if one of them pressed me / suddenly against his heart: I would be consumed / in that overwhelming existence."[22] It is easier to "embrace" skepticism, to suffer the negative, than to endure the certain prospect of justification.[23] Here, the fact that the finite personality Kafka is unable to realize the task of belief is less strongly marked than the knowledge that the right thing to do is real, readable, and a terrible burden. At this point, during the writing of the Zürau aphorisms entitled by Max Brod "Reflections on Sin, Suffering, Hope, and the True Way" (1917–18), Kafka's conviction of both the necessity and the unendurable burden of hope and belief is at its strongest. The (im)moral skepticism induced by a present "sinful" state of affairs could never produce, meanwhile, the "calm" of "a cessation of wind" ("einer Windstille") (GW 6:207). What is more enticing—and, indeed, more crushing—is the fact that "theoretically there is a perfect possibility of happiness: believing in the indestructible element in oneself and not striving towards it" (DF 41). But there is little suggestion that such happiness is meant for him.

For Kafka the salvaging of the world in the Nietzschean sense is not a thing that his or any art might accomplish: it is rare that he wanders along this edge, and when he does so, it is in the optative. He wrote, in a diary entry for September 25, 1917, "I can still have passing satisfaction from works like *A Country Doctor*. . . . But happiness only if I can raise [heben] the world into the pure, the true, and the immutable."

(Note, in "raising," the necessity of striving.) The latter qualities are not, by any stretch, the attributes of Nietzsche's world.

The value of Kafka's art, once it has been detached from its root in an aesthetics of skepticism, is not irrefutably great. But this does not preclude Kafka's subtler claim that its value is not irrefutably small. Writing at the limit might engender "consolation," and even "more than consolation" — it might engender "weapons"; one could say: weapons against moral skepticism (D2 233, GW 11:236). Writing towards the limit appears to support the moral struggle. Kafka, then, is clearly not a moral skeptic in the sense of doubting the possibility, as Bernd Hüppauf puts it, of living "a life in pursuit of the moral good."[24] His life as an artist, however, as it has been actually lived, is a matter of skepticism toward the question of whether that life could satisfy the chief desideratum: "to become," as we have read, "a good man and answer to the Highest Court." For in his hands writing might also be a baser thing as, "quite to the contrary," it strives "to know the entire human and animal community," an enormous-sounding conceptual effort yet not innocent of a craving for justification for small stakes, since it is done, Kafka continues, "so that this way I should become thoroughly pleasing to all, . . . so pleasing, that, without sacrificing this general love, I might finally . . . parade the meanness that dwells in me, openly, before all eyes" (LF 545 [translation modified], BF 755).

Note the conjunction of two terms belonging to the practice of writing: art gives pleasure — it is an aesthetic practice — that is old — and it displays a certain "meanness," too — that is new. That writing, in giving pleasure, might attract love is not an obscure idea; in *Père Goriot*, Balzac, for one, remarks that "love is perhaps simply gratitude for pleasure."[25] That an aesthetic display could amount to a "parading of meanness," however, calls for some reflection.

This argument appears to build on the equation of "aesthetic display" and "self-display." An aesthetic display is an exhibition of a self in pursuit of gratification; it is, according to Freud, a kind of daydreaming in public. The Laurenziberg fable verges on such dreaming, on "vanity" ("Eitelkeit") and "sensuality" (the craving for pleasure [Genußsucht]) (Br 385). This would be to wish the wish improperly. Is this true of any aesthetic display of which Kafka might be capable? This will forever be the key question. "What is essential to life is only to forego complacency," he wrote to Max Brod, "to move into the house instead of admiring it and hanging garlands around it" ("statt es zu bewundern und bekränzen") (L 334, Br 385).

Kafka suspected moral skepticism of being no more than the alibi of a certain self, the family self, from which he had always sought to take leave. But in taking leave of it, for writing, he was not certain that he had landed in a truthful place:

> The existence of a writer is an argument against the existence of the soul, for the soul has obviously taken flight from the real ego, but not improved itself, only become a writer. Is it possible that separation from the ego can so weaken the soul? (L 334)

and here what is meant, surely, is the ego as it might have constituted itself in family action of its own. The letter continues, however, with this important proviso: "I don't dare let this stand. Put this way it is also wrong" (L 334).

Consider the various aspects of Kafka's uncertainty on this point: they have a recurrent structure. His aperçu concerns the strengthening of the soul; the conclusion speaks of its being ruined for having been separated from the ego. The optimal relation would then appear to be a sort of staying at home of the soul in the domains of the real ego — the ego of family, food, sex, music, and philosophy. If there is still a notion of writing alive here, it is as one that also stayed at home in the domains of the ego and thrived there. But this idea sounds outlandish and calls for revision. So now the question is: what prompts so inglorious a surmise?

It is prompted by suffering. One should not forget the costs of provisioning the journey of the soul that has "taken leave" of the ego — a killing anxiety arising not so much from "shaking off" the real ego but its rebellion: the ego will no longer tolerate being discarded for the sake of the self alleged to be higher, "the writer in me." It makes itself felt *as* the nullity it has been forced to become.

And how, then, to keep it quiet, while it is being abandoned? It must be duped, it must be appeased. It could be appeased by feeding it the social reward of its exclusion — specifically, the love of women (for women cannot resist loving the martyr of art, the ascetic priest) and the fame conferred by princes (the reward of "recognition" for one's "cultural" achievement). In Kafka's ideolect this becomes the display by which, as a writer, he should become pleasing to all while parading his meanness before all eyes.

This must not be the case. The ego must suffer — for its own good, of course — which means: its moral justification. It must suffer at the hands of the real writer even when the ascetic path of real writing can seem a ruse and a delusion. And it could not fail to seem so. If the existence of the writer is conceived as a salvaging of the empirical self, how much, finally, could its achievements matter? On the one hand, the (derelict) empirical ego is glad to cast its fate with the pure self, the writing agency. But if the degree of wholeheartedness required for this surrender is perfect, then precisely its measure of success — the distance opened between the empirical self and its transcendental mutation — leaves the empirical self behind. So how can acts accomplished by the writing self, whose existence is based on the abandonment of the empirical self, count toward its "ensouling"? Can we be saved by what we do in our sleep or when our ghost wanders abroad?

This argument, too, must not stand. Kafka has a rebuttal ready, in principle, to prove it wrong. Imagine contracting to nothing the "distance" between the real empirical ego and the transcendental writing self — the distance Kafka calls "separation from the ego." This distance can be figured as zero when it is cast as the precondition of an impersonal art. The empirical self disappears into the higher self: the ego loses itself in the writer where the soul is joined to it. Think again of Stephen Dedalus's account of "the personality of artist" that "finally refines itself out of existence, impersonalizes itself, so to speak."[26] Joyce's "self-refinement" forecasts Kafka's "self-consumption." The goal is not now the ego's salvation but its ecstatic submission to this movement for the sake of its truth — "a higher type of observation" evoked with the predicates "pure, truthful, immutable" (D2 212, 187). To the degree that the movement is impersonal, to the degree that its intention is pure, it could contribute — an "intensified soul" — to Kafka's justification, for "the spirit becomes free only when it ceases to be a support" (DF 42). Kafka will take up such a logic of sacrifice in his final diary entry, with its spears and skewers that have something to *do* with the truth. But the point would seem to require that all calculations be let go and that writing be reckless.

The point about abandoning calculation is nicely illustrated in a comment made by Erich Heller about the manuscript of *The Castle*, a work composed in 1922, less than a year before Kafka's final diary entry of June 12, 1923. Heller notes that Kafka deleted a number of coldly calculating passages from the manuscript as not in keeping with "the muted meaning of the book," for they are too explicit in indicting K. They would leave nothing, not even a suspicion, of the intensity of his inwardness, which seems damnably muted throughout. One such passage, Heller explains, is contained in

the protocol about . . . [K.'s] life in the village which Momus has drawn up, and in which K. is accused of having made up to Frieda out of a "calculation of the lowest sort": because he believed that in her he would win a mistress of Klamm's and so possess "a pledge for which he can demand the highest price." On the margin of the protocol there was also "a childishly scrawled drawing, a man with a girl in his arms. The girl's face was buried in the man's chest, but the man, who was much the taller, was looking over the girl's shoulders at a sheet of paper he had in his hands and on which he was joyfully inscribing some figures."[27]

The exemplary final diary entry I am about to address has nothing of this: it is the very antipode of calculation and also of the struggle to purify the self of the spirit of calculation. It begins by identifying the resistance of the "spirits," who "twist" the writer's every word; their gesture is inescapable. Yet the faithful meditation on such a movement — "Every word, twisted in the hands of the spirits — this twist of the hand is their characteristic gesture — becomes a spear turned against the speaker" — might constitute a "way," a "practice," in line with the Gnostic ethic that entertains as positive the destruction of the world as given. This complex is further hinted at in a late fragment from Kafka's Notebook "H": " — If I seek in his runes / To fathom the theater of change / Word and weight . . ." (GW 6:225). But we need not go only to the end of Kafka's life to find the balance mooted.

These runes could also frame the earliest extant piece of Kafka's writing. In 1897, at the age of fourteen, he wrote lines in a poetry album belonging to his friend Hugo Bergmann: "There is a coming and a going / A parting and often no — meeting again" ("Es gibt ein Kommen und ein Gehn / Ein Scheiden und oft kein — Wiedersehn") (BrM 380). The vision of an immense coming into being and of an equally potent vanishing accompanied Kafka throughout his life. It is his great and central experience: an abundance of creative things rising up in him and this same abundance of creative things vanishing away — a marked experience of creation and destruction, so that the category of "a destruction that is not destructive but constructive" would repeatedly occur to him (DF 103).[28] Kafka made this point directly in an aphorism: "The world can be regarded as good only from the place from which it was created, for only there was it said: And behold, it was good — and only from there can it be condemned and destroyed" (DF 95). Remarkably, this standard translation does not quote the sentence fragment with which the aphorism concludes: "If I want, therefore, to enter into a correct relation with it . . ." (GW 6:210). But "it," surely, means "writing": the relation adduced here is the basis of an act of writing.[29] His sense of this movement appears to be the injunction to act accordingly, to incorporate this movement. Kafka, writing, enacts such a privileged moment — the glimpse of creative abundance, of "the tremendous world [die ungeheure Welt] I have in my head" (D1 288), and then of its strong dissolution, followed by a glimpse of the sense of what has happened. Such representations recur throughout Kafka's work both thematically and formally in structures I have called "chiastic" and "recursive." The constructive moment consists in his standing firm and registering his annihilation by reading destruction as a sort of rhetorical deconstruction. The inner affinity of this structure with that of an aesthetics of skepticism is apparent.

It is true that Kafka took a dim view of artistic "truth": "Our art is a way of being dazzled by truth." But, especially in his final aphorism, "truth" might be a matter of grasping and acknowledging a certain sort of destruction in writing, a frenzy of deconstruction. In registering degrees of annihilation — "the spear turned against the speaker," the threat poised against the mask of art — the possibility appears of an opening out to the light, discernible not only to another's eyes (the mask cannot see the light that glances off it) but discernible to the speaker; for "slanting through the words there come vestiges of light" ("Quer durch die Worte kommen Reste von Licht") (DF 261, H 293). Here, the tension is plainest in Kafka between an "aesthetics of skepticism" as a moral force and an "immoralism of skepticism" — "immoralism," since, as Kafka alleges in the theological aphorisms, there are none but contingent, empirical grounds for unbelief.[30]

Believing in the necessity of a movement of world assertion (the fiction) and world extinction (its deconstruction) becomes a weapon of sorts ("You too have weapons") in the struggle for ethical justification. Here we glimpse an aesthetics of skepticism en route to an ethics through a mimesis of being and its vanishing. Kafka puts chiastic recursion in play, in a kind of skepticism that has not yet definitively lost its balance, or a sort of belief that has no footing except in the inevitability of recursion.

A final question needs to be asked: in what way might this aesthetic of a higher mimesis — the rhythmic dawning and vanishing of a constellation of the mind — represent an advance on the aesthetic of Laurenziberg by assisting the "real ego" in its moral struggle? The difference is present in the agonistic dimension of a skepsis that, in the act of writing, grasps itself as a weapon against the annihilating "spirits." These are the inhuman, noncontingent adversaries that a false consciousness once attempted to socialize as "the authorities." They are better seen as a riot of Gnostic devils, owners of "the false hands that reach out to one in the midst of writing."[31]

This entire argument aims at a blunt conclusion: Kafka is not a skeptic in moral matters. We have seen that on occasion he is uncertain of his ability to believe and repeatedly uncertain of his ability to act on his belief. This would mean to live and above all to write with an unheard of degree of wholeheartedness, rigor, and crystalline awareness. But his claim that, as a finite individual, he is unable to realize the task — of doing the right thing — is inferior to the claim that the right thing to do is real, transparent, and an authentic burden. In this sense Kafka is not a moral skeptic. In this sense, too, he must pursue an unanxious aesthetics of skepticism.

*Chapter 8*

---

# KAFKA AND THE DIALECT

# OF MINOR LITERATURE

> In one's own language, however, were one only to say
> something as exactly and as uncompromisingly as possible,
> one might also hope through such relentless effort to
> become understandable as well.
> —Theodor Adorno, *"On the Question: 'What is German?'"*

THE IMMEDIATE THRUST of this chapter and the next, unlike the preceding chapters, is social and political. Both chapters deal with the categories of social being that are held to embed literature—linguistic capital and ecommodity capital, respectively. And both chapters conclude by subordinating the political, agonistic component of Kafka's thought to a philosophy of writing as gnostic ecstasy.

They proceed by addressing two of the most influential politically minded essays written on Kafka during the last half century. The first is Gilles Deleuze and Félix Guattari's *Kafka: Toward a Minor Literature* (*Kafka: Pour une littérature mineure*), 1975; the second, in the chapter that follows, is Theodor Adorno's essay "Notes on Kafka" ("Aufzeichnungen zu Kafka"), 1953.[1] Both essays present us with Kafka as an anticapitalist resister. The special target of Deleuze and Guattari's Kafka is capitalist literature; the special target of Adorno's Kafka, the culture of disintegrating commodities under monopolistic capitalism. This perspective on Kafka, in claiming centrality for itself, deserves to be resisted.

We begin with Deleuze and Guattari. The phrase in my title "the dialect of minor literature," which alludes to their work, is meant to convey two things at once. It refers, first of all, to the mistaken idea that Kafka wrote in a dialect called "Prague German"; and, second, to the mistaken idea that in doing so, he intended to contribute to the construction of a "minor literature" rebelliously aimed at a "major" or master literature.

The claim that Kafka wrote in dialect has recently been advanced by Joachim Neugroschel in the introduction to his new translations of Kafka's stories:

Kafka's oeuvre has now become a monument to Prague German, which, like so many dialects and regional variants of German, was liquidated along with the Fascist era.[2]

For this argument to work, one has to ignore the most immediately transparent sense of the phrase "Prague German" — the fearsome jargon spoken by Prague Czech-speaking butchers and scullion maids in conversation with their generally more affluent German-speaking customers and employers. In Kafka's case, therefore, the "Prague German" he allegedly wrote has got to mean something else — it has to mean the German that Kafka spoke and therefore presumably wrote, because he did not write downward into dialect.

This claim, however — even if there were some original minor language called "Prague German" that Kafka spoke — is dubious, first, on general conceptual grounds; it relies on a dogmatic notion of style as a quasi-biological fact, à la early Barthes — as if Kafka, being a Prague German(-Jew), could not but speak the language of others and, furthermore, did indeed write in the language he spoke. The most striking feature of Kafka's prose, however, as the linguist Marek Nekula observes, is its "*range* of regional, phonic, morphological and syntactical as well as lexical characteristics," the outcome of a series of choices driven by "Kafka's conscious (self-) stylization" (emphasis added).[3] Second, the Prague German that Kafka presumably *spoke* was only a faintly dialectical coloration of High German, audible as a regional sociolect but certainly not the distinctive language of a people. Max Brod, a trustworthy authority in such matters, reports that Kafka, along with almost all Germans in Prague, strove not to be recognized as speakers and especially as writers of Prague German of whatever description: "The German of the Prague German-speaker was distinctive only for its somewhat harsh accent; on the other hand, we were extremely careful not to let locally-conditioned deviations get into the written language."[4]

Whatever Brod's and Kafka's intention, some of these "locally-conditioned deviations," it is true, have surfaced in Kafka's manuscripts and even in his published works. When, for example, Gregor Samsa interprets his metamorphosis into a giant vermin as a sign of the onset of a cold, Kafka writes the word "Verkühlung" for "cold" — both in the manuscript and in the published text — whereas the more nearly standard German word is "Erkältung" (GW 1:97). But "Verkühlung" is Austrian and not unique to Prague, as are such locutions as "Kasten" for "Schrank" (cupboard) and "Kanapee" for "Sofa" (GW 1:95, 116). In the uncorrected manuscript of *The Trial*, Kafka writes the Austrian "nachtmahlen" for "Abendessen einnehmen" (have supper) and the more nearly Prague "trotzdem" for "obwohl" (although);[5] but, gener-

ally speaking, the line between such Prague locutions and the same locutions in Austria and so-called Upper Germany (Bavaria, Swabia, etc.)
is invisible.[6] In any case, the list of such possible Prague variants is small
and carries no discernable semantic weight: Kafka agreed with Brod
that they should not appear in his published texts. The manuscripts that
display such variants should therefore perhaps not be described as a
"monument" to a lost dialect, as Neugroschel has it, since Kafka was at
work destroying this monument — let alone as verbal atoms of revolutionary potential, as Deleuze and Guattari will argue.

Meanwhile, Kafka's relation to the *literary* German of Prague authors
is another matter — one of considerable interest, especially as it might be
contrasted with the work, for example, of Rilke, Brod, and Werfel.
Kafka's reaction points chiefly to his discreet repugnance with regard to
its perfumed literariness. Kafka had an entirely different idea of what he
called, appreciatively, "the most individual High German," which, as it
happens, he distinguished precisely from "dialect." (He thought them
both sources of liveliness as compared with the jejune middle ground of
daily spoken German ["nothing but embers"].) But, though he might
have considered his own work a derivative of "mauscheln" — German
spoken with a Yiddish flair, a "fine . . . , organic compound of bookish
German and pantomime" — he meant this grimly pejorative word to describe his literary language in an only ironic and elliptical way, as taken
only in the broadest sense of the phrase ("im weitesten Sinn genom-
men") (L 288, Br 336–37). Kafka's relation to Yiddish literature, a literature that he could read but not write, is another story altogether — one
now being studied by many scholars.[7] In no plausible way, though, did
Kafka consider his work to have been written in dialect.

The phrase "the dialect of minor literature" also alludes to another
sense of "dialect" — a certain theory-dialect or discursive type as it is
found in Deleuze and Guattari's popular *Kafka: Toward a Minor Literature*. By claiming that Kafka wrote in the distinctive dialect of turn-of-
the-century Prague, they mean to provide him with the linguistic vehicle
of a so-called minor literature and hence with revolutionary authority.
In their view, Kafka's literary German figures as a kind of polemical
ideolect aimed against high German literature — the literary language of
Greater Germany (*Großdeutschland*). Kafka's work, they claim, is informed by the pathos of political defiance, and this claim is implied
whenever it is said that Kafka meant to contribute to a so-called minor
literature. But this thesis is aberrant because what, after all, is this subversive Prague German literature that Kafka wrote? Deleuze and Guattari offer no philological descriptors at all.

Despite its inaccuracy, Deleuze and Guattari's view of Kafka as an
author working within the constraints of a minor literature has now

located Kafka exemplarily within a certain dialect — or, perhaps, pidgin — of critical theorizing. This is a political criticism empowering the literature of small nations, a literature said to be exemplary of strategies for exploding power at the underside. The thesis has found a home primarily in and around postcolonial studies, but it has also impacted Kafka studies as well, since, according to Deleuze and Guattari, Kafka's work constructs "linguistic Third World zones by which a language can escape" (DG 27). Deleuze and Guattari's eponymous figure of the "anti-Oedipus" also belongs to this claim of the political efficacy of the literature of small nations — a claim in which Kafka turns out, somewhat surprisingly, to figure as the primal anti-Oedipus.

This reading of Kafka as a local revolutionary figures further in the larger event of self-reflection taking place in Central and Eastern Europe since the 1990s, where critics and writers have been displaying an acute awareness of the long suppressed factor of national identity. What was at first a backlash against Soviet-Communist domination is now a backlash against American-spurred globalization. After decades of prohibition, East European writers are bent on defining their sense of national and ethnic specificity — as, for example, in Prague and Vilnius and Kiev; this is true, too, of cultural Croatians, Romanians, Estonians in and outside their homeland. I am alluding here to the phenomenon that Professor Timothy Reiss has called "falling back into the local."[8]

In this context, the retranslation and reinterpretation of Kafka's own stories and novels have acquired a special significance. Consider, for example, the project of Kafka's Czech translators in the light of Václav Havel's allusions to Kafka as the inspiration for a necessary, an authenticating anxiety-in-government. The ongoing Central and Eastern European use of Kafka aims chiefly to open a source of political and polemical impulses heightening the self-consciousness of peoples living on the margin of great powers. In all this, another sort of reading of Kafka is implicitly taking place. For when Central and Eastern European intellectuals address questions of ethnic or national identity, they are commenting willy-nilly on Kafka's now famous essay on the literature of small nations. This essay — a five-page diary entry written in 1911 — also occupies a central position in Deleuze and Guattari's account of Kafka's own work as the project of someone writing within the boundaries of a minor literature.[9] Both inside and outside Central and Eastern European countries, it is used to justify the claim that ethnic and linguistic difference can *as such* resist hegemonic powers, institutions, and discourses.

I said at the outset that I have little sympathy with much of the use made of Kafka's work in the critical dialect of so-called minor literature. But before saying what might be wrong about such applications —

this reaching out to and totalizing *a postmodern literature and politics as such* from points allegedly made by Kafka about minor literature—it will be important to get hold of Kafka's views as he states them. This will not be easy, since this essay too is a sort of prose poem written by Franz Kafka. I am concerned chiefly with highlighting difficulties in the way of its most immediate political appropriation.

The diary entry composed on December 25, 1911, opens by declaring that "many of the benefits of literary activity [. . .] can be produced *even by* a literature whose development is not in actual fact *unusually broad in scope*" (my emphasis). This, we can say, is a minor literature. What minor literature does Kafka actually have in mind? He gives the examples in 1911 of contemporary Yiddish literature in Warsaw—or as much as he knows about it from Löwy, one of the actors appearing in Yiddish plays in Prague that year—as well as "contemporary Czech literature," as he has experienced it. I stress: typical minor literatures for Kafka are Yiddish and Czech—and certainly not, pace Deleuze and Guattari, the literature written in the German of Prague authors, through which Kafka intends to make a unique contribution to world literature as one whose very essence is literature (Kafka wrote: "Not a bent for writing, my dearest Felice, not a bent, but my entire self" [LF 309]).

The benefits of literary activity are significant even when that literature is minor. Kafka's essay begins with an engaging list of its advantages, put together anarchically, like the Chinese taxonomy of animals quoted from Borges by Foucault at the beginning of *The Order of Things*.[10] Literature, for Kafka, "stirs minds [bewegt die Geister] and brings about the unity and solidarity [das einheitliche Zusammenhalten] of national consciousness, which, in social life, is often inactive and [whether active or not] is forever disintegrating there" (D1 191, GW 9:243). Literature could therefore never reflect or contain—it would more nearly constitute—a national consciousness always in the process of dissolving outside its frame. From this constitution arises "the pride and support that the nation gains for itself in the face of a hostile environment" (D1 191, GW 9:243). Literary production could therefore be likened to "keeping a diary by a nation—something entirely different from historiography," because this diary keeping amounts to a "detailed spiritualization" ("detaillierte Vergeistichung" [*sic*]) of the broad scope of public life.[11] (The orthographical slip—the loss of the "l" from "Vergeistlichung"—is bemusing; it releases a *Stich*, the stab of a knife, the sting of an insect, the pang of a pain—the stroke of a pen; and just some eighteen months before, Kafka had begun keeping *his* diary in order to strengthen his hurt pride, as a blocked writer, in the "face of a hostile environment.") The process of diary keeping, however, is crucial,

for by means of it "dissatisfied elements are assimilated and immediately become useful, since it is only the slack tolerance [Lässigkeit] of
them that can do harm" (D1 192, GW 9:243). This is literary idealism
in the service of national unity, and at this moment Kafka does not
sound very different from a Dilthey writing in Germany around 1867.[12]

The view, I might point out, is expressly opposed to that of another
rigorous Gnostic writer; Herman Melville, who notes in *Billy Budd* of
"such events [as mutiny]": they "cannot be ignored, but there is a con-
siderate way of historically treating them. If a well-constituted individual refrains from blazoning aught amiss or calamitous in his family, a
nation in the like circumstance may without reproach be equally discreet."[13] Not so for Kafka, who will pay more than lip service to this
view a year later in writing about the metamorphosis of a Prague textile
salesman into a giant dung beetle, which, as he himself noted, did
blazon abroad things more than a little amiss in the family apartment.[14]

What is at stake in the domestic as well as the national sphere is the
redemption of dissonance ("die Bindung unzufriedener Elemente"), occurring through "a continual articulation of a people with respect to its
experience." In this development "the incessant bustle of the literary
magazines plays a key role." Here Kafka's focus appears to be slipping
onto the German-speaking Prague scene, with its literary journals and
cafés, displaying the fact that the focus throughout this essay is unde-
cidably *bi*nocular. Kafka is, after all, dealing with *literature* as such and
also even and especially *the literature of small nations*. But we should
be clear on this point: if Kafka shifts focus to the literary production of
Prague authors writing in German, he does so because their work comes
under the head of *literature*. The shift is not evidence that Kafka construes his own literary work in German as the literature *of a small nation* of Jewish Prague writers minded to revolt against writing in the
German of Goethe and his acolytes (thus Deleuze and Guattari).

The list of literary benefits continues unexpectedly. Literature brings
about a "narrowing down of the attention of a nation upon itself [auf
ihren eigenen Kreis] and the acceptance of what is foreign only in reflection [in der Spiegelung]." Literature is, therefore, *as such* less a medium
for preserving foreign differences than for producing unity, solidarity,
and the assimilation of the foreign within an intimate circle, mirror, or
hearth. This point will irritate, of course, any generally postmodern assimilation of this essay to a brief for literature's principled generosity to
alien differences, negation of its own thing, breakup of the illusion of
intimacy, and so forth.

Literature induces crucial changes in the subjective consciousness of
family members: it marks "the birth of a respect for persons active in
literature" and brings about

the transitory awakening in the younger generation of higher aspirations, which nevertheless leaves its permanent mark. Furthermore, it produces the acknowledgment of literary events as objects
of political concern, the dignification of the antithesis between fathers and sons and the possibility of discussing this; the presentation of national faults in a manner that is especially painful, to be
sure, but also liberating and deserving of forgiveness;[15] and the beginning of a lively and therefore self-respecting book trade and the
eagerness for books.

Kafka now sounds as if he is telling the story of his own literary beginnings.

The above list mingles benefits from various spheres: nationalist ideology; aesthetic education; the economics of art, such as the book trade;
and generational struggles. Benefits accrue at different levels. One bo-
nus — nothing less than a total unification of national consciousness —
mingles with a homelier one: a nicer sort of quarreling between father
and son. Under the influence of literature you will no longer find a
father saying to his son, around the dinner table, "I'll tear you apart
like a fish!" (thus Hermann Kafka of Prague).[16] Perhaps.

This mixing of benefits at different levels could be explained from the
different impulses of the writer Kafka at work on this extended diary
entry. One could see him here jotting things down rapidly for a future
tract on literature and especially small literature — an essay that will be
correctly worked out only when its general program has been confirmed
or been adjusted by Kafka's own literary production. (Deleuze and
Guattari interpret this jotting as if it had already been saturated with
such a future literary experience and hence as Kafka's official poetics,
omitting reflection on the time gap; it was written months before he had
even written "The Judgment.") On the other hand, the disparities of
register in Kafka's list of literary benefits could point to the spontaneity,
swiftness, and gaiety of its composition. The essay on minor literature
would then have been written by Kafka not as a writer solemnly projecting in outline his future work but as one gaily and slyly crafting a
piece of his work as the writing of a single night and day. The essay is
(1) a Christmas caprice — it was composed half on Christmas and half
on Boxing Day; (2) a gift to Löwy, the Yiddish actor, and to Mrs.
Tchissik, the Yiddish actress, with whom Kafka had fallen in love the
previous month (D1 139); and (3) a celebration in advance of the joys
of nativity of the writer he was about to become. Nine months later, in
the early morning of September 23, 1912, Kafka would complete "The
Judgment" — his breakthrough — in a single sitting.

There is evidence of high spirits. The definition of a minor literature as one "whose development is not in actual fact unusually broad in scope" is incomplete, for Kafka adds, "but [whose development] *seems* to be [broad in scope] *because it lacks outstanding talents*" (my emphasis, D1 192, GW 9:244). Stop and consider: Yiddish literature in Warsaw is, according to Kafka, an instance of a literature without major talents, one exemplarily not dominated by a single major talent, the struggle with which might conceivably define its whole future direction. In other words, Yiddish literature does not have its Goethe, does not live in the shadow of a single indomitable father talent (not even Mendele).

Of the mighty figure of Goethe Kafka writes in his journal in the midst of composing this entry:

> Goethe probably retards the development of the German language by the force of his writing. Even though prose style has often traveled away from him in the interim, still, in the end, as at present, it returns to him with strengthened yearning and even adopts obsolete idioms found in Goethe but otherwise without any particular connection with him, in order to rejoice in the *completeness of its unlimited dependence.* (my emphasis, D1 197, GW 9:247)

Such a power, semidivine, of the single instance is a crucial mark of the major literature. Quite otherwise minor literature — or . . . ?

When I discussed this point with the Professor of Slavic Literatures at the University of Tel Aviv, he looked at me curiously. Modern Yiddish literature — i.e., Yiddish literature — was without its great precursor? Quite the contrary, he said. For whereas German writers had to contend (only) with Goethe, Yiddish writers had to contend with God: did Kafka mean to suggest that Goethe was a greater writer than God?

This perspective, I might note, would make God — leaving aside all questions of proportion — at least a writer; and sometimes Kafka indeed appears to think so, as when he writes, "God doesn't want me to write — but I, I must" (L 10); and, indirectly, too, when he remarks that nothing can compare with the conclusion of Flaubert's *L'education sentimentale* except the conclusion of the Fifth Book of Moses, for both works record the failure of a man to arrive at his goal — Frédéric Moreau and Moses too, "not because his life was too short but because it was a human life" (D2 196, GW 11:190).[17] If my colleague's objection is true, it would be a mark of the irrefragable irony of Kafka's program.

The benefits of literary work are mixed — and by no means easily assimilated in a contemporary climate favoring the fragmentation of integral personality, the radical entitlement of what is left, and the cultivation of difference. We say it is an altogether worthy enterprise *to understand difference* however hard — an understanding not easily achieved and certainly not by means of such intellectual labor-saving devices (following Walter Benjamin) as empathy (*Einfühlung*) or being in accord (*Einverständnis*) but rather through an obsessional immersion (*Versenkung*) into otherness with all holds barred. This being the case, what are we to make of minor literature's facility in reflecting what is different only in its own mirror? This point will make it impossible, I believe, to grant minor literature, according to Kafka, a subversive prestige vis-à-vis major literature.

We read on, stressing, again according to Kafka, the absence of a dominant talent in minor literature and, as a consequence, its compensatory strength or what he calls its "liveliness" (*Lebhaftigkeit*). The word belongs importantly to his poetics.

> The liveliness of such a literature exceeds even that of one rich in talent, for, as it has no writer whose great gifts could silence at least the majority of cavillers, literary competition on the greatest scale has a real justification. A literature not broken into [von keiner Begabung durchbrochen, i.e., ohne Durchbruch, "breakthrough"] by a great talent has, therefore, no gap through which the irrelevant or indifferent might force its way. (D1 192, GW 9:244)

It has no room for diatribe or aping.

Kafka's fine insight points up the negativity—the gap—that is the flip side of every genius's breakthrough in a literary tradition, though it did not stop Kafka from courting nine months later a breakthrough of his own. It creates an entrance for indifferent talents, whose task will be to dispute with and, equally, to imitate uselessly or complete speciously the work of that genius. Let us agree that Kafka's essay is here at its least Bloomian and most anti-Oedipal and hence most Deleuzian and Guattarian.

The claim to attention of the specifically small literature now becomes more compelling. In it the independence of the individual writer—within national boundaries—is better preserved. The lack of irresistible national models keeps out writers without genuine talent—polemical types inspired by *ressentiment*. Equally, however, there appears to be a danger associated with writing within a minor literature that arises despite its democracy of talent (in minor literatures, remember, no writers are completely untalented and none are extravagantly talented). Kafka conjures the temptation of exotic influence (the "exotic" and "influence" are the same thing). This is the risk of being "influenced by the indistinct qualities of the fashionable writers of the moment, or of introducing the works of foreign literatures, or of imitating the foreign literature that has already been introduced." It appears to be less a temptation for writers in a major literature; "this is plain," writes

Kafka, "in a literature rich in great talents, such as German [. . .], where the worst writers limit their imitation to what they find at home." The difference between minor and major literature cannot yet be made to support a distinction of greater authenticity if this means resistance to influence.

The fact that some writers have little talent, whether in a minor or a major literature, does not affect the degree of their mimetic desire for the exotic of the moment—fashion—or the exotic from abroad. Even without extreme talents (including extremely weak talents), a minor literature suffers this influence, which has nothing to do with genius. Kafka does not say what the root of this susceptibility is: it is very likely an aspect of character—of an assimilationist bent. If this text were about Kafka, it could identify something like the temptation of "Zionism" that was to interfere with his elaboration of "a new secret doctrine, a Kabbalah" (D2 203).[18]

Kafka forces his way past this present difficulty of making a value distinction by turning to the past—to tradition.

> The force [. . .] of a literature poor in its component parts proves especially effective when it begins to create a literary history out of the records of its dead writers. These writers' undeniable influence, past and present, becomes so matter-of-fact that it can take the place of their writings. One speaks of the latter [their writings] and means the former [their influence], indeed, one even reads [their writings] and sees only [their influence]. But since that influence cannot be forgotten, and since the writings themselves do not act independently upon the memory, there is no forgetting and no remembering again. Literary history offers an unchangeable, dependable whole [einen Block] that is hardly affected by the taste of the day.

The literary history of small nations is a "whole" because it exhibits no hysteresis between two histories: between the popular consciousness of a writer's work—a kind of sediment of the history of its reception—and an actual knowledge of it—the inner history of the work studied. Gerald Bruns writes appositely: Words in literature "echo or resonate with their historicality, that is, [. . .] are expressive or reflective of their contexts"; even more, they "situate you in their historicality in the sense of exposing you to it, placing you under its claims. . . ."[19] Agreed, the manufacture of literary history in small nations does not follow a model guaranteeing good results either as history or as textual knowledge—and hence is not exemplary. Still the beautiful outcome, however illusory, is that literary history becomes the sacramental time of small nations. This view, too, will not be attractive to the postmodern interest in revising canons, and indeed it has its down side for Kafka as well: congregational bias. Observe the fall.

> A small nation's memory is not smaller than the memory of a large one and so can process [verarbeiten] the existing material more thoroughly. There are, to be sure, fewer experts in literary history employed, but literature is less a concern of literary history than of the people; and thus, if not purely, it is at least reliably preserved. For the claims that the national consciousness of a small people makes on the individual is such that everyone must always be prepared to know that part of the literature which comes down to him, to support it, to defend it — to defend it even if he does not know it and support it.

High spirits, gaiety, irony!

> The old writings acquire a multiplicity of interpretations; despite the mediocre material, this goes on with an energy that is restrained only by the fear that one may too easily exhaust them [an ecological reverence hard to find in the postmodern scene], and by the reverence they are accorded by common consent. Everything is done very honestly, only within a bias that is never resolved [. . .], and is broadcast for miles around when a skillful hand is lifted up. But in the end bias interferes not only with a broad view [Ausblick] but with a close insight [Einblick] as well.

"So that" — concludes Kafka — "all these observations are cancelled out"[!].
Finally,

> since people [of small nations] lack a sense of context, their literary activities are out of context too. (They depreciate something in order to be able to look down upon it from above, or they praise it to the skies in order to have a place up there beside it. Wrong.) Even though something is often thought through calmly, one still does not reach the boundary where it connects up with similar things, one reaches soonest the boundary with politics, indeed, one even strives to see it before it is there, and often sees this limiting boundary everywhere. The narrowness of the field, the concern too for simplicity and uniformity, and, finally, the consideration that the inner independence of the literature makes the external connection with politics harmless, result in the dissemination of literature throughout a country on the basis of its clinging to political slogans [sich an den politischen Schlagworten festhält].

"Festhalten" ("clinging") is also the word Kafka uses to describe in 1912 the relation of Gregor Samsa, the transmogrified salesman, to his fetish—the glass-encased woman in furs whom he once pinned up on his bedroom wall. The gesture suggests the most primitive attempt at covering up a loss of authority, of holding on to the rhetoric of lost identity.

In wanting to celebrate this aspect of minor literature—its ineluctably, instantaneously political character—Deleuze and Guattari are required to leave out these last sentences, for they damage their valorization of minor literature on radical grounds. These sentences say that *the literature of small nations disseminates itself by means of clinging to political slogans.* Kafka concludes:

> There is [in minor literature] universal delight in the literary treatment of petty themes whose scope is not permitted to exceed the capacity of small enthusiasms and which are sustained by their polemical prospects and resources. Insults, given literary treatment, roll back and forth; in circles of writers with a great deal of temperament, they fairly fly. What in great literatures goes on down below, constituting a not indispensable cellar of the structure, here takes place in the full light of day, what is there a matter of passing interest for a few, here absorbs everyone not less than as a matter of life and death. (D1 194, GW 9:250)

I want to stress now Deleuze and Guattari's use—not reading—of this essay, their misprision of Kafka's already quite idiosyncratic and varied views on minor literature, and shall proceed by way of personal experience. Some time ago, in Philadelphia, I lectured to an audience on Kafka's aphorisms, analyzing the shapes of their chiasmi and double helixes. The subject matter was formal, the question period, however, unexpectedly substantial. I was immediately asked, in the spirit of a small nation, for additional information about the character and personality of Kafka—for example, had he played basketball? I replied, no; although he was quite tall (six feet) and supple from exercise and, furthermore, in a remote sense, Czech, living in Prague, he was not a Croatian: it is Dalmatian Croatia that has produced excellent basketball players. This prompted an elderly woman, tired of those fumbling German translations, to ask, "Well then, can you tell us what Kafka is like in the original Czech?"

This question could have been prompted by her reading of Deleuze and Guattari. Their appropriation of Kafka's essay begins: "The problem of expression is staked out by Kafka not in an abstract and universal fashion but in relation to those literatures that are considered minor, for example the Jewish literature of Warsaw and Prague." Note: "the

Jewish literature of Prague." This is entirely Deleuze and Guattari's invention! In his own essay, of course, Kafka literally wrote "Czech literature," something of which he was not a part. These critics continue: "A minor literature doesn't come from a minor language [but of course it does, for Kafka: it comes from Yiddish and from Czech]; it is rather that which a minority constructs within a major language" (DG 16). This last point would have come as a great surprise to Kafka—that throughout his life he was at work constructing a Jewish Prague literature, meaning to do so by heightening the idiomatic disparities of Prague German. Deleuze and Guattari assert this thesis via a claim for the dignity of writing in a minor language. "Using the path that Yiddish opens up to him"—Yiddish, according to Deleuze and Guattari, being "intermixed with the German language in Czechoslovakia [*sic*]" (DG 20)—"Kafka takes it in such a way as to convert it into a unique and solitary form of writing" (DG 25). But this idea, even apart from the absurd implication that the German Kafka spoke in the office and café was "intermixed" with Yiddish, will not do, for it leaves out too baldly the elected influences of Goethe, Hegel, and Nietzsche, not to mention Kafka's "blood relations" Kleist, Grillparzer, Dostoevsky, and Flaubert in developing the "uniqueness and solitude" of Kafka's writing. And even if, in Deleuze and Guattari's sense, "unique and solitary," Kafka's writing would have amounted to a minor literature of one. In the end Deleuze and Guattari substitute the powers of dialect for what in Kafka are more truly the powers of dialectic—and here point up the decline, in their hands, of Benjamin's concept of the dialectical image.

The theory of the dialectical image, a moment of explosive historical meaning, is spelled out in *The Arcades Project (Passagenwerk)*, where Benjamin writes:

> It is not that what is past casts its light on what is present, or what is present its light on what is past; rather, image is that wherein what has been comes together [zusammentritt] in a flash with the now to form a constellation. In other words, image is dialectics at a standstill. For while the relation of the present to the past is purely temporal, the relation of what-has-been to the now is dialectical; not temporal in nature [Verlauf] but figural [bildlich]. . . . The image that is read—which is to say, the image in the now of its recognizability—bears to the highest degree the imprint of the perilous critical moment on which all reading is founded.[20]

This concept, nourished by Benjamin's understanding of Kafka, has been narrowed, especially under the impact of views on the national revolutions of the 1990s, into an idea of determinative dialect, into the idea of the gesture that resists a dominant political and linguistic power by means of dialect. An ideological image of the dialect undeservedly called "historical" replaces the idea of the dialectical image. This idea is then turned back onto Kafka with the purpose of coloring him as a Yiddish-Czech political dissident—qualities that are then said to reemerge in his work written in German—and stripping him of the universality that an allegedly lazy tradition of criticism has ascribed to him.

Is the concrete universality of the dialectical image to be found in its local color? I think not. What is truly dialectical in Kafka, as Benjamin suggests, is his *destruction* of metaphors and of the given image. Kafka's "images" are not properly images—they are not positives. Rather, they are negatives: they are the fission products of the destruction (metamorphosis, deconstruction) of the imagery of standard metaphors. Kafka's explosion of the image suggests the force contained as a history of repressions in each such figurative nucleus. This is quite in line with Benjamin's own perspective, for Kafka's tropes are dialectical in the Benjaminian sense of continually liberating the repressed implications of dead metaphors. This procedure does not require dialect to be carried through.[21]

Deleuze and Guattari confuse an automatic potential in Prague German—as idiom or dialect—with Kafka's *own* German. Kafka wrote, "As soon as a man comes along who has something primitive about him, so that he does not say: One must take the world as it is [. . .], but who says: However the world is, I shall stay with my original nature, which I am not about to change to suit what the world regards as good; the moment this word is pronounced, a metamorphosis takes place in the whole of existence" (L 203). (There is in Deleuze and Guattari no such category of "original nature.") It is important to note that the word stubbornly pronounced does not have to come from dialect (L 277).

Deleuze and Guattari enthusiastically politicize literature. But it is not so much that Kafka's work, being, allegedly, minor literature, permits of this appropriation as that Deleuze and Guattari are themselves writing in the *ideolect* of minor literature, politicizing wherever they go. This is a feature of life in a minor literature, but it is not true that Kafka's essay defends it.

Deleuze and Guattari deny, in Kafka's name, the subjective aspirations of individuals. Kafka says exactly the opposite: minor literature encourages "the independence of the individual writer" (D1 192).

I conclude: On the strength of Kafka's views on minor literature, no argument can be made for the politicization of literature—for justifying its polemical use in heightening the adversarial consciousness of being minor and marginal with respect to a major language or literature. It is true that literature, for Kafka, "brings about the unity and solidarity of

national consciousness [. . .]," whence there arises "the pride and support which the nation gains for itself in the face of a hostile environment" (D1 191, GW 9:243). But at what cost to its quality! "There is
[in minor literature] universal delight in the literary treatment of petty
themes whose scope is not permitted to exceed the capacity of small
enthusiasms and which are sustained by their polemical prospects and
resources" (D1 194, GW 9:250). Kafka does not teach you that a consciousness of ethnic or dialect-ical peculiarity increases your chances of
building escape routes, across a sense of oppression, from a hegemonic
literature, let alone exploding its authority.

Reading Deleuze/Guattari on Kafka suggests that you can read in order to formulate political slogans—that might be useful. Or you can
prefer to close-read texts. That might have only the slightest of political
effects yet still produce a sense of power, in the way, say, that reading
Kafka or a critic like Benjamin reading Kafka gives you a sense of
power. But it is wrong to say that the closely read text gives authority to
political slogans.

Kafka's relation to the traditions of his literary community is no different in principle from that of other German and European writers
who turned for inspiration to non-European sources (thus Goethe to
Persian poetry, Schopenhauer to Sanskrit literature, Yeats and Brecht to
No, Pound to Chinese ideograms). This field covers Kafka's increasing
sensitivity to the themes of Jewish mysticism and the argumentative gestures of Talmud, as these come to him through Yiddish literature from
the East, as well as his attraction to Lao-Tzu.[22]

In general, his relation to his literary past is marked neither by anxiety nor querulousness—nor of excessive playfulness. He is, in the first
instance, prone to be awed by a consciousness of the specialness of his
gift. "The tremendous world that I have in my head. But how free myself and free it without being torn to pieces."[23] He describes a persona
of himself: "All that he does seems to him, it is true, extraordinarily
new, but also, because of the incredible spate of new things, extraordinarily amateurish . . ." (GrW 263–64). Kafka is eager to discover in
other writers comparable passions; he searches not so much for mastery
and guidance as something sharable in them, upon which his own
nightmares can be reflected. He is strengthened by the consciousness
that others have suffered even more than he for the same great cause. It
is wonderful when another's strangeness can be less strange than he is
to himself. The danger is not so much that other writers prove more
massively truthful than he as that they might be trivial, bad, or irrelevant—and he is once again condemned to selfhood. He is less bent on
fighting off the supposed knowledge that the great hold on humanity of
canonical writers excludes him—robs him of his right to "settle"—than

he is anxious to greet the spirit of other writers to whom he might raise a flag, like Robinson, considering them terra firma and in principle a harbor for his wandering bark. The claim of Deleuze and Guattari that Kafka is a deterritorializer of the territorializations of the cultural masters who oppress him flows from a contemporary paranoia insensitive to the finer shades of Kafka's literary schizophrenia, which is to say, to the "monstrosity" he called literature.[24]

# Chapter 9

## ADORNO'S "NOTES ON KAFKA"

### A CRITICAL RECONSTRUCTION

Den visionären Blick habe ich nur bei Blitzlicht.
(It's the flash that gives me that visionary look.)

I BEGIN WITH a precis of my argument about Theodor Adorno's essay "Notes on Kafka" ("Aufzeichnungen zu Kafka") that should suggest why I must address it.[1] Adorno's Kafka espouses, theologically speaking, a Gnosticism *without relief*; in fact, Kafka saw remnants of light come "slanting through the words." Adorno ignores Kafka's intermittent yet felt, redemptive immersion in the act of writing (DF 261), claiming, instead, to uncover in Kafka's work a prime "inverse-theological" fable—a Marxian-Freudian story that tells of the collaboration of bourgeois commodity culture in its own extinction under fascism. Although Adorno pleads for a nonallegorical, a *literal* reading of Kafka's stories, he in fact proceeds allusively, by fits and starts, to "mortify" the text to fit his fable. The outcome is that Kafka's texts are seen as offering a form of socially redemptive resistance. But if they amount to an index of the falsity of Kafka's time and place (in Adorno's *Aesthetic Theory*, to a moment of truth), it remains hard to see how this moment of insight could be recovered, since, for Adorno, the benighted bourgeois reader has been "unable to find a successor"—and we are all bourgeois (260). In general, the question of how Kafka's texts, embedded as they are in the falsity of their historical moment, may be said to convey insight remains notably obscure. My sense is that this shortcoming is founded on Adorno's own devotion to a hieratic, exclusionary style, poised to warn the reader: "Understand me at your own risk!" One is then dismayed to discover one's failure, even as a bourgeois, to have qualified as an exception.

Adorno's essay is foremost an event of style; hence, the style of any critique that claims to do justice to it calls for critique in its own right. Thinking of Kafka's request to Max Brod to have his writings destroyed, Adorno remarks that Kafka had a horror of being copied, since "the work that shatters individuation will at no price want to be imitated" (254).[2] The reader of Kafka, Adorno continues, finds himself in the same predicament: he may not imitate Kafka, least of all if he has not suffered for his insight as has Kafka.

A comparable question arises: how to write on Adorno on Kafka? His essay by no means "shatters individuation," but it is in many places as hermetic as Kafka, the effect of marmoreal fragments fused together under rhetorical pressure to something solid and resisting entry. Hence, we may not write epigrammatically, imitating him. But if we then write systematically — "rationally" — about Adorno, eschewing all half-in-love-with-easeful-death profundity (the *difficult* epigram being the least sociable of forms), we will have to put on the silk gown and begin to pronounce him, here, "Right!" here, "Wrong!" But this may amount to exactly that sort of instrumentalized reason that he comminates, as merely adding to "the soothing façade to which a repressive reason [rationale Kontrolle] increasingly conforms" (252, G 312).

The constraints under which one writes on Adorno in America also call for reflection. Contemporary scholarly publishing requires that this essay be cited in English and treated in English. What the reader reads is Adorno in translation — ergo, Adorno in exile — the condition that such an essay as "Aufzeichnungen" ("Notes") is supposed to get past. That is not the same thing as to "escape from": Adorno's only proper home, we know, is homelessness; and yet the change of address in 1945 from Los Angeles to Frankfurt portends a lesser degree of displacement. "Notes on Kafka" breathes in German; its ductus is freer; the exquisiteness of its word choice — the Parnassian face of a negative Reason — gives it a lustrous obscurity that for Adorno, I believe, marks precisely its origin in Europe — in Germany. But here a negative dialectic is also at work, for the traditionless Germany of the 1950s can no longer read such a diction, one that produces the resonances of meaning only as it alludes to the conventions that this same Germany has annihilated — in short: a style — or, precisely what, with the best will in the world, is lost in translation. Reading this essay in American is to enter a spectral space inhabited by two absences: the absence in the American idiom of room for so odd a monument of epigrammatic compression, and the historical absence of tradition to which it is offered in the spirit of defiant retribution. These aspects of Adorno's thought, except as they are conjured here, must, alas, go by the board — be carried away at sea — in what follows.

The American translation of this essay by Sam and Shierry Weber is competent, often admirable, up to the late point where it translates "Ladenhüter" (G 341) as "shopkeepers" (271), aiming for sensuous similarity with Kafka's word "Türhüter" (doorkeeper or doorkeepers), who — in the episode in *The Trial* "Before the Law" — guard the door that opens toward the Law.[3] The word "Ladenhüter" actually means, however, not "shopkeepers" but "white elephants," unsalable things that lie about gathering dust in abandoned shopwindows or in the back; and this mistake does grievously misread Adorno's thought, for Adorno has written: "As in the 'Natural Theater of Oklahoma,' Kafka's world of ideas resembles a world of white elephants" (271). This is a different idea from saying that Kafka's world is like the world of petty shop-keepers. Think of the lawyer-horse Bucephalus, Josephine the singing mouse, or even Gregor Samsa the giant vermin, none of whom are shopkeepers, though perhaps one does not want to think of them too insistently as white elephants either. Odradek—that hybrid, inorganic, irrepressible spool- and starlike creature (is he a *dredl*?)—fits better.[4] But the Webers' mistake has an unexpected tutelary value: it is better than a mistake, it is an error, or part of the error throughout Adorno's essay, which presses all of Kafka's stories and parables into the service of a vast fable, told in Freudian and demonic terms, of the capitalist reification of human consciousness.

Kafka's world of motifs and ideas is like a world of white elephants, Adorno continues, because "no theological principle comes so close to him as the title of an American film comedy: '*Shopworn* Angel.'" (271). Here, the "inner logic" is more persuasive than the logic. But, as I have suggested, part of the blame for the mistranslation is Adorno's, who compels his reader to read Kafka's parabolic figures as ciphers of the modern class history of goods and their relations—something that Kafka pejoratively called "property and its connections" ("Besitz und seine Beziehungen"), those things that "language" treats only because it is forced by its own practices to abandon its wish to address things "outside the sensate [sinnlich] world" (GrW 291–92).

Adorno first speaks of this "other sort of theology" in his correspond-ence with Benjamin, conjuring a Marxist-Freudian fable into which, un-like "existentialism"—or, for that matter, dialectical theology—Kafka does fit.[5] This "inverse" theology reads traces of "the Law" in the devolu-tion of commodities under monopolistic capitalism. I want to examine this *other* theology of economic cipher reading, while repeating my con-cern as to the right way of producing a verdict. Consider the following case in detail. Adorno is writing of a domain of experience common to both "the Third Reich" and "Kafka's world":

Acts of unbridled violence are performed by figures in subordinate positions, types such as non-commissioned officers, prisoners-of-war, and concierges. They are in each case déclassés, in the collapse caught (or absorbed) by the organized collective and permitted to survive, like Gregor Samsa's father. (translation modified, 259)[6]

The acts of violence Adorno has in mind as occurring in both the Third Reich and Kafka's world are performed, among others, by types such as noncommissioned officers, prisoners of war, and concierges. But I do not know of any noncommissioned officers or prisoners of war in Kafka's works.[7] So one is prepared to say that the analogy is false, but that would also be wrong, because the analogy is not completely false. In *Amerika (The One Who Sank Out of Sight)*, a sort of concierge, the head porter, is gratuitously violent to Karl Rossmann, more sinned against than sinner.

"They are in each case declassés," Adorno continues, saved from total collapse "by the organized collective and permitted to survive, like Gregor Samsa's father" (259). But they are not in each case members of a class, even as declassés, since the subjects referred to in this sentence do not belong together: some belong only to the empirical reality of the Third Reich and others to both the Third Reich and Kafka's world. How then are we to understand Adorno's likening them "in each case" to Gregor Samsa's father, who is neither a noncommissioned officer nor a prisoner of war though, if you will, he is a kind of head porter in the Samsa household. The latter point might be granted, and the figure of Herr Samsa then grafted onto the head porter of *Amerika (The One Who Sank Out of Sight)*, whereby we can begin to construct a significant constellation of spasmodically aggressive, vacuous, politically instrumentalizable adults — sublimations, presumably, for Kafka, of his very own Herr Herrmann Kafka. The link is an interesting one and owed to Adorno's logic. And yet, the passage continues, "As in the era of defective capitalism, the burden of guilt is shifted from the sphere of production to the agents of circulation or to those who provide services, traveling salesmen, bank employees, waiters." But what, now, is the relation of "the era of defective capitalism" to either the Third Reich or to Kafka's world? Is this era a third thing, to which these two worlds are likened, on the basis of the fact that in all three worlds "guilt is shifted from the sphere of production to the agents of circulation"? Or is it a thing that already pervades both halves of the binary of the Third Reich and Kafka's world? But this thing now sounds very little like the Third Reich, which was not notoriously set against "its agents of circulation," so long as these were not wandering Jews or Gypsies (certainly, traveling salesmen, bank employees, and waiters did their share in filling the Party's rolls). And this characterization sounds very little like Kafka's world, although on the point of making this judgment one must hesitate, too, since in one instance the "agents of circulation" in Adorno's text are correctly illustrated by Gregor Samsa, who is indeed a traveling salesman. Yet "traveling salesmen" in this sentence are also associated with "bank employees," but the latter — bank employee — is not what Gregor Samsa is but just what Gregor Samsa's *father* is, so Gregor and his father are now being tarred with the same brush as creatures rendered subordinate by the vagaries of capitalism. (One hopes, surely, under "bank employee," that Adorno cannot have in mind Joseph K., since he is a bank official of high rank, comparable with Kafka himself, who was Senior Legal Secretary of the Workers' Accident Insurance Institute of Bohemia.) But we recall that Adorno's preceding point was to *distinguish* Gregor's father from Gregor as the type of the senselessly violent subaltern. Gregor must not be included in this mix, for it is crucial that, in the story in which he is the hero, he is not subaltern, not a noncommissioned officer at all. *The Metamorphosis* reads: "On the wall directly opposite hung a photograph of Gregor from his army days, in a lieutenant's uniform, his hand on his sword, a carefree smile on his lips, demanding respect for his bearing and his rank" (M 12). The entire purpose of this representation cannot be Kafka's desire to establish Gregor Samsa as prima facie a reject of capitalism but surely to exploit the mad, carnivalesque humor of the moment: having Lieutenant Samsa demand respect from the very bug into which he has been changed. This motive lies far to one side of the Marxist parable that Adorno wants it to illustrate. And yet, threading through this Adornian text is a set of images and claims with an indisputable propadeutic charge, an invitation to cultural study, a suggestiveness that here, as in almost every instance, is nonetheless rebutted by the detail and the logic of the Kafkan text itself.

With these examples we have found ourselves in the midst of the main complex of themes in Adorno's essay: Kafka's world is a cryptogram of a decaying capitalist social order. To judge from the details noted above, however, this complex has a peculiarly imprecise, rather only allusive relation to Kafka's texts. Consider, further, the internal logic, the syntax, of this cryptogram as Adorno draws it. I shall attempt to reconstruct this profane fable from pieces scattered throughout Adorno's essay.

Kafka's world is a representation of late capitalism through the waste products it excretes: "Kafka unmasks monopolism by focusing on the waste-products of the liberal era that it liquidates" (257). Under the head of "waste products" are shabby and contingent things — "human" and material — extruded from the circulation of commodities.

These categories — shabbiness and contingency (in one word, obsolescence) — are distinctive markers of late capitalism when they are read as a sort of mirror writing of its "untruth." (The term "untruth" is not the excluded opposite of "truth.")[8] Insofar as Kafka's representation is perfectly — completely and hermetically — clamped onto the capitalist thing itself, it reveals a certain truth: capitalism's systematic untruth. This truth is masked when capitalism is depicted immediately — which is to say, ideologically — through the newness and not the shabbiness of its commodities and through its appearance not of contingency but of "law" — such "ideological custom," as Adorno points out, that makes the parasitic employer the ostensible "Arbeitsgeber," the source of labor. Those "heroes" in Kafka who do not work — viz., the vermin Gregor; the ineffectual Joseph K.; the land surveyor who surveys nothing and is indeed bent only on the transgression of boundaries — heroes who are promptly identified by the powers in whose web they are caught as dangerous, expendable outsiders — are the waste products of capitalism and constitute the genuine experience of capitalism behind its ideological façade.

If this argument is to be coherent, everything turns on the fact that Adorno's claim to Kafka's truthfulness depends on the prior claim that Kafka's representation of capitalism is perfect, airless, viz. "No world could be more homogeneous than the stifling one which he compresses to a totality by means of petty-bourgeois dread; it is logically air-tight and empty of meaning like every system" (256).[9]

But there is trouble here in what we have noted as Adorno's casual use of the rhetorical figure of displacement — in the example, for one, of the displacement of the parasitism of the figure of power onto the creature on whom it feeds, the displacement of what is verminous in Herr Samsa onto the vermin Gregor. Kafka's "perfect" representation of the untruth of capitalism turns out to be a "twisted," because trope-riddled, text, requiring interpretation — and for being interpretable, vulnerable to reideologization. The hermetically perfect seal on this representation of the substance of late capitalism turns out to be "open" to interpretation, pliable under the assault, especially, of Freudian tropic ratios. Indeed, writes Adorno, "At times the power of the images he [Kafka] conjures up cracks through their protective covering" (254). And so Adorno's reading begins to take on the character of a dream analysis with respect to the latent content of Kafka's text, in which the logic of the unconscious is fully operative and the law of noncontradiction does not hold: the Kafkan moment, for example, may be the moment of high capitalism in its late, incipiently fascist stage; a recrudescence of prehistory; and also the moment as such, the eternal moment, endlessly self-repeating. Hence, the mention of Spain as a getaway in *The Castle* is, for Adorno, scandalous in its particularity, violating the homogenous nonspecificity of Kafka's space-time; and yet Kafka's world is illuminated, according to Adorno, by the world of Auschwitz (which is not an anytime and everywhere) and bombed-out Frankfurt, seen in cubistic, bird's-eye perspective, which is not any perspective. There is really no consistency to Adorno's procedure of matching elements from Kafka to his vast fable of social and economic history, an uncertainty that highlights the fundamental oscillation in Adorno's reading of the matter of the power, the exemplarity, owed to the "substance" (*Gehalt*) of the text on the one hand and the reader's work on the other (269).

This difficulty can be put as a question: Is the "demolition" (*Abbau*) of the ideological façade of capitalism an event conveyed in the text of Kafka through the fate of its heroes who are crushed or cast aside; or is it produced by the critical reason of the reader who must interpret to save himself lest he too be crushed and cast aside? But what, after all, gives him or her the margin of superiority to interpret what the K.'s were unable to, if "the bourgeois was unable to find a successor" (260)? One would ordinarily be inclined to say that Kafka articulates for the reader what the victim in the story was unable to articulate himself, for "if there is hope in Kafka's work, it is in those extremes [viz., "Metamorphosis," "In the Penal Colony"] . . . , in the capacity to stand up to the worst *by making it into language*" (emphasis added, 254). But what is the relation between *this* language and the language that the overwhelmed reader must produce to save himself?

The relation of the putative substance of the work to its interpretation is an insistent question. It could be asked again in terms of the *Aesthetic Theory*.[10] Readers of that work, recently made famous through its retranslation, will find in it a good deal of celebratory mention of Kafka.[11] Kafka is cited as a healing counterexample to the discreditable hedonism of Kant's aesthetic judgment. Kant's so-called disinterested pleasure, the ostensible promise of "contemplation," is exposed as mere submission to the "mythic powers."[12] Kafka's stories, on the other hand, assault the viewer like a locomotive shooting out at him from an Expressionist film, abolishing "aesthetic distance" and hence the possibility of the pleasurable detachment that would allow for "identification" (246).[13] Here, the reader risks becoming, not the victim *in* the text but the victim *of* the text; for, as Adorno says, "Kafka's texts are designed not to sustain a constant distance between themselves and their victim but rather to agitate his feelings to a point where he fears that the narrative will shoot towards him like a locomotive" (246). But since the heroes of Kafka's pieces are also victims, a problem comes explicitly to the fore, which turns on Adorno's reluctance to distinguish between a bad thing being arraigned (here, the reader's victimhood) and the value of authorial depictions of such bad things as victimhood, absolute estrangement, objectless inwardness, submission to the mythic powers, reification, and so on. Briefly: why is it a bad thing for the reader to be steamrolled for having failed to produce the interpretive word, but not a bad thing if Kafka steamrolls Georg Bendemann, Gregor Samsa, Joseph K., a country doctor, a hunger artist, etc.?[14] And then again it is not perfectly obvious that this is what Adorno thinks Kafka is doing to his K.'s.

Is this complication the result of the negative dialectic, or is it an epistemological issue that has been sped past? On the one hand, Kafka (and his fictional world) are found in a state of alienation from which he (and it) cannot be liberated by any imaginable activity on the part of its "heroes." Only the reader battling for a perspective higher than the bourgeois can salvage it. On the other hand, Kafka (and Kafka's world) fictively mime their alienation and hence provide the framelike distance that the reader needs to perform a demolition. Where, then, in this scene of instruction, should the reader's power of interpretation be situated? "Instead of curing neurosis," writes Adorno, "he [Kafka] seeks in it itself the healing force, that of knowledge: the wounds with which society brands the individual are seen by the latter as ciphers of the social untruth, the negative of truth" (252). (We already know what this truth for Kafka is supposed to be: the Marxistically inflected historical process that surfaces sterotypically in Althusser, too, as "the bourgeoisie's shattering entry into history before 'traversing' the Weimar Republic and entrusting itself to Nazism.")[15] But if the inverse of this social untruth can be registered by the canny "individual"—the critic Adorno—then it can also be registered, in principle, by other individuals able to read the brandings on the backs of Kafka's victims: "Out of this nettle, danger; we pluck this flower, safety."[16] Yet it is hard to see how this reading could be performed, because in Kafka's case we are faced with a text *at all times* threatening to annihilate the reader and rob him of the crucial hermeneutic composure that Adorno calls "Versenkung" ("concentration," 252, G 313; "immersion," 270, G 340). The source of this threat is never specified but appears to arise from the image that means to annihilate the victim *within the text*, who lacks the will to resist his tormenter, e.g., the father in "The Judgment" or the torture machine in "In the Penal Colony." And yet, here where the possibility of a fatal "identification" between hero/victim and reader would appear to exist, Adorno denies it a priori: "Such aggressive physical proximity undermines the reader's habit of identifying himself with the figures in the novel" (246). A Kantian world of detached aesthetic contemplation would provide the leisure (and masochistic bliss) of identification, but Kafka's text, which "agitates the feelings," denies him any such safety (or gratification). Indeed, it is exactly the achievement of the *text*, and certainly not of the *victim*, to *express* an imminent collapse of "intellectual equilibrium" (246), viz. "[He, Kafka] drives through to the bare material existence that emerges in the subjective sphere through the *total collapse* of a submissive consciousness, *divest of all self asser-*

*tion*" (emphasis added, 252). On the other hand, the destitution of the subject produces a certain positive result. "The decline of genius, the spasmodic lack of resistance," consistent with the above, "which so completely converges with Kafka's morality, is paradoxically rewarded by the compelling authority of its expression" (252). The expressiveness of the *text* arises from the failure of the hero's self-assertion as a form of resistance. The hero, a void of active consciousness, asserts nothing; only his reification is expressive of the truth of social untruth, of domination. And yet, as we have seen, it is this very lurid expressiveness that *inhibits* the identification of the endangered reader with the victim. So what, we may ask, is the expressive form of the danger that comes at the reader? Is it the victim-laden, corpse-laden, locomotive of the text *as a whole*, the aggressive cryptogram itself of late capitalist society? But, if so, by what cognitive means could the unredeemed reader resist such an assault?

This difficulty is fundamental but not entirely consistent in its form. In yet another respect, the essay complicates the question of where and how knowledge is produced, for it offers still another view of the victim, one that upsets the hierarchy adapted to the structure of communicated knowledge—the hierarchy of author, crushed victim-hero, and yearning reader. A different set of relations comes off different claims, viz. "The crucial moment, however, towards which everything in Kafka is directed, is that in which men become aware that they are not themselves—that they themselves are things" (255). "The subject seeks to break the spell of reification by reifying itself" (270). Who are these "men," and which "subject" is meant? They do not appear to exclude the victim at all. In this case, however, what does it mean that so alienated and thinglike a subjectivity "becomes aware," "seeks," "reifies itself"? Yet if the victim is to go through his victimization "knowledgeably," then he becomes, precisely, an exemplary figure for the reader, a figure commanding identification. And this is what Adorno appears to be asserting when he writes that Kafka "reports what actually happens, though without any illusion concerning the subject, which, possessing the greatest degree of self-awareness—of its nullity—throws itself on the junkpile," until he adds, then, the entirely disruptive analogy, "no different from what the death-machine does to its victims" (266)—the same torture machine adduced, above, as an example of the blind, entirely crushing, entirely overwhelming, threat to the victim and, by implication, to the reader. But there is a world of difference in whether we are to conceive a subject as the helpless victim of late capitalist domination or as the strategic victim of his own sacrificial logic—viz. "Kafka seeks salvation in the incorporation of the powers of the adversary; . . . the subject ['that postulates the self by the self, officially sanctioned by philosophy'] seeks to make amends by abandoning this ['mythic'] defiance" (270).

It would finally seem that we lack the salutary solitude to survey the scene of knowledge according to Adorno. He writes: "That above which individuation lifts itself, what it conceals and what it drove from itself, is common to all but can only be grasped in solitude and undistracted concentration [Versenkung]" (252). "Immersion [Versenkung] in the inner space of individuation, which culminates in such self-contemplation, stumbles upon the principle of individuation" (270). The requirement is good contemplation, good self-immersion, which "the subject" elects as a prelude to self-destruction. Yet who, finally, is this subject — author, critic, victim, reader — all of them? — and where and how are the conditions of contemplation achieved? Adorno's way of saying that art under capitalism is alienated and that it is also a scene of instruction into the truth that capitalism estranges is to say both things simultaneously, but these arguments are opposed, and no conjuration of negative dialectics, to my mind, can sublate their difference.[17] Adorno's final summary formulation reads, "Kafka's artistic alienation [Verfremdung] [is] the means by which objective estrangement [Entfremdung] is made visible" (this alienation is moreover legitimated by "the work's inner substance") (269). What does this mean? If "inner substance" only reproduces hermetically the "soul" of capitalism — i.e., petty-bourgeois dread — then it repeats, it does not resist, the fault.

This capitalist hell is elaborated by means of Marx and Freud.[18] The grand sociological fiction does not arise from immersion in the details of Kafka's texts, including their titles, nor does Adorno's reading of the moment of cognition in Kafka arise from the secure status of any such thing in Kafka as a eudaemonic principle of steadfast articulation (the point of "In the Penal Colony" is that the brandings on the back of the prisoner *cannot* be read to their conclusion).[19] We shall address instead the source of the great sociological fable as it has been adapted to Kafka: much of it is found in Adorno's early correspondence with Benjamin.

Recall that the central figure in this story is the bourgeoisie, which died ingloriously: it liquidated itself in fascism. And when the bourgeoisie died, there died with it the ideology of "the liberal era," the ideology of "civilization and bourgeois individuation" (257, 251). "The obsolete liberal traits that Kafka put in relief [überhöht] . . . reappeared in the forms of fascist organization" (translation modified, 259). Such a development would appear to have been inevitable, since the capitalist machine functions as the "anarchic" circulation of commodities, a mode of "exchange [that] unremittingly reproduces injustice" (259, 270). Dysfunctional persons and personal aptitudes and qualities are thence expelled from the collective into a "subordinated state" (249), whence they become capable of "acts of unbridled violence . . . , types such as non-commissioned officers, prisoners of war, and concierges." Adorno concludes:

> The unemployed—in *The Castle*—and emigrants—in *America*—are dressed and preserved like fossils of the process of *déclassement*. The economic tendencies whose relics they represent even [or already] before those tendencies had prevailed were by no means as foreign to Kafka as his hermetic procedure might suggest. (translation modified, 259–60)[20]

The metaphors of this last argument—"fossils," "relics"—invite commentary, especially together with the zigzag temporality of the phrase, "even [or already] before these tendencies had prevailed." What is the chronology here? This "before" appears to be an ideological conduit phrase to the "*Vorwelt*," the preworld of the swamp with which these alleged "relics" are identified.[21] For, after all, according to Adorno: "In the latest phase of this force [the mythically represented monopolistic apparatus of distribution], that of bureaucratic control, Kafka recognizes the earliest stage: its waste-products as belonging to primal history" (translation modified, 260).

What is being evoked here is the connection of the modern historical period (*Zeitalter*) to a world aeon (*Weltalter*), a link that helps to explain why, for Adorno, there are so few explicit references in Kafka to actual history. We are watching Adorno connect *Zeitalter* (ages, generations) to *Weltalter* (aeons, cosmic periods). Under *Zeitalter* come such epochs as Antiquity, the Middle Ages, the Renaissance, Modernity; under *Weltalter* such periods as primal history (*Urgeschichte*, *Mythos*) and history, writing (*Schrift*). These ages and aeons are, according to Adorno, to be more than contrasted, which is all that Benjamin has done: they need to be put in dialectical relation. "For *us*," wrote Adorno to Benjamin, "the concept of the historical period [Zeitalter] is simply nonexistent (as little as we recognize Decadence or Progress in an overt [offenen] sense); . . . rather, it is solely that the world-aeon exists as the extrapolation *from* the petrified [versteint] present" (B 103). Why is this so, and why is what Adorno calls in his letter to Benjamin "the relation of primal history and modernity" "the gold standard of any successful Kafka interpretation" (B 102)? Benjamin, who reads "the *anamnesis*—or 'forgetting'—of primal history in Kafka in an archaic and not thoroughly dialectical [durchdialektisierten] sense," has not elaborated this connection (B 103). It is by providing such an interpretation that Adorno's "Notes" essay means to stand or fall, and its crux is his identification of fascism with the new archaic and Kafka as a herald of this New.

The fable becomes more interesting when Adorno asks Benjamin to make the connection between primal history and myth, on the one hand, and also reproductive technology on the other. Adorno approaches this issue through an arresting image that alludes to an earlier essay of his on Kafka, written in 1925 and "most likely unpublished and gone missing" (B 101).[22] Adorno remembers the perspective of this lost essay as Kafka's own. It is "a photograph of earthly life from the perspective of the redeemed life, of which nothing appears in it except a corner of the black cloth, while the ghastly tilted optic of the image is none other than that of the oblique camera itself" (B 101). This image crops up, metamorphosed, in the "Notes" in the oblique camera of the *child's* vision (255). After the experience of World War II, childhood is expropriated by the hell of self-reflecting technology.

In Benjamin's essay, "Franz Kafka: On the Tenth Anniversary of his Death," Benjamin mentioned the famous photograph of Kafka as a child in a photographer's studio, something between "a torture chamber and a throne room" (B 16). This figure centers Adorno's criticism of Benjamin's alleged failure to dialecticize the archaic, which would include his failure to interpret the flash (*Blitzlicht*) of the studio camera. The interpretation of the flood-lit image, writes Adorno, had it been provided, "would be equivalent to the neutralization of the aeon [Weltalter] in the flash"—presumably of that aeon that Benjamin has in mind as forgotten or encrusted in the present: the swamp (B 103). This is suggestive on Adorno's part: the flash signals the camera's own inscriptive interpretation of the swamp world that drags it into modernity. The interpretation made by the photograph is equivalent to the "neutralization" of the aeon produced by the camera flash in the sense that the interpretation explicitly undoes the immediate violence of the swamp world present in "symptoms of captivation by the archaic, [modernity's] failure to execute the mythic dialectic" (B 103). Interpretation and camera flash mark the reversal (*Umkehr*) that brings the preworld into written history. For Benjamin such "reversal is the direction of the moment of study [Studium] that transforms existence into script [Schrift]" (B 37).[23] Adorno will maintain (scil. *The Dialectic of the Enlightenment*) that the relation of mythos and script is not one or just one of reversal. The flash may be the warning light of an Enlightenment reason turned repressive and the mark of this moment, the scriptlike ciphers or stigmata of rational or economic oppression. This, according to Adorno, is the coded halakah or Law of the inverse theology that informs Kafka's "history" of capitalism.

This story also projects the (anti)theology that Adorno discovers in Kafka. Kafka's theology exists chiefly as what is not the case: it must not be dialectical theology. This thrust is aimed at the Karl Barth–brand of crisis theology advanced by Hans-Joachim Schoeps, who wrote on Kafka in the 1930s. Adorno's quarrel with Schoeps has the acrimony of a sectarian dispute on how Kierkegaard's "infinite qualitative distinction" is to be applied to Kafka's case: it is *not* to be applied!

> Dialectical theology fails in its attempt to appropriate him except for the mythical character of the powers at work [which it rightly catches], an aspect that it is correct to treat, because in Kafka, unlike *Fear and Trembling*, ambiguity and obscurity are attributed not only to the Other as such but to human beings and to the conditions in which they live. Precisely that "infinite qualitative distinction" taught by Kierkegaard and Barth is levelled off; there is no real distinction, Kafka writes, between town and castle. (translation modified, 259)

"Human beings and the conditions in which they live," something quite particularly emphasized above, returns us to the sociological reality.

Kafka's theology—"if one can speak of such at all," continues Adorno—is antinomian with respect to the God of the Enlightenment, the deistic *deus otiosus*, who is also—in Adorno's aperçu—a *deus absconditus*. Both are instances of a God total, abstract, and indeterminate, whom Kafka finds finally "mythic"; the "absolute difference" of the hidden God "converges with the mythic powers" (268). As such it will be terrifying. Divine as well as human abstraction flipflops into the monstrous; the extreme point of rational demythification invokes the archaic terror of the unknown. This analysis departs from Adorno's hermeneutic dictum drawn from Benjamin in regard to Kafka: "neither natural nor supernatural" be; but Adorno, in concerning himself with Kafka's Freudianism as well as his theology, sins against the whole of the dictum. If Adorno follows Benjamin in sacking dialectical theology, he clings to his own theological paraphrase: Kafka's world is "hell seen from the perspective of salvation" (269).[24]

This account of Kafka's "theology," though, is unsatisfactory, because Adorno does not attend to Kafka's Gnostic aphorisms (let alone the entire strain of gnosticism throughout). It may be that he intuitively wants to exclude Kafka's plainly theological writings because they authorize ecstatic self-destruction, but one should not ignore the power of this thought. Adorno speaks of such a category when he writes, "Integration is disintegration, and in it the mythic spell converges with the rationality of domination" (257). But the Gnostic category of destruction is not an affair of *Abbau*, of the demolition of social illusions, of the demystification that rends the maya of commodity culture. Kafka wants not cultural critique but mortification: "profession, love, family,

income" illumine him as they disintegrate entirely. Recall the great fi-
nale to " 'You,' I said . . .":

> Already, what protected me seemed to dissolve here in the city. I
> was beautiful in the early days, for this dissolution takes place as
> an *apotheosis*, in which everything that holds us to life flies away,
> but even in flying away illumines us for the last time with its hu-
> man light. (emphasis added, D1 28)

He does not seek pacification of the familial and social trauma but explosion of the traumatically scarred personality, the destruction of personality and not the registering, through "making into language," of the
"adversary powers," the agents of that suffering; nor "incorporating"
them; nor simply "making amends" for the "mythic" defiance of its
postulating itself as subject. In this self-destruction there is a mystic bliss
that Adorno does not heed. It is present in Kafka as early as the conclusion of "The Judgment."

In one respect, Adorno is right to criticize a reading of Kafka as the
dialectical theologian of "absolute difference." For Kafka, the way to
the absolute is not systematically barred; the boundary between the existent and the absolute fluctuates, meaning: there is another history — a
history of approaches, of traversing the space between. On the other
hand, pace Adorno, neither is this absolute wholly immanent as the
demonic grimace of the real. (Indeed, Adorno appears to have corrected
himself, or at any rate inflected this "identity" differently, in writing of
Kafka in "Charakteristik W. Benjamins" as one who "got deus absconditus and devil confused."[25]) Kafka does have a powerful god-word: it is
"truth" (*Wahrheit*). Truth is figured, early and late, as light, and the
relation to it of art and the artist is a variable one, inassimilable to
polemic or to doctrine. It is shifting and elliptical: "Slanting through the
words there come vestiges of light" (DF 261).

At times the light does figure as an "infinite qualitative distinction,"
to which the human has no conscious access. "Truth is indivisible, hence
it cannot recognize itself; anyone who wants to recognize it has to be a
lie" (DF 43).[26] Only "the light on the . . . grimacing face is true" (DF
41); it cannot be glimpsed, yet might it be caught, as light is caught in
silk? "Art flies around truth, but with the definite intention of not getting burnt. Its capacity lies in finding in the dark void a place where the
beam of light can be intensely caught, without this having been perceptible before" (DF 87). But here, even to say that art surely catches the
beam, is to say too much; art directs you to the place where the beam
"can" be caught.

On the other hand, most passages imply that the distinction is not final; rather, it is an affair of approximation, "mercifully quantitative" (DF 38, H 43)![27] At times the light is trapped in matter, yet their distinction is never finally eliminated, pace Adorno's alleged indistinction "between town and castle." In the early diary entry of 1910, a "human light" is impacted even in the products of commodity culture (the condition of the apotheosis is detachment from "everything that holds us to life"), and it is not hard to imagine that the engine of this detachment is writing fiction. Hence, when Kafka writes fiction, in the manner in which he wrote "The Judgment," he is pursuing an apotheosis, he is not throwing himself on the junkpile in order to pacify the social forces that have already turned him into junk.

There is most certainly a live consciousness in Kafka of difference (268), even as it coexists with the lure of transcendence. This attraction is a term of art for him in all its senses, for it is activated in the field of artistic work, as a theme and a practice. Here, too, in writing about art, Kafka introduces the concept of a difference "varying from itself," writing, "The point of view of art and that of life are different even in the artist himself" (DF 86). This inserts a potentiated factor of difference into that high thing, the relation of the artist to his art. The difference that varies from itself makes sense as the "boundary" (Grenze), and Kafka's varying relation to it, of which Kafka often writes. So we get such formulations as these touching his "creative abilities," of which we have heard: "mysterious powers which are of an ultimate significance to me." "In the literary field I have "experienced states . . . in which I completely dwelt in every idea, . . . and not only felt myself at my boundary, but at the boundary of the human in general" (D1 58).

I agree that Adorno means to concentrate on Kafka's fiction and not the sort of texts I have been citing. He chooses from that preponderance of works in which there is next to nothing about writing. Kafka is absent as a reflective medium on the act of writing, which invariably includes the notation of ecstasy. But how adequate is Adorno's essay even to the works of fiction it invokes? The way the light in *The Trial* is figured will not encourage one to think that Kafka collapses to zero the distinction between God or light and the human supplicant, the man from the village.

Earlier, I said that Adorno breaks his contract with Benjamin not to adduce "nature," because he makes much of the "psychoanalytical verism" of Freud. Here Adorno borrows from psychoanalysis the logic or system that "derives the individual from amorphous and diffuse drives, the Ego from the Id. Personality is transformed from something substantial into a mere organizational principle of somatic impulses" (251). This is supposed to explain Kafka's animal stories or subaltern stories: in Adorno's text they come to the same thing through the gesture that turns the rejects of monopoly capitalism into the creatures of primal history. This Freudian narrative is superimposed on fragments of Marx. Recall that Adorno criticized Benjamin for not dialecticizing the archaic in Kafka: "The antithesis of the historical age [Zeitalter] and the world-era [Weltalter] [in your study] could not become fruitful as a mere contrast but only dialectically" (B 103). Yet I do not find in Adorno more than one stage of the dialectic he missed in Benjamin. Objectless inwardness, relics of writing [Schrift], "the enigmatic [Expressionist] image [of] reality composed of its scattered fragments," somatic impulses, sought-after reification, myth all tend to be agglutinated in a protofascist modernity. Categories of barbarism (Marx, technology) and savagery (Freud, bestializaton) are freely interchanged. Yet the residue of the somatic consciousness cannot be at once badger, shy mouse, and anti-skidding devices on trucks ("Antiderepants") (V 140).[28] The side by sideness of technological terror and animal regression requires one or two more mediations.

If one further outcome of medial technology is to proliferate new gestures, it might seem that Adorno could introduce these mediations into his account of Kafka's gestures, which for him have a nonlinguistic basis. But his actual discussion of gestures in Kafka is mythic: he wants them to have an original power and the status of bedrock: "Gestures often serve as counterpoints to words: the pre-linguistic that eludes all intention upsets the ambiguity" (248). "The experiences sedimented in the gestures will eventually have to be followed by interpretation, one which recognizes in their mimesis a universal which has been repressed by sound common sense" (249). Adorno gives authority to the gesture, as mimetically sedimenting prelinguistic experience; but Kafka, in *The Trial*, for example, takes pains to demystify this claim. Perhaps the gesture "upsets" ambiguity — by introducing yet more. The claim for an alternative human history of gesture surpasses any claim that Kafka was willing to make on behalf of his characters. The point about many, if not all, of Kafka's depicted gestures is that they are as opaque to the parties involved as anything else in their situation.

Here are some examples from *The Trial*.

"Good heavens!" said the guard, "you just can't accept your situation; you seem bent on annoying us unnecessarily, although we're probably the human beings closest to you now." "That's right, you'd better believe it," said Franz, not lifting the coffee cup in his hand to his mouth but staring at K. with a long and *no doubt meaningful, but incomprehensible*, look. (emphasis added, T 8)

K., arrested in his bedroom, glares at and reproves the people from across the street staring at him through an open window.

"Obnoxious, thoughtless people!" said K., turning back to the room. The inspector may have agreed with him, as he thought he noticed a sideways glance. But it was equally possible he hadn't been listening at all, for he had pressed his hand firmly down on the table and seemed to be *comparing the length of his fingers*. (emphasis added, T 16)

A cryptogram of mensurative capitalism in its middle and not so glossy late phase?[29] The knowledge suppressed by common sense? Such a question might be shallow, or it might be exactly what Adorno asks for. There is a spectacular decalage between Adorno's mythy-minded abstractions and the examples he fails to mention.

The end of the "Notes" is grisly: it is illuminated by the pyres of World War II that "through all the dusky air / . . . thick-flaming shot a dismal glare."[30] Adorno reflects this light back onto Kafka's world: "The light-source which shows the world's crevices to be infernal is the optimal one"; "Kafka allies himself with death" (269, 271). And yet Adorno also finds something "salutary" in Kafka's submission to the dark powers (L 333): "Instead of human dignity, the supreme bourgeois concept, there emerges in him [Kafka] the salutary recollection of the similarity between man and animal" (270). This sentence should be read in conjunction with his remark, "The boundary between what is human and the world of things becomes blurred" (262). This descent of the subject could serve as a reminiscence of the token of hope Adorno saw at the end of his most important letter to Benjamin on Kafka. There is hope in the hybrid Odradek, the "thing" without dignity; it has no fixed abode and yet conjures the idea of its immortality:

As the reverse side of the world of things, [Odradek] is a sign of disfigurement—is as such, however, precisely a motif of transcendence—the erasure of boundaries and the reconciliation of the organic and the inorganic or the sublation [Aufhebung] of death. Odradek "survives." In other words, it is only to the topsy-turvy [verkehrt] life of things that an escape from the bonds of nature is promised. (B 104)

Benjamin, Adorno wrote, had rendered Odradek entirely in the properties of the "preworld" (*Vorwelt*), but a full commentary would see this figure as a "prolegomenon" to issues of text, script, and "study" (*Studium*), implying the flash of a reversal. Adorno's cluster of concerns, aspects of the great fable of world ages that Kafka needs to illustrate, all surface here. Benjamin had failed to mention the main feature of the Odradek figure: that it survives. And its survival is a function of the "concern" (*Sorge*) of the "warden" of the house to which the creature always faithfully returns: the story in which it figures is called "The

Cares of a Family Man" ("Die Sorgen eines Hausvaters"). Odradek has entered into the care of its father, and such care is a token of hope, projected, as it were, from the dialectical form of its being "without fixed abode" (CS 428). "It is so dialectical," writes Adorno, "that one can also really say of it, 'almost nothing has made everything good'" (B 104). It has the appearance of a derelict commodity ("the reverse side of the world of things") and of a thing inscribed, for it is a "sign" (*Zeichen*). And yet, though it bears the disfigurement of modern script (according to Adorno), its surface is, for Kafka, "unbroken"; it is "in its own way perfectly finished," and it is alive with a primordial, inextinguishable life (CS 428). The dialectic of these elements promises more for Adorno than that "neutralizing" of the mythic world that Benjamin, he predicts, would discover in the camera flash.

What Adorno fails to mention here, however, is how the outcome of this dialectic is viewed by the narrator of Odradek's story himself. This temporal product of the inscribed sign and the miraculously "unbroken" surface — namely, Odradek's immortality — prompts him to reflect, "The idea that he is likely to survive me I find almost painful" (CS 429).

Let us leave Adorno with his token of hope; it is an exigency in 1934. But now, in 1953, some twenty years later? The final sentence of "Notes on Kafka" reads, "The name alone, revealed through a natural death, not the living soul, vouches for that in man which is immortal" (271). It speaks of death, and not the living soul — and not even the soulless creature who is alive. The Kafka whom Adorno now has in his sights is he, who, not himself ecstatic, casts the light that brings hell to light. He brings in the light cast *past him* from the standpoint of redemption. The famous concluding aphorism of *Minima Moralia* conjures this light source:

> The only philosophy which can be responsibly practiced in face of despair is the attempt to contemplate all things as they would present themselves from the standpoint of redemption. Knowledge has no light but that shed on the world by redemption; all else is reconstruction, mere technique. Perspectives must be fashioned that displace and estrange the world, reveal it to be, with its rifts and crevices, as indigent and distorted as it will appear one day in the messianic light.[31]

This is a perspective not unfaithful to Kafka who wrote, "Our art is a way of being dazzled by truth; the light on the flinching, grimacing face is true, and nothing else" (DF 41). And yet this perspective is incomplete. It ignores the light impacted in the creature and liberated by "constructive destruction" (DF 103). Through the very particular, rigorous act of writing fiction, *that* light is cast back upon his lifted face.

# Chapter 10

# ON TRANSLATION MISTAKES, WITH SPECIAL
# ATTENTION TO KAFKA IN AMERIKA

> Graphology has taught us to recognize in handwriting
> images that the unconscious of the writer conceals in it.
> — Walter Benjamin, *"On the Mimetic Faculty"*

IF WE DO not read Kafka in the original, then our understanding of him
will be only as good as its translation. And then the question arises of
what "the original" would be. If we do not read Kafka in the original
manuscripts, would we still be reading him in the original? And would
we be reading him in the original if we did not read them in *his* place
and time? And can we even imagine what this place and time would be?
What moment of *his* reading . . . or writing of them? The chapter that
follows arises from a reflection on this predicament, which has of late
become a public event.

In dealing with "translation," one is tempted to imagine the relationship between two texts as filial, in which translations figure as the offspring of a primary text. But here caution is advised: embedded in this
metaphor are unentitled naturalistic consolations of the kind discussed
in chapter 5. Such an objection belongs to the history of translation
theory, which amounts to a continually adjusted redescription of the
relation between two texts. This is not surprising since, no less than
originals, translations do not stand alone but mediate intricately associated worlds or fates or languages. As a result, accounts of translation
may focus on the relation of worlds or fates or languages brought on by
the shock of juxtaposition. Walter Benjamin's essay "The Task of the
Translator" ("Die Aufgabe des Übersetzers"), for example, disrupts the
reproductive model in describing translation as a relation between two
*languages*, the goal of which is to bring to light a third language —
"pure language" ("reine Sprache"). In this enterprise the translator's
task is least of all the salvaging of an original meaning, a quasi-genetic,
progenitive substance, through "accurate communication" ("genaue
Mitteilung"), for

> all information, all sense, and all intention finally encounter a stra-
> tum in which they are destined to be extinguished. This very stra-

tum furnishes a new and higher justification for free translation; this justification does not derive from the sense of what is to be conveyed, for the emancipation from the sense is the task of fidelity.[1]

This thesis is striking as much for the way it dislodges the customary translation paradigm of text-begat-text as for the way it smuggles it back in, in the congenial form of the metaphor recurrent in theories of translation—figures of ethical intersubjective relation (here: "fidelity" [Treue]). The appearance of this metaphor in even so "inhuman" a description as Benjamin's suggests the operations of the propadeutic identified by Goethe in his advertisement to his novel *Elective Affinities* (*Die Wahlverwandtschaften*):

> The author . . . might have noticed that in the natural sciences ethical analogies [Gleichniße] are very often used to make things that are far remote from the circle of human knowledge more accessible.[2]

To judge further from such recent sources as George Steiner's *After Babel* and Wolfgang Iser's reflections on "translatability" as the enabling feature of cultural communication, the "far remote" character of translation lies less in its distance from human affairs than in the inscrutable ubiquity of its embeddedness: it cannot be fully identified because it always already indwells each attempt to understand it.[3] Steiner puts the governing "postulate" of his work as follows: "Translation is formally and pragmatically implicit in *every* act of communication, in the emission and reception of each and every mode of meaning, be it in the widest semiotic sense or in more specifically verbal exchanges" (emphasis added).[4] Interestingly, Steiner's wide sense of the concept also includes the illuminations of "inadequate" moments of translation supplied by writers who "articulate the conventions of masked or failed understanding which have obtained between men and women, between women and men, in the lineaments of dialogue we call love or hatred."[5] Here, translation once again falls under the head of intersubjective relations—"love or hatred." If we include uninhibited sexuality under the head of such relations, then Goethe's famous apothegm settles the matter: translators are those "industrious pimps who, in extolling the adorable charms of a partly clothed beauty, excite in us an irresistible desire for the original."[6]

It is precisely the irritation with such prosopopeia that motivates the thrust in recent translation theory towards erasing the distinctiveness of the so-called primary text, the original, vis-à-vis the secondary text, the translation proper. For, as the distinction between them tends to disappear, so does the pertinence of ethical categories to their relation. Certainly this is plain in the aims of so-called deconstructive translation theory, which arise from a general demythification of notions of originality and secondariness in favor of a universal and unrepresentable *différance*.[7] An especially pointed application of deconstructive ideas to translation theory shapes Paul de Man's reading of Benjamin's essay, which situates both original and translation at the *same* radical depth of unintelligibility.[8] Finally, under the head of this leveling tendency comes an observation by the American translator and theorist of translation Willis Barnstone:

> The translated poem need not be secondary to the original. The Dao de Jing, the Kabbalah, and the Bible in English, Shakespeare in German, Whitman in Spanish, Poe in French, Tolstoi and Kafka in most languages [sic] — books and authors live as much abroad as in their native tongue, and abroad they live only in translation. If they are to live well in their foreign habitat, then Poe finds Baudelaire to translate his stories and Mallarmé his poems, Whitman finds Borges for *Leaves of Grass*, Eliot finds Guillén and Seferis for *The Waste Land*, Valéry finds Rilke, and Shakespeare finds Schlegel in German, Gide in French, and Pasternak in Russian.

Even here, though, Barnstone's diction of "finding" continues to verge on a higher prosopopeia, on a transcendental variation of the ethically scandalous metaphor of "elective affinities."[9] We shall have occasion, too, to wonder at the implicit claim that Kafka "has found" his English translator in Edwin and Willa Muir.

In the following pages I want to address events of an associated order, events of an empirical kind that in their own right force a redescription of the relation of original and translated work, a redescription that in fact upsets current doxa about the lack of firm distinction between them. These are the publishing events (mentioned earlier in segue 1) that are transforming this relation in ways still difficult to conceptualize. I am referring to the publication of the works of Franz Kafka first by the Fischer Publishing House and now more recently by the Stroemfeld/Roter Stern Publishing House on the "basis" of Kafka's manuscripts. I put "basis" in quotation marks because disputes have arisen around these editions concerning just what the concept of a basis is supposed to mean.

The edition that first provoked this crisis is the Fischer version of Kafka's work calling itself "the manuscript version" (*Kritische Ausgabe in der Fassung der Handschrift, KKA*) — an edition that has been appearing over the last twenty years under the editorship of Hans-Gerd Koch, Michael Müller, and Malcolm Pasley. (The first volume in the series, Malcolm Pasley's edition of *Das Schloss* [*The Castle*], appeared in 1982, followed by Jost Schillemeit's edition of *Der Verschollene* [*Amerika* or *The One Who Sank Out of Sight*] which appeared in 1983). Now, in 2004, the right to print many of Kafka's manuscripts, hitherto the exclusive property of Schocken Books, has entered the public domain; and the dispute over the clarity of the editorial practices guiding the critical edition — more particularly, the aptness of the claim to authenticity that the phrase "manuscript version" suggests — has become more acute, since large publishing fortunes are at stake. Quite particularly, we have recently seen the appearance of several volumes in the rival edition of the Stroemfeld/Roter Stern Publishing House — *Franz Kafka — Ausgabe*, *FKA* — including the so-called Oxford "Quartal" notebooks, the manuscript bundles of the "Description of a Struggle" ("Beschreibung eines Kampfes"), "The Judgment" ("Das Urteil"), and the totality of *The Trial* (*Der Process*); and Stroemfeld/Roter Stern means to produce an entire series of facsimile editions of Kafka's manuscripts, entitled *Franz Kafka, Historisch-Kritische Ausgabe sämtlicher Handschriften, Drucke und Typoskripte* under the editorship of Roland Reuß and Peter Staengle, who have set down their editorial principles in their first volume as well as in the journal *TEXT: Kritische Beiträge*.

Some of the criticism that has been addressed to the Fischer Critical Edition is evidently reasonable. For the very notion of a "manuscript version" is a paradoxical notion — or, more harshly put, a mystified one — a hybrid whose elements pull in opposite directions. There cannot be a "manuscript version" of an author's writings if the qualifier "manuscript" is supposed to guarantee the authenticity of the version and hence establish it as radically less a "version" than some allegedly second-order, explicitly editorialized edition of Kafka's writings, like Brod's *Sämtliche Werke* (Complete works). Put otherwise: the paradoxical "manuscript edition" cannot in good faith pretend to banish, once and for all, the spook of the merely approximate text of Kafka's writings, one hitherto — and *only* hitherto — marred, it is said, by editorial intervention. It cannot banish editorial intervention as a thing appropriate only to a more sentimental and less technically refined age for the simple reason that its version must also differ from the original.

We should not fail to note, certainly, the variety of ways in which the *KKA* is tangibly richer than Brod's *Sämtliche Werke*: for example, in its inclusion of texts such as "Man darf nicht sagen . . ." in the unpublished writings and a good deal of *Amerika* (*The One Who Sank Out of Sight*) in an orthography more nearly faithful to Kafka's own.[10] On the other hand, the *KKA* obviously does "correct" what it takes to be inadvertent oversights; makes no attempt to indicate in its apparatus where Kafka's crossed-out "mistakes" are located on the line; adds periods when there are none in the manuscripts; adds quotation marks to form pairs of such marks when one is missing; and substitutes "ß" for "ss" when deemed appropriate to normal orthography. It makes many of these changes without informing the reader.

In what follows, I am particularly interested in changes in that sector of the conceptual field (original/translation) occupied by the concept of a translation-*mistake*. The phenomenon of the mistake is linked to the alleged loss of difference between original and secondary texts inside the translation relation, since a radical elimination of the difference would amount to the claim that a secondary text could arise free of mistake, as a text in which the concept of the "mistake" (as opposed to "error") would have no place. The lesson of the recent empirical events I am describing, however, in fact appears to produce a precisely contrary result. It drives a cleft of unsuspected magnitude between original and translation, destroying at its source the very possibility of a translation without mistakes. This transformation, I have said, is occurring even now, as you read this, so we do not yet have before us the definite form of a new concept of a translation mistake. It may be that in Kafka's case, as in the many cases like his where manuscripts survive and reveal pen strokes not hitherto incorporated into standard editions (e.g., the cases of Kleist, Nietzsche, Trakl, Proust, Musil), the concept of a translation mistake will mutate into a form scarcely resembling the old.

Until recently, several generations of Kafka's American readers have depended on the work of a few highly accomplished translators, among whom the Muirs, Edwin and Willa, husband and wife, have been most prominent. They are the translators of *The Castle* (Knopf, 1930); *The Trial* (Knopf, 1937); and *Amerika* (*The One Who Sank Out of Sight*) (New Directions, 1940). These versions are generally considered very good and adequate according to basic standards of accuracy, although it has also been noticed that they display "tendencies" of their own. According to Ronald Gray,

> The Muirs were strongly influenced by the view of Kafka as a modern Bunyan which dominated most early interpretations. . . . The more optimistic view taken by the Muirs is reflected almost from the outset, in *The Trial*. . . . K. is altogether a better-disposed character, as he emerges from the translation, than he is in the original.[11]

Joyce Crick has noted that "the Muirs have overlooked certain problems of idiom. . . . [Their] vocabulary is more vivid than Kafka's neu-
tral speech."[12] S. S. Prawer elaborates both critiques:

> Scholar after scholar has told us of the Muirs' tendency to tone
> down Kafka's ominousness and make his central figures more kindly
> than they are in the original. . . . [The Muirs] misunderstood some
> of Kafka's phrases and sentences . . . [and] tended to obscure Kaf-
> ka's cross-references by elegant variation. . . . At other times, they
> import connections where there are none in the original.[13]

To say that they "misunderstood" means, putting it bluntly, that the
Muirs made mistakes; and yet these mistakes were never felt to be so
numerous or egregious as to have prompted Schocken, their publishers,
to commission a single major retranslation of Kafka before the mid-
1990s — i.e., during a period of some sixty years. Typical of Schocken's
halfway stance was its sponsoring in 1989 Arthur S. Wensinger's "revision" of several shorter pieces — but nothing more.[14] Wensinger tugs
shut the modest mantle of his task as translator by arguing (like Barnstone) as follows:

> Among the countless examples of translation of modern European
> literature into English there are few critically influential and truly
> potent texts. The Muirs' translations of Kafka are surely among
> them. It is no exaggeration to say that the English Kafka — from the
> 1930s through the 1950s especially — was at least as well known,
> at least as much read, and subjected to at least as much interpreta-
> tion as the German Kafka. One does not idly tamper with such
> texts; in a sense, they have become a kind of holy writ, for better or
> worse. And taken all in all, it has been for the better, we are bound
> to say. It would be neither fair nor, indeed, well informed to call
> them inadequate or to dismiss them out of hand as outdated. They
> contain passages of great brilliance and solutions that still cannot
> be improved upon.[15]

Still, of course, mistakes keep sticking out — mistakes that Wensinger,
among others, have detected, as well as "awkward passages, evasions,
lapses in cadence and rhythm, avoidances of deliberate humor, and a
few hopelessly snarled sentences."[16] Wensinger's task, therefore, will be
to eliminate the few striking errors but aside from smoothing out a few
stylistic infelicities leave the text alone. "Instead of retranslations," he
concludes, "we have made adjustments."[17] The reasoning is what it is,
and the mistakes, in at least four of Kafka's stories, are gone.

Recently, however, more and more of Kafka's texts have come into
the hands of new American and English translators. In the last few

years we have had, most notably, provocative new versions of *The Trial* by Breon Mitchell and of *The Castle* by Mark Harman, based on Kafka's original manuscripts. And yet, as versions have appeared that are more nearly mistake-free, it may be that we shall begin to look back at the mistakes of the Muirs less in sorrow than in wistful gladness, as betokening a happier time when a mistake was identifiable as a mistake and not part of an unboundable field of generalized error, à la Proust's "perpétuelle erreur, qui est précisément la 'vie.'"[18] The new era will know translation mistakes, if it all, in a quite different guise.

I will explain this paradox as I proceed, but I shall say, first, what, generally speaking, are such old-style, Muir-style translation mistakes. They are in a special sense at once particular and general. As particular mistakes, they are finite, specifiable deviant substitutions. As general mistakes, they appear to expose a motive for their commission: they open up to a worldview seen to have seized on the "mistake" as an opportunity to express itself. Mistakes, in other words, which are in the first instance corrigible, become in the second instance interesting as the occasion through which the translator's motives and interests reveal themselves — in distortion — become interesting as aberrations with respect to a posited, conventional, more nearly homogeneous "ordinary" language in the way that, for example, neurotic symptoms (slips, but also dreams and witty flashes) crop up within an everyday hermeneutic field. In the extreme case, such mistakes capture the reader's attention, as do works of art or privileged moments in worklike constellations and cast their spell. In this light, mistakes in works of art can appear as interesting as, or even more interesting than, "the works themselves," standing in relation to the finished work as the work does to the language of the everyday. Thus, especially in deconstructively influenced literary criticism, aporias or single oddities in the texture of works can function as privileged starting-off points for concentrated analysis or unraveling.[19]

Let us look at some of these mistakes. The first is simple though typical. In the middle of "The Judgment" the following sentences appear:

Endlich steckte [. . . Georg] den Brief in die Tasche und ging aus seinem Zimmer quer durch einen kleinen Gang in das Zimmer seines Vaters, in dem er schon seit Monaten nicht gewesen war. Es bestand auch sonst keine Nötigung dazu, denn er verkehrte mit seinem Vater ständig im Geschäft. Das Mittagessen nahmen sie gleichzeitig in einem Speisehaus ein, abends versorgte sich zwar jeder nach Belieben; doch saßen sie dann noch ein Weilchen, meistens jeder mit seiner Zeitung, im gemeinsamen Wohnzimmer,

wenn nicht Georg, wie es am häufigsten geschah, mit Freunden bei-
sammen war oder jetzt seine Braut besuchte.[20]

The words that are interesting are "Das Mittagessen nahmen sie
gleichzeitig in einem Speisehaus ein," which the Muirs translate as:
"They took their midday meal together at an eating house" (CS 80–81).
But this is not what the German says: Georg and his father do not take
their meal "together" but "at the same time." The nuance of estrangement is crucial, and it attunes in advance the hollow notion of a "*ge-
meinsames* Wohnzimmer" (a living room that both of them use). Perhaps the sharp edges of such estrangement are displeasing to the Muirs.

A second example:

In the episode of *Amerika* (*The One Who Sank Out of Sight*) called
"A Country House near New York," Karl Rossmann is seen playing the
piano for the amazon Klara with some difficulty:

> Er mußte ja tatsächlich wie bei jedem Lied die nötigen Tasten mit
> den Augen erst zusammensuchen, aber außerdem fühlte er in sich
> ein Leid entstehn, das über das Ende des Liedes hinaus, ein anderes
> Ende suchte und es nicht finden konnte. (GW 2:94)

The Muirs translate the second part of this sentence as follows: "[Karl]
felt rising within him a *song* [sic] which reached past the end of this
song, seeking another end which it could not find," as if Kafka had
written "[Karl] fühlte in sich ein *Lied* [sic] entstehn, das über das Ende
des Liedes hinaus, ein anderes Ende suchte und es nicht finden konnte"
(emphasis added).[21] The translators have proceeded with a sort of official dialectical alacrity to spirit away Karl's pain, turning "Leid" into
"Lied," his sorrow into song.

The particular aspect of the mistake is plain, the general aspect more
interesting. One can put it this way: in their version the Muirs have
been too swift to *objectify* Karl's suffering. Yet in doing so they are not
entirely insensitive to Kafka's concerns. It is as if they were responding
to Kafka's diary entry for September 19, 1917, which puts forth a key
poetological principle:

> Have never understood how it is possible for almost everyone who
> writes to objectify his sufferings in the very midst of undergoing
> them; thus I, for example, in the midst of my unhappiness, in all
> likelihood with my head still smarting from unhappiness, sit down
> and write to someone: I am unhappy. Yes, I can even go beyond
> that and with as many flourishes as I have the talent for, all of
> which seem to have nothing to do with my unhappiness, ring sim-
> ple, or contrapuntal, or a whole orchestration of changes on my
> theme. And it is not a lie, and it does not still my pain; it is simply,

a merciful surplus of strength at a moment when suffering has
raked me to the bottom of my being and plainly exhausted all my
strength. But then what kind of surplus is it? (D2 183–84)[22]

Pain is objectified in writing, in a sort of lament (*Klage*) or song
(*Lied*), even in the very moment of suffering pain. This points to a
power of psychic conversion that, in a quite incomprehensible manner,
mutates pain but, in doing so, does not bring about the slightest remis-
sion: "it does not still my pain." And yet this action is real—not a lie,
redounding to an increase in the power that directs it: it is part of a
perpetual motion machine or is, in other words, a perpetual surplus that
maintains a relation with pain by objectifying it, *but it does not translate it*. The surplus itself is a source of perpetual translation mistakes,
ever more elaborate ones, evoking, with its *Verschnörkelungen* (flourishes), more sentences, a failure of the literal; "for if the sentence," as
Benjamin writes, "is the wall before the language of the original [the
pure language], literalness is the arcade."[23] In the Muirs' version, song
displaces suffering, which now can no longer be felt: this full conversion
has proceeded, then, in opposition to Kafka's *intentio* in his diary entry,
inexcusable even if, in the riddle of Hölderlin's Empedocles that we
cited apropos the writing machine in "In the Penal Colony": "Nothing
is more painful . . . than unriddling suffering."[24]

My next example of a translation mistake cannot be laid at the door
of the Muirs. As translators they have inherited a kind of mutation
made without any fanfare at all by Max Brod upon Kafka's original
manuscript of *Amerika* (*The One Who Sank Out of Sight*), but its
thrust will be familiar and the shock of discovery for the American
reader the same. Karl, having been forced out of his uncle's house, joins
two rogues, Delamarche and Robinson, who are traveling on foot with
the alleged purpose of finding work. Before too long the reader finds
this geographical perspective:

> They now came to rising country, and when they stopped here and
> there they could see on looking back the panorama of New York
> and its harbor, extending more and more spaciously below them.
> The bridge connecting New York with Brooklyn hung delicately
> over the East River, and if one half-shut one's eyes it seemed to
> tremble.[25]

Since, as it happens, the author of this chapter grew up in Brooklyn, I
still cannot suppress, on rereading this sentence, a thrill of crosscultural
intimacy: Just think! The word "Brooklyn" crossed Kafka's lips, if si-
lently, as he was writing *Amerika* (*The One Who Sank Out of Sight*).
Kafka knew (my) Brooklyn—intimately! Or did he? I cannot suppress

another sort of emotion upon seeing the translation demythified by the original: "Die Brücke, die New York mit Boston verbindet hieng zart über den Hudson und sie erzitterte, wenn man die Augen klein machte" (The bridge that connects New York with Boston hung gently over the Hudson and trembled when one squeezed one's eyes closed) (GW 2:113). What has happened to Brooklyn? And to the Brooklyn Bridge, suspended so delicately over the East River? Of course one can see through the lens of the editor: there is no bridge between New York and Boston, which is 200 miles from New York as the crow flies; and even if there were one, it is doubtful that one could make it out very clearly after half a day's march away from it somewhere in upstate New York. So Brod (and the Muirs, helplessly in his wake) have corrected Kafka in case his aberrant geography should seem absurd in an epic. But by this logic, should not Frieda's allusion, too, in *The Castle*, to "Spain," as another place affording possible refuge to her and K., not be better translated as "S.," so as to guard the reader against the same sort of disorientation? (C 136). I would be against it. The road leading from an invisible castle to Spain, like the bridge over the Hudson connecting New York and Boston, cannot be crossed over so lightly as Brod (and the Muirs) have done, and Kafka's manuscripts do not need such planing down.

It is not hard to sense the uniformity of the perspective generating such mistakes from behind the scenes. It is the impulse to produce humane, sedative effects, to produce a Kafka who will not insist too nicely on distinguishing the merely simultaneous from the shared and who can sublimate his sorrows in song while remaining geographically well informed. In truth Kafka appears to want to assign at least this latter sort of knowledge to an inauthentic domain: in the original manuscript of *The Metamorphosis*, Gregor Samsa is heard complaining about the other traveling salesmen, who, like "harem women" ("Haremsfrauen"), can be found still lingering over breakfast late in the morning, where "yawning [they] discuss world politics" ("[sie] besprechen gähnend die Weltpolitik"). True, Kafka subsequently crossed out this phrase, but more for the reason, I believe, that it jars with the habits of harem women than that he wished to spare the world political situation the bad press of a yawning salesmen.

Here, now, are a few more eye-catching old-style mistakes: again, though not the fault of the Muirs, these mistakes can be readily assimilated to a certain kind of normalizing impulse. The translators, by and large very capable, of Kafka's *Diaries* are Joseph Kresh (D1) and Martin Greenberg (with the assistance of Hannah Arendt) (D2). In 1915 Kafka wrote about the different fates of the heroes of *Amerika* or *The One Who Sank Out of Sight* and *The Trial*: "Roßmann und K., der Schuldlose und der Schuldige, schließlich beide unterschiedslos strafweise umgebracht, der Schuldlose mit leichterer Hand, mehr zur Seite geschoben als niedergeschlagen" (GW 11:101). The translator wrote as follows: "Rossmann and K., the innocent and the guilty, both executed without distinction in the end, the guilty [*sic*] one with a gentler hand, more pushed aside than struck down," as if Kafka had written that Roßmann, not Joseph K., were "the guilty one" or that Joseph K., not Roßmann, had been executed "with a gentler hand, more pushed aside than struck down" (D2 132). Joseph K. does not need the translator's posthumous vindication.

The translators of the "Letter to His Father" ("Brief an den Vater"), finally, are Ernst Kaiser and Eithne Wilkins, who succeeded the Muirs as the foremost translators of Kafka in America; but the thrust of their unwitting rectification is familiar: it too aims to cover up moments that jolt and shock. In the letter Kafka wrote: "Mein Schreiben handelte von Dir, ich klagte dort ja nur, was ich an Deiner Brust nicht klagen konnte. Es war ein absichtlich in die Länge gezogener Abschied von Dir, nur daß er zwar von Dir erzwungen war, aber in der von mir bestimmten Richtung verlief."[26] Kaiser and Wilkins translate the second sentence as follows: "All I did there, after all, was to bemoan what I could not bemoan upon your breast. It was an intentionally long-drawn-out leave-taking from you, yet, although it was brought about by force on your part, it did *not* [*sic*] take its course in the direction determined by me," as if Kafka had written, "nur daß er zwar von Dir erzwungen war, aber in der von mir bestimmten Richtung *nicht* [*sic*] verlief" (emphasis added, DF 177).[27] The translators contribute to the fable of Kafka's massively helpless dependency on his father's will, as if the "Letter to His Father" itself were not also "a lawyer's letter," full of "lawyer's tricks," attesting as such to Kafka's ability to determine anew the direction of *everything*. Especially the feeling of being hunted and pursued by a devilish oppressor, viz. "Dieses Jagen nimmt die Richtung aus der Menschheit. . . . Wohin führt sie? Sie kann, dies scheint am zwingendsten, zum Irrsinn führen. . . . 'Jagd' ist ja nur ein Bild, ich kann auch sagen 'Ansturm gegen die letzte irdische Grenze' " ("This pursuit, originates in the midst of men. . . . Where is it leading? The strongest likelihood is, that it may lead to madness. . . . 'Pursuit,' indeed, is only a metaphor. I can also say, 'assault on the last earthly frontier' ") (GW 11:198–99, D2 202). Kafka here visibly determines the direction of his art. His weapon is the "turnabout" (*Umschwung*): "Mehr als Trost ist: Auch Du hast Waffen" ("More than consolation is: You too have weapons") (GW 11:236, D2 233). These mistranslations converge on producing a kinder, gentler, more *familiar* Kafka, as if *family* language were not among the chief evils in the sensate world.

I shall give one closing instance of a mistranslation — it is the Muirs' — that aims, consciously or not, to flatten out an extraordinarily radical thought of Kafka's. Earlier, we examined Kafka's great commentary on the Fall, beginning, "We do not have the strength to do the right thing," in which Kafka speaks of the strength *in* death.

The point is so counterintuitive — that only in death, with death, one might succeed in doing the right thing — that the Muirs' mistranslation could seem understandable, even though it robs the passage of its thanotropic force. The Muirs write,

> The strength to do so, however [to act in accordance with the knowledge of good and evil], is not likewise given him [man], consequently he must destroy himself *trying to do so*, at the risk of not achieving the necessary strength even then; yet there remains nothing for him but this final attempt. (emphasis added, GW 299)

With a vividness scarcely to be exceeded, this "translation" amounts to an *interpretation* that etiolates and levels the audacity of Kafka's statement. The words, "trying to do so," have been interpolated into Kafka's text in order to clear things up, with the result that what Kafka literally says is hidden: namely, that the final attempt to acquire the right degree of strength to do good is *by means of* destroying oneself, by taking one's life. The Muirs make this action an accessory, a cost or wretched by-product of the attempt to "try to do good," and dissolve its force into the vacuous counterfactual of "I'll try, even if it kills me." On their reading, the "last attempt" mimes some action at the brink of exhaustion, whereupon nothing but death follows, but that is not what Kafka says. Kafka says that the last action is willing one's own death; and hence it is no accident that, in *The Trial*, Joseph K.'s disgrace coincides with his reluctance to take the knife of his executioners into his own hand. Kafka imagines a gain of strength by a kind of sinking down in advance as death's representative — a willing and comprehending accession to death. The Muir translation elides the insane radicalism of this Gnostic position.

In all this I have described portions of an earlier state of affairs, where the notion of a mistake had a more or less definite sense. But now I want to explore briefly the fate of the mistake in the new editorial situation.

The Kafka text of Stroemfeld/Roter Stern, the original (or facsimile of the original), is now one *in* which there are mistakes, for these pages demonstratively contain Kafka's crossings-out. The "mistake," now least of all the marginalized and proscribed term in translations, has a constitutive virtue for the original. For example: at a certain point in the Cathedral chapter of *The Trial*, one encounters the following conversation between Leni and K.

> "[w]Warum denn in den Dom?" fragte Leni. K. suchte es ihr in Kürze zu erklären, aber kaum hatte er damit angefangen ["ehe er noch damit fertig" crossed out] war, sagte Leni ["plötzlich" inserted]: "Sie hetzen Dich" ["Unerwartetes" crossed out] Bedauern, das er nicht ["ge" crossed out"] herausgefordert und nicht erwartet hatte, vertrug K. nicht [. . .].

> . . . . .

> "[w]Why the cathedral?" asked Leni. K. tried to give her a brief explanation, but he had hardly begun ["before he {was} finished with it" crossed out] when Leni ["suddenly" inserted] said: "They're hounding you." ["Something unexpected" crossed out] K. could not stand pity that he neither ["re" crossed out] desired nor expected. (T 205, Pr 17)

In the *FKA*, manuscript pages are faced by ingeniously conceived "Typoskripte" constituting an "inoffensive transcription" ("diplomatische Umschrift"), which Peter von Matt erroneously calls "an exact transcription" ("eine genaue Transkription"): this category mistake is not unlike the category mistake built into the concept of the "manuscript version," *KKA*.[28] On the one hand, the typescript does look something like the manuscript, structurally speaking: interpolations, for example, appear in the same relative position with respect to other words on the line. On the other hand, the graphic character of manuscript remains irreducible to type: here we come face to face with what is termed the "materiality of the letter," what Paul de Man calls, in his Benjamin essay, "the uncontrollable power of the letter as inscription."[29] The typescript is itself a necessarily imprecise translation, yet another *version* of the original.

In this situation, what is the poor translator to do? He must translate the mistakes visibly caught by Kafka in the manuscript and not only literally: he must decide on the kind of intention informing the mistake. He needs a theory of mistakes: Is the crossed out grapheme just a mistake, effectively worthless for author and reader? Or a subliminal revelation that must not be allowed to become explicit? Is it an interesting hypothesis that Kafka meant to keep in reserve, readable, for him, under its crossing out, or a productive error untimely cut off—a mistaken mistake? The translator must translate this mode of intention with different sorts of marks.

For the translator in his deliberations the kind of line that Kafka literally draws through the mistake may be of help, and hence it is obvious that the line needs its own responsive translation. This is not a problem, however, addressed by the *KKA*, which also includes mistakes but removes them in a body from the finished work, registering them cleanly in a separate volume (the apparatus) without informing the reader as to their status or position on the line. This apparatus can be translated according to normal criteria — but not so even the pertinent portions of the *FKA* typescript ("the inoffensive transcription") of the manuscript. That is because in the *FKA* typescript and manuscript inescapably mediate one another; the typescript (including the barred word or words) cannot be read except in the process of its being rapidly referred back to the manuscript. In *Beyond Good and Evil*, Nietzsche wrote: "Was sich am schlechtesten aus einer Sprache in die andre übersetzen läßt, ist das *Tempo* ihres Stils" ("What is most difficult to render from one language into another is the *tempo* of its style").[30] This is now particularly true, in a quite unsuspected sense, of the reading of the manuscript/typescript couple. The translation of the typescript alone misrecognizes its relation to the manuscript.

How to translate Kafka's mistakes, now that they are embedded in his texts? So far I have indicated only subtypes of one category of mistakes — those caught by Kafka. But mistakes come in (at least) these three categories: (1) those caught by Kafka; (2) those caught by Kafka but not so marked (these are the not yet crossed-out graphemes hovering uninserted over the line); and (3) those uncaught by Kafka, hence, putative inadvertencies, inconsistencies.

One can reproduce the mistake, letter for letter, but how is one to reproduce the spirit of the mistake — without mistake? To reproduce the "mistaken" word by means of its lexical counterpart is not to reproduce the spirit, intention, or meaning of the mistake in the original, for Kafka's intention in crossing out a word could be, for one thing, to annihilate it as a mistake, whereas the "correct" translation aims to reproduce the mistake as something like a microhistory of the engendering of the word that survives it, a highly abbreviated Bildungsroman. (I write "Roman" to stress the intralinguistic character of these relationships, their constructive character.) The reader's reading of this manuscript is therefore in many places sheerly opposed to Kafka's own reading; in reading his manuscript, Kafka re-reads *out* of existence his crossed-through mistakes, but in reading this manuscript (mechanically reproduced), the modern reader reads *into* existence the crossed-through mistake. Kafka reads the line running through the mistakes: this line identifies the mistake. The modern reader omits reading the line, seeing no mistake — seeing, indeed, more. He situates the crossed-out word in a different, elliptical relation to the word or blank that survives it. The question remains: how is this different, elliptical relation to be conceived within the norm of a correct translation? The answer appears to be a paradox: with respect to the manuscript, it ceases to be a mistake. In this sense Kafka's mistakes, in being transparently reproduced, are systematically rendered as translation mistakes, for they engender relations between reader and text that are not in the original.

## CHIPS FROM THE TRANSLATOR'S WORKSHOP

Some years ago I proposed translating Kafka's *Der Verschollene* (*Amerika* or *The One Who Sank Out of Sight*) for an American publisher, feeling that a new translation of a work last translated in 1940 (by the Muirs) was overdue, especially as that version, worthy as it is, did not even include several especially brilliant fragments belonging to the manuscript of *Der Verschollene*, signally, the passage entitled "Ausreise Bruneldas" ("Brunelda's Journey") (GW 2:289), and one beginning as follows:

> 'Auf! Auf!' rief Robinson, kaum daß Karl früh die Augen öffnete. Der Türvorhang war noch nicht weggezogen, aber man merkte an dem durch die Lücken einfallenden gleichmäßigen Sonnenlicht, wie spät am Vormittag es schon war. Robinson lief eilfertig mit besorgten Blicken hin und her, bald trug er ein Handtuch, bald einen Wasserkübel, bald Wäsche- und Kleidungsstücke und immer wenn er an Karl vorüberkam, suchte er ihn durch Kopfnicken zum Aufstehn aufzumuntern und zeigte durch Hochheben dessen was er gerade in der Hand hielt, wie er sich heute noch zum letzten mal für Karl plage, der natürlich am ersten Morgen von den Einzelheiten des Dienstes nichts verstehen konnte. (GW 2:274)

I made this translation:

> "Get up!" shouted Robinson, as Karl, thinking it was early, had just barely opened his eyes. The door-curtain hadn't been drawn yet, but it was clear from the sunlight falling evenly through the gaps how late the morning already was. Robinson was rushing back and forth with a frantic look on his face, carrying now a towel, now a water bucket, now underwear and articles of clothing. Whenever he passed Karl, he tried by nodding his head to encourage him to get up, signaling with a wave of whatever he happened to have in his hand that today was the last time he would be slaving away for Karl, who, of course — it being his first morning — could not be expected to know all the details of the service.

The translation project got mired down and did not come to fruition, chiefly from the skepticism of the editor (whom I shall call "Mr. J.") toward the very notion of replacing the Muirs' version, on the view: "if it ain't broke, don't fix it"; partly, too, for the solider reason that the Muirs' work commands a good deal of well-founded affection. My editor's disaffection with my own efforts was actually expressed in a series of concrete objections to my rendering of each of Kafka's sentences shown above. As it happens, there is no Muirs' version to serve as a standard against which my own translation of these pages of *Der Verschollene* could be tested, but Mr. J., on the strength of his long association with the Muirs' translation, had an intuition about how such a text should sound—or better, not sound.

I think there is something exemplary in our disagreements, and I should like to set them down here. Arthur S. Wensinger, whom I mentioned above as the author of an improved version of the Muirs' translations of the stories making up Kafka's projected volume *The Sons*—namely, "The Stoker" ("Der Heizer"), "The Judgment" ("Das Urteil"), *The Metamorphosis* (*Die Verwandlung*)—said about the Muirs' versions that they were "a kind of holy writ." Well, if this is so, what then of Kafka's originals? This was Mr. J.'s view, who required *literalness* at all costs: "You must stay with Kafka's actual words," he said; "treat them like the Bible." Therefore I produced some consternation right at the outset.

In my translation of the first words of the text—"Auf! Auf!"—Mr. J. was disturbed by my violation of literalness, since I translate these words as "Get up!" Mr. J. felt the right translation should be "Up! Up!"

I replied: "The meaning of 'Auf! Auf!' is not twice 'auf' ('up!' then 'up!' again). Let us consult the Muret-Sanders Encyclopedic German-English dictionary of 1910—i.e., an important reference work essentially contemporaneous with the writing of *Der Verschollene*. You will see that 'Up! Up!' is not an option (pp. 86–87). It wasn't English then, and it isn't now. The expression 'auf! auf!' means 'look alive!,' 'let's go!' My translation 'get up' is good enough; 'let's go!' might be better."

The word "früh," Mr. J. then told me, means "the next morning," and that is how it must appear in the translation. Unfortunately, this suggestion wouldn't work, for several reasons.

Kafka does not use the German word for "morning" in this sentence or the next, although the following sentence does require the English word "morning" ("spät am Vormittag"—"late in the morning"). To use "morning" in the first sentence is to insert it twice in the text at the outset, even though, once again, it is not a word whose literal German equivalent Kafka uses.

More important, to say "the *next* morning" is to speak from the standpoint of a narrator over the head of the protagonist Karl. This violates the inner principle of this novel/fragment — and indeed of all of Kafka's novel/fragments. They are not narrated by an omniscient narrator but, with the exception of a few minor — although interesting — breaks, arise from a standpoint congruent with the perspective of the hero. This device is called *Einsinnigkeit* (monopolized perspective); the hero, *die Aspektfigur* (the figure furnishing the perspective). This means that everything that appears in the fictional world is registered in Karl Rossmann's consciousness — some would say, produced by it.

"Thus," I declared, "you say my translation of 'früh' ('thinking it was early') puts thoughts into the head of Karl. But all the images and scenes and temporal indicators in the novel are already in the head of Karl.

"It is true that Kafka did not emphasize the point as explicitly as I did; and it would be lucky if one could just insert the word 'early' in this sentence. But one cannot write 'early' without a qualification, first, because there is no place in the English sentence for it; and, furthermore, the *next* sentence tells us, precisely, that it isn't early — it's late.

"The opening sentence *means* that Karl opens his eyes and registers that it is 'early (in the day).' This is what my translation says. The difficulty prompted the great French translator Alexander Viallate to omit the word entirely."

Mr. J. continued by saying " 'door-curtain' should read 'curtain over the door.' " This, however, is not what Muret-Sanders gives for *Türvorhang*. (See p. 977: *Türvorhang* = door-curtain.)

Mr. J. also felt that "gleichmäßiges Licht" should be translated as "bright light," despite the violation of literalness. "But," I wrote him, "the light is 'gleichmäßig' = 'uniform' or 'even' — because at midday the sun is shining fully into the window of the room where Brunelda and Delamarche are sleeping; hence it shines with equal intensity through all the gaps in the curtain. The point is not the intensity of the light at any one of its entrances but its regularity from entrance (gap) to entrance (gap)."

Mr. J. declared that the light which "fällt ein" 'breaks in' or 'bursts in' through the gaps and doesn't 'fall.' This is not what Muret-Sanders (and the Random House dictionary) say. *Einfallen* is a word belonging to optics: "einfallende Lichtstrahlen" = "incident rays of light" (p. 296). The Random House dictionary gives: "incident" = "falling or striking on something, as light rays" (p. 966).

Mr. J. objected to the expression "with a wave."

I replied: "To follow your suggestion in this instance yields, to my mind, a wooden sentence: 'By lifting up (high) whatever he happened to have in his hand in order to indicate. . . .' What exactly is Robinson doing? He is not, presumably, lifting high a water bucket since we're told he can barely lift the buckets off the floor.

"When I lift high an object already in my hand—such as an article of clothing—in order to signal something with it, I am signaling with a 'wave' of it.

"Furthermore, 'by lifting up' would repeat the previous construction: 'by nodding his head.' It's very awkward to do so."

"You are surprised," I added, finally, "that I translate 'Dienst' as 'service,' yet 'Militärdienst' is, of course, 'military service.' Waiters are instructed in details of 'the service.' The *Dienst* which Kafka is talking about is not 'Karl's duties' but *the* (morning) routine. Karl does not yet know the details of the 'drill.' But this is too newfangled. 'Service' is my choice, and a good choice, because it anticipates the word 'serve' (*bedienen*) in the next sentence and reminds the reader that Karl and Robinson are *Diener* ('servants'). Your suggestion, 'details his duties entailed,' is not elegant."

I realize that in now setting down my own versions and meanings I am only pointing to the maelstrom of dialectic that every translating decision rightly calls up. My joy in welcoming the authorized (facsimile) manuscript version of Kafka's works is tempered by my sadness that it may prove an end to such discussions.

# Chapter 11

## THE TROUBLE WITH CULTURAL STUDIES

> In no case does art reproduce its age. To pass from the art
> of a time to the time itself is the great mistake that all
> historians commit.
> —Oscar Wilde, *"The Critic as Artist"*

> The work belongs in that domain which is opened up by it.
> —Martin Heidegger, *Der Ursprang des Kunstwerkes*

THE TWO CHIEF obstacles to a good grasp of Kafka's work are bad translations — including bad editions — and bad interpretations. There will be little profit in having purified texts of Kafka if the dominant optic through which they are read is that of so-called cultural studies, which reads the specificity of these texts through the generalities of political coercions and cultural stereotypes. In discussing the allusions to *writing* in Kafka's works, Bill Dodd has put forward "The Case for a Political Reading":

> The demonstrable existence of such veins of meaning in Kafka's writing appears . . . to point towards an introverted meaning system, and thus to question the notion that Kafka engages in some substantial way with an external, social world. Taken to an extreme, this can suggest a picture of Kafka as a solipsist, and some critics tend to endorse this view by reading, for example, *The Trial* and "In the Penal Colony" substantially as extended metaphors for the trials of writing in general, and writing the work in question in particular.[1]

This is the ideological watermark of cultural studies.

Dodd begins his challenge to an older "consensus" by turning to *Amerika* (*The One Who Sank Out of Sight*) as a prize witness for his claim that Kafka was above all "political" and engaged by an "external" world. But this move flies in the face of Kafka's own view of the worth of such testimony, for Kafka considered this book as adrift in the "lowlands of writing" and literature, in general, as the founding of a "homeland on the moon":

> When we write something we have not coughed up the moon [den Mond ausgeworfen], whose origins might then be investigated.

Rather, we have moved to the moon with everything that we have. . . . The only separation that can be made, the separation from the homeland, has already taken place. (L 204, Br 240–41)

The hobgoblin of Kafka as "solipsist" is not an impressive argument, either, since the solipsist's attention circles around the "self" and its various "modifications and states," these being, for him, the form of "all real entities."[2] This view supposes the presence of a fixed personal being around which Kafka's reflection and interest revolve (the moon that interests him is *not* fixed). But even if the point about fixity is rejected, and the person is said to wander, then the mobility of this self as center shatters the solipsist metaphor of circular motion. If we must spring for a geometrical figure, Benjamin's dual-centered ellipse is more nearly apt.[3]

In fact, it is precisely the location of any sort of Kafkan self that is in question from the start. "How pitiful my knowledge of self," he wrote,

when compared, for example, with my knowledge of my room. Why? There is no observation of the inner world as there is of the outward one. On the whole, psychology is probably an anthropomorphism, a nibbling at the borders. (NS2 32)[4]

In the absence of a self, Kafka is at work *constituting* one, wide and general enough to contain even the elucidated empirical tensions of his time. His first task is the creation of a being supple and capacious enough to absorb these tensions without shattering. And the means to this constitution of self is a will to stylize a conversation with himself or a dream—in short, to write. It is to get things backwards to suppose that Kafka's writing strives in the first place to give accounts of "the political."

You find in a recent study of Kafka an answer to the question of "what was it about Kafka that enabled him to depict modern life more tellingly than his contemporaries." It is, writes Jeremy Adler, "the *identity* of his personality and his writing, and of his writing with a modern impersonal world" (emphasis added).[5] How well does such a gnome answer to Kafka that unquiet dreamer?

Who is it? Who walks under the tress on the quay? Who is quite lost? Who is past saving? Over whose grave does the grass grow? Dreams have arrived, upstream they come, they climb up the wall of the quay on a ladder. One stops, makes conversation with them, they know a number of things, but what they don't know is where they come from. It is quite warm this autumn evening. They turn towards the river and raise their arms. Why do you raise your arms instead of clasping us in them? (DF 226)

This is the relation of the dreamer to his dream, and it is precisely this figure that Walter Sokel uses to characterize Kafka's relation to his age. The historian's mistake of "pass[ing] from the art of a time to the time itself" is here corrected by another mediation — the dream of the time itself. Sokel concludes:

> Kafka's writing corresponds to the age on a level far below explicit articulation. It relates to the age as dreams do to waking life. The latter permeates them in a manner not conceptualized and articulated, but allusive and concealing. In the same estranging and mystifying way, Kafka's mythos alludes to and expresses historical reality.[6]

If we add to this account Walter Benjamin's remark that his morning's writing was shadowed with the fear of a too quick "combustion of the dream," we will have arrived at a better formula for Kafka's writing: *the combustion of the dream of his age*. But this combustion implies the dislocation of both self and world: "Far, far away world history takes its course, the world history of your soul" (DF 243). It has gone to the "moon," to the lunar system of works.

Dodd's piece is too brief and recent to have engaged the field as has the work of senior critics writing in a comparable way. Earlier, in my preface, I said that cultural studies' overexplicit way of approaching the "substance" of Kafka's world as "external and social" had reached its apogee in the work of two redoubtable scholars: Elizabeth Boa and Sander Gilman, both authors of vivid and influential works conforming to a tendency. Boa is the author of *Franz Kafka: Gender, Class, and Race in the Letters and Fictions* and Gilman, of *Franz Kafka: The Jewish Patient*.[7] If I study them here, it is because this tendency, with its distinctive way of being at once impersonal and interest-driven, strikes me as a matter for concern. It is significant, as part of the Zeitgeist, and it is a provocation.

The fact that Boa's book is a work of cultural studies could not be plainer: the cultural studies statement is embedded in its title. As verbal objects for analysis and commentary, Kafka's letters — which, for Boa, are essential as testimony of his empirical preoccupations — have the same or higher rank than the fiction. That work of Kafka matters most that can be most swiftly excavated for attitudes on gender, class, and race. Boa's approach invites critique, because her polemical, social-critical arguments lead to contradictions that reveal some of the signature difficulties of cultural studies.

Boa's account of social stereotypes in Kafka's work begins with his bachelor types in their "parasitic dependence . . . upon the institution of marriage." The point, however, is soon inflected differently, for Kafka also represents "the bachelor's heroism [as] . . . functional to patriarchal marriage." This new idea appears to make marriage (parasiti-cally?) dependent on "bachelordom," a thesis that seems more nearly correct, since for Kafka bachelorhood is not parasitic on marriage but is its indispensably reciprocal cooperating feature, marriage being the in-stitution whose purpose is to engender initially bachelor men and women.[8] My point now is that such things as social stereotypes do not and can-not display the reciprocally cooperating features of persons and *also* their presumed opposites (bachelors *and* married persons, and, thereaf-ter, men *and* women, workers *and* bosses, Jews *and* Germans): stereo-types are unambiguous, or they are nothing. Or, better, since they are unambiguous, but social reality — let alone its refraction in literature — is not, stereotypes *are* nothing, or worse. In the most radical formula-tion — that of Paul de Man, for instance — even the social reality from which they are derived is a "a waste of time from a critical viewpoint," but his position is possibly distorted by embitteredness.[9]

From time to time throughout her book, Boa gives an account of her methodology, rightly considering the "bodily features" of Gregor Samsa, the hero of Kafka's *The Metamorphosis*, as "signs in a literary text, not symptoms in a medical handbook." But she thereafter speaks of the "incorporation" in literature of such physical symptoms of degenera-tion, noting, though, that even before this pseudo-embodiment,

> the symptoms became signs in a culturally constructed body lan-guage and spoke aloud of secret vices. . . . As signifiers rather than symptoms, the signs wandered around. . . . (111)

Kafka's literary text is dependant on the allegedly wider social text, of which it is the plagiarism. But everything crucial depends, I think, on visualizing how the cultural construction of symptoms (en route to be-coming signs) actually "wandered" into Kafka's fiction. The matter surely calls for a good deal of reserve: Did Kafka, then, have so little individual relation to these border crossings, so little power to admit these signs or to refuse them? But without a view on Kafka's writerly intentions (his horror precisely of such ungoverned "metaphoric" wan-derings from "culture" to "writing"), the alleged collapse of Kafka's body and his work is trivialized: he just went slack and ruptured, he took in the collapsing patriarchal social and cultural order as the flailing swimmer takes in the water in which he drowns. For Boa, Kafka's expe-rience is in fact not of "signifiers" but the a priori experience of stereo-types — of other peoples' "signifieds." A more melancholy inflection of the neo-Romantic view of the artist's privileged capacity for experience can hardly be imagined: Kafka's questionable distinction survives in the completeness with which he incorporates the banalities of his age. This is a Kafka who offers us the New Woman, the shapely ephebe, the Jewish ape, the priapic bachelor, the circus artiste in decline, but there is no tension in his figure, nothing specifiable that comes from his "existence as a writer." Even as the writer, Kafka is the male of his time, reprehensibly incapable of the prescriptive change that would have qualified him for an exemplary marriage with his fiancée Felice Bauer.

Sander Gilman's project, in *Franz Kafka: The Jewish Patient*, shares the methodology of Boa's but with implications that are farther reaching. Gilman's account of Kafka's Jewish "patienthood" offers a detailed report of the cultural climate in which Kafka lived worked, grew ill, and died. This climate was pitilessly anti-Semitic. As a result, according to Gilman, Kafka lived in shame and worked in fear, as he watched his body sicken in a way he could not fail to understand (he became tubercular, even though Jews were by and large supposed to be immune to tuberculosis). This "Jewish self-hatred" can be found throughout Kafka's stories, letters, and diary entries.[10] Despite all manner of twisting and turning, Kafka himself adhered to an anti-Semitic view of himself, and this became the obsessive content of his work.

Gilman is writing on the cusp of a sea change in literary scholarship that he, more than anyone else in German studies, has helped to bring about. The approach is iconoclastic: literary works are to be read no differently from any sort of notes and jottings by the author in question or, for that matter, from articles, speeches, and books written by the author's contemporaries, such as professors and doctors and journalists and also political agitators and crackpots. It is less important to show how the literary work might differ from such writing than the way they amount to the same thing.[11] All texts in a given period have like testamentary value for a prevailing "discourse" of race, gender, sexuality, and disease; and in the case of Kafka as well, all contribute to the Central European obsession with the otherness of Jews—their ugly otherness, an ugliness that "explains" (one may say this, speaking from the standpoint of the sources Gilman cites, *Kafka included*) the murderous hatred they reaped. For "the Jew," whom Gilman constructs on the basis of his freewheeling reading of his sources, is a dirty, scabrous, fetid, diseased, effeminate male of the third sex, on whose body his difference from all good and healthy things is indelibly inscribed.

Now, it is true that contemporary sources do paint this picture of the Jew. And to suppose that every Jew necessarily holds this opinion of himself, having "internalized" it as his own, might be useful as a working assumption. But the thesis offered as the "unique contribution" of *The Jewish Patient* is that Kafka's work reproduces this vile caricature of himself and that a glance at his novels, stories, letters, and diary entries reveals that they are saturated with such (ugly) things as Jewish tuberculosis, barbaric circumcision, bloody kosher slaughtering, ritual murder, and flat feet. In truth, this thesis has been *inflicted* on Kafka's work.

Toward the end of his life, in the "Letter to his Father," Kafka directly addressed his destiny as a writer, saying to his father:

> My writing was all about you; all I did there, after all, was to bemoan what I could not bemoan upon your breast. It was an intentionally long-drawn-out leave-taking from you, only although it was brought about by force on your part, *it did take its course in the direction determined by me*." (emphasis added, DF 177)

If Kafka's literary achievement, however, amounted to anything more than the reproduction of bits and pieces of the hate speech prevailing in mid-Europe at the fin de siècle, it is not something easy to find in Gilman's work. What finally matters is what Kafka's literature, an itself negligible medium, embeds: the "hanks of hair and bits of bone" of the prevailing discourse of anti-Semitic slur and pseudoscience.[12] Yet, if you look more precisely at Gilman, nothing he quotes from Kafka is literally about bloody circumcision, kosher slaughtering, ritual murder, and so forth. The citations may be suggestive of such things for what Theodor Adorno sardonically called "an orientated understanding," but just as often they suggest no such things. Kafka's "The Vulture," a fantasy of self-mutilation, in which a predatory bird attacks the victim's feet, nowhere allows that they are "ugly, Jewish feet." Gilman is projecting other peoples' views of Jewish feet and Gentile vultures.

Now, how is it possible that a scholar as astute as Gilman can have ridden so roughshod over Kafka's works? It is partly because Gilman possesses the stereotype of the anti-Semitic Jew in such depth and detail that he cannot imagine any contemporary as sensitive as Kafka not being persuaded by it. Such dogmatism is in ample supply in his study, but so, too, is something more humanly engaging. It is the kind of concern that you find at the root of the cultural studies enterprise at its best—a passion for justification, suggested by the extraordinary image quoted above—the image of hanks of hair and bits of bone that Gilman imposes on Kafka's writings and which refer to fragments of the dominant discourse of anti-Semitism that Kafka was not entirely able by literary means "to mask and efface."[13]

These hanks of hair and bits of bone suggest what a visitor to Auschwitz could scrape out of the ground. These hanks of hair and bits of bone are the surviving fragments (it may well be) of Jewish victims of genocidal anti-Semitism. What is startling about Gilman's use of this image is that in his hands they represent fragments of the vicious discourse that found their way into Kafka's writing. They are the topics of a racist anti-Judaism brought to a murderous point; and as it was not Jews who originated this discourse, then Gilman's fragments are the fragments of their murderers. Here, Gilman's rhetoric itself masks and effaces a crucial movement of his own thought: a fin de siècle anti-

Semitic rhetoric has become the remains of its *victims*. The concern that appears to have driven Gilman's project all along emerges now as something he has judged to be dishonest or feeble or deficient in Kafka's writing, that only so little of this (murderous) anti-Semitic discourse can be recovered from it. Kafka's ultimate victimhood now seems explained — "deserved," almost — by his readiness to hide that discourse. Kafka's "literature" — that is, everything that cannot be reduced to the "discourse" — is a mendacious diversion or flight from the truth that he could just as well, being perspicacious or courageous enough, have acknowledged. At some level Gilman is saying that if the Jews of Europe had not fled into High Modernism or some version of this option available to nonwriters they could have better resisted their annihilation. And I believe he resents Kafka for having spent so much energy stubbornly resisting the clearest possible consciousness of this view.

I linger so long on the work of another scholar, because Gilman's hidden argument reveals the strongest source of the drive to the cultural studies that dominate literary studies today: the social mood of *ressentiment*. Because literature, it is supposed, has never been explicit enough in arraigning the crimes of men and women, it will not satisfy the scandalized ethical man or woman who wants to see these crimes arraigned, especially those against his or her own people. And so such critics are quick to identify literature with the ideological and physical struggles of its time in order to make explicit what otherwise appears to be hidden in it. For Boa, Kafka is antifeminist; for Gilman, he is not anti-Semitic enough.[14]

This passion for retribution has taken a special impetus from a crisis in recent literary studies; it is a drive abetted in America by the fall from grace in 1987 of a powerful rival critical tendency, the deconstructionism of Paul de Man. This thinker and writer, a professor of comparative literature at Yale, was shown to have written collaborationist newspaper articles for the Belgian press between 1939 and 1943. And for the deconstructionist critic, we recall,

> considerations of the actual and historical existence of writers are a waste of time from a critical viewpoint. These regressive stages can only reveal an emptiness of which the writer himself is well aware when he begins to write.[15]

What certainly does not fill the writer, let alone his work, are the epochal themes of his ethnic personality, sex life, and attitudes to work and class. But when de Man fell, so, for many, did the authority of his position.

At this point, we could seem to be traveling away from the concerns of a book on Kafka and Kafka studies, but we are not. Several paths lead back and forth between them. One of the most curious has actually given this book its title "Lambent Traces." The English critic Gilbert Adair has written a novel called *The Death of the Author*, a mystery that cleverly plays on the literary-critical thesis that modern writing implies the "death" of the empirical self of the author—his needs and personal interests—and introduces a character who is a parody of Paul de Man.[16] Yet it is with a good deal of acuity that Adair puts these words in his hero's mouth:

> There could be no doubt, I repeat, about my opposition to the Nazi movement. Nevertheless, detectable in my discourse, there remained the lambent traces, the still flickering embers, of an occult and certainly unconscious attachment to the very codes and practices of the ideology I claimed to oppose.[17]

*These* lambent traces, traces of self-seeking, are the antipode of the Gnostic—they turn the words embedding them against the Gnostic.

Meanwhile, in thinking of de Man with Kafka, we should be perfectly clear that it is useless to speak of a specific de Manian reading of Kafka, for this does not exist.[18] Yet, even while, in 1943, de Man was dismissing Jewish writers for their "meddling" in the core of literature—this core consisting of a certain purity, atrociously miscast as a *European* "originality and character"—de Man chose to protect from his attack, in a list of acceptable modernists, a writer of undetermined ethnicity named "Kafha."[19] Even then, Kafha's or Kafka's literary work seemed to him exempt from the intrusions of extraneous ("Jewish") needs and social demands that had otherwise invaded "all aspects of European life." I say "even then" because, though de Man never wrote about Kafka during his mature years, it is hard to believe that he did not know that many of Kafka's key words and insights describe and perpetuate the ascetic mood of deconstruction. Here is an especially explicit example from Kafka's letters:

> Any criticism that deals in concepts of authentic and inauthentic, and seeks to find in the work the will and feelings of an author who isn't present—any such criticism seems to me nonsensical and follows only from the critic's also having lost his homeland. (L 204, Br 240–41)

The true homeland of the critic is exile. Meanwhile, I hope to have made clear throughout this book Kafka's affinity with the ethos of a rigorous deconstruction but also the point that Kafka surpasses the limits of theoretical deconstruction. "Lambent traces" marks the place where the writer (Kafka) and the critic's writer ("Kafha") intersect, a place of resistance and idealism, of resistance *as* idealism, "however meager and marginal that freedom may be."[20]

We have been concerned with the lines that lead to cultural studies from political resentment, from an irritation with deconstruction's exclusion of social contents, and from a curiosity to expose the violent and erotic roots of these repressed stereotypes. These lines, too, are elliptical, yet they help to explain why Gilman's and Boa's work on Kafka has found the resonance it has. The desire to rectify inherited social evils—the longstanding sufferings of marginalized Jews, women, proletarians, colonials, gays, and persons of color—has animated critics, but they are wrong to imagine that they will finally find in Kafka either an ally or a foe. There is an altogether different substratum of concern in him that I have called "gnostic" and that guides my way of reading him. It happens to connect, too, with aspects of de Man's teaching: the view that literature strives for an autonomy apart from social experience on the strength of its knowledge of this difference.

What so strikingly marks the cultural studies I criticize is a certain grievous disparity—the gap between the rigor that Kafka brought to his enterprise of moral and aesthetic purity and the ease with which these authors suppose him to have been merely contaminated by "the dross of the phenomenal world" ("Abhub der Erscheinungswelt").[21] Boa and Gilman are in this sense de Man's antipodes. They project narrative personae of a perfect liberality and rectitude, they have lived their lives (for all I know) with exemplary ethical rigor, but they write as if contamination were the most self-evident, least avoidable thing. De Man, on the other hand, was guilty of a terrible form of such contamination—active collaboration with the Nazi occupiers of the city in which he lived—but thereafter broke a lance for purity, for the only purity he could presume to speak of, but which he imagined intensely: the stringency with which the work of art, as a fiction, distinguishes its artist-maker from a world of empirical entanglements and specious consolations. How, in the optic of Boa and Gilman, is one to understand Kafka's claim that he would have complete satisfaction from nothing less than "raising the world into the pure, the true, and the immutable" ("die Welt ins Reine, Wahre, Unveränderliche heben") (D2 187, GW 11:167)? What relation has this desire to the satisfaction that Gilman posits for Kafka in the knowledge that with his tuberculosis he had at last come into possession of the effete, scabrous, and effeminate—because Jewish—body of his father, a desideratum that had long lived in him an unwholesome underground life of denial? The crux in positing an origin for Kafka's art is the change in direction that he was able to give his being, a change away from the natural perspective of a body sunk in the toils of reproduction.[22]

I conclude with this parable, unpublished in Kafka's lifetime.

> Before setting foot in the Holy of Holies you must take off your
> shoes, yet not only your shoes, but everything; you must take off
> your traveling garment and lay down your luggage; and under that
> you must shed your nakedness and everything that is under the
> nakedness and everything that hides beneath that, and then the
> core and the core of the core, then the remainder and then the
> residue and then even the glimmer of the undying fire. Only the fire
> itself is absorbed by the Holy of Holies and lets itself be absorbed
> by it; neither can resist the other. (DF 87)

Can we not say that the perversity of cultural studies is precisely to run
backwards through the stages of this "consuming of self" before the
Holy of Holies—to assume the failure of the traveler's enterprise and
re-dress him with the (cultural) baggage he had put down (DF 87, GW
6:198)? (Mark Anderson's seminal work of cultural studies is significantly entitled *Kafka's Clothes*).[23] In light of Kafka's parable, however,
surely more courtesy is owed to Kafka's idealism. You must listen to it.
You cannot refuse every last drop of credence to the enterprise of purity
that creates Kafka the writer and his work.

And so my own chapters have gone another route, in order to introduce a different way of thinking and writing about him. Certainly, it is
easier to say the things I take to be wrong with cultural studies than to
say how Kafka, and his crucial relation to his own writing, must be
represented. I would need more chapters, because the matter can be put
only allusively and by indirections, and so it is actually interminable. As
Keats observed: "A Man's life of any worth is a continual allegory—
and very few eyes can see the Mystery of his life—a life like the scriptures, figurative."[24]

But here we have arrived once again at the point that justifies a resistance to cultural studies. What it fails to grasp is the way that literature
is less testimony to the dead letter of the stereotype in any given age
than the "continual allegory" of a new beginning. Kafka described this
point explicitly in writing about "a good book" when "it rouses me,
satisfies me, suffices me":

> Proofs that previously I did not include this book in my eternity, or
> had not pushed on far enough ahead to have an intuitive glimpse of
> the eternity that necessarily includes this book as well.—From a
> certain stage of knowledge [Erkenntnis] on, weariness, insuffi-
> ciency, constriction, self-contempt must all vanish: namely at the
> point where I have the strength to recognize as my own nature
> what previously was something alien to myself that refreshed me,
> satisfied, liberated and exalted me. (DF 91–92)

# NOTES

### PREFACE

1. Hartmut Binder, "'Man muss die Nase dafür haben': Kafka und seine Bücher," *Kafkas Bibliothek: Expressionismus* (Stuttgart: Antiquariat Herbert Blank, 2001), 6.

2. For an illuminating discussion of the metaphor of "the way," from the pre-Socratic philosophers to Heidegger, Blanchot, and, especially, Kafka, see David Schur, *The Way of Oblivion* (Cambridge, Mass.: Harvard University Press, 1998).

3. A number of critics — Jeremy Adler, among others — have recently emphasized this point. "Although Kafka constantly stresses the conflict between his writing and his profession," writes Adler, "this perceived dualism . . . provides the premise for his authorship, enabling him to write about modernity and its discontents from the inside. . . . His job brought him into direct contact with industrialization, mechanization, and bureaucracy, as well as with the struggle between capital and labor, and his official writings antedate his literary breakthrough." Jeremy Adler, "In the Quiet Corners," *Times Literary Supplement*, no. 5140 (5 October 2001), 6–7.

4. "[A] destruction of the world that is not destructive but constructive" (DF 103, GW 6:220).

5. "Letter to Gershom Scholem on Franz Kafka" (12 June 1938), trans. Edmund Jephcott, in *Walter Benjamin, Selected Writings, Volume 3, 1935–1938*, ed. Howard Eiland and Michael W. Jennings; trans. Edmund Jephcott, Howard Eiland, et al. (Cambridge, Mass.: Harvard University Press, 2002), 325. The approach is caught up in the lustrous words of Theodore Weiss, "[Kafka's] is the microscope that by the bright obliquity reveals in our daily conventions the unsuspected horror." "Franz Kafka and the Economy of Chaos," *The Man from Porlock: Engagements 1944–1981* (Princeton: Princeton University Press, 1982), 254.

6. See "Introduction: Beginnings."

7. Hanns Zischler, *Kafka Goes to the Movies* (Chicago: University of Chicago Press, 2002). The importance of *Schaffsteins Grüne Bändchen* (Schaffsteins little green books) for satisfying Kafka's imaginative needs is richly discussed in John Zilcosky's *Kafka's Travels: Exoticism, Colonialism, and the Traffic of Writing* (New York: Palgrave, 2003).

8. Think of Stephen Daedalus's stance, in James Joyce's *A Portrait of the Artist as a Young Man*. I have used the edition of R. B. Kershner (Boston: Bedford, 1993).

9. In a new biography, *Kafka — Die Jahre der Entscheidungen* (Frankfurt a.M: Fischer, 2002), Reiner Stach writes: "The richness of Kafka's existence unfolded essentially at the order of the mind (*im Psychischen*), hence, invisibly, in a *vertical* dimension, which seems to have nothing whatsoever to do with the social landscape and yet penetrates this realm *at every point*" (emphasis added)

(xiv). This sentence asserts that Kafka's "depth" manifested itself at every point in the social landscape of the Bohemian Lands, but this is hard to conceive. The thrust of Stach's remarks is to fuse the two dimensions, but that is precisely the idea that I wish to contest in insisting on the primacy of the "vertical."

I would like to develop this point by imagining the reader's objections to what he has so far read. How can Kafka's interest in the media possibly exclude the relevance to his work of cultural studies in the media of fin-de-siècle Prague? But here it is again a question of origin and intention: Kafka's interest in the media is driven by an ontology of writing. It is his most marked contribution to high modern literature: the way in which the subject of writing has become Writing, the way in which reflection on the act of writing has become ontological not psychological. Kafka downloads into culture; he does not upload its givens. (See the introduction to my *Franz Kafka: The Necessity of Form* [Ithaca: Cornell University Press, 1988]).

Again, one could ask why a book that aims to interpellate cultural studies should nonetheless insist that the relative immortality that Kafka sought through his writings is culturally determined. For what follows, surely, is the necessity of exploring Kafka's views on this very culture as the bearer of a secular immortality of sorts. And that would mean filling in the gaps in his only partially embodied account by a detailed historical reconstruction, especially of the institutions of writing and reading in his time. But such detailed empirical representations are not what his stories, parables, and meditations strive for. His conjuring of a contemporary parliament in "In the Penal Colony" is precisely what he afterwards excoriated as a construction; and the law represented in *The Trial* is not the Roman civil law of the Czech Lands but an archaic *lex talionis*. In a word, the term "culture" in Kafka's work is in Heidegger's sense an "existentiale," a constitutive category of being. Kafka was not ignorant of this category! But its empirical givens do not go far toward explaining the tendency of his art, which is the metamorphosis he calls *Schriftstellersein* ("the *being* of a writer") (emphasis added, Br 383). Furthermore, in this respect cultural studies harbors a more grievous tendency: to read Kafka in its lens is to bypass the specificity of his art-language and see it as a means to provide the empirical ego with substitutive gratifications—a compensatory profit not otherwise obtainable. All this is discussed further in chapter 11 below.

10. James Joyce, *Finnegans Wake* (New York: Viking Press, 1947), 298.


INTRODUCTION
BEGINNINGS

1. A wise saying by the Kafka scholar Ritchie Robertson, which I heard at "Kafka 2000," an international conference held at the University of Bergen (Norway) on 12 May 2000.

2. Erich Heller, *Franz Kafka* (New York: Viking Press, 1974), 82.

3. Friedrich Hölderlin, *Hyperion, Or the Hermit in Greece*, trans. Willard R. Trask, adapt. David Schwarz, in *Hölderlin: Hyperion and Selected Poems*, ed. Eric Santner (New York: Continuum, 1990), 4.

4. *Franz Kafka. Schriftverkehr*, ed. Wolf Kittler and Gerhard Neumann (Freiburg: Rombach, 1990).

5. Jean-François Lyotard, "Answering the Question: What is Postmodernism?", trans. Regis Durand, in *The Postmodern Condition* (Minneapolis: University of Minnesota Press, 1984), 81.

6. Compare the activity of the badger-hero of "The Burrow" ("Der Bau"), the burrow, too, being a house of art. Here, too, the connection is strengthened by the link between the scratching, digging activity (*scharren*) of the burrowing creature and the act of writing (*schreiben*); both verbs derive from the common Indo-European root *sker*. See my *Franz Kafka: The Necessity of Form* (Ithaca: Cornell University Press, 1988), 282. Furthermore, Gregor Samsa, in *The Metamorphosis* (*Die Verwandlung*), is described as "scrabbling [scharrte] on the leather [of his sofa] for hours on end." Kafka associated lying on the sofa with his nightly preparations for writing (M 21).

7. Walter Sokel, *The Myth of Power and the Self* (Detroit: Wayne State University Press, 2002), 110–11.

8. The seed of these reflections was planted by Walter Sokel's powerful essay "Between Gnosticism and Jehovah: The Dilemma in Kafka's Religious Attitude," *South Atlantic Review* 50 (1985), 3–22. This essay is reprinted in *The Myth of Power and the Self*, 292–310; see especially 303–4. This essay (along with other works by Walter Sokel) has inspired a good deal of the thinking of this book.

9. "Letter to Gershom Scholem on Franz Kafka" (12 June 1938), trans. Edmund Jephcott, in *Walter Benjamin, Selected Writings, Volume 3, 1935–1938*, trans. Edmund Jephcott, Howard Eiland et al.; ed. Howard Eiland and Michael W. Jennings (Cambridge, Mass.: Harvard University Press 2002), 325.

10. In a late diary entry for 28 January 1922, Kafka calls himself a foreigner (*Ausländer*), a perpetual wanderer in the Land of Canaan (D2 213, GW 11:211). Jeremy Tambling, professor of comparative literature at the University of Hong Kong, calls Kafka an "American" in "Orphans in America: Kafka Reading Dickens" (an unpublished MS).

11. The theme of doubling is well served in Kafka scholarship. Henry Sussman, for one, discusses Kafka's "aesthetics of doubling." "The doubles," he writes, "are not perfect lookalikes; instead their contrary activities and attitudes . . . ultimately bracket and question the protagonist's articles of faith." The "kitten/lamb of 'A Crossbreed,'" is such an exemplary double, "an unwanted 'remarkable legacy' from the narrator's father, which, despite an anomalous status . . . bears an uncanny affinity to the narrator. 'It sometimes gazes at me with a look of understanding, challenging me to do the thing of which both of us are thinking' (CS 427). The kitten/lamb is precisely the narrator's double in anomaly, Otherness, and a perverse posture toward the protocols of everyday existence. [They] . . . share in the . . . economy of writing, which is a universe and worldview as well as a vocation." The latter point is instructive if it is held to mean that the "economy of writing" accommodates doubles that at once resemble one another and differ from one another. This would point to writing's "two souls": it is worldly, because it participates in a practical economy aiming at the relative cultural immortality of literary fame, and it is otherworldly because it is

an ascetic practice aimed at "the heavens." "Kafka's Aesthetics: A Primer: From the Fragments to the Novels," in *A Companion to the Works of Franz Kafka*, ed. James Rolleston (Rochester: Camden House, 2002), 130–31.

12. See chapter 9 for a discussion of Benjamin and Adorno on this point.

13. Max Brod, *Franz Kafka: A Biography*, trans. G. Humphreys Roberts (New York: Schocken, 1947), 129.

14. Silke Weineck, "The Laius-Complex: Towards a Theory of Fatherhood," an unpublished MS, 6.

15. It would not be enough as a rule to attribute to writers who *say* that they have an antipathy to antitheses that their work will be without them, as if that dogmatic statement as such had scourged and purified the text, but in Kafka's case it appears to hold true—grounds perhaps for attributing to his theoretical statements an unwonted truthfulness and efficacy.

16. Mark Anderson, "Virtual Zion: The Promised Lands of the Kafka Critical Editions" (*http://www.kafka.org/essays/anderson.htm*). The entry for "Zion" in the *OED* reads: "In biblical and derived use, allusively for: The house or household of God; and hence connoting variously, the Israelites and their religious system, the Christian Church, heaven as the final home of believers, a place of worship or meeting-house."

17. It is *this* Kafka in whose company Primo Levi finds himself: "By writing I found peace for a while and felt myself become a man again, a person like everyone else, neither a martyr nor debased nor a saint: one of those people who form a family and look to the future rather than the past." *The Periodic Table*, trans. Raymond Rosenthal (New York: Schocken, 1984), 151. The phrase "new and improved existence" is an echo of Nietzsche's understanding of the "Greek concept of culture . . . as a new and improved/transfigured *physis* or physical nature (einer neuen und verbesserten Physis)." See "Vom Nutzen und Nachteil der Historie für das Leben," *Unzeitgemäße Betrachtungen* ("On the Use and Disadvantage of History for Life," *Thoughts out of Season*), *Friedrich Nietzsche, Werke in Drei Banden*, ed. Karl Schlechta (Münich: Hanser, 1954–56), 1:285.

18. Sokel, *Myth of Power*, 302–3.

19. Kafka would call this world one "of God's bad moods." See Walter Benjamin, *Illuminations*, ed. and introd. Hannah Arendt, trans. Harry Zohn (New York: Schocken, 1969), 116.

20. Raj Ayyar, "Kafka's Angst," *The Great Namaste Bazaar* (*http://www.namaste-bazaar.com/generic38.html*).

21. Klaus Wagenbach, *Franz Kafka: Eine Biographie seiner Jugend, 1883–1912* (Bern: Francke, 1958), 262–63.

22. *The Austrian Mind: An Intellectual and Social History* (Berkeley: University of California Press, 1972), 270.

23. Sokel is concerned to stress that Kafka's gnosticism is nourished by the Gnosticism readable in the first books of the Old Testament, before the covenant in which God appears as a transcendent, otherworldly being not yet bent on a return to his creation. Kafka's "gnostic sensibility" shows the greater affinity with Gnosticism of the Syro-Egyptian (not Marcionite) kind because he is *not* a simple dualist. Especially in the Zürau aphorisms of 1917–18, entitled by Max Brod "Reflections on Sin, Suffering, Hope and the True Way," Kafka con-

jures "evil" as dwelling in the heart of the principle of goodness. *Myth of Power*, 292–310.

24. "What have I in common with Jews? I have hardly anything in common with myself. . . ." (D2 11).

25. Franz Kuna, *Franz Kafka: Literature as Corrective Punishment* (Bloomington and London: Indiana University Press, 1974), 46. To complicate matters yet further, in light of recent research, there is nothing like a consensus that Marcionism *is* a Gnosticism. One would not have suspected this from reading Hans Jonas's *The Gnostic Religion* (Boston: Beacon, 1958). In Michael Williams's *Rethinking "Gnosticism": An Argument for Dismantling A Dubious Category* (Princeton: Princeton University Press, 1996), Williams quotes Giovanni Filoramo, among authorities who dispute that Marcionism is a Gnosticism: "There is a profound difference, though not an insuperable one, between Marcion and Gnosticism (though they are in some ways linked)." See Giovanni Filoramo, *A History of Gnosticism*, trans. by Anthony Alcock (Oxford: Basil Blackwell, 1990), 166. Williams adds: "I find Filoramo's wording to be indicative of the frustrated ambivalence about the treatment of Marcion often induced by problems with the very category of gnosticism itself" (274).

26. The principle of an irreducibly unique refraction of images and themes from Kafka's "feverish and unbroken reading" is stressed in Benno Wagner, "Ende oder Anfang? Kafka und der Judenstaat," forthcoming in *Conditio Judaica*, ed. Hans Otto Horch (Niemeyer: Tübingen).

27. Blackman, *Marcion and His Influence* (London: Society for the Propagation of Christian Knowledge, 1948), 66.

28. Ibid.

29. Gerhard Kurz, *Traum-Schrecken. Kafkas literarische Existenzanalyse* (Stuttgart: Metzler, 1980), 150.

30. Stephan Hoeller, "What is a Gnostic?" *Gnosis: A Journal of Western Inner Traditions*, vol. 23 (spring 1992), 26.

31. Clark Emery, *William Blake: The Book of Urizen* (Coral Gables, Fla.: University of Miami Press, 1966), 13–14.

32. See, above all, chapter 6.

33. William Blake, *Jerusalem, The Emanation of the Giant Albion*. One finds a chiastic reminiscence of "O Rose, Thou art Sick," in Kafka's story "A Country Doctor," where a patient sports a wound like a rose.

34. A comparable distinction is time honored in the literature on Gnosticism. E. C. Blackman cites authority "that distinguishes a broad sense, according to which any religion of redemption might be called gnostic; and a narrower sense, viz., the specifically Christian gnosticism with which we are made familiar in the Christian literature of the second and third centuries A.D." *Marcion and His Influence*, 83, n. 1.

35. In *Franz Kafka. Ein Schriftstellerleben* (Frankfurt a.M.: Fischer, 1984), Joachim Unseld takes on "the legend of an impossible author, who would rather burn his texts than make them accessible to the public; in fact we encounter, again and again, and beyond any doubt, *the author's will to be published*" (emphasis added, 14). I owe the idea of an "articulation" of long-held concerns to my colleague Arnd Wedemeyer.

36. Ritchie Robertson, "Kafka as Anti-Christian: 'Das Urteil,' 'Die Ver-wandlung,' and the Aphorisms," in *A Companion to the Works of Franz Kafka*, ed. by James Rolleston (Rochester: Camden House, 2002), 120.

37. Mark Anderson, personal correspondence, 10 December 2002.

38. This is a view that gains support from Hartmut Binder's critique of Karl Erich Grözinger's widely circulated thesis that Kafka's work is inspired by Kabbalah through and through. Binder points out that until 1915 Kafka had next to no experience of Kabbalah. Hartmut Binder, "Jüdisches In Kafkas Werk? Zu einer Publikation von Karl Erich Grözinger" (a review of Karl Erich Grözinger, *Kafka und die Kabbala*), *Neue Zürcher Zeitung*, 22 February 1993.

CHAPTER 1
IN THE CIRCLE OF "THE JUDGMENT"

1. On August 14, 1916, Kafka wrote to Mr. Meyer of the Kurt Wolff publishing house, asking to have "The Judgment" published as a book in its own right. "'The Judgment,' which means a great deal to me, is admittedly very short, but it is more a poem than a story; it needs open space around it and, moreover, deserves that, I think" (L 125). Five days later, Kafka added, "The story . . . needs open space around it if it is to exert its force. It is also my favorite work and so I always wished for it to be appreciated if possible by itself" (L 126).

2. Erich Heller, *Franz Kafka* (New York: Viking, 1974), 95.

3. This point is discussed in Mark Anderson, *Kafka's Clothes: Ornament and Aestheticism in the Habsburg Fin de Siècle* (Oxford: Clarendon Press, 1992), 186.

4. In citing this passage, Heller comments: "The German original alludes to the idiom *'etwas am eigenen Leib zu spüren bekommen'* — 'to come to experience something at first hand, i.e., on one's own body.'" And he adds: "Once again Kafka takes a figurative saying literally, and reveals the horror underlying . . . this particular phrase" (*Franz Kafka*, 18–19). But the prisoner will not get to experience his sentence on his own body (see chapter 4); so much for Kafka's alleged "literalization" of metaphor.

5. This point was made earlier by Anderson, *Kafka's Clothes*, 185. The consciousness of this mythic power only dawned gradually to Kafka. At first, in the letter to Felice Bauer dated October 24, 1912, he denied that there was the slightest connection between her and the events and persons of the story. This démenti is not surprising, since at the time Kafka contemplated an affiancement with her, but the bitter truth of the story is that, in the words of his own commentary of February 11, 1913, "The bride, who lives in the story only in relation to the friend, that is, to what father and son have in common, is easily driven away by the father" (D1 278–79). Afterwards, when the thought of the failure of the engagement had become apparent to him with an habitualness that made it no longer terrifying, he was content to change his mind. In the same diary, he wrote: "'Frieda' has as many letters as 'Felice' and the same initial, 'Brandenfeld' has the same initial as 'Bauer' [peasant] and in the word 'Feld' [field] a certain connection in meaning, as well" (D1 279). Furthermore,

in a letter to Felice Bauer of June 2, 1913, he repeated this discovery in almost the same words, adding, then, the pleasant observation: "'Friede' [peace] and 'Glück' [happiness] are also closely related" (LF 265). A most suggestive feature of this letter is the error of fact it contains. Kafka says to Felice, "It was written at a time when I had not yet written to you, though I had met you and the world had grown in value owing to your existence" (LF 265). In fact "The Judgment" was written two days *after* his first letter to Felice. It is as if Kafka were inclined to suppress the possibly germinative effect of his (first) letter to Felice on the production of "The Judgment." If letters have a status more or less similar to diary entries, then the thought that his first letter to Felice had preceded the writing of "Das Urteil" would not be subsequently attractive to Kafka, as perhaps impugning the mythic autonomy of its production and condemning all his poetic inspiration in principle to its heteronomous dependence on the preparatory work of diary writing.

6. Gerhard Neumann, "Eine höhere Art der Beobachtung": Wahrnehmung und Medialität in Kafkas Tagebüchern," *Franz Kafka: Zur ethischen und ästhetischen Rechtfertigung*, ed. Beatrice Sandberg and Jakob Lothe (Rombach: Freiburg i. B., 2002), 33–58.

7. For the writer of fictions, however, death is "secretly a game. . . . In the death enacted, [he] rejoice[s] in [his] own death." But the condition of his rejoicing is that the death he enacts be someone else's and that the artist survive to "display [his] art" in the "lament . . . [that] dies beautifully and purely away" (D2 102).

8. Hans-Gerd Koch is general editor of the Fischer, so-called Manuscript Edition of Kafka's works (*KKA*); volumes in this edition began appearing in 1983. The philological principles informing this edition have been criticized by Roland Reuß, among others; Reuß is the editor of a rival edition, the *FKA*, published, also in Frankfurt a.M., by Stroemfeld/Roter Stern, beginning 1995. Through their scrupulous work, both editors have vastly enriched our understanding of Kafka's texts.

9. Max Brod, *Franz Kafka: A Biography*, trans. G. Humphreys Roberts (New York: Schocken, 1947), 104.

10. Ibid., 105. Max Brod, *Franz Kafka — Eine Biographie, Über Franz Kafka* (Frankfurt a.M.: Fischer, 1966), 95.

11. Brod, *Franz Kafka: A Biography*, 95.

12. Walter Benjamin wrote, "Keeping silent is the inner boundary of the conversation. . . . The unproductive one never arrives at the boundary; he keeps his conversations for monologues. From out of the conversation he steps into the diary or into the café." *Gesammelte Schriften*, ed. Rolf Tiedemann and Hermann Schweppenhäuser (Frankfurt a.M.: Suhrkamp, 1974–89), 2:92. It is interesting to oppose to this Kafka's movement of coming to his journal *in order to* begin a conversation with himself.

13. The notion of an *obligation* to pose questions, however unanswerable, arises in one of Kafka's earliest letters to Felice, whom he will invite to "let questions and answers entangle themselves to their hearts' content." On October 13, 1912, he declares, "I write this letter not so much in the hope of a reply as to discharge a duty towards myself" (LF 105). This is the very logic of the diary.

14. Brod, *Franz Kafka: A Biography*, 106.

15. Cf. Kafka's aphorism, "Psychology is the description of the reflection of the terrestrial world in the heavenly plane, or, more correctly, the description of a reflection such as we, soaked as we are in our terrestrial nature, imagine it, for no reflection actually occurs, only we see earth wherever we turn" (DF 65–66). Logically, Kafka would thereafter exclaim, "Never again psychology!" (DF 45).

16. The category of ontological "kinds" might seem exalted, but in his decisive letter to Brod of July 5, 1922, Kafka speaks of his condition as a kind of "being" — *Schriftstellersein* [writerly being, one's being (as) a writer] (Br 383).

17. I do not claim to distinguish as precisely as Malcolm Pasley the modalities of consciousness — self-observation and self-consumption — in Kafka's writing. The moment of transition cannot be fixed. See Malcolm Pasley, *"Die Schrift ist unveränderlich . . .": Essays zu Kafka* (Frankfurt a.M.: Fischer Taschenbuch, 1995), 151ff.

18. Koch alludes to the brief notes left by Kafka that served as a source, as occasions for him to practice a "literarizing form of elaboration" (GW 9:353). By contrast, Kafka could not return to revise what he had written because there was no bridge back to that state of mind (produced by the destruction of an empirical self-consciousness) in which he had conceived what he wrote. Compare J. M. Coetzee: "What I say is marginal to the book [his novel *Michael K.*], not because I as author and authority so proclaim, but on the contrary because it would be said from a position peripheral, posterior to *the forever unreclaimable position* from which the book was written" (emphasis added). *Doubling the Point: Essays and Interviews*, ed. by David Attwell (Cambridge, Mass.: Harvard University Press, 1992), 206. One can easily imagine Kafka's going back to a diary entry to revise it (that was precisely what Kafka did with his "Stichworte," his preliminary jottings); but returning to a literary text could mean only: adding something on to it. This is just what he despaired of, and why only that work famously written in a single sitting, "The Judgment," struck him as authentic. See Hartmut Binder, *Kafka: Der Schaffensprozess* (Frankfurt: Suhrkamp, 1983).

19. Brod, *Franz Kafka: A Biography*, 106.

20. Yitzchak Löwy was the main player in the Yiddish Theater that so much interested (and influenced) Kafka during its performances in Prague in 1911–12.

21. Brod, *Franz Kafka: A Biography*, 106.

22. "In their conversations with themselves persons of spirit sometimes imagine as present an absent friend to whom they communicate their inmost feelings, and thus the letter too is a sort of conversation with oneself (*Selbstgespräch*)." Johann Wolfgang Goethe, "Vorrede," *Winckelmann und sein Jahrhundert* (1805), *Sämtliche Werke*, Abt. I, vol. 19 (Frankfurt a.M.: Deutscher Klassiker, 1998), 13. Cited in Reiner Stach, *Kafka — Jahre der Entscheidungen* (Frankfurt a.M.: Fischer, 2002), 620.

23. It might also prepare for the magnificent, sad diary entry of 19 September 1917, in which Kafka writes of taking aesthetic (but not moral) pleasure from "the various flourishes I might have talent for, . . . ringing simple, or contrapuntal, or a whole orchestration of changes on my theme" (D2 183–84).

24. See Heidegger's aperçu, in *Being and Time*: "In 'poetic' discourse, the communication of the existential possibilities of one's state-of-mind can become

an aim in itself, and this amounts to a disclosing of existence." Martin Heideg-ger, *Being and Time*, trans. John Macquarrie and Edward Robinson (New York: Harper and Row, 1962), 205.

25. Could a writer feel otherwise? Yes. Consider Primo Levi: "Alongside the liberating relief of the veteran who tells his story, I now felt in the writing a complex, intense, and new pleasure, similar to that I felt as a student when penetrating the solemn order of differential calculus. It was exalting to search and find, or create, the right word—that is, commensurate, concise, and strong; to dredge up events from my memory and describe them with the greatest rigor and the least clutter. Paradoxically my baggage of atrocious memories became a wealth, a seed; it seemed to me that, by writing, I was growing like a *plant*" (emphasis added). Primo Levi, *The Periodic Table*, trans. by Raymond Rosen-thal (New York: Schocken, 1984), 153.

26. Kafka read *The Lord Chandos Letter* and discussed it with Max Brod on the evening of their first meeting. Max Brod, *Streitbares Leben 1884–1968* (Munich: F. A. Herbig, 1969), 180.

27. *The Lord Chandos Letter*, trans. Russell Stockman (Marlboro, Vt.: Marl-boro Press, 1986), 19, 21.

28. For Kafka's Orientalism, see Rolf Goebel, *Constructing China: Kafka's Orientalist Discourse* (Columbia, S.C.: Camden House, 1997). For Kafka's rep-resentation of varieté performers in the context of "the problem of art," see Gerhard Neumann's lustrous " 'Nachrichten vom Pontus': Das Problem der Kunst im Werk Franz Kafkas," in *Franz Kafka: Schriftverkehr*, ed. Wolf Kittler and Gerhard Neumann (Freiburg: Rombach, 1990), 164–98.

29. It is not that Kafka is incapable of going to the social-empirical world for "ideas"; he is capable of going to the social–empirical world when it offers apt enough metaphors for what is emerging in him. The world does this best in the moments of its dissolution.

30. "Nicht Selbstabschüttelung sondern Selbstaufzehrung" (GW 6:198). Some-thing like this distinction no doubt exists in many other languages. It appears to exist in Tamil, in a terrifying perversion of context, suggesting all the same its inspiration in theological discourse: "The Tigers [who are Sri Lankan revolu-tionaries] abjure the phrase suicide bombing. Mr. Thamilchelvam [the Tigers' po-litical leader] cited two words in Tamil. One, 'thatkolai,' means to kill yourself. The other, 'thatkodai,' means to give yourself. That was the word the Tigers used, and preferred." (From Amy Waldman, "Masters of Suicide Bombing: Tamil Guer-rillas of Sri Lanka," *New York Times*, 14 January 2003, A8.)

31. "Selbstvergessenheit ist erste Voraussetzung des Schriftstellertums" (Br 385).

32. Paul de Man's reflections on the "fragility of poetic transcendence" and the "ontological self," arising from a contemporary phenomenological tradition marked by early Lukács, Husserl, and Oskar Becker, provide a suggestive paral-lel. See "The Sublimation of the Self," in *Blindness and Insight: Essays in the Rhetoric of Contemporary Criticism*, 2d ed. rev. (Minneapolis: University of Minnesota Press, 1983), 46, 50. See, too, Cyrena N. Pondrom, "Kafka and Phenomenology," in *Twentieth Century Interpretations of The Trial*, ed. James Rolleston (Englewood Cliffs, N.J.: Prentice-Hall, 1976), 70–85; and Arnold

Heidsieck, *The Intellectual Contexts of Kafka's Fiction: Philosophy, Law, Religion* (Columbia, S.C.: Camden House, 1994).

33. *"Vielleicht sind es Tenöre": Kafkas literarische Erfindungen in den frühen Tagebüchern* (Bielefeld: Aisthesis, 1995).

34. Consider Benjamin's remark: "Kafka's entire work constitutes a code of gestures which surely had no definite symbolic meaning for the author from the outset; rather, the author tried to derive such a meaning from them in ever-changing contexts and experimental groupings. The theater is the logical place for such groupings." Walter Benjamin, *Illuminations*, ed. Hannah Arendt, trans. Harry Zohn (New York: Schocken, 1968), 120; the original in Benjamin, *Gesammelte Schriften*, 2:2, 418. Meanwhile, diary entries of an almost purely discursive kind, as the opposite sort of limiting idea, also recur, like the manic Hegelian dialectic beginning "I feel too tightly constricted in everything that signifies Myself" (DF 91–92).

35. The narrative beginning " 'You, I said . . . ,' " was begun sometime between 19 July and 6 November 1910, when Kafka was twenty-seven. In his edition of Kafka's *Diaries* (*Tagebücher*) (Frankfurt a.M.: Fischer, 1951, 7ff.; D1 22–29), Max Brod printed as a continuous text—a story with a beginning and an end—what in fact is a number of fragments strewn through Kafka's notebooks, the *Oxforder Quarthefte 1 and 2*. The notebooks can now be read in facsimile in Franz Kafka, *Oxforder Quarthefte 2, Historische-Kritische Ausgabe sämtlicher Handschriften, Drucke und Typoskripte*, ed. Roland Reuß and Peter Staengle (Frankfurt a.M.: Stroemfeld/Roter Stern, 2001). Hans-Gerd Koch argues that the fragments of " 'You,' I said" in fact constitute approaches to a second version of Kafka's unfinished "novella" "Description of a Struggle" (See GW 9:302). Brod preferred, however, to organize them into an independent work, and the outcome is a compelling narrative. The story " 'You,' I said . . ." is, therefore, an apocryphal Kafka text, but it is a text well worth preserving and noting under the head of the author Brod-Kafka. This idea is not anomalous when one recalls that Kafka and Brod did in fact collaborate on the novel "Richard and Samuel," of which the first chapter survives (Kafka, however, did not find it good [L 119]). In *Kafka's Travels: Exoticism, Imperialism, Modernism* (New York: Palgrave, 2003), John Zilcosky offers a persuasive reading of the "modernity" of this project of dual authorship.

36. Parts of the following argument concerning " 'You,' I said . . ."—and, thereafter, "The Judgment"—first appeared in my *Franz Kafka: The Necessity of Form* (Ithaca: Cornell University Press, 1988). But here my overall concern is different: I want to show the contribution made by various of Kafka's thought experiments to the writing of "The Judgment" by examining in detail the mode and argument of the earlier diary entries.

37. This objection has been forcefully raised in a recent study by Ronald Speirs and Beatrice Sandberg: *Franz Kafka*, Macmillan Modern Novelists (London: Macmillan, 1997), 27–28.

38. Gerhard Kurz, *Traum-Schrecken: Kafkas literarische Existenzanalyse* (Stuttgart: Metzler, 1980), 133.

39. The last phrase was crossed out by Kafka. See the *Oxforder Quarthefte 2*, 53.

40. This piece is discussed incisively by Clayton Koelb, in *Kafka's Rhetoric: The Passion of Reading* (Ithaca: Cornell University Press, 1989), 208–10. Koelb perceives its seminal importance as a treatise on rhetoric.

41. More than once, Kafka was preoccupied by another's irrational, excessive, intransigent hostility. See, for example, his story "A Little Woman" (1923), discussed in chapter 6.

42. Grimm illustrates the word *zudecken* with the phrase "ein Gedanke, ein Sinn, eine Wahrheit wird durch Worte zugedeckt" (a thought, a meaning, a truth is covered up [or closed off] by words) and further cites a phrase from Goethe: "die verschiedenen Auslegungsarten . . . die man auf den Text anwenden, die man dem Text unterschieben, mit denen man ihn zudecken konnte" (the various kinds of interpretation, . . . which are applied to the text, which are attributed, imputed or stuck on to the text, with which it could be covered-up [or closed off]). *Deutsches Wörterbuch von Jacob Grimm und Wilhelm Grimm* (Leipzig: Hirzil, 1954), 16:319.

43. Gilbert Ryle, *The Concept of Mind* (Chicago: University of Chicago Press, 1984), 195–98.

44. According to the narrator of Saul Bellow's novel *Ravelstein* (for Ravelstein, read: Alan Bloom, or Wolfowitz's mentor): "I had made the discovery that if you . . . spoke of someone as a gross, belching, wall-eyed human pike you got along much better with him thereafter, partly because you were aware that you were the sadist who took away his human attributes. Also, having done him some metaphorical violence, you owed him special consideration" (New York: Viking, 2000), 152.

45. "Through the power with which Kafka commands interpretation," Adorno writes, "he collapses aesthetic distance. He demands a desperate effort from the allegedly 'disinterested' observer of an earlier time, overwhelms him, suggesting that far more than his intellectual equilibrium depends on whether he truly understands; life and death are at stake." Theodor W. Adorno, "Notes on Kafka," in *Prisms*, trans. Samuel and Shierry Weber (London: Spearman, 1967), 246. (See further chapter 11.)

46. Max Brod, *Franz Kafka: A Biography*, 129.

47. The Muirs' translation is unfortunate since it tends to associate the water in which Georg drowns with the "stream" of traffic going over it. There is no "stream" in the German.

48. Further: "It was an intentionally long-drawn-out leave-taking from you, only although it was brought about by force on your part [note: the vitality, the violence], it did take its course in the direction determined by me" (DF 177). Note that the translators actually write: "it did *not* take its course. . . ." This is a bad mistake.

49. I published the gist of the preceding paragraph in *Franz Kafka's The Metamorphosis* (New York: Bantam, 1972), xv–xvi. I present it now as if it were written by another person, since I no longer hold to its argument.

50. Consider Martin Amis's aperçu: "The distance between author and narrator corresponds to the degree to which the author finds the narrator wicked, deluded, pitiful or ridiculous." *Money* (Penguin: New York, 1984), 229.

51. Such a "reader"—the critic I have chiefly in mind—is David Schur,

whose lustrous *The Way of Oblivion* (Cambridge, Mass.: Harvard University Press, 1998) concludes with a reading of "The Judgment" that has stimulated my own, especially, his pages 246–65. The flow of traffic, which in the moment of George's drowning goes over the bridge, propels, for Schur, Kafka's afterlife. This is something of which Kafka was aware, to judge especially from the diary entry he wrote the morning after, in which he identifies the aura of ecstatic composition as the fulfilled pledge of literary achievement. The poor immortality (Mallarmé's "faux manoir") imagined by the businessman/fiancé and presumptive father must go under for the sake of the author's craved-for afterlife. A paradoxical fusion of the full time of the Now (*Jetztzeit*) ("at this moment" [in *diesem Augenblick*]) and the historical detachment of the preterite (*"was . . . going* over the bridge" [*ging* über die Brücke]) that alleges infinitely ongoing process ("an *unending* stream of traffic" [ein geradezu *unendlicher* Verkehr]) evokes the afterlife transcending the ecstasies of ordinary temporal distinction: it is the *Zug*, the draught that moved Kafka along as he wrote "The Judgment" in a single sitting, and the flow of the greater traffic of the world—sexual, commercial, epistolary, vehicular. With this "giving birth" of "The Judgment" ("a *regular* birth" [ein regel*rechtes* Geburt]), Kafka shall now enter this flow, truly and for good: the traffic is "ein *gerade*zu unendlicher"—the word *geradezu*, difficult to translate, can mean "downright" and contains the word *gerade* (direct, straight).

52. Ibid.

CHAPTER 2

*THE TRIAL*: THE GUILT OF AN UNREDEEMED LITERARY PROMISE

1. Detlef Kremer, *Kafka: Die Erotik des Schreibens* (Frankfurt: Athenaeum, 1989), 7.

2. Leo A. Lensing, *Frankfurter Allgemeine Zeitung* (23 August 1997), no. 195, "Bilder und Zeiten," 1.

3. Erich Heller, *Franz Kafka* (New York: Viking Press, 1974), 105.

4. "The expressionless is the critical violence which, while unable to separate semblance from essence in art, prevents them from mingling." "Goethe's Elective Affinities," trans. Stanley Corngold, in *Walter Benjamin: Selected Works*, vol. 1 (1913–1926), ed. Michael Jennings and Marcus Bullock (Cambridge, Mass.: Harvard University Press, 1997), 1:340.

5. This is Nietzsche's etymology in *On the Genealogy of Morals, Basic Writings of Nietzsche*, trans. and ed. Walter Kaufmann (New York: Random House, 1968), 507.

6. For "uncanny," Kafka wrote literally "in a normal state in no way recognizable [*erkennbar*]." Cited in Rainer Stach, *Kafka. Die Jahre der Entscheidungen* (Frankfurt a.M.: Fischer, 2002), xv.

7. Some of the ideas and phrasing that follow are adapted from "*The Trial*/ 'In the Penal Colony': The Rigors of Writing," in my *Franz Kafka: The Necessity of Form* (Ithaca: Cornell University Press, 1988).

8. As Christopher Bradley has noted, "K. depends too much on the inter-

pretations of others, he believes in the interpretations of others; he forgets the
indestructible self, the that-it-is, which has the status of *Schrift* vis-à-vis its interpretations. But this is not a *Schrift* humanly accessible." From an unpublished
paper, Princeton University, spring 2000.

9. G.W.F. Hegel, *Grundlinien der Philosophie des Rechts, Werke in zwanzig
Bänden*, ed. Eva Moldenhauer and Karl Markus Michel (Frankfurt: Suhrkamp,
1978), 7:263. This note, by the way, is not included in the capable translation of
S. W. Dyde, G.W.F. Hegel, *Philosophy of Right* (Amherst, NY: Prometheus,
1996). I am grateful to Professor Mark Roche for alerting me to this passage.

10. For Joseph K. as a "reader," see the following chapter 3.

11. *Franz Kafka, Der Process: Die Handschrift redet*, prepared by Malcolm
Pasley *Marbacher Magazin 52/1990* (Marbach: Deutsche Schillergesellschaft,
1990), 22.

## Segue I
### On Cultural Immortality

1. "The medial-technical world of modernity consumes the substance of the
subject, . . . a world of senselessly circulating medial messages in which the
subject trickles away." Gerhard Neumann, in *Franz Kafka. Schriftverkehr*, ed.
Wolf Kittler and Gerhard Neumann (Freiburg: Rombach, 1990), 17, 20.

2. Ibid., back cover.

3. Kafka's phrases for such an agency: "the heavens" (GrW 285), "a higher
life" (DF 45–46), "some fabulous yonder" (CF 457).

4. Pace Slavoj Žižek, who detects a new religiosity everywhere and has called
on "Christianity" to stay the ruin.

5. This famous passage from Foucault is cited and discussed in Alexander
Nehamas, *The Art of Living: Socratic Reflections from Plato to Foucault*
(Berkeley: University of California Press, 1998), 171. In speaking of the late
Nietzsche, I am thinking in particular of Nietzsche's 1888 "Attempt at a Critique of Myself," his short essay on his earlier "The Birth of Tragedy" (1872),
in which he utterly repudiates a main idea advanced there—the "metaphysical
consolation" supplied by tragedy. His repudiation is made in the name of another value, his late chief predilection: laughter.

6. After September 11, 2001, it now seems evident that some combination of
computerized signaling and a lethal agent will bring about the destruction of a
good deal of the world as we know it.

7. See John Zilcosky, who writes: "Kafka's autobiographical travel novel
*Richard and Samuel* and his travel essay about an Italian air show (attended
also by Marinetti) disclose his participation in the fads of tourism and technophilia." *Kafka's Travels: Exoticism, Imperialism, Modernism* (New York: Palgrave, 2003), 15.

8. The Germanist and philosopher of culture Jochen Hörisch has written in-
defatigably and with great originality of the modern technological media as belonging to a history of modes of transmission and exchange shaping the deep
cultural history of the West and distinctive for promising salvation. The inven-

tion and proliferation of modern technological media is in this sense no different from the invention and proliferation of the "media" of salvation — viz. the taking of the Eucharist — of the Christian Church. (Hörisch has noted the odd afterlife of Rome [in German, "Rom"] in the CD-ROM). Consult, among his many works: *Ende der Vorstellung: die Poesie der Medien* [The end of representation in the idea: the poetry of the media] (Suhrkamp: Frankfurt a.M., 1999) and *Kopf oder Zahl: die Poesie des Geldes* (Suhrkamp: Frankfurt a.M., 1996), trans. Amy H. Marschall as *Heads or Tails: the Poetics of Money* (Wayne State University Press: Detroit, 2000).

9. Noting the speed and breadth of response from the "rational" members of his profession after he had circulated by email a petition urging resistance to the Republican initiative to impeach ex-President Clinton, Sean Wilentz, professor of history at Princeton University, declared, "The glories of the e-net have overwhelmed my powers of understanding." This bold admission, belonging as it does to theological talk, to the language of sublimity, sublates an entirely rational-seeming enterprise. The Charlie Rose Show, WNET, 28 October 1998.

10. Andrew Piper, "The Invisible World Order," *Atlantic Unbound* (online archive of the *Atlantic Monthly*, accessed 29 July 1998, at *http://www.theatlantic. com/unbound/digicult/dc980729.htm*. Compare, further, Walter Benjamin in *Arcades*: "Multiplication of traces through the modern administrative apparatus. Balzac draws attention to this: 'Do your utmost, hapless Frenchwomen, to remain unknown, to weave the very least little romance in the midst of a civilization which takes note, on public squares, of the hour when every hackney cab comes and goes; which counts every letter and stamps them twice, at the exact time they are posted and at the time they are delivered; which numbers the houses . . . ; which ere long will have every acre of land, down to the smallest holdings . . . , laid down on the broad sheets of a survey — a giant's task, by command of a giant.' Balzac, *Modest Mignon*, cited in Régis Messac, *Le 'Detective Novel'* <*et l'influence de la pensée scientifique*> (Paris, 1929), p. 461." Walter Benjamin, *The Arcades Project*, trans. Howard Eiland and Kevin McLaughlin (Cambridge, Mass.: Harvard University Press, 1999), 225.

11. How do I know? I consulted the Web, in a sort of loop-the-loop. This ostensibly benevolent divinity assists your understanding of him — god in his Talmud.

12. Jonathan Rosen, *The Talmud and Internet* (New York: Farrar, Straus, and Giroux, 2000).

13. Friedrich Kittler, *Discourse Networks 1800/1900*, ed. David Wellbery, trans. Michael Metteer with Chris Cullens (Stanford: Stanford University Press, 1990); trans. of Friedrich Kittler, *Aufschreibesysteme* 1800/1900 (Munich: Fink, 1987). Franz Kafka, *Historisch-Kritische Ausgabe sämtlicher Handschriften, Drucke und Typoskripte*, ed. Roland Reuß with Peter Staengle, Michel Leiner, und K.D. Wolff (Basel/Frankfurt a.M.: Stroemfeld/Roter Stern, 1995). Franz Kafka, *Der Process. Historisch-Kritische Ausgabe sämtlicher Handschriften, Drucke und Typoskripte*, ed. Roland Reuß with Peter Staengle (Basel/Frankfurt a.M.: Stroemfeld/Roter Stern, 1997).

CHAPTER 3
MEDIAL INTERVENTIONS IN *THE TRIAL*; OR, *RES* IN MEDIA

1. The question of Kafka's theatricality was originally posed by Walter Benjamin in 1934: "Kafka's world is a world theater. For him, man is on the stage from the very beginning." "Franz Kafka: On the Tenth Anniversary of his Death," trans. by Harry Zohn, in *Illuminations*, ed. by Hannah Arendt (New York: Harcourt, Brace and World, 1968), 124. In an exchange of letters with Benjamin, Theodor Adorno found much to criticize in this idea: "The form of Kafka's art . . . is the most extreme antithesis to the theatrical," perceiving in Benjamin's remark the (for him) pernicious presence of Brecht's idea of epic theater. *Benjamin über Benjamin*, ed. Hermann Schweppenhäuser (Frankfurt a.M.: Suhrkamp taschenbuch wissenschaft, 1981), 105. Since then, there have been many rich discussions of the theatrical character of Kafka's literary imagination, especially James Rolleston's *Kafka's Narrative Theater* (University Park: Pennsylvania State University Press, 1974). The theatrical character of the opening of *The Trial* is an often acknowledged fact. The American translator of *Der Process*—Breon Mitchell—terms it "farce": "*The Trial* begins as farce and ends as tragedy" (T xxi). Theodore Ziolkowski considers the whole of *The Trial* a "burlesque" of Austrian legal procedure. *The Mirror of Justice: Literary Reflections of Legal Crises* (Princeton: Princeton University Press, 1997), 226. Still, a great many details of the theatrical opening of *The Trial* call for further exploration.

2. Mark Anderson points out that theatricality raises questions different from those of the media—questions of performance and representation—whereas media raises questions of originality, dissemination, and the decay of aura. It is fruitful to think these distinctions back to a common root, since "theatricality" in the modern period (according to Nietzsche, from Euripides on) implies, precisely, a loss of origin. What is illuminating about Kafka's theater of Joseph K. is that it means to stage an origin, as I hope to explain.

3. Stanley Corngold, *The Commentators' Despair: The Interpretation of Kafka's "Metamorphosis,"* National University Publications (New York: Associated Faculty Press, 1975), v.

4. Anna, it will be recalled, was last seen fleeing the Samsa household after having gone in search of a locksmith and/or doctor; now she has evidently taken up lodging at Frau Grubach's. There's the trace here of an unwritten Prague epic of the demimonde: *Anna Mutzenbacher*—but this is an only virtual medial intrusion.

5. Jean-Jacques Rousseau, *Oeuvres Complètes*, "Bibliothèque de la Pléiade" (Paris: Gallimard, 1959) 1:1004–1005.

6. Jean-Jacques Rousseau, *The Reveries of the Solitary Walker*, trans. Charles E. Butterworth (New York: New York University Press, 1979), 15–16.

7. "Im Kampf zwischen Dir und der Welt sekundiere der Welt" (GW 6:236).

8. John Zilcosky, *Kafka's Travels: Exoticism, Colonialism, and the Traffic of Writing* (New York: Palgrave, 2003), 34.

9. Ernst Pawel, *The Nightmare of Reason: A Life of Franz Kafka* (New York: Farrar, Straus, Giroux, 1984), 10.

10. Mark Anderson, "Kafka in America: Notes on a Travelling Narrative," in *Kafka's Clothes: Ornament and Aestheticism in the Habsburg Fin de Siècle* (Oxford: Clarendon Press, 1992), 98–122. To these senses of the word *Verkehr*, one should add "the flow and exchange of commodities." This idea was to my knowledge first identified by Gayatri Chakravorty Spivak, who wrote: "In Kafka's code the word translated as 'traffic' (*Verkehr*) is also the word for 'commerce,' and it is the word that is used everywhere in all the literature of political economy (including, most significantly, Marx) in German." *Literature and Anthropology*, ed. Jonathan Hall and Ackbar Abbas (Hong Kong: Hong Kong University Press, 1986), 192.

11. Anderson, *Kafka's Clothes*, 161.

12. Zilcosky, 75.

13. The rape is a suggestion but more than a "mere" suggestion: it is the powerful apparition of a cathexis and fully part of the atmosphere throughout *The Trial* of a more than free-floating sexual violence. Compare such moments as K.'s assault of Fräulein Bürstner in the scene following, the scene of the whippers, the prurient behavior of the girls who pursue K. in Titorelli's chambers. Perhaps it is such an atmosphere of waxing sexual violence that now fixates the bystanders in their window. They seem worried, ashamed of their curiosity. Consider such details as that the curiosity of the old woman in the window is "quite unusual for her" (T 3); subsequent scenes of their gaping always include acts of nervous or physical agitation.

14. Especially in the months before the composition of *The Trial*, Kafka was involved in an intricate correspondence with Grete Bloch, the friend of his fiancée Felice Bauer, bearing on reasons for and against his marrying Felice. In Ernst Pawel's subtle account of their relations, Grete was "his most solid human contact." Pawel, *The Nightmare of Reason*, 309.

15. "Alte untergeordnete Schauspieler schickt man um mich: . . . An welchem Teater spielen Sie[?]" (Pp 306).

16. "Nur Ihr Urteil [der Frau Grubach], das Urteil einer vernünftigen Frau wollte ich hören und bin sehr froh, daß wir darin übereinstimmen" (Pp 34).

17. "Du suchst zuviel fremde Hilfe . . . und besonders bei Frauen" (Pp 289).

18. Franz Kafka, *Der Prozeß*, ed. Max Brod (Frankfurt a.M.: Schocken, 1950), 11.

19. Franz Kafka, *The Trial* (New York: Modern Library, 1956), 5–6.

20. Clayton Koelb, "Kafka's Rhetorical Moment," *PMLA* 98, no. 1 (1983).

21. "Pre-Reading *The Trial*," Annual Meeting of the Modern Language Association of America, San Francisco, December 1998.

22. "Pre-reading *The Trial*," MS, 10.

23. *Franz Kafka, Der Process: Die Handschrift redet*, prepared by Malcolm Pasley, *Marbacher Magazin 52/1990* (Marbach: Deutsche Schillergesellschaft 1990), 22.

24. Ibid.

25. "[D]en ruhig einteilenden Verstand behalten," says K., adding: "Soll ich nun zeigen, daß nicht einmal der einjährige Process mich belehren konnte? . . .

Soll man mir nachsagen dürfen, daß ich am Anfang des Processes ihn beenden und jetzt an seinem Ende ihn wieder beginnen will" (Pp 308).

26. *Franz Kafka, Der Process: Die Handschrift redet*, prepared by Pasley, 24.

27. "Wenn er im Bureau keine Zeit für sie fand, was sehr wahrscheinlich war, dann mußte er sie zuhause in den Nächten machen. Würden auch die Nächte nicht genügen, dann mußte er einen Urlaub nehmen. Nur nicht auf halbem Wege stehn bleiben, das war nicht nur in Geschäften sondern immer und überall das Unsinnigste" (Pp 170).

28. "Was für Tage standen ihm bevor! Würde er den Weg finden, der durch alles hindurch zum guten Ende führte? Bedeutete nicht eine sorgfältige Verteidigung . . . gleichzeitig die Notwendigkeit sich von allem andern möglichst abzuschließen? Würde er das glücklich überstehn? Und wie sollte ihm die Durchführung dessen in der Bank gelingen? Es handelte sich ja nicht nur um die Eingabe, für die ein Urlaub vielleicht genügt hätte, . . . es handelte [in the ms. "handelt"] sich doch um einen ganzen Process, dessen Dauer unabsehbar war" (p 177).

29. "Zudecken" is a key word uttered by the son Georg Bendemann to his father in Kafka's "breakthrough" story, "The Judgment." It has the connotation of "covering up" a dangerous, adversarial truth. See chapter 1.

30. Ibid., 24.

31. Theodore Ziolkowski has shown that the word/concept "Böses" (evil, deep wrong), if it alludes to the phrase "böser Vorsatz" (malicious intent), is, in Austro-Hungarian jurisprudence, also a technical term of law: the malicious intention indispensable to a punitive judgment. Ziolkowski, *The Mirror of Justice*, 236.

32. Kafka appeared to waver in deciding whether to write, in the so-called "Legend of the Doorkeeper," a portion of the chapter "In the Cathedral": "der Türhüter . . . fragt ihn [den "Mann vom Lande"] "nach seiner Heimat aus" or "über seine Heimat aus," both expressions meaning: "the doorkeeper inquired about his home" (T 216). The manuscript passage can be read in facsimile in Pr, in the fascicle entitled "Im Dom," 45. Pasley, in his edition, settles the matter by simply choosing "über seine Heimat aus" (Pp 293). The manuscript, however, does not support either decision. Roland Reuß observes that once an edition, like Pasley's, is governed by the idea of producing a reader's text—a book—it is going to have to make univocal decisions, whether or not it respects cases like these where Kafka evidently wavered. At this point supplementary apparatuses can make very little difference. Roland Reuß, "Zur kritischen Edition von 'Der Process' im Rahmen der Historischen-Kritischen Franz Kafka-Ausgabe," *Franz Kafka—Hefte 1* (Frankfurt a.M.: Stroemfeld, 1997), 23.

33. Günther Anders, "Franz Kafka—pro und contra," *Die neue Rundschau*, 58 (spring 1947), 119–57. Incorporated in *Kafka, pro und contra* (Munich: Beck, 1951). English version (not a literal translation) in Anders, *Franz Kafka*, trans. by A. Steer and A. K. Thorlby (London: Bowes and Bowes, 1960). See Brod's hostile reply: "Ermordung einer Puppe namens Franz Kafka," *Neue Schweizer Rundschau* (Zurich), 19, no. 10 (Feb. 1952), 613–25, and further contributions to this discussion by Anders and Brod. "Franz Kafka: pro und contra," *Neue Schweizer Rundschau*, 20 (May 1952), 43–50. See, too, Michael

Kowal, "Kafka and the Emigrés: A Chapter in the History of Kafka Criticism," *The Germanic Review*, 41 (Nov. 1966), 291–301.

34. See chapter 1.

35. "In diesem Augenblick ging über die Brücke ein geradezu unendlicher Verkehr" (GW 1:52).

36. "'Wünscht der gnädige Herr etwas? Soll ich den Vater holen?' 'Nein, nein,' sagte K., in seiner Stimme lag etwas Verzeihendes, als habe der Bursche etwas *Böses* ausgeführt, er aber verzeihe ihm. 'Es ist gut,' sagte er dann und gieng weiter, aber ehe er die Treppe hinaufstieg, drehte er sich noch einmal um" (emphasis added, Pp 31).

37. An unpublished Princeton University paper entitled "Arguing with a Friend: Writing and Reading Kafka's 'Process' in a New Edition," delivered at the Colloquium "Authorship and Work in the Age of New Media" at Princeton University, February 19, 2000.

38. Dorrit Cohn, *The Distinction of Fiction* (Baltimore: The Johns Hopkins University Press, 1999), 22.

39. This is Clayton Koelb's term of art. Clayton Koelb, *The Incredulous Reader: Literature and the Function of Disbelief* (Ithaca: Cornell University Press, 1984), 41–42.

40. After having written this chapter, I was alerted by Peter Beicken to a very suggestive passage from his *Franz Kafka, Der Proceß: Interpretation* (Munich: Oldenbourg, 1999). Here Beicken identifies and interprets another authorial intersection from the archive at the close of *The Trial*. The passage from *The Trial* begins with a chain of questions: "War noch Hilfe? Gab es Einwände, die man vergessen hatte? Gewiss gab es solche" (Pr, fascicle entitled "Ende," 22) ("Was there still help? Were there objections that had been forgotten? Of course there were" [T 230–31]). This is followed by a sentence of interior monologue: "Die Logik ist zwar unerschütterlich, aber einem Menschen, der leben will, widersteht sie nicht" ("Logic is no doubt unshakable, but it can't withstand a person who wants to live" [T 231]). After this gnome, which could also be attributed to a superior, commenting authorial narrator, we have the further questions: "Wo ist der Richter? Wo ist das hohe Gericht?" (Pr, "Ende," 22) ("Where is the judge? Where is the high court?"). Here, Beicken comments:

Kafka, however, changed this interior monologue into "erlebte Rede" [in French "style indirect libre," whereby the intimate thoughts of fictional characters are narrated in the third person], with the exception of one sentence, and added relative clauses: "Wo war der Richter den[n] er nie gesehen hatte? Wo war das hohe Gericht bis zu dem er nie gekommen war?" ("Where was the judge he'd never seen? Where was the high court he'd never reached?") (T 231). He then crossed out the protesting sentence: "Ich habe zu reden!" ("I have something to say"). Instead, in the original, a gesture is indicated: "Ich hebe die Hand" ("I raise my hand"). This sentence, which preserves the "I" of the interior monologue, raises it to the level of the narrating "I"; but as the revision proceeds, it is also promptly changed into "erlebte Rede": "Ich hob die Hände und spreizte alle Finger" (Pr, "Ende," 22) ("I raised my hands and spread out all my fingers") (cf. T

231) "K.'s letztes Lebensgefühl" (K.'s final feeling of life) . . . is especially emphasized by this change from the prevailing narration to that of an "I"-figure (Pr, "Ende," 25). From the standpoint of narrative and rhetoric, Joseph K. comes to his self, to his identity, to himself. This [is] a striking existential moment before the imminent death of the protagonist. . . . For one brief moment at the close, Joseph K.'s voice rises to the level of the narrator . . . (107).

Now it is perfectly clear that this interpretation jeopardizes my own. I have been insisting that at the close Kafka's text does everything in its power to repudiate K. and to deny him anything like "existential awareness." How can this difficulty be solved? It is true that with the appearance of the word "I," together with the past tense, the voice of K. fuses with that of the authorial narrator, whom I have been calling Kafka himself, and who generally represents the thoughts and actions of Joseph K. in the preterite tense. But what is crucial to note, and what needs even greater emphasis, is that the instant this fusion of voices occurs, Kafka the narrator does everything in his power to crush it. In the sentence in question, it is true, he has failed to change the "I" of the interior monologue to the "he" of "erlebte Rede"; but what he does do simultaneously, as soon as he has noted the repetition of *Ich hebe*—a probably musical reminiscence of the *Ich habe* of the interior monologue—is scratch into the word "hebe" with his pen, in an unaccustomedly forcible manner, the word "hob" ("[I] raised"). This scriptive gesture takes the text securely out of the present tense, which connotes an identity with K. This entire passage is, in my view, far less a sign of Kafka's abiding by a discovered intimacy of voices than of his swift effort to flee that intimacy for the superior-sounding mode of "erlebte Rede." What Kafka needed to do to secure this distance absolutely was replace the "I" with the "he"; he did not. But his energetic physical revision of the "hebe" as all wrong on two counts would have been enough for the moment to get clear of any connotation of a respectful identity with K. This interiority, by the way, Beicken describes as "resistant," but I see it rather as instinctive, plaintive, and ordinary. Everything points to the fact that Kafka is not murdering himself (the narrator) along with K. but bolting away from the danger of contamination by this guilty mask of himself.

41. comparable, perhaps, to the entertainment that awaited Sancho Panza after "diverting the attentions of his devil . . . Don Quixote" (CS 430, translation modified).

## CHAPTER 4
### ALLOTRIA AND EXCRETA IN "IN THE PENAL COLONY"

1. Friedrich Hölderlin, *Sämtliche Werke* (Kohlhammer: Stuttgart, 1961), 4:21.
2. Lionel Trilling, "Introduction" to *Anna Karenina*, cited in Leon Wieseltier, "Get Smart: Lionel Trilling's Exhilarating Pursuit of Moral Realism," *Los Angeles Times Book Review*, 11 June 2000, 4.

3. According to Malcolm Pasley and Klaus Wagenbach, Kafka composed "In the Penal Colony" between October 4 and 18, 1914. *Sämtliche Erzählungen*, ed. Paul Raabe (Frankfurt a.M.: Fischer Taschenbuch, 1970), 398. Citations in German from this edition of "In the Penal Colony" ("In der Strafkolonie") will be given in the text of this essay as page numbers in parentheses.

4. And so we are promptly in a bind, needing to be pedantic about the non-pedantic.

5. "Kretzschmar hatte nichts dagegen und begünstigte es sogar, daß dieser von Gescheitheit vibrierende Jüngling auch musikalisch vorauseilte und sich mit Dingen zu schaffen machte, die ein pedantischer Mentor als Allotria verpönt haben würde" (would have forbidden as time-wasting). Thomas Mann, *Doktor Faustus* (Frankfurt a.M.: Fischer Taschenbuch, 1991), 101. For an English language version, see *Doctor Faustus*, trans. H. T. Lowe-Porter (New York: Vintage, 1948), 73.

6. So much for Theodor W. Adorno's claim that Kafka's characters are all subaltern (all "Gestalten der Subalternität") in "Aufzeichnungen zu Kafka," in *Prismen: Kulturkritik und Gesellschaft* (Frankfurt a.M.: Suhrkamp, 1955), 324. Cf. "Notes to Kafka," in *Prisms*, trans. Samuel and Shierry Weber (Spearman: London, 1967), 259.

7. Kafka read it at the Hans Goetz Gallery on November 10, 1916 — a fact drawn from a catalogue translated from the Catalan of the exhibit "Kafka/Prague" arranged at the Jewish Museum in New York in fall 2002. Kafka's applications for permission from the police to leave Prague for Munich have been preserved.

8. John Wesley, *The Good Steward, A Sermon* (London, 1768), 5.

9. Kafka studied medieval German literature at the University of Prague in 1902. Klaus Wagenbach, *Franz Kafka, Eine Biographie seiner Jugend (1883–1912)* (Bern: Francke, 1958), 100. He assiduously consulted Grimms' etymological dictionary; cf. Max Brod, *Über Franz Kafka* (Frankfurt a. M.: Fischer, 1966), 110, 213.

10. D. D. Guttenplan, *The Holocaust on Trial* (London: Granta, 2002), 17.

11. This word is, incidentally, conspicuous in the opening scene of *The Trial* describing K.'s arrest (15).

12. Allotria and excreta have this in common: they are distinctively, nonexclusively human, being common to both human beings and animals, especially to children and childlike beings who have no natural dislike of what Kafka calls *Schmutz* — what adults term physical and moral filth.

13. And not for the first time. In *The Decay of Lying*, Wilde wrote: "Personal experience is a most vicious and limited circle," which resonates perfectly with the view of the prison chaplain in *The Trial*. Joseph K. has attempted to defend his low opinion of the court as based on his "personal experiences," to which the priest responds with chilly silence. *The Decay of Lying*, in *Oscar Wilde: Selected Writings* (London: Oxford University Press, 1961), 26.

14. *Oscar Wilde*, ed. Isobel Murray (The Oxford Authors) (Oxford, New York: Oxford University Press, 1989), 65.

15. *Kafka Handbuch in zwei Bänden*, ed. Hartmut Binder (Stuttgart: Alfred Kröner, 1979), 229.

16. Ibid.

17. Detlev Kremer, *Kafka: Die Erotik des Schreibens* (Frankfurt a.M.: Athenäum, 1989), 7.

18. Terry Eagleton, *The Gate Keeper: A Memoir* (New York: St. Martin's Press, 2001), 113.

19. This life-in-death connects to the peculiar life-in-death of the corpse of the officer at the close. The face of the corpse "was as it had been in life" (CS 166). Mark Anderson has written suggestively of this aspect of the piece, "the existential condition of being caught between death and life," in "The Ornaments of Writing: 'In the Penal Colony,'" in *Kafka's Clothes: Ornament and Aestheticism in the Habsburg Fin de Siècle* (Oxford: Clarendon Press, 1992), 187–88.

20. J. M. Coetzee writes of history as "a society's collective self-interpretation of its own coming-into-being," against which "the freedom of textuality, however meager and marginal that freedom may be," might be asserted. *Doubling the Point: Essays and Interviews*, ed. David Attwell (Cambridge: Harvard University Press, 1992), 206.

21. Recall the phrase, "Jetzt geschieht Gerechtigkeit" (111). Also see Friedrich Kittler on Faust's feckless attempt to interpret the *sign* of the Earth Spirit. "For once, Faust does not just glimpse and gaze at signs. The first unperformable stage direction in European theatrical history declares that 'he seizes the book and mysteriously pronounces the sign of the spirit.' 'Mysteriously,' indeed. This event, speaking out loud, is possible for books composed of letters, but not for a collection of magic ideograms." *Discourse Networks 1800/1900*, ed. David Wellbery, trans. Michael Metteer with Chris Cullens (Stanford: Stanford University Press, 1990), 6.

22. See Margot Norris, "Sadism and Masochism in Two Kafka Stories," *Modern Language Notes*, 93 no. 3 (1978), 430.

23. The hunger artist nourishes himself on his own flesh; the flesh of the culprit in "In the Penal Colony" is scraped out of his body and excreted as so much useless blood and tissue.

24. In later editions, the parentheses have disappeared. Until there is a general access to the manuscripts, we cannot say why.

25. "I will put my law in their inward parts, and write it in their hearts" (Jer. 31.33). Cited in Malcolm Pasley, "In the Penal Colony," in *The Kafka Debate: New Perspectives for our Time* (New York: Gordian, 1977), 302.

26. The phrase is Milton's, at the close of *Samson Agonistes*; to Samson is attributed "new acquist / Of true experience." *John Milton: Complete Poems and Major Prose*, ed. Merritt Y. Hughes (New York: The Odyssey Press, 1957), 593.

27. Benjamin's aperçu is superbly apt: "Darum ist bei Kafka von Weisheit nicht mehr die Rede. Es bleiben nur ihre Zerfallsprodukte. Deren sind zwei: einmal das Gerücht von den wahren Dingen [. . .]; das andere [. . .] die Torheit, welche zwar den Gehalt, der Weisheit zuzeigen ist, restlos vertan hat, aber dafür das Gefällige und Gelassene wahrt, das dem Gerücht allerwege abgeht" ("Hence, in Kafka's case there can be no further talk of wisdom. There remain only the products of its decay. Of these there are two: one, the rumor of true

things [. . .]; the other, foolishness, which to be sure has squandered the substance of wisdom but, in recompense, preserves what is obliging and complai-
sant, which escapes rumor always and everywhere").

SEGUE II
DEATH AND THE MEDIUM

1. A fictional exegesis of lines from Wordsworth's *The Prelude*. J. M. Coetzee, *Disgrace* (London: Secker and Warburg, 1999), 22. Coetzee is also an outstanding Kafka scholar, the author of "Time, Tense and Aspect in Kafka's 'The
Burrow,'" *Modern Language Notes*, 96 (3) (Apr. 1981), 556–79, among other
works.

2. James Joyce, *A Portrait of the Artist as a Young Man*, ed. R.B. Kershner
(Boston: Bedford, 1993), 187.

3. "Murderer's row," the lower type of observation, proceeds by associating
"deed-observation deed observation." In writing this sentence, Kafka can have
been recollecting the kind of vision he assigned to Grete Samsa, in *The Metamorphosis*, who has a murderess's eye for her brother, the monster Gregor. It is
precisely in this manner that she observes him, with her accustomed pseudo-
benevolence, "Of course it was not only childish defiance and the self-confi-
dence she had recently acquired so unexpectedly and at such a cost that led her
to make this demand [that all Gregor's furniture, with the exception of the
couch, his hiding place, be removed]; she had in fact noticed [*sie hatte doch
auch tatsächlich beobachtet*(!)] that Gregor needed plenty of room to crawl
around; and on the other hand, as best she could tell, he never used the furniture at all" (M 25, GW 1:129).

4. This point is made incisively in one of Gerhard Neumann's many luminous
studies of Kafka, "'Nachrichten vom "Pontus"': Das Problem der Kunst im
Werk Franz Kafkas," in *Franz Kafka: Schriftverkehr*, ed. Wolf Kittler and Gerhard Neumann (Freiburg: Rombach, 1990), 164–98.

5. The rule brooks at least one exception: In "The Judgment," we read: "At
this moment he [Georg] recalled this long-forgotten resolve and forgot it again,
like a man drawing a short thread through the eye of a needle" (CS 85). This
trope for forgetting is wonderful.

6. This passage is cited in full, page 87.

7. Max Brod, *Franz Kafka: A Biography*, trans. G. Humphreys Roberts (New
York: Schocken, 1947), 139–40.

8. Walter Sokel, *The Myth of Power and the Self: Essays on Franz Kafka*
(Detroit: Wayne State University Press), 97.

9. "[D]ie Welt ins Reine, Wahre, Unveränderliche [zu] heben" (GW 11:167).

10. *The Periodic Table* (New York: Schocken, 1984).

11. See the letter to Max Brod of early April 1918 (cited in chapter 11), in
which Kafka describes his writing as the journey to a lunar homeland (L 204, Br
240–41).

12. For a contrary view, see Kafka's aphorism beginning, "We do not have
the strength to do the right thing," which is discussed in chapters 6 and 10.

13. Silvio Vietta, *Neuzeitliche Rationalität und moderne literarische Sprachkritik: Descartes, Georg Büchner, Arno Holz, Karl Kraus* (München: Fink, 1981), 215–16.

14. This a task generally assigned to live cultures: to create and preserve forms of ecstasy. Sublimation à la Kafka's writing ecstasy would be the best of all the good deaths. But all narcotically induced toximanias, including writing, are preferable to the alleged transfiguration of self-inflicted death: the sacrificial death of a religiously inspired self-immolation (Al Qaida) or the patriotic death owed to medially inspired retaliation (the U.S. Marine Corps following September 11, 2001).

15. "But for me, who believe that I shall be able to lie contentedly on my deathbed, such scenes are secretly a game" (D2 102).

16. This phrase, though written in 1922, is a refrain that sounds repeatedly, especially in the years after 1917.

17. I have mentioned that a kind of Gnosticism called Marcionist was rampant in Prague during Kafka's lifetime and a matter of intermittent interest to him. (See introduction.) Kafka was also interested in Eastern mysticism; at the end of his life he read Lao-tzu and Hsüan-tsang and absorbed the Tao.

18. Joachim Unseld, *Franz Kafka — Ein Schriftstellerleben* (Frankfurt a.M.: Fischer, 1984), 192.

19. And what is the definition of the real empirical ego if not its wounds? But these wounds are by the same token inscriptions; and so the empirical ego is defined by its inscriptions — but not by all possible inscriptions — and those by which it is not defined are those that kill it.

20. See "Introduction: Beginnings" and chapters 6 and 7.

21. Cited in *Franz Kafka, Über das Schreiben*, ed. Erich Heller and Joachim Beug (Frankfurt a.M.: Fischer, 1983), 160.

22. Ibid.

23. Sokel, *The Myth of Power*, 26.

## CHAPTER 5
### NIETZSCHE, KAFKA, AND LITERARY PATERNITY

1. Peter Mailloux, Kafka's American biographer, believes that the section of *Thus Spoke Zarathustra* that Kafka read aloud to Selma Robitschek née Kohn was the "Dionysus Dithyrambs," that is, hot, seductive inducements. For my part, I am fairly confident that the text that Kafka recited was "On Child and Marriage" (Nietzsche's anticonjugal thesis), because, as we know from Selma Robitschek's letter to Max Brod, Kafka tried very hard to induce her to study at the university (Br 495). Kafka owned a copy of *Also Sprach Zarathustra*. In his description of Kafka's library, Jürgen Born records "Item 180: Nietzsche, Friedrich: *Also Sprach Zarathustra*. Ein Buch für Alle und Keinen. Von Friedrich Nietzsche [= *Nietzsche's* [sic] *Werke*. Erste Abteilung, Bd. VI). 38, 39. u. 40. Tsd. Leipzig: Verlag von C.G. Naumann, 1904. 531 S." *Kafkas Bibliothek: Ein beschreibendes Verzeichnis* (Frankfurt: Fischer, 1990), 119.

2. Kafka also subscribed to *Die Kunstwart* from 1900–1904, a journal with

a Nietzschean presence, and a year before his death put Ernst Bertram's *Nietzsche: Versuch einer Mythologie* on a list; see Jürgen Born, *Kafkas Bibliothek*, 183. But still these are fugitive signs. Significantly, Steven E. Aschheim, in *The Nietzsche Legacy in Germany: 1890–1990* (University of California Press: Berkeley, 1993), has nothing to say about Kafka's reception of Nietzsche, for his is the historian's view.

3. On the relation of Nietzsche's and Kafka's thought generally, Gerhard Kurz asserts: "Having discovered him while in Gymnasium, Kafka remained faithful to Nietzsche's thinking until his death." "Nietzsche, Freud, and Kafka," trans. by Neil Donaghue, in *Reading Kafka: Prague, Politics, and the Fin de Siècle*, ed. Mark Anderson (New York: Schocken, 1988), 138. This approach also has its own rigor, as witness the study by Jacob Golomb, "Kafka's Existential Metamorphosis," *Clio* 14 (1985), 271–86. In the matter of Thomas "Mann as a Reader of Nietzsche," see the chapter of this title in my *The Fate of the Self: German Writers and French* (Durham, N.C.: Duke University Press, 1994).

4. The creative Kafka scholar Benno Wagner would no doubt claim that he is doing more than following his own bias in asserting that Kafka's work "is engaged almost line by line with Nietzsche, in the most intimate and intense dialogue." "Der Bewerber und der Prätendent. Zur Selektivität der Idee bei Platon und Kafka," in *Hofmannsthal Jahrbuch zur europäischen Moderne* (2000), 8:274. Wagner's ongoing discovery of source texts for Kafka in Nietzsche — better, problems, discourses, "crypto-networks" — points toward an objective basis for this "bias." Consider, for example, lines from *Zarathustra*'s "The Other Dancing Song": "Ich bin der Jäger, / willst du mein Hund oder meine Gemse sein" ("I am the hunter; would be my dog or my doe [better: chamois]"). *Thus Spoke Zarathustra: Third Part*, in *The Portable Nietzsche*, trans. and ed. Walter Kaufmann (New York: Viking, 1969), 337. The figure of the chamois symbolizing life resurfaces in metonymical refraction without an otherwise discernable origin in Kafka's "The Hunter Gracchus," who "followed a chamois and fell from a precipice" (CS 229). This would be only one in a webwork of shared images. In another essay, Wagner writes: "Nietzsche not only *outlined* a set of critical issues relevant for the Kafka-generation of intellectuals; for Kafka, he, Nietzsche, himself *constituted* a crucial problem." Recalling that Kafka spent half his writing life composing accident reports and propaganda for workmen's compensation, Wagner concludes: "It is not the metaphor of danger — and insurance — that leads from Kafka to Nietzsche, but the insurance of metaphor; not as sign but as a discourse, i.e., a wholly new way of writing." "Insuring Nietzsche: Kafka's Files," an unpublished MS.

5. *Beyond Good and Evil*, in *Basic Writings of Nietzsche*, trans. and ed. Walter Kaufmann (New York: Random House, 1968), 193. According to J. M. Bernstein, Nietzsche has it precisely wrong; Bernstein writes, "Philosophy began with Plato's challenge to the authority of Homer, and with the expulsion of the poets from the republic that was to be grounded in reason, truth, alone. *That challenge and expulsion stand over and constitute modernity*." *The Fate of Art: Aesthetic Alienation from Kant to Derrida and Adorno* (University Park: Pennsylvania State University Press, 1992), 1. The matter is clarified when we grasp that the modernity to which Bernstein refers is Nietzsche's postmodernity, the

modernity that Nietzsche brought about. But the separation of the energies of *art* and the energies of *truth* was not something Nietzsche was serenely able to accept. Bernstein cites a remark of Nietzsche unpublished in his lifetime: "Very early in my life I took the relation of art to truth seriously: even now I stand in holy dread in the face of this discordance" (1).

6. *The Works of Plato*, trans. B. Jowett (New York: Tudor, n.d.), 368. Alexander Nehamas generously discussed the *Phaedrus* with me; see his lustrous translation of the *Phaedrus* (Indianapolis: Hackett, 1995).

7. *The Works of Plato*, ibid., 446–47.

8. The full text reads: "The author of a kindness feels affection and love for the recipient even if he neither is nor is likely to be of any use to him. This is just what happens in the crafts too. Every craftsman loves the work of his own hands more than it would love him if it came to life. Probably this happens most of all with poets, etc." *The Ethics of Aristotle: The Nichomachean Ethics*, trans. J.A.K. Thomson (London: Penguin, 1976), 299. Earlier in *The Ethics* Aristotle wrote: "All people are fonder of what they have produced themselves — just like parents and poets" (ibid., 144).

9. We should not leave this fight against Plato without distinguishing, though, the early modern stance of Nietzsche and Kafka from the late modern associated with Derrida, precisely through his deconstruction of the *Phaedrus*. "Plato's Pharmacy," in *Dissemination*, trans. Barbara Johnson (Chicago: University of Chicago Press, 1981), 61–171. The elicitation of a postmodern literature, which Derrida seems to sponsor in deconstructing Plato's valorization of speech over writing (literature being, in this sense, the postmodern as such), occurs not to reverse the prestige and propriety of speech over writing, a reversal that gives predominance to exterior writing over self-reflective speech. Rather, Derrida's deconstruction proceeds in a spirit of (quietly maniacal) irony that makes it impossible to assert either Plato's seeming value judgment against writing — or the reverse. That is because, for Derrida, the topics of speech and writing are snarled in a boundless Greek, Egyptian, and Western textuality, whose ruling order cannot be grasped in a perception but only unraveled by an interminable reading that postpones the appearance of any conclusion having the form of progeny. A sharp interpreter of such procedures, Edward Said, remarks on the superannuated logic of "classical" writing:

> The classical novel contained the molestations of psychology and language in the pattern of procreation and generation found in the genealogically imagined plot, the family, and the self. But such a pattern cannot properly begin or order writing once the human subject is no longer given as capable of such procreation, once as a subject its major feature is not the author's faith in it but the fact that it, and its author, are fictions together being produced during the writing. (*Beginnings* [New York: Basic Books, 1975], 157).

But if the argument against the procreative power of writing has to rest on the view that the human self is a fiction, then the argument cannot be grounded on either Nietzsche or Kafka (for neither writer is the self a fiction). See Stanley Corngold, "Self and Subject in Nietzsche" and "The Author Survives on the

Margin of His Breaks: Kafka's Narrative Perspective," in *The Fate of the Self*, 95–128, 161–79. These differences are a ready marker of the distinction between early modern and late modern.

10. *Nietzsche: Life as Literature* (Cambridge, Mass.: Harvard University Press, 1985), 234.

11. *Ecce Homo*, in *Basic Writings*, 715.

12. There is a fine sardonic formulation of this distinction in Dostoevsky's *Notes from Underground*, where it takes the form of polemic. The Underground Man says, to conclude,

> Why we don't even know where the living lives today, or what it is, or what its name is. Leave us on our own, without a book, and we shall instantly become confused and lost—we shall not know what to join, what to believe in, what to love and what to hate, what to respect and what to despise. We even feel it's too much of a burden to be men—men with real bodies, real blood *of our own*. We are ashamed of this, we deem it a disgrace, and try to be some impossible "generalhumans." We are stillborn; for a long time we haven't even been begotten of living fathers, and we like this more and more. We have developed a real taste for it. We'll soon invent a way of somehow getting born from an idea. But enough; I do not want to write any more "from Underground." (*Notes from Underground*, trans. Mirra Ginsburg [New York: Bantam, 1983], 153).

Here, Dostoevsky is conjuring a condition contrary-to-fact, whose rhetorical force is chiefly comminatory, meaning to warn against any deeper immersion into the book-madness of modern life. Kafka and Nietzsche are not infected with this despair: and both have a good deal to say about the benefits of a disappearance of living fathers.

13. *Nachgelassene Fragmente* (8/6), *Kritische Studienausgabe* 10:326, cited in *Nietzsche über die Frauen*, ed. Klaus Goch (Frankfurt a.M. and Leipzig: Insel, 1992), 228.

14. *Beyond Good and Evil*, in *Basic Writings*, 408.

15. Importantly, the passage leaves open the question of whether personality can ever be assigned to a work of art. On the other hand, it rules out the possibility of assigning any comparable (greatness of) personality to the so-called creator. Hence, since reproduction implies production in kind, there is no kinship in this relation of author to book beyond the illusion of kinship, an illusion that can be seen through in the way that the factitiousness of the wretched minor fiction can be seen through.

16. *On the Genealogy of Morals*, in *Basic Writings*, 537.

17. Walter Sokel, *The Myth of Power and the Self: Essays on Franz Kafka* (Detroit: Wayne State University Press, 2002), 71.

18. Compare these lines from *Twilight of the Idols*: "If there is to be art, if there is to be any aesthetic doing and seeing, one physiological condition is indispensable: frenzy. . . . What is essential in such frenzy is the feeling of increased strength and fullness. Out of this feeling one lends to things, one *forces* them to accept from us, one violates them—this process is called *idealizing*." *The Portable Nietzsche*, 518.

19. *On the Genealogy of Morals*, in *Basic Writings*, 538.

20. If it is true that the act previously conjured—of "laying hold of actuality" (*das Übergreifen ins Wirkliche*)—suggests a sexual clasp and incursion, then Wagner will already have scandalously displaced this scene of violence into the interior of the music drama.

21. *On the Genealogy of Morals*, in *Basic Writings*, 539.

22. Like the upstart in Kafka's *The Castle* also a *Landvermesser*: a surveyor and also a hubristic mismeasurer.

23. Compare the similar conclusion that Geoff Waite comes to, after taking a different route of reflection—namely, Nietzsche's reflections on Baudelaire: "It seems, in any case, that the music of Wagner, now as mediated by Baudelaire, possessed for Nietzsche the quasi-sexual, and certainly phallocentric, power not merely to *disseminate* but also to *re/produce* the (semiotic and illocutionary, if not also physiological) *tools* of dissemination." Geoff Waite, "Nietzsche's Baudelaire, or the Sublime Proleptic Spin of His Politico-Economic Thought," *Representations* 50 (spring 1995), 22.

24. *Thus Spoke Zarathustra: A Book for All and None*, in *The Portable Nietzsche*, "On Little Old and Young Women," 178. I owe this reference to Peter Burgard's introductory essay—"Figures of Excess"—in *Nietzsche and the Feminine*, ed. Peter Burgard (Charlottesville/London: University Press of Virginia, 1994), 7.

25. "Supposing truth is a woman—what then?" *Beyond Good and Evil*, in *Basic Writings*, 192.

26. See *Twilight of the Idols*, in *The Portable Nietzsche*, 518.

27. Sarah Kofman, "A Fantastical Genealogy: Nietzsche's Family Romance," in *Nietzsche and the Feminine*, 49.

28. The phrase is assigned sardonically to Gundolf, Goethe's hagiographer, in Walter Benjamin, "Goethes Wahlverwandtschaften," in *Gesammelte Schriften*, ed. Rolf Tiedemann and Hermann Schweppenhaüser (Frankfurt a.M.: Suhrkamp, 1972), 1.1:199. "Goethe's Elective Affinities," trans. Stanley Corngold, in *Works*, ed. Michael Jennings and Marcus Bullock (Cambridge, Mass.: Harvard University Press, 1996), 354. (The editors chose to translate the phrase as "sham frankness").

29. *Genealogy of Morals*, in *Basic Writings*, 543.

30. *The Gay Science*, trans. Walter Kaufmannn (New York: Vintage, 1974), 35–36.

31. Ibid., 129.

32. *Looking After Nietzsche*, ed. Laurence Rickels (Albany: SUNY Press, 1990), xv.

33. *Ecce Homo*, in *Basic Writings*, 678.

34. Ibid., 684.

35. Kierkegaard, *Fear and Trembling/Repetition*, ed. and trans. H. V. and E. H. Hong (Princeton: Princeton University Press, 1983), 27.

36. *Human, All Too Human*, trans. R. J. Hollingdale (Cambridge: Cambridge University Press, 1986), 150.

37. Friedrich Nietzsche, *The Birth of Tragedy*, 74.

38. Henry Staten writes aptly of *Ecce Homo* in addressing Nietzsche's fear of

being a ghost: "Has there ever been a more cunning project of self-representation? Nietzsche does not say 'here I am, look at me, I display my portrait to you'; he leaves everything to be inferred from hints, allusions, tones of voice, from the structure of the masks he wears when he speaks, not the man himself but his traces. And yet these traces project the strange illusion of a being of infinite pathos whose pathos is that he cannot quite become real, a being of flesh and blood. He remains a kind of phantasm or ghost who does not inhabit the text but *haunts* it: 'Example: one reaches out for us but gets no hold of us. That is frightening. Or we enter though a closed door. Or after all the lights have been extinguished. Or after we have died' (G[ay] S[cience] 365). What makes this phantasm disturbing is that it seems to be the 'real' Nietzsche, the only Nietzsche that ever managed to come into being, as though this were not only all that is left of him but also all there ever was." *Nietzsche's Voice* (Ithaca: Cornell University Press, 1991), 184.

39. *Thus Spoke Zarathustra*, in *The Portable Nietzsche*, "On Child and Marriage," 181–83.

40. *Beyond Good and Evil*, in *Basic Writings*, 211.

41. Jochen Hörisch, "*Die Armee, die Kirche und die alma mater. Eine Grille über Körperschaften*," *Merkur* 44, 7 (Juli 1990), 553.

42. Johannes Urzidil recalls that while out walking one day, he met Kafka, who asked, "What are you pulling in that little wagon?" while pointing to its contents, an apparatus of black steel and glass.

"It's an enlarger," said Urzidil.
"What is it used for?" Kafka asked.
"I take photographs, and I enlarge them."
"Whom do you photograph?"
"Oh, my sister, my mother, my father."
For a moment Kafka was still. "And you want to *enlarge* them?"

This story was told by Urzidil to the German poet, Reinhard Paul Becker, and Becker told it to me.

43. Maurice Blanchot, "The Diaries: The Exigency of the Work of Art," trans. Lyall H. Powers, in *Franz Kafka Today*, ed. Angel Flores and Homer Swanders (Madison: The University of Wisconsin Press, 1964), 195–220.

44. Ibid., 197–98.

45. Max Brod, *Franz Kafka: A Biography*, trans. G. Humphreys Roberts (New York: Schocken, 1947), 139–40.

46. Bernhard Böschenstein's independent analysis of "Eleven Sons" comes to a similar conclusion. Böschenstein argues that the rhetoric of the father-narrator is designed to seize possession of his children by confining their *being* to a few marked sensory attributes. The result is that "every assertion about the eleven sons contains judgments by Kafka the author on his eleven stories and at the same time cancels out these very judgments in denying the legitimacy of the father's procedure." Bernhard Böschenstein, "Elf Söhne," in *Franz Kafka: Themen und Probleme*, ed. Claude David (Göttingen: Vandenhoeck & Ruprecht, 1980), 150.

47. "This feeling of those who have no children: it perpetually rests with you, whether you will or no, every moment to the end, every nerve-racking moment,

it perpetually rests with you, and without result. Sisyphus was a bachelor" (D2 205).

48. Compare Benjamin who, in "Der Erzähler" (The Storyteller), speaks of "die Kette der Tradition, welche das Geschehene von Geschlecht zu Geschlecht weiterleitet" (the chain of tradition, which passes on that which has happened from generation to generation). *Gesammelte Schriften*, ed. Rolf Tiedemann and Hermann Schweppenhaüser (Frankfurt a.M.: Suhrkamp, 1972), 2:453. Compare, further, Nietzsche, who wrote to Strindberg, proposing a translation of *Ecce Homo*: "Es ist eine Sache allersten Ranges. Denn ich bin stark genug dazu, die Geschichte der Menschheit in zwei Stücke zu zerbrechen" (It is a matter of the first rank. I am strong enough to shatter the history of humanity into two pieces). Nietzsche, *Sämtliche Briefe: Kritische Studienausgabe, Friedrich Wilhelm Nietzsche*, ed. Giorgio Colli and Mazzino Montinari (Berlin: De Gruyter, 1986), 8:509. My thanks to James McFarland for pointing out this text that "suggests a cataclysmic destruction of historical continuity." See McFarland, *Constellation: Nietzsche/Benjamin* (Ph.D. dissertation, Princeton University, 2002), 196.

49. This Kierkegaardian link of sexuality and history is found in *The Concept of Anxiety*. See Jacob Taubes, "Der dogmatische Mythos der Gnosis," in *Poetik und Hermeneutik IV, Terror und Spiel: Probleme der Mythenrezeption*, ed. Manfred Fuhrmann (Fink: Munich, 1971), 150ff.

50. According to Klaus Wagenbach, Kafka heard a number of lectures by Rudolf Steiner in Prague in 1911 employing such expressions as "Ahrimanian forces." Kafka's diary entry for March 28, 1911, describing his visit to "Dr. Steiner," cites, in free indirect discourse, the following opinion of Steiner's followers: "The efforts of Dr. Steiner will succeed if only the Ahrimanian forces do not get the upper hand" (D1 57). Moreover, reported Berta Fanta, in whose mother's house the event took place, "I remember noticing how during the lectures Kafka's eyes flashed and gleamed and a smile lit up his face." Klaus Wagenbach, *Franz Kafka: Eine Biographie seiner Jugend, 1883–1912* (Bern: Francke, 1958), 175.

51. Michael Schreiber, "*Ihr sollt euch kein Bild . . .*": *Untersuchungen zur Denkform der negativen Theologie im Werk Franz Kafkas* (Frankfurt a.M.: Peter Lang, 1988), 92. Walter Sokel, "Between Gnosticism and Jehovah: The Dilemma in Kafka's Religious Attitude," in *The Myth of Power and the Self*, 292–310.

52. *Ecce Homo*, in *Basic Writings*, 783–84.

53. Ibid., 784.

54. "All such writing is an assault on the frontiers," wrote Kafka; "if Zionism had not intervened, it might easily have developed into a new secret doctrine, a Kabbalah" (D2 202–203).

55. Harold Bloom, "Introduction," *Franz Kafka's* The Trial, Modern Critical Interpretations (New York: Chelsea House, 1987), 17, 4.

56. Sokel, *The Myth of Power and the Self*, 298.

57. *Ecce Homo*, in *Basic Writings*, 784. On the distinction between truth and truthfulness in Nietzsche, see Jacob Golomb, "Nietzsche on Authenticity," *Philosophy Today* 34 (1990), 243–58.

58. By refusing the fiction of literary paternity, Nietzsche and Kafka become,

according to Roland Barthes, "*modern* scriptors" par excellence: "The Author is thought to *nourish* the book, which is to say that he exists before it, thinks, suffers, lives for it, is in the same relation of antecedence to his work as a father to his child. In complete contrast, the modern scriptor is born simultaneously with the text, is in no way equipped with a being preceding or exceeding the writing, is not the subject with the book as predicate; there is no other time than that of the enunciation and every text is eternally written *here and now*." Roland Barthes, "The Death of the Author," in *Modern Criticism and Theory: A Reader*, ed. David Lodge (London and New York: Longman, 1980), 170.

59. Kafka evokes "a living magic or a destruction of the world that is not destructive but constructive" (DF 103).

CHAPTER 6
SOMETHING TO DO WITH THE TRUTH:
KAFKA'S LATER STORIES

1. For the categories "dream story" and "thought story," see Martin Greenberg, *The Terror of Art: Kafka and Modern Literature* (New York: Basic Books, 1968).

2. The English phrase in brackets is translated from GW 11:210. It is not found in D2, the English translation by Martin Greenberg. On the other hand, the phrase in parenthesis is found in the English and not in the German.

3. "I am learning to see. I don't know why it is, but everything enters me more deeply and doesn't stop where it once used to. I have an interior that I never knew of. Everything passes into it now. I don't know what happens there." Rainer Maria Rilke, *The Notebooks of Malte Laurids Brigge*, trans. Stephen Mitchell (New York: Vintage, 1990), 5.

4. Compare K.'s judgment on the power relationship between himself and the Castle authorities, which in one instance consoles him for his inaction: for he would have despaired "if he had not been obliged to tell himself that the difference between himself and the authorities in terms of power was so enormous that all the lies and cunning he would have been capable of wouldn't have produced any significant reduction of that difference to his advantage" (C 166).

5. In such a spirit another Gnostic Herman Melville wrote, in *Billy Budd*: "Well, for all that, I think that to try and get into X. — enter his labyrinth and get out again, without a clue derived from some source other than what is known as 'knowledge of the world' — that were hardly possible, at least for me." Herman Melville, *Billy Budd, Sailor, and Other Stories* (Harmondsworth, Middlesex: Penguin, 1986), 327.

6. Friedrich Nietzsche, *The Birth of Tragedy*, in *Basic Writings of Nietzsche*, trans. Walter Kaufmann (New York: Random House, 1968), 97. Norman O. Brown, *Life Against Death* (New York: Vintage, 1959), 8.

7. Walter Benjamin, *Illuminations*, trans. Harry Zohn (New York: Harcourt, Brace & World, 1968), 117.

8. Maurice Blanchot, "The Diaries: The Exigency of the Work of Art," trans. Lyall H. Powers, in *Franz Kafka Today*, ed. Angel Flores and Homer Swanders (Madison: The University of Wisconsin Press, 1964), 195–220.

9. Slavoj Žižek assigns to Freud a theory of culture that provides a suggestive counterpoint: "All culture is ultimately nothing but a compromise formation, a reaction to some terrifying, radically inhuman dimension proper to the human condition itself." *Looking Awry: An Introduction to Jacques Lacan through Popular Culture* (Cambridge, Mass.: MIT Press, 1991), 37.

10. Theodor W. Adorno, "Notes on Kafka," in *Prisms*, trans. Samuel Weber and Shierry Weber (London: Spearman, 1967), 246.

11. "Kafka" means "jackdaw," a crowlike bird, and Kafka's unfinished story "The Hunter Gracchus" (1917) literally translates into Latin the word "crow."

12. Friedrich Hölderlin, "[Reflexion]," in *Sämtliche Werke und Briefe*, I (Munich: Carl Hanser Verlag, 1970), 855.

13. Wallace Stevens, "The Snow Man," in *Harmonium* (New York: St. Martin's Press, 1975), 24.

14. Compare J. M. Coetzee: "As for writing and the experience of writing, there is a definite thrill of mastery—perhaps even omnipotence—that comes with making time bend and buckle, and generally with being present when signification, or the will to signification, takes control over time." *Doubling the Point: Essays and Interviews*, ed. David Attwell (Cambridge, Mass.: Harvard University Press, 1992), 204.

15. Cited in Arturo Pérez-Reverte, *The Flanders Panel*, trans. Margaret Jull Costa (New York: Bantam, 1996), 1.

16. Kafka's logic here might be grasped as an extension of the famous diary entry (15 September 1917) in which he meditates on the confirmation of his tuberculosis: "If the infection in your lungs is only a symbol, . . . a symbol of the infection whose inflammation is called F. [his fiancée Felice Bauer], and whose depth is its deep justification; if this is so, then the medical advice (light, air, sun, rest) is also a symbol. *Lay hold of this symbol* [*Fasse dieses Sinnbild an*]" (emphasis added, D2 182, GW 11:161).

17. Here, to reinforce the mood of this recovery, is Kafka's relay station, Nietzsche, in *Thus Spoke Zarathustra*: "The time is gone when mere accidents could still happen to me; and what could still come to me now that was not mine already? What returns, what finally comes home to me, is my own self and what of myself has long been in strange lands and scattered among things and accidents." *The Portable Nietzsche*, trans. and ed. Walter Kaufmann (New York: Viking, 1969), 264.

CHAPTER 7
"A FAITH LIKE A GUILOTINE":
KAFKA ON SKEPTICISM

1. William M. Johnston, *The Austrian Mind: An Intellectual and Social History* (University of California Press, 1972), 271.

2. *Pyrrhoneioi hypotyposeis* (*Outlines of Pyrrhonism*), 18. Cited in A. A. Long, *Hellenistic Philosophy: Stoics, Epicureans, Sceptics*, 2nd ed. (Berkeley: University of California Press, 1986), 75.

3. Compare Max Weber: "The fact that there are works of art is a given for aesthetics, which attempts to explore the determining conditions of the facts of

the matter we have before us. But it does not pose the question whether the realm of art is not perhaps a realm of devilish splendor, a realm of this world and therefore contra the sacred [widergöttlich] in its inmost depths and in its innermost aristocratic spirit contra community [widerbrüderlich]. Hence it does not pose the question of whether works *ought* to exist." *Gesamtausgabe*, ed. Horst Baier, i.a., Abteilung I: *Schriften und Reden*, vol. 17, ed. Wolfgang Mommsen and Wolfgang Schluchter (Tübingen: J.C.B. Mohr Verlag, 1992– , 94–95. Cited in Daniel Jiro Tanaka, "Forms of Disenchantment: Kant and Neo-Kantianism in the Early Work of Walter Benjamin" (Ph.D. diss., Princeton University, 2002), 33.

4. See Segue 2, note 3.

5. Paul Valéry, "The Evening with Monsieur Teste," in *Paul Valéry: An Anthology*, ed. James Lawler (Princeton: Princeton University Press, 1977), 14.

6. W. B. Yeats, "Lapis Lazuli," in *Collected Poems of W. B. Yeats* (London, 1958), 338.

7. Paul de Man, *Allegories of Reading: Figural Language in Rousseau, Nietzsche, Rilke, and Proust* (New Haven: Yale University Press, 1979), 19.

8. The entire disquisition may be inspired by a subliminal reminiscence of the passage in Plato's *Republic* in which Socrates develops the idea of the (Form) of the Bed and the (Form) of the Table into a dim view of the poet as a producer of representations two degrees from the real: the poet imitates the carpenter's table, which is an imitation of the original Form of the table designed by the divine Demiurge of the creation myth in the *Timaeus*. Kafka's argument is not inconsistent with this Platonism, for Kafka will see the poet's table as at once a solid something (a well-made table) and a "non-entity" (a third-order imitation of the Form of the Table). *The Republic of Plato*, trans. by F. M. Cornford (New York and London: Oxford University Press, 1951), 325.

9. An example of this modernist mood would be the themes and tones of Rilke's *The Notebooks of Malte Laurids Brigge* (1910). Another point of interest: In reflecting on Hölderlin's "terrifyingly lucid irony," Paul de Man implicitly criticizes the marriage of skepticism and madness as a playing at art for too low stakes: "Who will dare say," he writes, "whether this madness" out of which Hölderlin produced little or no poetry "was [not] Hölderlin's way of experiencing totally absolute skepticism?" *Blindness and Insight: Essays in the Rhetoric of Contemporary Criticism*, 2d ed. rev. (Minneapolis: University of Minnesota Press, 1983), 263.

10. See Wittgenstein on parallel "worlds": "It is obvious that an imagined world, however different it may be from the real one, must have *something*—a form—in common with it"—thus Nature, thus Art. Ludwig Wittgenstein, *Tractatus Logico-Philosophicus*, with a new edition of the translation by D. F. Pears and B. F. McGuinness (London: Routledge and Kegan Paul; New York: Humanities Press, c1971, 1974), 2.022.

11. "I am on the hunt for constructions. I come into a room and find them whitely merging in a corner" (D1 311).

12. Cultural studies of Kafka has also seen Kafka's dreamwork and, hence, his writing, as a representation of a granting of social acceptance to the Jews, to the Czechs, to the German speakers in Prague, but leaves Nothingness, which was Kafka's acknowledged concern, to one side. See chapter 11.

13. "Literatur nach der Skepsis," *Cultura Tedesca* (1998), 181–207.

14. "The original sin, the ancient wrong committed by man, consists in the complaint, which man makes and never ceases making, that a wrong has been done to him, that the original sin was once committed upon him" (GW 270).

15. "Characteristics," in *Critical and Miscellaneous Essays* (London, 1899), 3: 7, 40. Cited in J. M. Coetzee, *Doubling the Point: Essays and Interviews*, ed. David Attwell (Cambridge, Mass.: Harvard University Press, 1992), 423.

16. One way to understand this aphorism might be to retrace its logical formation. The aphorism reads, once more: "Puny life-force, misleading education, and bachelorhood produce the skeptic, though not necessarily; in order to salvage skepticism, many a skeptic marries, at least the idea thereof [ideel], and becomes a believer" (DF 251, H 282). Reduced, and with its complicating qualifiers eliminated, it reads: "X. produces the skeptic: in order to salvage skepticism, many a skeptic marries and becomes a believer." The irreducible complication is the skeptic's wanting to salvage skepticism itself. But this is the condition resulting from a set of negative factors, intolerable contingencies; what interest could the skeptic have in salvaging such a product? Consider, then, the phrase "to salvage skepticism" as having the banal sense of "to salvage oneself from skepticism." Then the aphorism makes transparently clear, common sense: the skeptic takes refuge in marriage from his corrosive skepticism. But this is not Kafka. *Kafka* is in the improvement of the idea of saving "the skeptic" by means of saving "skepticism," a position worth the saving that evidently needs all the help it can get. This refinement is Kafka's signature. We advance in this matter by alerting ourselves to the obstinate pride that the skeptic takes in his condition. Everywhere else (presumably outside marriage) there are seductions, distractions in store, to weaken the resolve of such self-respecting skepticism. The skeptic takes it to marriage—where it is bound not to fail, bound to maintain its superiority, in the spirit of Hegel's *comic* figure of the "married philosopher." But there, contrary to expectations, it least of all survives. There is the huge, frightening hope in this that marriage will indeed transcend an after all tormenting position.

17. Michael Wood, "Start Thinking," a review of *Dicta and Contradicta* by Karl Kraus, trans. by Jonathan McVity, *London Review of Books* (7 March 2002), 11.

18. Compare J. M. Coetzee: "Returning to Kafka: I have no objection to thinking of alienation as not only a position but a practice as well. From that point of view, alienation is a strategy open to writers since the mid-eighteenth century, a strategy in the service of skepticism." *Doubling the Point*, 203.

19. For an excellent discussion of the presence of Pascal in Kafka's work, see Richard Gray, *Constructive Destruction: Kafka's Aphorisms: Literary Tradition and Literary Transformation* (Tübingen: Niemeyer, 1987), 190–96.

20. Freud notes that for past writers, dreams appear to narrate, fancifully, external stimuli suffered by the dreamer in the course of his night's sleep; Maury reports an elaborately horrible dream of decapitation at the guillotine, then registers, on awakening "in a torment of fear," that a piece of his bed has fallen on his neck. *The Interpretation of Dreams*, trans. Joyce Crick (Oxford: Oxford University Press, 1999), 25. But then it is also apparent that the "fanciful" element is decisive; given the *same* external stimulus—the morning's alarm, for

example—the dreamer constructs, night after night, a variety of different dream narratives. The guillotine is the invention of Maury's dream. Could we say, following Kafka, that he, Maury, did wish-dream his dream properly?

21. A negative variant of the famous apothegm stated by Nietzsche in the positive, in *The Birth of Tragedy*, in *Basic Writings of Nietzsche*, trans. and ed. Walter Kaufmann (New York: Modern Library, 1968), 52.

22. Rainer Maria Rilke, *Duino Elegies*, in *The Selected Poetry of Rainer Maria Rilke*, trans. and ed. Stephen Mitchell (New York: Random House, 1982), 151.

23. I do not suppose that it will be easy to get our minds completely around any one of these aphorisms; this is so on Einstein's own account, who is supposed to have said, after reading *The Castle*, "The human mind is not designed to deal with such complexity."

24. In the *Program* for a conference on "Skepticism and the Literary Imagination," New York University, 22 September 2000.

25. "Infamous or sublime, whichever she was, he [Eugène] worshipped her [Delphine] for the delight he had received from her." Honoré de Balzac, *Père Goriot*, trans. Henry Reed (Signet: New York, 1962), 244.

26. James Joyce, *A Portrait of the Artist as a Young Man*, ed. R. B. Kershner (Boston: Bedford, 1993), 187.

27. Erich Heller, *Franz Kafka* (New York: Viking Press, 1974), 121–22.

28. See Nietzsche, in *Ecce Homo*: "Has anyone at the end of the nineteenth century a clear idea of what poets of strong ages have called *inspiration*?", in *Basic Writings*, 756.

29. The idea that the "correct relation" to the world into which Kafka means to enter is *writing* is discussed in a rich essay on Nietzsche's creativity (with asides to Kafka) in Isak Winkel Holm, "Konstruktive Ästhetische Rechtfertigung: Überlegungen zu einem 'anzüglichen' Satz in der 'Geburt der Tragödie,'" *Text + Kontext*, 23 (Munich: Wilhelm Fink Verlag, 2001).

30. The introduction of "weapons" at the close of Kafka's speculative career marks a definitive abandonment of the hope of ending, at least without a fight, on a note of "freedom from disturbance."

31. Cited in *Franz Kafka, Über das Schreiben*, ed. Erich Heller and Joachim Beug (Frankfurt a.M.: Fischer, 1983), 160.

CHAPTER 8
KAFKA AND THE DIALECT OF MINOR LITERATURE

1. Gilles Deleuze and Félix Guattari, *Kafka: Pour une littérature mineure* (Paris: Minuit, 1975), trans. Dana Polan, *Kafka: Toward a Minor Literature* (Minneapolis: University of Minnesota Press, 1986). Quotes from this work in English translation are indicated in the text by DG plus page number. Some of the most relevant pages have been reprinted in the anthology *Reading Kafka: Prague, Politics, and the Fin de Siècle*, ed. Mark Anderson (New York: Schocken, 1988). Theodor Adorno, "Notes on Kafka," trans. Sam and Shierry Weber, in *Prisms* (London: Spearman, 1967). "Notes on Kafka" is a translation of Ador-

no's essay "Aufzeichnungen zu Kafka," which appeared in the *Neue Rundschau* (Frankfurt), 64 (July–Sept. 1953) and was reprinted in *Prismen: Kulturkritik und Gesellschaft* (Frankfurt a.M.: Suhrkamp, 1955).

2. Franz Kafka, *The Metamorphosis and Other Stories*, trans. Joachim Neugroschel (New York: Scribners, 1993), xi.

3. In an important essay, the linguist Marek Nekula points out that "the term 'Prague German' has so many possible references that in this [intricate] case of Kafka it had better not be used at all." "Franz Kafkas Deutsch," *Linguistik online* (13, 1/03), 6, 33 (*http://www.linguistik-online.de/13—01/nekula.html*).

4. Max Brod, *Streitbares Leben* (Munich, 1960), 219. Cited, along with other valuable materials, in Pavel Trost, "Das später Prager Deutsch," *Acta Universitatis Carolinae-Philologica—Germanistica Pragensia* 2 (1962), 35.

5. Peter Beicken, *Franz Kafka, Der Proceß: Interpretation von Peter Beicken* (Munich: Oldenbourg, 1999), 226.

6. In Nekula's words, "so-called 'Pragueisms'—in their syntactical as well as lexical aspects—are as a whole sooner interpreted as Austrianisms or northern German (oberdeutsche) forms. "Franz Kafkas Deutsch," 33.

7. Among many works bearing on this important subject are Giuliano Baioni, *Kafka: letteratura et ebraismo* (Turin: G. Einaudi, 1984); Ritchie Robertson, *Kafka: Judaism, Politics, and Literature* (New York: Oxford University Press, 1985); Jean Jofen, *The Jewish Mystic in Kafka* (New York: Peter Lang, 1987); and Régine Robin, *Kafka* (Paris: P. Belfond, 1989). For an overview of this material, see Iris M. Bruce, *A Life of Metamorphosis: Franz Kafka and the Jewish Tradition* (Ph.D. dissertation, University of Toronto, 1990).

8. On the occasion of the Eastern Comparative Literature Conference held at New York University on 5 May 1990. This point is further developed in Timothy J. Reiss, "Mapping Identities: Literature, Nationalism, Colonialism," *Debating World Literature*, ed. Christopher Prendergast (New York and London: Verso, 2004), 110–47.

9. Deleuze and Guattari defend the idea of a so-called minor literature (*littérature mineure*). This concept, which they apply to Kafka's work, appears on their account to derive from Kafka's explicit analysis of just such a literature. There is some usefulness to their idea; but its application to Kafka's work as a whole is tendentious, and the claim that it derives from Kafka's own reflections on his writing goals is unjustified. The concept of "minor literature" as "revolutionary literature"—Deleuze and Guattari write that "there is nothing that is major or revolutionary except the minor" (DG 26)—is essentially their invention.

Kafka's sources, for Deleuze and Guattari, consist of letters and diary entries which Kafka wrote at widely different times. The earliest are three closely linked diary entries on "*small* literatures" which Kafka began writing early on December 25, 1911 (the first entry has no heading, the second is headed "Continuation," the third, "Character Sketch") (D1 191). The German text is found in GW 9:243–45, 249–50, and 253, to which I refer (I have made a number of small changes to the translation). In these entries Kafka does not stress, à la Deleuze and Guattari, the distinction between "major" and "minor" in the strict sense. What he does refer to is a "literature whose development is not in actual fact unusually broad in scope" ("Litteratur . . . , die sich in einer tatsächlich zwar nicht ungewöhnlichen Breite entwickelt") (D1 192, GW 9:243–44); "a small nation's memory" ("das Gedächtnis einer kleinen Nation"); and "the national consciousness of a small people" ("das Nationalbewußtsein innerhalb eines kleinen Volkes") (D1 193, GW 9:245). In the "Continuation," the literature of small nations is implicitly opposed to "great literatures" ("große Litteraturen"); and the "Character Sketch," too, speaks of "small literatures" ("kleine Litteraturen"). Something of the interdependence and confrontational tension in the English terms major/minor — the effort of the minor to usurp the major — is not present in Kafka's usage "great/small." Deleuze and Guattari's rhetorical strategy has been trenchantly exposed by Christopher Prendergast, who writes: "They have made Kafka's essay an early version of the script in which the Empire-writes-back, by the simple expedient of converting the concept of 'small literature' into that of '*minority* literature,' which is then attributed explosive 'revolutionary' potential" (emphasis added). "Negotiating World Literature," *New Left Review,* 8 (second series) (March/April 2001), 112.

10. Michel Foucault, *The Order of Things: An Archaeology of the Human Sciences,* a translation of *Les Mots et les choses* (New York: Athenaeum, 1971).

11. Recall J. M. Coetzee, who defines "history" as "a society's collective self-interpretation of its own coming-into-being," against which "the freedom of textuality, however meager and marginal that freedom may be," might be asserted. *Doubling the Point: Essays and Interviews,* ed. by David Attwell (Cambridge, Mass.: Harvard University Press, 1992), 206.

12. In Dilthey's inaugural lecture in Basel in 1867, political consciousness and the idea of a German Classicism lend themselves to an ideology of empire. See Bernd Peschken, *Versuch einer germanistischen Ideologiekritik* (Stuttgart: Metzler, 1972), 134.

13. Herman Melville, "Billy Budd, Sailor (An Inside Narrative)," in *Billy Budd, Sailor, and Other Stories,* ed. Harold Beaver (Harmondsworth, Middlesex, England: Penguin, 1970), 333.

14. "What do you say to the terrible things going on in our house?" Kafka is reported to have said to Professor Thieberger apropos of *The Metamorphosis.* Johannes Urzidil, *Da Geht Kafka* (Munich: Deutscher Taschenbuch Verlag, 1965), 11. And then, allegedly, to Gustav Janouch: "Is it perhaps delicate and discreet to talk about the bugs in one's own family?" Gustav Janouch, *Conversations with Kafka* (New York: New Directions, 1971), 32. But Kafka did also say to his sister, in dismissing her view that the apartment described in the linked novella "The Judgment" was the Kafka family's own, "In that case, then, Father would have to be living in the toilet" (D1 280). Thus "one man fights at Marathon, the other in the dining room." *Letters to Milena,* ed. Willi Haas, trans. Tania and James Stern (New York: Schocken, 1953), 174.

15. Compare Walter Benjamin on "contemporary" Russian literature, ca. 1927. "The Russian literature of today fulfills, one might say, the physiological task of redeeming the body politic [Volkskörper] from this excessive burden of themes, experiences, and conjunctures (a monstrous process of excretion)." *Gesammelte Schriften,* ed. Rolf Tiedemann and Hermann Schweppenhäuser (Frankfurt a.M.: Suhrkamp, 1974–89), 2/1:761.

16. *Letter to his Father/Brief an den Vater*, trans. Ernst Kaiser and Eithne Wilkins (New York: Schocken, 1953), 35.

17. There is furthermore the sense that Kafka as a writer rivals the author of the Old Testament when Kafka thinks of his characters (and indeed of himself) as prophets. See Malcolm Pasley, "Kafkas Ruhm," *Neue Rundschau* 98 (Jahrgang 87, Heft 3), 79–92.

18. "All such writing [his writing] is an assault on the frontiers; if Zionism had not intervened, it might easily have developed into a new secret doctrine, a Kabbalah" (D2 203).

19. Gerald Bruns, *Heidegger's Estrangements* (New Haven: Yale University Press, 1989), 15.

20. Walter Benjamin, *The Arcades Project*, trans. Howard Eiland and Kevin McLaughlin (Cambridge, Mass.: Harvard University Press, 1999); in German as "Konvolut N: Erkenntnistheoretisches, Theorie des Fortschritts," *Gesammelte Schriften*, ed. Rolf Tiedemann and Hermann Schweppenhäuser (Frankfurt: Suhrkamp, 1972ff.), vol. 5 (*Das Passagenwerk*), N3, 1. For further discussion, see Michael Jennings, *Dialectical Images: Walter Benjamin's Theory of Literary Criticism* (Ithaca: Cornell University Press, 1987).

21. See my *Franz Kafka: The Necessity of Form*, esp. chapters 3 and 10.

22. On the back cover of the Czech novelist Bohumil Harabal's *Too Loud a Solitude*, trans. Michael Henry Heim (San Diego, New York, and London: Harcourt, 1990), there is this account of the hero of the novel: "Hanta may be an idiot, . . . but he is an idiot with a difference—the ability to quote the Talmud, Hegel, and Lao-tzu." These are cautionary words for readers of Kafka too quick to see in his "system" of writing an affair of received religion on the strength of such tags, as if, once more, Kafka did not know that he "must create a System, or be enslav'd by another Man's" (Blake).

23. "And a thousand times rather be torn to pieces than retain it in me or bury it. That, indeed, is why I am here, that is quite clear to me" (D1 288).

24. See segue 2, "Death and the Medium."

CHAPTER 9
ADORNO'S "NOTES ON KAFKA":
A CRITICAL RECONSTRUCTION

1. Theodor Adorno, "Notes on Kafka," trans. Sam and Shierry Weber, in *Prisms* (London: Spearman, 1967). Citations from this essay will henceforth be indicated in the text with page numbers in parentheses. "Notes on Kafka" is a translation of Adorno's essay "Aufzeichnungen zu Kafka," which appeared in the *Neue Rundschau* (Frankfurt), 64 (July–Sept. 1953), and was reprinted in *Prismen: Kulturkritik und Gesellschaft* (Frankfurt a.M.: Suhrkamp, 1955). Citations from "Aufzeichnungen zu Kafka" are taken from *Prismen* (1955) and indicated in the text with "G" and page numbers in parentheses.

2. Adorno's German reads: "Das Werk, das die Individuation zerrüttet, will um keinen Preis nachgeahmt werden" (G 315).

3. Throughout this essay I have modified a number of the Webers' translations in light of the fine distinctions pointed out to me by Matthias Gockel.

4. I owe this suggestion to Professor Iris Bruce of McMaster University.

5. *Benjamin über Kafka, Texte, Briefzeugnisse, Aufzeichnungen*, ed. Hermann Schweppenhäuser (Frankfurt a.M.: Suhrkamp Taschenbuch Verlag, 1981). Citations from this volume will henceforth be referred to directly in the text with "B" and the page number in parentheses.

6. The Webers' translation reads: "They are all declassés, caught up in the collapse of the organized collective and permitted to survive, like Gregor Samsa's father." But Adorno wrote: "Das sind allemal Deklassierte, die im Sturz vom organisierten Kollektiv aufgefangen werden und überleben dürfen gleich dem Vater Gregor Samsas" (G 324). It is not the collective that collapses but the collective that sustains them.

7. Neither category quite fits the humble dyad of soldier and prisoner in "In the Penal Colony."

8. Compare Paul de Man, who writes: "It is easy enough to see that this apparent glorification of the critic-philosopher in the name of truth is in fact a glorification of the poet as the primary source of this truth; if truth is the recognition of the systematic character of a certain kind of error, then it would be fully dependent on the prior existence of this error." "Semiology and Rhetoric," in *Allegories of Reading* (New Haven: Yale University Press, 1979), 17.

9. Compare this passage: "What is enclosed in Kafka's glass ball is even more monotonous, more coherent, and hence more horrible than the system outside, because in absolute subjective space and in absolute subjective time there is no room for anything that might disturb their intrinsic principle, that of inexorable estrangement" (261). This image maintains the point that Kafka's world is an *essential* repetition of the capitalist world, whose principle is "inexorable estrangement." At the same time, the representation, being marginally *unlike* the capitalism contemporary with Kafka, could allow Adorno the freedom to associate it "allegorically" with other ages and social conditions (the swamp world, the Third Reich, war-devastated Europe). This is Michael Jennings's argument: Adorno is not claiming to expose a genuine referential base for Kafka; in fact it is precisely the absence of such a binding web that allows him to read allegorically. The argument is interesting but squares badly with Adorno's other claim that "the first rule is: take everything literally; cover up nothing with concepts invoked from above. Kafka's authority is textual. Only fidelity to the letter, not oriented understanding, can be of help" (247). Many of Adorno's "allegorical" connections are obtained only by distorting the jumping-off point in Kafka's texts — a distortion directly traceable to an "oriented understanding"; and the pattern of his allegorical references is internally incoherent.

10. Theodor Adorno, *Aesthetic Theory*, trans. Robert Hullot-Kentor (Minneapolis: University of Minnesota Press, 1998).

11. The most useful of these allusions to Kafka in *Aesthetic Theory* are found in the English edition on pages 12, 13, (16), 19, 112, 126, 127, 195–96, 230–31, (304), 318, (322), 333, and (339). Page numbers in parentheses are less interesting.

12. Kafka's resistance to Kant is a point that evidently matters greatly to

Adorno; it is one of the few points repeated inside the "Notes on Kafka" (page 246 and then page 254). I am quite opposed to Adorno's reading of Kant's disinterested pleasure in the beautiful as an invitation to the "habitual reader" to submit to the mythified powers of rational domination. I recommend Walter Biemel's *Die Bedeutung von Kants Begründung der Ästhetik für die Philosophie der Kunst* (Cologne: Kölner-Universitäts-Verlag, 1959) for antisepsis. With help from Heidegger, Biemel focuses on two Kantian key words — *Gunst* and *gönnen* — to define the active respect which the aesthetic judgment shows toward the form-object that prompts it. Adorno's claim is troubling, moreover, because he, too, will see as a source or resistance the pleasure of the sublime transposed to art-experience (Kant having been too "timid" to have made this transposition): "Aesthetic hedonism is to be confronted with the passage from Kant's doctrine of the sublime, which he timidly excluded from art: Happiness in artworks would be the feeling they instill of standing firm." *Aesthetic Ideology*, 15.

13.  Compare Primo Levi: "Translating *The Trial*, I have understood the reason for my hostility towards Kafka. It is a form of defense born of fear. Perhaps for the very particular reason that Kafka was a Jew and I am Jew. *The Trial* opens with a surprise and unjustified arrest and my career, too, opened with a surprise and unjustified arrest. Kafka is an author I admire — I do not love him, I admire him, I fear him, like a great machine that crashes in on you, like the prophet who tells you the day you will die." *The Voice of Memory, Primo Levi, Interviews, 1961–1987*, ed. Marco Belpoliti and Robert Gordon, trans. Robert Gordon (New York: New Press, 2001), 156.

14.  Matthias Gockel and Michael Jennings have argued that it is in no way evident that Adorno means to defend the reader who falls victim to the text, i.e., arraign his fate as "a bad thing." It is true that the matter calls for some nuancing. Adorno writes: "Anyone who sees [Kafka's text bearing down on him like a locomotive] and does not choose to run away must stick out his head, or rather try to batter down the wall with it at the risk of faring no better than his predecessors. As in fairy-tales, their fate serves not to deter but to entice. As long as the word has not been found, the reader must be held accountable [bleibt der Leser schuldig]" (246). What is "bad" about this situation, a judgment to which Adorno presumably adheres, is that every reader (including, of course, himself), *must*, whether coward or fool or brave hermeneut, be annihilated and *deservedly* so, since no reading can attain to the status of "the word." But to accept this situation is to be compelled to consider this, Adorno's essay, as the futile lament of one about to die of it. Is not a "better" reading situation thinkable, one in which the reader is spared annihilation as his reading approaches an authentic rapport with Kafka's texts? In "Notes," Adorno speaks of the reader of Kafka's rebuses as one who understands "more of Kafka" than the one who takes his work as illustrated ontology (249). Marton Dornbach points out that "throughout *Ästhetische Theorie*, Adorno insists on the dynamic, dialectically 'layered' (*schichtenweise*) 'prozessual' character of aesthetic experience: it is never 'pure,' it always involves a non-aesthetic moment, that of 'real,' immediate, 'interested' experience, and it always follows a temporal trajectory between the aesthetic and non-aesthetic poles." *Gesammelte Schriften*,

ed. Gretel Adorno und Rolf Tiedemann, vol. 7 (Frankfurt a.M.: Suhrkamp, 1970), 513, 262.

15. Louis Althusser, *Ideology and State Apparatuses*, in *Lenin and Philosophy and Other Essays*, trans. Ben Brewster (London: New Left Books, 1971), 145.

16. William Shakespeare, *Henry IV, Part One*, 2.3.

17. I presume to speak of a "truth" in its absence, as Adorno does, when he writes apropos of gesture, that "language, the configuration of which should be truth, is, as a broken one, untruth" (249). In "Notes" Adorno is frugal in his appeal to "truth" as realized in Kafka's art. He is far less reticent, however, in *Aesthetic Theory*, where one reads: "What opened up to, and overpowered, the beholder [of works of art] was their truth, which as in works of Kafka's type outweighs every other element" (13). Further: "In the judgment of history, domination in the form of prevailing opinion entwines with the unfolding truth of artworks. As the antithesis to existing society, truth is not exhausted according to society's laws. Rather, truth has its own laws, which are contrary to those of society; and in real history it is not only repression that grows but also the potential for freedom, which is unanimous with the truth content of art" (195). But these dicta might be criticized in turn according to the Adornian logic that speaks against any such thing as knowledge of the truth. Marton Dornbach puts the matter as a question of degree: "It is not that truth is *not* a category in Adorno's conception of art. 'Verstanden werden Kunstwerke erst, wo ihre Erfahrung die Alternative von wahr und unwahr erreicht oder, als deren Vorstufe, die von richtig und falsch' (*Ästhetische Theorie*, 515). On the other hand, it is only in a very attenuated sense that Adorno allows us to think of art as 'a scene of instruction into the truth that capitalism alienates' and to think of truth as something self-sufficiently present in works of art. Art cannot unproblematically lay claim to such presence because it cannot occupy a perspective external to the untruth of 'the existing order.' Only the critical act can articulate art's relation to truth (and critique too is bound to remain mired in untruth to some extent); and though Adorno views critique as something immanent and implicit in the work of art itself, the latter's relation to truth is not one of symbolic implication, as in Hegel: 'Ein Kunstwerk als Komplexion von Wahrheit begreifen, bringt es in Relation zu seiner Unwahrheit, denn keines ist, das nicht teilhätte an dem Unwahren ausser ihm, dem des Weltalters' (515). Perhaps one may speak of a revelation or a self-unmasking of untruth in art; but this does not yet amount to truth. To say that recognizing an untruth qua untruth (and thus negating it) already constitutes 'the' truth would be a violation of the logic of determinate negation." Paul de Man, on the other hand, proposes truth as "the recognition of the systematic character of a certain kind of error." "Semiology and Rhetoric," in *Allegories of Reading*, 17. This perspective, when brought to a reading of the "Notes," makes cogent the category of the truth (of capitalism) in art. In the matter, though, of "sublating the difference" between the thesis (art is alienated) and the antithesis (art represents the truth of capitalist estrangement), Stathis Gourgouris stresses the Adornian point that one will not discover in art or critique a final sublation; art does not repair—it refracts the fault. This refraction is a type of resistance and the result of a continuous articulation of the

difference. In this way critical understanding can and does advance — dialectically. Yet I am concerned that Adorno's account of Kafka's world as perfectly informed by the principle of estrangement and the affect of petty bourgeois dread does not provide the space for dialectical articulation.

18. A propos of his forthcoming essay on *The Brown Book of the Hitler Terror* of 1934, Anson Rabinbach comments on the wide circulation on the Left of "the image of the 'embryonic' Fascist (freudomarxist man), the declassé swamp creature between heterosexuality and homosexuality, bourgeois and proletariat, who became the key figure of the antifascist myth. Adorno takes Kafka as prime witness for the thesis that only the radical reification of the bourgeois world (history and nature fused) can reveal the 'fable' of economic man and shatter the façade of bourgeois society. In fact, however, historians of fascism have long since jettisoned the 'petty bourgeois' thesis, e.g., that supporters of the Nazis came from that social borderland, from the declassés, degenerates, etc. Most historians now accept the "Sammelpartei" view — e.g., that the Nazis appealed widely and not just to the disenfranchised. In fact, the Communists got the unemployed (despite what old Fallada thought). The myth is ubiquitous in the 1930s–50s though." Personal correspondence, 19 May 2001.

19. In his correspondence with Benjamin, Adorno writes "Aufzeichnungen eines Hundes" (Notes of a Dog) for "Forschungen eines Hundes" (Investigations of a Dog) (B 96).

20. For "even" (*schon*, literally, "already"), the Webers write "almost."

21. The term "preworld" is prominent in Benjamin's magisterial essay on Kafka "Franz Kafka: Zur zehnten Wiederkehr seines Todestages" (On the tenth anniversary of his death) and in the letters on Kafka exchanged between Adorno and Benjamin between 1934 and 1940. These letters are indispensable to a full appreciation of "Notes on Kafka." They are found in B 100–10.

22. This letter is dated 12 December 1934.

23. And yet the concept of "Studium" in Benjamin does not answer simply to "reason in its ambiguous relation to myth." "The activity of study," notes James McFarland, "far from being a rational debunking of myth, is first of all an ascetic religious vigil, a staying awake. When the students do write, it is not in order to express the results of their studies, but merely to transcribe another text. . . . Study, in Benjamin's reading, is to stay awake and to remember, and involves an irreducible moment of passivity. These motifs are not scientific, but messianic. And that is because, unlike Adorno, Benjamin has room for more than an opposition of reason to superstition. In his letter on Kafka to Gershom Scholem, Benjamin wrote: 'Kafka's work is an ellipse, whose farflung foci are determined on the one hand by mystical experience (which is above all the experience of tradition) and on the other by the experience of the modern big city dweller.' 'Letter to Gershom Scholem on Franz Kafka' (12 June 1938), trans. Edmund Jephcott, *Walter Benjamin, Selected Writings, Volume 3, 1935–1938*, ed. Howard Eiland and Michael W. Jennings (Cambridge: Harvard University Press 2002), 325. The position of reason is not coordinated with either of these foci." (Personal correspondence, 17 May 2001.)

24. We recall this trope from his correspondence with Benjamin where the perspective is figured as a camera!

25. "Kafka, dem deus absconditus und Teufel sich verwirrten" (*Prismen*, 292).

26. Kafka's antinomianism is remarkable. Compare, however, a classical German position: according to that famous logic found paradigmatically in Hölderlin's hymn *Der Rhein*:

But their own immortality
Suffices the gods, and if
The Heavenly have need of one thing,
It is of heroes and human beings
And other mortals. For since
The most Blessed in themselves feel nothing,
Another, if to say such a thing is
Permitted, must, I suppose,
Vicariously feel in the name of the gods,
And him they need;

The gods *need* us, says Hölderlin, who feel *for them*. (Kafka's first publication was in the journal *Hyperion* in 1908 and 1909 — that is just by the way.) According to Kafka, the gods cannot possibly "need" us, except as targets on which to sharpen their spears: "Every word, twisted in the hands of the spirits — this twist of the hand is their characteristic gesture — becomes a spear turned against the speaker" (D2 233).

27. "It is comforting to reflect that the disproportion of things in the world seems to be only arithmetical [better, the disproportion in the world appears mercifully to be only quantitative]" ("Das Mißverhältnis der Welt scheint tröstlicherweise nur ein zahlenmäßiges zu sein").

28. "Badger" refers to the hero of "The Burrow" ("Der Bau"); "mouse," to the heroine of "Josephine the Singer, or The Mouse Folk." "Antiderepants" is Kafka's word in *Amerika* (*The One Who Sank Out of Sight*) for antiskid devices on trucks (cf. the French adjective "antidérapant," nonskidding).

29. "But the shabbiness in Kafka goes further. It is the cryptogram of capitalism's highly polished, glittering late phase, which he excludes in order to define it all the more precisely in its negative" (256).

30. Homer, *The Iliad*, trans. Alexander Pope (1715), 1.72.

31. Theodor Adorno, *Minima Moralia*, trans. E.F.N. Jephcott (New Left Books: London, 1974), 247.


CHAPTER 10
ON TRANSLATION MISTAKES, WITH SPECIAL ATTENTION TO KAFKA IN AMERIKA

1. Walter Benjamin, "The Task of the Translator," trans. Harry Zohn, in *Selected Works*, ed. Michael Jennings and Marcus Bullock (Cambridge, Mass.: Harvard University Press, 1997), 1:261. "Die Aufgabe des Übersetzers," *Gesammelte Schriften*, 4:1, ed. Rolf Tiedemann and Hermann Schweppenhaüser (Frankfurt a.M.: Suhrkamp, 1980), 19.

2. "[Der Verfasser] mochte bemerkt haben, daß man in der Naturlehre sich

sehr oft ethischer Gleichnisse bedient, um etwas von dem Kreise menschlichen Wissens weit Entferntes näher heranzubringen." Johann Wolfgang von Goethe, *Sämtliche Werke*, Munich Edition, vol. 9 (Munich: Hanser, 1987), 285. The full English translation of this passage in its context reads: "It seems that this strange title was suggested to the author by the experiments he carried on in the physical sciences. He might have noticed that in the natural sciences ethical analogies [Gleichniße] are very often used to make more accessible things far remote from the circle of human knowledge; and therefore he was very likely inclined, [in dealing here] with an ethical case, to refer back to its spiritual origin a chemical discourse of likenesses [eine chemische Gleichnisrede] [I follow Muret-Sanders (1910) in translating this archaic term "Gleichnisrede" as "figurative speech or allegory," and not just as a single simile] — all the more so, since, indeed, everywhere there is but One Nature, and also the traces of disturbing [or opaque (Trübe)] passionate necessity incessantly run through the serene empire of rational freedom — traces that can only be entirely extinguished through a higher hand, and perhaps not in this life either." The stress on what is "inhuman" in Benjamin's account of pure language is prominent in Paul de Man's tendentious commentary on "The Task of the Translator," viz.: "Now it is this motion, this errancy of language which never reaches the mark, which is always displaced in relation to what it meant to reach, [. . .] that Benjamin calls history. As such, history is not human, because it pertains strictly to the order of language." Paul de Man, *The Resistance to Theory* (Minneapolis: University of Minnesota Press, 1986), 92.

3. George Steiner, *After Babel: Aspects of Language and Translation*, 2d ed. (Oxford: Oxford University Press, 1992). Wolfgang Iser, "On Translatability: Variables of Interpretation in the Human Sciences," a special session held on 18 March 1995 at the annual meeting of the American Comparative Literature Association, University of Georgia, Athens, Georgia.

4. Steiner continues: "But although we 'translate' at every moment when speaking and receiving signals in our own tongue, it is evident that translation in the larger and more habitual sense arises when two languages meet." *After Babel*, xii.

5. Ibid.

6. "[G]eschäftige Kuppler . . . , die uns eine halbverschleierte Schöne als höchst liebenswürdig anpreisen; sie erregen eine unwiderstehliche Neigung nach dem Original." *Maximen und Reflexionen. Nach den Handschriften des Goethe- und Schiller Archivs*, ed. Max Hecker (Weimar, 1907), Nr. 299.

7. Edwin Gentzler, *Contemporary Translation Theories* (London: Routledge, 1993), 144–80. Emil Angehrn, "Dekonstruktion und Hermeneutik," in *Philosophie der Dekonstruktion*, ed. Andrea Kern and Christoph Menke (Frankfurt a.M.: Suhrkamp, 2002), 177–99.

8. "Any work is totally fragmented in relation to this *reine Sprache*, with which it has nothing in common, and every translation is totally fragmented in relation to the original. The translation is the fragment of a fragment, is breaking the fragment — so the vessel keeps breaking, constantly — and never reconstitutes it; there was no vessel in the first place, or we have no knowledge of this vessel, or no awareness, no access to it, so for all intents and purposes there has never been one." De Man, *The Resistance to Theory*, 91.

9. Willis Barnstone, *The Poetics of Translation: History, Theory, Practice* (New Haven and London: Yale University Press, 1993), 106.

10. "Man darf nicht sagen" is a critique of two essays on aesthetic theory, *Zur Ästhetik*, by Max Brod, published in the Berlin weekly "Gegenwart" on 17 and 24 February 1906. See Max Brod, *Der Prager Kreis* (Stuttgart: Kohlhammer, 1966), 93. "Man darf nicht sagen" is reprinted in GW 5:11–13. One finds a more faithful orthography in *Der Verschollene, Roman (Amerika* or *The One Who Sank Out of Sight)*, ed. Jost Schillemeit (GW 2).

11. "But Kafka wrote in German," in *The Kafka Debate*, ed. Angel Flores (Gordian: New York, 1977), 248–49.

12. Joyce Crick, "Kafka and the Muirs," in *The World of Franz Kafka*, ed. J. P. Stern (New York: Holt, Rinehart, 1980), 166.

13. "Difficulties of the Kafkaesque" [review/essay on Kafka in translation], *Times Literary Supplement*, 14 October 1983.

14. Franz Kafka, *The Sons: The Metamorphosis, The Judgment, The Stoker, and Letter to His Father*, introduction by Mark Anderson (New York: Schocken Books, 1989).

15. *The Sons*, xxi.

16. Ibid.

17. Ibid.

18. This phrase appears as the epigraph to the first edition, but only the first edition, of Paul de Man, *Blindness and Insight: Essays in the Rhetoric of Contemporary Criticism* (New York: Oxford University Press, 1971).

19. An example: one finds in the version of *Die Verwandlung* published in Kafka's lifetime the following sentence just after the opening of section 3: "Mit einer Art Eigensinn weigerte sich der Vater, auch zu Hause seine Dieneruniform abzulegen." The critic Eric Santner has observed: "The ambiguity of Kafka's diction makes possible the reading that the father has refused to remove his uniform not just at home but in public as well; his recent 'investiture' with a kind of official status and authority, low though it might be, might, in other words, be a sham." This observation contributes importantly to Santner's reading of *Die Verwandlung* as the representation of a crisis in the constitution of authority. "Kafka's *Metamorphosis* and the Writing of Abjection," in *Franz Kafka, The Metamorphosis*, ed. Stanley Corngold, Norton Critical Edition (New York: Norton, 1996), 201. Interestingly enough, despite its claim to authenticity, the *KKA* normalizes the crucial sentence thus: "Mit einer Art Eigensinn weigerte sich der Vater auch, zu Hause seine Dieneruniform abzulegen" (GW 1:137).

20. Ibid., 43–44.

21. *Amerika*, trans. Willa Muir and Edwin Muir (New York: New Directions, 1946), 90.

22. "Mir immer unbegreiflich, daß es jedem fast, der schreiben kann, möglich ist, im Schmerz den Schmerz zu objektivieren, so daß ich z.B. im Unglück, vielleicht noch mit dem brennenden Unglückskopf mich setzen und jemandem schriftlich mitteilen kann: Ich bin unglücklich. Ja, ich kann noch darüber hinausgehn und in verschiedenen Schnörkeln je nach Begabung, die mit dem Unglück nichts zu tun zu haben scheint, darüber einfach oder antithetisch oder

mit ganzen Orchestern von Associationen phantasieren. Und es ist gar nicht Lüge und stillt den Schmerz nicht, ist einfach gnadenweiser Überschuß der Kräfte in einem Augenblick, in dem der Schmerz doch sichtbar alle meine Kräfte bis zum Boden meines Wesens, den er aufkratzt, verbraucht hat. Was für ein Überschuß ist es also?" (GW 11:163). The reader may wish to consult my discussion of this passage in *The Fate of the Self: German Writers and French Theory*, 2d revised (paperback) edition (Durham, N.C: Duke University Press, 1994), 163–68.

23. Benjamin, "The Task of the Translator," 260.

24. "[N]ichts ist schmerzlicher . . . denn Leiden zu enträtseln." Friedrich Hölderlin, *Empedokles I*, in *Sämtliche Werke (KTA)*, vol. 12 (Darmstadt: Luchterhand, 1986), 192.

25. *Amerika* or *The One Who Sank Out of Sight*, 111.

26. Franz Kafka, *Brief an den Vater, Faksimile*, ed. by Joachim Unseld (Frankfurt: Fischer Taschenbuch Verlag, 1994), 160.

27. The translators corrected their error in a subsequent edition of *Letter to His Father*, viz. "It was an intentionally long-drawn-out leave-taking from you, yet, although it was enforced by you, it did take its course in the direction determined by me." *Letter to His Father/Brief an den Vater*, trans. Ernst Kaiser and Eithne Wilkins (New York; Schocken, 1966), 87.

28. Peter von Matt, "Wie Kommt der Kaviar zum Volk?: Vom Verschwinden des Werks in der Editionspraxis—Bemerkungen zur neuen Kafka-Faksimile-Ausgabe im Stroemfeld Verlag," *Die Zeit* (3 February 1995), 5:15.

29. De Man, *The Resistance to Theory*, 89.

30. Friedrich Nietzsche, *Werke in Drei Bänden*, ed. Karl Schlechta (Munich: Hanser, 1954–1956), 2:593. *Beyond Good and Evil*, in *Basic Writings of Nietzsche*, trans. and ed. Walter Kaufmann (New York: Random House, 1968), 230.

CHAPTER 11
THE TROUBLE WITH CULTURAL STUDIES

1. Bill Dodd, "The Case for a Political Reading," *The Cambridge Companion to Kafka*, ed. Julian Preece (Cambridge: Cambridge University Press, 2002), 137.

2. See "solipsism," definition 1b2, *Webster's Third New International Dictionary* (1963).

3. One would sooner be willing to keep with "solipsism," taking the Wittgensteinian (and, thereafter, Adornian) provision that "solipsism, when its implications are followed out strictly, coincides with pure realism. The self of solipsism shrinks to a point without extension, and there remains the reality coordinated with it." Ludwig Wittgenstein, *Tractatus Logico-philosophicus*, with a new edition of the translation by D. F. Humanities Press, c1971, 1974), 5.64.

4. Translation by Stephen Dowden, in his excellent *Kafka's Castle and the Critical Imagination* (Columbia, S. Car.: Camden House, 1995), 83.

5. Jeremy Adler, *Franz Kafka* (New York: Overlook, 2001), 4.

6. Walter Sokel, *The Myth of Power and the Self: Essays on Franz Kafka* (Detroit: Wayne State University Press, 2002), 30.

7. Elizabeth Boa, *Franz Kafka: Gender, Class, and Race in the Letters and Fictions* (Oxford: Clarendon, 1996). Sander Gilman, *Franz Kafka: The Jewish Patient* (New York and London: Routledge, 1995).

8. Boa, *Frank Kafka*, 23, 28.

9. Paul de Man, *Blindness and Insight*, rev. 2d ed. (Minneapolis: University of Minnesota Press, 1983), 35. Tom Cohen puts the matter in an even graver rhetorical register: "'Cultural studies' appears vital, extremely present, alive; yet as an archive of that present it defers and fetishizes it like a corpse." *Ideology and Inscription* (Cambridge: Cambridge University Press, 1998), 104.

10. *Jewish Self-Hatred: Anti-Semitism and the Secret Language of the Jews* (Baltimore: The Johns Hopkins University Press, 1991) is the title of another of Gilman's major studies.

11. I leave to one side Gilman's undiscussed notion of the "ironical distance" found in some of Kafka's novels and stories.

12. Gilman, *Franz Kafka*, 238.

13. Ibid., 9.

14. In a review of Gilman's book, in which Gilman's enterprise is seen as brilliantly faithful to its aim—a judgment that no one would dispute—Walter Sokel remarks suggestively that "Gilman's strict socio-historical and cultural determinism loses sight of what is unique about Kafka as well as of the crucial role the notion of uniqueness plays in Kafka's world." Walter Sokel, a review of *Franz Kafka: The Jewish Patient by Sander Gilman, Modern Fiction Studies* 43.2 (1997), 526. Indeed Gregor, Odradek, the cross-breed are one of a kind.

15. De Man, *Blindness*, 35.

16. See, for example, Roland Barthes, "The Death of the Author," in *Roland Barthes: Image, Music, Text*, trans. Stephen Heath (New York: Hill and Wang, 1977); and Michel Foucault, "What Is an Author?" in *Language, Counter-Memory, Practice*, ed. and trans. D. F. Bouchard (Ithaca: Cornell University Press, 1977).

17. Gilbert Adair, *The Death of the Author* (London: Heinemann, 1992), 61.

18. In an early essay called "Le Roman anglais contemporain," which is much indebted to Aldous Huxley's *Music at Night* (1931), de Man mentions Kafka's *Castle* as a novel of "analysis" separated from Thomas Mann's *Buddenbrooks*, a novel of "character," by an abyss, all in Kafka's favor. *Wartime Journalism, 1939–1943 by Paul de Man*, ed. Werner Hamacher, Neil Hertz, and Thomas Keenan (Lincoln and London: University of Nebraska Press, 1988), 16.

19. "Les Juifs dans la Littérature actuelle," *Le Soir* (Brussels), 4 March 1941, in *Wartime Journalism, 1939–1943 by Paul de Man*, 45.

20. Here I purge de Man's postwar criticism of its sinister reminiscences and his wartime writings of its downright fascist viciousness to focus on what he consistently defended: "real" writing. I quote J. M. Coetzee in *Doubling the Point: Essays and Interviews*, ed. David Attwell (Cambridge, Mass.: Harvard University Press, 1992), 206.

21. This phrase is found in Theodor Adorno, "Aufzeichnungen zu Kafka," in *Prismen: Kulturkritik und Gesellschaft* (Frankfurt a.M.: Suhrkamp, 1955), 312.

Adorno appears to be quoting Freud and pointing to objects *redeemed* by Freud . . . and Kafka.

22. On this matter of "divergence," two of de Man's propositions are eloquent—first, a sympathetic paraphrase of an argument by the early Georg Lukacs:

> The totality of the [artistic] form by no means implies a corresponding totality of the constitutive self. Neither in its origin, nor in its later development does the completeness of the form proceed from a fulfillment of the person who constitutes this form. The distinction between the personal form of the author and the self that reaches a measure of totality in the work becomes concretely manifest in these divergent destinies. The divergence is not a contingent accident but is constitutive of the work of art as such. Art originates in and by means of the divergence. (*Blindness*, 41)

This passage speaks of the distinction between the self and the work. A second passage speaks of the distinction between the signs of the work and the meaning dependent on the constitutive activity of *these* signs:

> [The beauty of Helen] prefigures the beauty of all future narratives as entities that point to their own fictional nature. The self-reflecting mirror-effect by means of which a work of fiction asserts, by its very existence, its separation from empirical reality, its divergence, as a sign, from a meaning that depends for its existence on the constitutive activity of this sign, characterizes the work of literature in its essence. (*Blindness*, 17)

This sought-after "divergence" is exactly how Kafka conceives of himself and his art.

23. Mark Anderson's innovative book amounted to a new beginning in Kafka studies: it opened out to new possibilities of representing the effect on Kafka's work of Kafka's readings in the artistic and political culture of his time. The tendentious way in which refractions have since been turned into stereotypes was not a foregone conclusion.

24. John Keats, letter to George and Georgiana Keats, 18 February 1819, in *John Keats, Selected Letters*, ed. Robert Gittings (Oxford: Oxford University Press, 2002), 203.

# ACKNOWLEDGMENTS

SOME OF THIS material has previously been published, but here it is fitted into a new order of argument and reflection. Passages from the Introduction will appear in *The Cambridge Companion to the Modern German Novel*, ed. Graham Bartram (Cambridge: Cambridge University Press) and *The New History of German Literature*, ed. David Wellbery (Cambridge, Mass.: Harvard University Press). A briefer version of chapter 1 was published in *Skrift* (Oslo), 12, no. 24 (2000), 39–62. Chapters 1 and 2 refer to pages in my *Franz Kafka: The Necessity of Form* (Cornell University Press, 1988). Much of chapter 2 will appear in Harvard's *The New History of German Literature*. Most of chapter 3 was published in *A Companion to the Works of Franz Kafka*, ed. James Rolleston (Rochester: Camden House, 2002), 149–70. A shorter version of chapter 4 was published in *Modernism/Modernity*, 8, no. 2 (April 2001), 281–93; a considerably shorter version of chapter 5 appeared in *Nietzsche and Jewish Culture*, ed. Jacob Golomb (London and New York: Routledge, 1996), 137–57. Much of chapter 6 appeared in *The Cambridge Companion to Kafka*, ed. Julian Preece (Cambridge: Cambridge University Press, 2002), 95–110. A briefer German version of chapter 7 was published in *Skepsis und literarische Imagination*, ed. Bernd Hüppauf and Klaus Vieweg (Munich: Fink, 2003), 217–29. A version of chapter 8 appeared in *College Literature*, 21, no. 1 (February 1994): 89–101. Chapter 9 was published in *Monatshefte*, 94, no. 1 (spring 2001), 24–42. Much of chapter 10 appeared in *Zwiesprache: Theorie und Geschichte des Übersetzens*, ed. Ulrich Stadler (Stuttgart: Metzler, 1996), 143–57. Finally, some pages of chapter 11 were previously published in reviews in *Shofar*, (summer 1997), 15:4; and in the *Journal of English and Germanic Philology* (1998) 410–12. All of the pieces mentioned above have been revised and a comparable number of new pages added.

For their incisive, timely, and encouraging criticism, I am grateful to Mark Anderson, Russell Berman, and Mary Murrell. David Allen and Deborah Tegarden, my editors, brought to the manuscript their courtesy and precision. I cannot have done without the graceful companionship of Regine Corngold.

# INDEX

In this Index an "f" after a number indicates a separate reference on the next page, and an "ff" indicates separate references on the next two pages. A continuous discussion over two or more pages is indicated by a span of page numbers. *Passim* is used for a cluster of references in close but not consecutive sequence.